and
**PERSONNEL
PRACTICES**

To my family: Anna and David Gutman,
Valerie McClain, and Phillip McClain Gutman

and
PERSONNEL
PRACTICES

Arthur Gutman

SAGE Publications
International Educational and Professional Publisher
Newbury Park   London   New Delhi

For information address:

 SAGE Publications, Inc.
2455 Teller Road
Newbury Park, California 91320

SAGE Publications Ltd.
6 Bonhill Street
London EC2A 4PU
United Kingdom

SAGE Publications India Pvt. Ltd.
M-32 Market
Greater Kailash I
New Delhi 110 048 India

Printed in the United States of America

Library of Congress Cataloging-in-Publication Data

Gutman, Arthur.
   EEO law and personnel practices / Arthur Gutman.
         p.   cm.
   Includes bibliographical references and index.
   ISBN 0-8039-5221-X (cl). — ISBN 0-8039-5222-8 (pb)
   1. Discrimination in employment—Law and legislation—United
States. I. Title.
KF3464.G87   1993
344.73'01133—dc20
[347.3041133]   93-21828

93 94 95 96 10 9 8 7 6 5 4 3 2 1

Sage Production Editor: Tara S. Mead

Brief Contents

Contents

4. CIVIL RIGHTS STATUTES FROM   125
   THE RECONSTRUCTION ERA

Foreword

The human resource management field has been dominated for the past 30 years by the various Congressional mandates generally lumped together as "civil rights legislation." Nothing has come close to having the impact on personnel management practices as have the various segments of civil rights legislation dealing with employment practices.

In today's business world, a real dilemma confronts the human resource executive. In the face of the specter (or reality) of courtroom confrontation, the executive's selection and promotion policies must demonstrate the creation of a work force that is representational of the diverse protected groups under equal employment opportunity law (i.e., racial, gender, ethnic, handicapped, etc.). On the other hand, in the face of growing global economic competition, which includes employment climates in other countries not quite so favorable to labor, the executive must assemble a workforce reasonably capable of ensuring the operational success of his or her organization. Similar, but not identical, considerations confront the human resource executive in the public sector. Although governmental bodies must be extremely sensitive to the dictates of EEO law, it is equally important that the unit function effectively to meet its assigned mission.

Facing as many pitfalls and traps as Indiana Jones, the human resource executive can successfully navigate his or her treacherous path only if armed with a clear understanding of EEO law.

One problem facing the executive attempting to keep abreast of the body of knowledge in the field is that most of the writing on the subject has been done *by* lawyers *for* lawyers and is full of the legal jargon that has meaning only to another EEO lawyer.

This book is a refreshing change on that score. Art Gutman certainly delves into the intricacies and implications of the applicable case law but does so in language that clearly presents the "real world" impact of the various judicial decisions and in terms understandable to the nonjurist. The reader comes away fully briefed on the present state of the law on the subject and with a better understanding of what the impact of the law is on the practice of human resource management.

My view has always been that the best operational solution for the human resource executive is to meld sound legal analysis with sound human resource management techniques. This book is a valuable tool to the executive in reaching that optimum level of effectiveness. It is also instructive reading for students and others who need to be informed and conversant on this timely subject.

David Morris
Morris & McDaniel, Inc.

Preface

In 1988, I developed a course in EEO law for our graduate program in Personnel Psychology. For the first course, I used a legal text and case law readings. The following year I developed a half-day workshop for human resource managers using excerpts from a legal handbook and personally written handouts. Both offerings were well received, but neither audience was totally satisfied. They enjoyed reading case law, but they felt that legal texts and/or handbooks were for lawyers and legal scholars. Therefore, in the graduate course the following year, I supplemented the text with personally written handouts. The students felt they learned more from the handouts than the text. After an exhaustive search for something better, I concluded that a book organized in accordance with my handouts would fill an important niche; it would teach nonlegal students and practitioners to understand and use EEO law in personnel practice, and if they so choose, how to further benefit from legal texts, handbooks, workshops, review materials, and, of course, case law. In writing this book, I observed the following organizational principles.

Beyond the introductory material in Chapter 1, Chapters 2 through 8 are organized in accordance with a major law (or executive order) as opposed to major targets of discrimination (i.e., protected classes such as race, sex, age, etc.). This is based on my classroom experience, which is that the picture for protected classes does not become clear until the various laws and orders are understood as a body.

I have used a number of pedagogical techniques generally seen in social and behavioral sciences books. Therefore, each new law or order is first overviewed in accordance with the key dimensions cited below, and in conjunction with a chart providing a quick pictorial reference to the law or order. Additionally, a brief summary is provided at major chapter breaks, and a chapter summary is provided at the end of each chapter.

My main references for the book are the written laws and regulation and case law. I occasionally use other references. I rely to a large extent on my own reading of legal texts and handbooks and on legal workshops I have attended. These sources have helped me frame my thinking; however, the case law tells most of the story. In this regard, I have focused my efforts on describing key cases in detail, as opposed to providing an exhaustive list of cases. More than 400 cases are represented, but this list does not exhaust the number one would normally find in legal text.

In ordering the chapters, I opted for a logical sequence as opposed to an historical one. Like many others, I believe that the conceptual comparison point for all EEO laws is Title VII of the Civil Rights Act of 1964. All other EEO laws and orders are either modeled after or fill gaps in Title VII—even those laws that pre-date Title VII. Therefore, Title VII receives more extensive treatment than any other law, and this treatment is provided early in the book (Chapters 2 and 3). Subsequently, Chapters 4 and 5 cover preexisting laws that are important Title VII gap fillers (the Reconstruction Civil Rights Acts and the Equal Pay Act), and two of the final three chapters cover Title VII-type laws for protected classes not covered by Title VII (chapter 6 on the Age Discrimination in Employment Act and Chapter 8 on the Americans With Disabilities Act). Chapter 7 covers Executive Order 11246 on affirmative action, which to some degree clashes with Title VII. One other law of interest is the Civil Rights Act of 1991. This law contributes to virtually all of the other laws and, therefore, is woven into the various chapters when applicable.

Beginning with Chapter 2, each law is organized in accordance with six major dimensions. These dimensions have proved to be useful to me both in the classroom and in workshops. Therefore, each law is analyzed in accordance with (a) who the law protects, (b) who provides the protection, (c) which practices are prohibited, (d) how claims are filed, (e) what remedies are obtainable, and (f) how the case is argued in court. An overview of these dimensions is provided in Chapter 1; therefore, it is absolutely essential to read this chapter first.

The goal with each law or order is to bring the reader up to date as of the end of the 1992 Supreme Court calendar. I feel, however, that historical developments are critical. Therefore, with each law and order, the evolution to current status is provided and, in some instances, heavily emphasized. For example, it would be difficult to understand the Americans With Disabilities Act of 1991 without foreknowledge of the evolution of the Vocational Rehabilitation Act of 1973.

A certain amount of "legalese" is necessary in writing such a book, but I have avoided unnecessary expressions where possible. The fact, however, is that key sources—namely laws, guidelines and regulations, and cases—contain these terms. I define these necessary terms in the text. Nevertheless, I recommend that the reader purchase a dictionary of legal terms to use much like one would use a thesaurus. Also, among these terms are commonly used acronyms (e.g., EEOC, OFCCP, ADEA, etc.). To ease this burden, I have created a list of acronyms that are frequently used throughout the text and/or in case law.

Legal books have a written style that generally includes a numerical ordering system with footnotes and references provided on each page. Rather than using this system of notation, I have opted for a standard American Psychological Association format with conceptual headings and subheadings. Chapter endnotes, when used, serve to emphasize or clarify a conceptual issue; occasionally, an endnote provides a book reference. All case references, however, are provided at the end of the book.

There are also pedagogical prompts and space savers. For example, even though it is correct to say "the Court" when referencing any specific court, the capital "C" will be reserved for reference to the Supreme Court or where a common noun directly precedes the word Court (e.g., the Smith Court); "court" (small "c") will be used for all lower courts. Additionally, numbers will be used in lieu of letters where possible (e.g., 1st Circuit Court rather than First Circuit Court, or the 14th Amendment rather than Fourteenth Amendment). Finally, when referring to court case decisions (e.g., the Roe decision), the case will not be italicized. Only references to the full name of the case will be italicized.

Finally, I consider my audience to be nonlegal students and practitioners in state or local government and private industry. Consequently, I focus more so on these entities and less so on federal employers. Moreover, as regards my audience, my goal is to preempt the need for litigation. Therefore, beyond Chapter 1, and aside from Chapter 4, each chapter ends with a discussion of application to personnel practice. My general belief, expressed throughout the book, is that understanding and forethought can satisfy two major goals: (a) avoidance of discrimination in the workplace and (b) a more effective workforce. I believe that this is possible and have geared my entire presentation to these ends.

A number of people have been helpful to me in completing this sojourn. To begin with, I have enjoyed working with the best editor in the business—C. Deborah Laughton. We have worked together before, but never on a project of this magnitude. Her guidance, support, and, of course, editorial expertise made this book possible. She pushed and prodded, listened and understood, and most importantly, treated me with the utmost dignity and respect, which happens to be difficult when a person is also a good friend.

I would like to thank Tara Mead (Production Editor), Nacy Hale (Assistant Editor), and Kristen Bergstad (Copy Editor) at Sage. Each was a joy to interact with, and each made significant contributions to the timely completion of this book.

Several people reviewed the manuscript at several stages of development. They provided invaluable feedback, and their thoughts and ideas were gratefully used. Therefore, my thanks to Edward L. Levine, Susan E. Jackson, Randall S. Schuler, David M. Morris, Martin W. Anderson, Darla C. Kirby, and Jonathon Marcy.

Although all of the reviewers were helpful, two of them were as much confidants as they were critics. My thanks to Ed Levine and Dave Morris for aid beyond the call of reasonable imagination. I picked their brains, sometimes at odd hours or on off days. They not only persevered but did so with pleasure and anticipation. I feel that together with my editor and students they are my partners in this venture.

I wish to thank my students. Unfortunately there are too many to mention by name. Therefore, refusing to insult any one of them, I want to cite all of them for constructive criticism provided during a 5-year stretch. In the same regard, there are several people in the government and business community in Brevard County, Florida, with whom I consulted and who, like my students, provided invaluable constructive criticism. Again, that list is too long to cite individuals.

The Legal System and EEO Law

F air Employment Practice (FEP) encompasses a broad range of issues, including labor standards and relations, employment benefits,
employment at will, workplace safety, and, of course, Equal Employment
Opportunity (EEO). EEO is the newest area of FEP, distinguished by
its focus on seven protected classes of people: race, color, religion, sex,
national origin, age, and disability. Title VII of the Civil Rights Act
of 1964 is the most critical EEO law,[1] protecting five of these classes—
race, color, religion, sex, and national origin. Other EEO laws address
gaps in Title VII, or provide Title VII-type protections for the two remaining classes, age and disability.

The language of EEO law is difficult for nonlegal scholars. Statutes
and executive orders are not written in standard prose, and therefore
lack a story-like quality. The purpose of this book is to present a conceptual framework of both EEO law and personnel practices for nonlegal but scholarly students and practitioners. The purpose of this
chapter is to overview the United States legal system and the EEO laws
to be covered in this book. Section I of the chapter overviews the legal
system, and Section II overviews the laws. Section III contains a brief
discussion on compliance with these laws.

SECTION I
THE U.S. LEGAL SYSTEM

The U.S. Constitution is the foundation of our legal system. Steeped in **common law** traditions (i.e., statutory and judicial precedents from England and colonial America), the Constitution defines our three-branch system of government and ground rules for creating and modifying laws. In addition, the federal government relies on agencies and commissions to regulate and enforce laws. State legal systems mimic the federal system. Therefore, most states have a constitution modeled after the federal Constitution,[2] the same three branches of government, and regulatory and enforcing agencies and commissions.

THE U.S. CONSTITUTION

After the American Revolutionary war, the original 13 colonies were joined under the "Articles of Confederation and Perpetual Union." Devastated by the recent tyrannical rule of the English king, the Articles created 13 sovereign states and a very weak central government. In fact, the central government lacked a chief executive officer. Functioning much like 13 independent republics, the states suffered financially, and were vulnerable to military invasion. Ratification of the Constitution was therefore necessary, but not necessarily joyous.

The originally ratified Constitution contains seven articles. Articles I, II, and III define the legislative, executive, and judicial branches, respectively, and Articles IV and V address states' rights and constitutional amendments, respectively. Article VI addresses prior debt, treaty procedures, and required oaths, and Article VII defines the ratification process (i.e., 9 of 13 states had to approve).

Federal Versus States' Rights

Article IV delegates control of interstate matters to the federal government, leaving (or implying) control of intrastate matters to the states. Article IV is supported by the 9th and 10th Amendments, which further protect the people (9th) and the states (10th). However, two clauses in the Constitution permit federal encroachment on states' rights. First, the **Commerce** Clause in Article I empowers Congress to:

regulate Commerce with foreign Nations, and among the several States, and with the Indian Tribes.

This clause motivates federal laws protecting private sector employees. Second, the **Supremacy** Clause in Article VI states:

The laws of the United States dealing with matters within its jurisdiction are supreme and the Judges in every state shall be bound thereby, anything in the Constitution or laws of any state to the contrary notwithstanding.

This clause invalidates state laws that contradict federal laws.

In essence, the federal government grows stronger as it enacts new laws. But the relationship between the federal and state governments is, for the most part, cooperative. The states serve three critical functions. First, state laws fill voids in federal laws (e.g., most states have laws protecting classes of people not covered in any of the EEO statutes). Second, federal and state agencies share regulatory responsibilities for federal laws (e.g., Title VII of the Civil Rights Act of 1964 relies on state agency investigation of private and state/local claims). Third, federal laws borrow from state laws (e.g., Title VII is modeled after FEP statutes in key states such as New York).

The Constitutional Amendments

The Revolutionary War was fought for individual rights, and a strong federal government was feared nearly as much as a foreign king. Therefore, the states retained the right to amend the Constitution. In 1787, it was understood that amendments guaranteeing individual and states' rights would follow shortly after ratification. The first 10 amendments (the Bill of Rights) were ratified in 1789 and offer various protections from the federal government (including the 9th and 10th Amendment provisions cited above).

In the Bill of Rights, EEO law has been most affected by the 1st, 4th, and 5th Amendments. The 5th Amendment grants due process from federal prosecution and motivates laws protecting federal employees. The 1st Amendment separates church and state, limiting federal coverage of religious entities. And the 4th Amendment prohibits unreasonable search and seizure, limiting modern-day electronic surveillance, polygraph testing, and encroachment on privacy in record keeping.

The subsequent amendments (11 through 26) cover a variety of issues, many of which relate to states versus citizens. EEO law has been most affected by the 11th, 13th, and 14th Amendments. The 11th Amendment grants state sovereign immunity, insulating states from private lawsuits. On the other hand, the 13th amendment prohibits slavery within the states, and the 14th Amendment provides equal protection for citizens against state violations of federal law. Both Amendments fueled post-Civil War civil rights statutes that, only recently, have become relevant to EEO. The 14th Amendment is particularly critical because it permits the federal government to override state sovereign immunity and is the primary motivator of federal laws protecting state and local employees.

THE THREE BRANCHES OF GOVERNMENT

The legislative role in creating laws is obvious to most people. Less obvious are the executive and judicial roles. In fact, as we will witness throughout the book, it is difficult to implicate only one branch in the history and evolution of any one EEO law.

The Legislative Branch

The Senate and House of Representatives enact statutes subject to executive approval and judicial interpretation. The Senate also approves executive appointments, and sometimes authorizes executive orders. Few statutes retain their original form. The President may veto or threaten to veto a congressional bill, thus altering its structure and meaning prior to enactment. Congress may reverse this pressure by threatening to, succeeding in, or even coming close to overriding the veto. Despite the odds (i.e., a two-thirds vote in both houses), Congress has overridden an EEO veto (the Civil Rights Restoration Act of 1987) and nearly succeeded again in 1990 (the aborted Civil Rights Restoration Act of 1990).

Once enacted, a statute may prove ineffective, prompting Congress to amend it. For example, in 1972, Congress amended Title VII to extend protections to federal, state, and municipal employees (it had originally protected only private employees).

Finally, courts occasionally misinterpret the meaning behind a statute. As a counter, Congress may enact new statutes to restore original meanings. For example, the Civil Rights Act of 1991, with amendments to

Title VII and other statutes, was motivated by congressional disagreement with six Supreme Court rulings.

The Executive Branch

In addition to the veto, the President can initiate legislation, issue executive orders, and make appointments to administrative agencies and the federal judiciary. The veto and legislative powers are obvious to most people; less obvious are the orders and appointments.

In 1965, President Johnson issued Executive Order 11246[3] (or E.O.11246) on affirmative action; a controversial practice when applied to minorities and women. In 1978, President Carter ordered[4] a sweeping reorganization of administrative enforcement of all federal EEO laws (and E.O.11246); an order that improved each law implicated.

The appointment powers are also important. Obviously, appointments can be political, and Supreme Court appointees are closely scrutinized by the media and press. Indeed, the current Supreme Court, containing five Reagan or Bush appointees, poses a significant threat to affirmative action for minorities and women, as we will witness in Chapter 7. But choices for lower courts and agencies are also important because they represent a pool from which higher level appointees are chosen. For example, Clarence Thomas, the newest Supreme Court Justice, had two prior appointments (director of the EEOC and federal judge) before his appointment to the Supreme Court.

The Judicial Branch

Law created by judicial ruling is termed **judicial** or **case** law. In addition to misreading statutory meaning, higher courts periodically reverse lower courts, and even themselves. For example, the most critical amendment in the Civil Rights Act of 1991 was motivated by a Supreme Court reversal of a prior Supreme Court precedent.

Structurally, the judiciary contains three tiers. The lowest tier contains district courts in each of the 50 states. District court rulings are routinely appealed in 1 of 12 regional circuit courts. Circuit court rulings are reviewed (or granted *certiorari*) by the Supreme Court, but not automatically. The Supreme Court reviews less than 200 cases a year, focusing on: (a) federal or state court rulings that threaten the Constitution; (b) contradictory rulings among circuit courts; (c) disputes among states; and (d) state laws that threaten federal laws.

Historically, all courts have followed the principle of *stare decisis*—the use of prior rulings to guide future rulings. Thus any ruling can serve as case law. Precedents are occasionally altered, but are generally followed. For example, the June 29, 1992, Supreme Court ruling that abortion is a fundamental right as initially deemed in *Roe v. Wade* (1973) was maintained only because one justice (Anthony Kennedy) refused to alter the Roe precedent, even though he was on record as being opposed to the *Roe v. Wade* ruling. In general, given the scarcity of Supreme Court rulings, many precedents follow from circuit court rulings, and there is often regional variation.

FEDERAL ADMINISTRATIVE AGENCIES

The legal system relies on federal agencies for two reasons. First, statutes are rarely whole and complete. Therefore, employers require guidance. Generally, regulations authorized by Congress have the force and effect of law, if fashioned consistently with the Administrative Procedures Act of 1946. Agency guidelines, though not as forceful legally, are often deferred to by the courts (e.g., the *Uniform Guidelines on Personnel Selection*).

A second important function of agencies is to settle claims short of litigation. Generally, agencies investigate complaints and use persuasion to gain conciliation. Most EEO laws require that federal agencies attempt conciliation before claimants access federal court. Some EEO laws require that state agencies attempt conciliation before federal agencies can intervene. On the other hand, some laws permit direct access to federal district court without intervention by either federal or state agencies.

Despite its positive functions, the consequence of administrative efforts can prove nightmarish. For example, in 1978 President Carter ordered the major reorganization among administrative agencies because:

> Eighteen Governmental units now exercise important responsibilities under statutes, Executive Orders and regulations relating to equal employment opportunity. . . . These programs have had only limited success. Some of the past deficiencies include . . . inconsistent standards of compliance; duplicative, inconsistent paperwork requirements and investigative efforts; conflicts within agencies . . . confusion on the part of workers . . . lack of accountability.

By the time Carter was finished, the vast majority of EEO administrative activity was transferred and reduced to three agencies: the Equal Employment Opportunity Commission (EEOC), the Office of Federal Contract Compliance Programs (OFCCP), and the Justice Department.

The EEOC

The EEOC is an independent commission mandated by Title VII. The EEOC focuses on acts of discrimination against identifiable victims. Its regulatory and persuasive powers are strong, but limited because it cannot impose strong remedies independently of court action. The EEOC investigates and conciliates claims in all sectors, and prosecutes private sector claims for remedies in the lower federal courts. The EEOC administers Title VII, the Equal Pay Act, the Age Discrimination in Employment Act, a portion of the Rehabilitation Act, and the Americans With Disabilities Act. The EEOC also administers affirmative action within federal agencies and has written guidelines interfacing Title VII with E.O.11246 on affirmative action.

The OFCCP

The OFCCP is the EEO arm of the Labor Department and its specialty is affirmative action. Unlike as under Title VII-type laws, individuals cannot directly seek judicial relief under affirmative action laws. And Unlike the EEOC, the OFCCP can impose strong remedies on employers. Thus the OFCCP regulates from a stronger base than the EEOC. The OFCCP administers E.O.11246 for minorities and women for nonfederal entities, as well as other orders and statutes on affirmative action for age and disability.

The Justice Department

The Justice Department interfaces with both the EEOC and the OFCCP. Its role in EEO was greatly reduced by Carter's reorganization plan. Currently, the Justice Department specializes in litigation against state, local, and federal governments, and in private sector EEOC cases that reach the Supreme Court. The Department also writes regulations when coordination among other agencies is required, and it can be called upon by the EEOC and the OFCCP to prosecute cases when information provided to these agencies is false or misleading.

SECTION II
SIX DIMENSIONS FOR EEO LAW

This book features major EEO laws impacting race, color, religion, sex, national origin, age, and disability. These laws will be structured in terms of six key dimensions. The following discussion overviews the dimensions, and then the laws.

THE SIX DIMENSIONS

The six dimensions are actually questions covering the boundary conditions within any given EEO statute or executive order. The questions are as follows:

(Q1): What classes of people are protected (or have rights)?

(Q2): What business entities are covered (or have duties)?

(Q3): What employment practices are covered?

(Q4): Is the law administered, and if so, how?

(Q5): What are the penalties (or remedies) for breaking the law?

(Q6): What are the attacks and defenses used in litigation?

Protected Classes (Q1)

By tradition, there are seven classes in EEO law. As noted previously they are race, color, religion, sex, national origin, age, and disability. In actuality, however, by 20th century thinking, race and color are synonyms. Modern-day statutes maintain this distinction because 19th century statutes treated color as mainly black versus white, and race as mainly ethnicity (e.g., Arabs and Jews), and sometimes as national origin (e.g., Swedes vs. Germans). Seven classes will be maintained in this book for reference purposes only.

No one law protects all seven classes.[5] As noted earlier, Title VII protects race, color, religion, sex, and national origin. The remaining laws protect: (a) one or more, but not all of the Title VII classes; (b) sub-groups within one or more of the Title VII classes; (c) only age; or (d) only disability.

Covered Entities (Q2)

EEO laws cover three general entities: (a) private sector employers, (b) the federal government, and (c) state and local governments. Some laws cover all three entities (e.g., Title VII and the Age Act), whereas others do not (e.g., Americans With Disabilities Act and the Civil Rights Acts of 1866 and 1871). Furthermore, some laws covering the same entities do so differently, basing coverage on size of the entity or the dollar amount and type of business conducted.

Covered Practices (Q3)

The list of covered practices is exhaustive. However, it reduces to three general concerns. The first concern is actually a trilogy of practices codified originally in Title VII. That trilogy includes: (a) terms, conditions, and privileges of employment; (b) segregation and classification of employees; and (c) retaliation for claiming EEO rights. Collectively, this trilogy addresses **nondiscrimination**. For example, to avoid race discrimination, an employer should treat all people as being of the same race. In addition, an employer should not use tests and policies that tend to screen out some groups more so than others unless it can be shown that these tests and policies are necessary to run the business. All laws since Title VII have codified the principle of nondiscrimination, either verbatim or by inference.

A second concern is **affirmative action**. Because of the history of discrimination in the United States (i.e., the pattern or practice of discrimination), certain groups (e.g., minorities and women) are at a disadvantage in the current marketplace. Thus affirmative action laws impose temporary requirements to correct underutilization of these groups (e.g., goals and timetables for increasing the number of minorities and women in a facility). A common by-product of affirmative action is the charge of reverse discrimination[6] by individuals who may suffer from affirmative practices even though they, as individuals, were not responsible for past discriminatory acts.

The third concern is **reasonable accommodation**. Technically speaking, reasonable accommodation is a form of affirmative action because it requires extra considerations from employers over and above the principle of nondiscrimination. More specifically, Title VII requires employers to reasonably accommodate sincerely held religious beliefs (e.g., permitting a religious person to observe a Sabbath), and the Rehabilitation Act and the Americans With Disabilities Act require that employers reasonably accommodate disabilities that serve to prevent people from working (e.g., modifying the workplace for people in wheelchairs). Reasonable accommodation, however, does not require that employers establish goals and timetables for correcting the under-utilization of employees who are entitled to it.

Administrative Procedures (Q4)

Title VII is noteworthy for its administrative procedures. To file a federal claim, the claimant must first exhaust EEOC filing and investigatory procedures. On the other extreme, statutes based on constitutional amendments permit direct access to federal court. Some post-Title VII statutes provide a choice between direct access and administrative procedures (the Age Act and the Equal Pay Act). Affirmative action laws, on the other hand, involve none of the above. Claimants are not permitted to access the court; instead, court cases emerge after a defendant has exhausted intra-agency appeals and then continues the appeal in federal court.

Remedies (Q5)

Most remedies fall into one of two classes: equitable or legal relief. **Equitable relief** includes injunction, back pay, reinstatement (or front pay in lieu of reinstatement), and legal fees.[7] Claims for equitable relief alone are usually decided by a judge. Claims for **legal relief** usually require a jury trial, and the awards are compensatory and/or punitive damages. Compensatory damages are for pain and suffering, and punitive damages punish the defendant for willfully breaking the law. Liquidated damages are a special form of punishment in which equitable monetary awards are doubled. Because of amendments in the recent Civil Rights Act of 1991, all EEO laws except for affirmative action permit both forms of relief.

There are three lesser known remedies. First, most EEO laws permit affirmative relief,[8] including either reasonable accommodation in a reinstatement action (e.g., religion or disability) or affirmative action in the form of goals and timetables to correct underutilization (e.g., in Title VII cases in which defendants are guilty of continuous and egregious acts of discrimination). Second, affirmative action laws such as E.O.11246 permit the enforcing agency to provide monetary relief to victims, as well as fines, suspensions, and debarment to defendants. The third lesser known remedy is the criminal fine, which is permitted in select statutes, and is almost never used.

Attacks and Defenses (Q6)

EEO trials involve a special three-phase scenario in which: (a) the employee (or plaintiff) satisfies a burden of attack; (b) the employer (or defendant) satisfies a burden of defense; and (c) the plaintiff tries to prove that the defense is pretextual. Generally, the balance between attack and defense is such that a more burdensome attack involves a more burdensome defense, and vice versa. The most common scenarios are adverse impact and disparate treatment.

Adverse impact occurs when a facially neutral policy screens out members of a protected class. In a typical adverse impact scenario the plaintiff demonstrates the impact persuasively (usually statistically), and the employer is forced to answer with persuasive evidence that the policy is job-related. For example, if a plaintiff demonstrates that a high school degree screens out blacks relative to whites, the employer must demonstrate that the degree is related to job requirements. If the employer succeeds, the plaintiff may persuade the court that there is an equally valid but less impactful policy. Although untypical, a plaintiff may use this latter strategy as part of the initial attack.

Employer motive is irrelevant in pure adverse impact cases, but is essential in **disparate treatment**. In disparate treatment, however, the plaintiff need only raise the inference of a violation (e.g., he was qualified and not hired) and the employer need only counter with an alternative inference (e.g., another candidate was better). The case is then settled in phase 3, where the plaintiff attempts to prove that the defendant's stated motive is pretext, or a cover-up for an illegal, discriminatory motive.

These are not the only scenarios and their applications can differ within and across laws. Also, adverse impact is not permitted in all laws, and some laws prescribe statutory defenses other than those permitted or required in adverse impact and disparate treatment. For example, failure to accommodate a disabled individual requires direct evidence that the disability cannot be accommodated or that accommodation would pose undue hardship on the employer.

Finally, most of the critical issues in this book will involve litigation. Litigation is, after all, the way in which case law is made. But not all litigation addresses issues of discrimination. Defendants may use any of the other five dimensions to ward off an attack. Thus defendants can challenge whether plaintiffs are **protected (Q1)** by a law, whether the challenged **entity (Q2)** or **practice (Q3)** is covered by that law, whether the plaintiff has exhausted **administrative procedures** and/or statutory limits **(Q4)** for a law, and/or whether the law in question permits a requested **remedy (Q5)**.

OVERVIEW OF THE LAWS

The laws to be featured in this book have been alluded to already. They include:

1. Title VII of the Civil Rights Act of 1964
2. Sections 1981 and 1983 of the Civil Rights Acts of 1866 and 1871
3. The Equal Pay Act of 1963
4. The Age Discrimination in Employment Act of 1967
5. Executive Order 11246 of 1965
6. The Americans With Disabilities Act of 1990

Each law has been amended at least once and some as many as half a dozen to a dozen times. Critical amendments will be featured as they become relevant. For example, the Civil Rights Act of 1991 will be referenced throughout the book. It is a major piece of legislation that has affected several of the laws cited above.

The following overview focuses on the current status of each law. The history and evolution of these laws will be discussed within the various chapters that follow.

Title VII

The Title VII **protected classes (Q1)**, as previously noted, are race, color, religion, sex, and national origin. It is critical to recognize that all groups in each class are protected. For example, the statute protects whites as well as blacks, and men as well as women.

The **covered entities (Q2)** include private and state or local "persons" with 15 or more employees for each day of 20 or more weeks of a given or preceding year, and most federal agencies (including Congress). The term *person* includes individuals, groups, partnerships, educational institutions, labor organizations, employment agencies, and overseas subsidiaries of American companies.

The **covered practices (Q3)** include the trilogy referenced earlier (terms/conditions, segregation/classification, and retaliation) as well as reasonable accommodation for sincerely held religious beliefs. However, there are exemptions for discriminatory practices based on bona fide occupational qualifications (BFOQs) for sex, religion, or national origin, and bona fide seniority systems (BFSSs).

Title VII permits a private right to sue in federal district court after preliminary EEOC **administrative procedures (Q4)** have been exhausted. In most states, nonfederal claims must satisfy preliminary state procedures prior to EEOC procedures. In claims against the federal government the EEOC shares administrative duties with the Merit Systems Protection Board.

The **remedies (Q5)** include equitable relief for unintentional discrimination (i.e., adverse impact) and equitable plus legal relief for intentional discrimination. Compensatory and punitive damages are capped, with limits varying in accordance with the size of the covered entities. Punitive damages are not recoverable under Title VII, or any other law, against federal or state/local entities.

The major **attack/defense balances (Q6)** are adverse impact and disparate treatment. However, there are two variations of disparate treatment in addition to the scenario described above. In the "pattern or practice" of discrimination, an employer is guilty of numerous and continuous violations. And in a "mixed motive" scenario, an employer has both legal and illegal motives for intentional discrimination. Additionally, the BFSS defense may be used against any class in any charge, and the BFOQ is the only defense to facial discrimination against sex, religion, or national origin, but *not* race or color.

Sections 1981 and 1983

Sec.1981 is a 13th Amendment statute and Sec.1983 is a 14th Amendment statute. Neither statute was designed for EEO purposes, neither statute produced EEO litigation until after Title VII, and neither statute is as comprehensive as Title VII. Both statutes, however, have strengths where Title VII has (or had) weaknesses.

Sec.1981 **protects (Q1)** race and ethnicity by 19th century standards, and the only realistically **covered entities (Q2)** are private sector employers. However, unlike Title VII, which requires 15 or more employees for coverage, there is no minimal requirement in Sec.1981. The **covered practices (Q3)** are the same as in Title VII, and there are no **administrative procedures (Q4)**. Sec.1981 permits both equitable and uncapped legal **remedies (Q5)**, and the only **attack (Q6)** is intentional discrimination (i.e., not adverse impact).

Sec. 1983 transcends EEO. For EEO purposes, however, it **protects (Q1)** each Title VII class; **covers (Q2)**, practically speaking, only state and local entities; and **covers (Q3)** each Title VII practice. Like Sec. 1981, Sec. 1983 requires no **administrative procedures (Q4)**, permits equitable and legal **remedies (Q5)** (subject to some 11th Amendment sovereign immunity constraints), and contains only intentional discrimination **attacks (Q6)**.

The Equal Pay Act (EPA)

The EPA is one of a series of legislative modifications to the FLSA (the Fair Labor Standards Act of 1938). Like the Civil Rights Acts of 1866 and 1871, the EPA predated Title VII. Subsequent legislation has connected the EPA to Title VII, an issue (i.e., "comparable worth") to be treated in Chapter 5. Like Sec. 1981 and 1983, the EPA addresses restrictions within Title VII.

The EPA is similar to Title VII in only one respect—it applies to all **entities (Q2)**. However, an entity need only employ two people (one of each sex). Otherwise, the only **protected class (Q1)** is sex (both of them), and the only **covered practice (Q3)** is wage discrimination. The **administrative procedures (Q4)** are complex and can involve a nonpetitioned EEOC suit for injunction; a petition to the EEOC for lost differences in wages and liquidated damages; or direct access for wages and liquidated damages. In other words, equitable and legal **remedies (Q5)** are both available, but not within a single suit. The **attack/defense balances (Q6)** are entirely dictated by statutory language.

The Age Discrimination in Employment Act (ADEA)

When Title VII was enacted in 1964, Congress authorized the Secretary of Labor to study age discrimination. The result was the Age Discrimination in Employment Act (ADEA), an FLSA act that shares dimensional principles with Title VII and the EPA. Aside from a little-used executive order for affirmative action, the ADEA is the only federal law protecting age.

Relative to Title VII, the ADEA **protects (Q1)** only age, and more specifically only those employees over 40 (i.e., a lower limit, but no upper limit). The **covered entities (Q2)** mimic Title VII except that the ADEA requires 20 or more employees (as opposed to 15) for non-federal entities. The **covered practices (Q3)** also mimic Title VII, as do most of the **administrative procedures (Q4)**. The ADEA uses Title VII equitable **remedies (Q5)**, but adds liquidated damages. The ADEA also uses Title VII **attack/defense (Q6)** balances, but with variations subject to substantive issues relating to age.

Executive Order 11246 (E.O.11246)

E.O.11246 contains three core parts. Part I addresses federal entities, and is rarely referenced. Parts II and III, however, have generated much action and controversy. Parts II and III, practically speaking, **protect (Q1)** minorities and women (e.g., blacks but not whites, and women but not men). The **covered entities (Q2)** are nonfederal procurement contractors (goods and services) in Part II and nonfederal construction contractors (roads and buildings) in Part III. Although the **covered practices (Q3)** include both nondiscrimination and affirmative action, the emphasis is on affirmative action (i.e., goals and timetables to correct underutilization of minorities and women). The OFCCP **administers (Q4)** Parts II and III, and can issue **remedies (Q5)** to benefit individual employees. However, the strongest remedies are used to threaten contractors into compliance. Therefore **attack/defense balances (Q6)** are de-emphasized, because individual rights are not the central issue in most affirmative action remedies.

A key issue in E.O.11246 is whether affirmative action for minorities and women raises valid reverse discrimination charges under Title VII and/or Sec.1983 (the 14th Amendment statute). A key issue among Supreme Court justices is whether affirmative action can legally benefit individuals who have never been victimized, particularly at the expense of nonpreferred groups (i.e., white males) who have never been found guilty of discrimination.

The Americans With Disabilities Act (ADA)

The Americans With Disabilities Act (ADA) is a recently codified statute designed to apply strong features in the Rehabilitation Act of 1973 to entities not strongly protected in that statute. More specifically, the Rehabilitation Act contained three core statutes: Sec.501 provided strong protections for federal employees; Sec.503 provided affirmative action for disability much as in Parts II and III of E.O.11246; but Sec.504 proved relatively ineffective in protecting private and state/local entities receiving federal assistance money. In essence, the

ADA extends to private and state local **entities (Q2)** the strong protections previously provided to federal employees in Sec.501. Beginning July 26, 1992, all nonfederal entities with 25 or more employees are covered. Beginning July 26, 1994, that number is reduced to 15.

The **protected class (Q1)** involves a broad and complex definition of "qualified individual with a disability." The individual must be disabled and must have the prerequisite knowledge, skills, and abilities for the essential functions of a job, with or without a need for reasonable accommodation.

The ADA covers the Title VII trilogy, but an additional key **covered practice (Q3)** is reasonable accommodation. Reasonable accommodation is mandated only if the disability interferes with performance of essential job functions and if accommodation can permit the individual to overcome that interference (i.e., to surmount barriers to job performance).

The **administrative procedures (Q4)** and **remedies (Q5)** mimic Title VII. Also, in addition to the adverse impact and disparate treatment **attack/defense balances (Q6)** from Title VII, many cases will likely feature an employer's failure to accommodate surmountable barriers. In these cases, courts will evaluate whether accommodations pose undue hardships (i.e., excess financial costs and/or interference with work efficiency), and/or whether a disabled person poses a direct threat to employer safety that, itself, cannot be reasonably accommodated (e.g., a person with an infectious disease).

The Civil Rights Act of 1991

Finally, most of the chapters will feature significant contributions from the Civil Rights Act of 1991. As previously noted, Congress passed the Civil Rights Restoration Act in 1990 to reverse six 1989 Supreme Court decisions. However, President Bush vetoed the bill. The House of Representatives overrode the veto, but the Senate failed to override by a single vote. The Civil Rights Act of 1991 represents a compromise between President Bush and his Republican leaders (most notably Senator Danforth), and Democratic leaders in both the House (Congressman Brooks) and the Senate (Senator Kennedy). In general, most of the amendments apply to Title VII and Sec.1981. Title VII amendments also affect the ADA, and to a lesser extent, the ADEA. The 1991 Act will be referenced, as applicable, in Chapters 2 through 8.

SECTION III
GENERAL ISSUES RELATING TO COMPLIANCE WITH EEO LAWS

EEO reflects basic changes in societal values. In the Declaration of Independence, discrimination was not a critical issue; all *men* were created equal. The Constitution did not provide equal rights for people other then Caucasian men until post-Civil War Amendments challenged racial discrimination and the 19th Amendment permitted women to vote. Still, well into the 20th century, employers were permitted to classify and segregate minorities and women into poorly paying jobs. Segregation was first addressed in society at large (e.g., housing, education, public facilities, etc.), and then in the workplace. Evidence of this delay is that no plaintiff thought to use Sections 1981 and 1983 for workplace discrimination until after enactment of Title VII.

The early Title VII years contained short-lived attempts to circumvent the law. To illustrate, although former slaves were given the voting right in the 15th Amendment, state and local requirements were created that were easier for whites to satisfy (e.g., poll taxes, reading tests, etc.). As late as 1971, in the famous *Griggs v. Duke Power* case, similar "badges" (in this case high school degrees and intelligence test scores) were used to prevent minorities from working.

Clearly, legal pressure is a major factor responsible for societal change. Although many people believe discrimination is wrong, the need for federal guarantees lies in the recent facts. While minorities and women were fighting their battles, there were not enough advocates for the aged or the disabled to incorporate these classes into Title VII.

In short, history reflects that strong EEO laws are necessary to ensure equal employment opportunity. Many employers do not understand the difference between a business versus a country club. If a business begins to grow, it begins to affect many people; country club policies generally affect only its members.

The ensuing chapters will reveal that federal EEO laws can actually facilitate business. No law requires employers to hire, train, or promote unqualified people, and no law insulates a given group from receiving the same discipline as any other group. The best protection against EEO violations is to use sound techniques for making personnel decisions.

At a general level, compliance with EEO laws requires: (a) an understanding of each law, including accompanying regulations and/or guidelines; (b) learning the common employer mistakes illustrated by case law; (c) knowing when to seek legal and technical assistance; (d) understanding the effect on the company of agents outside the company (e.g., unions and employment agencies); and (e) providing firm leadership and policy, through training if necessary, for agents within the company (i.e., supervisors and employees). Compliance will be a critical issue addressed at the conclusion of each chapter.[9]

NOTES

1. Strictly speaking, statutes are the only "laws." But broadly speaking, "laws" also include executive orders, precedents from court rulings, and federal regulations. This book uses the broader application.

2. Some states (e.g., Missouri) are common law states.

3. E.O.11246 was not directly authorized by Congressional statute, but has been approved by congress in other ways (e.g., funding).

4. Carter's order to reorganize in 1978 was authorized by the Reorganization Act of 1977.

5. Part I of E.O.11246 provides affirmative action based on race, color, religion, sex, national origin, age, and disability. However, affirmative action leaves certain groups within these classes unprotected (e.g., white males).

6. The most important affirmative action law is E.O.11246, which applies to minorities and women. But there are also affirmative action laws that apply to older and disabled workers. Reverse discrimination charges are a by-product mainly, if not exclusively, in E.O.11246.

7. Technically speaking, equitable relief refers mainly to injunction. Practically speaking, however, laws that permit injunction also permit other restorative remedies such as back pay and lawyer fees.

8. Using the same principle as in Note 7, affirmative remedies such as reinstatement, front pay, and even affirmative action are generally permitted where equitable relief is permitted.

9. The only exception is Chapter 4, where no new compliance issues will be raised relative to Title VII in the case law itself.

Title VII (Part I)
Boundary Conditions

CHART 2.1. TITLE VII

Q1	Q2	Q3	Q4	Q5	Q6
Race	Federal	Terms, conditions, & privileges	EEOC filing procedures	Injunction	Adverse impact
Color	State/local*		180 days in nondeferral states	Back pay	Disparate treatment
Religion	Private*	Segregation & classification		Reinstatement	Pattern/practice
Sex	*15 or more employees for each day, 20 or more weeks in current or prior year	Retaliation	300 days in deferral states	Front pay	Mixed motive
National origin		Religious accommodation		Legal fees	Statutory defenses: BFOQ BFSS
				Compensatory & punitive damages (capped)	Undue hardship in religious accommodation

(Q1): What classes of people are protected (or have rights)?
(Q2): What business entities are covered (or have duties)?
(Q3): What employment practices are covered?
(Q4): Is the law administered, and if so, how?
(Q5): What are the penalties (or remedies) for breaking the law?
(Q6): What are the attacks and defenses used in litigation?

The legislative history of Title VII[1] reveals that the statute was designed to protect minorities, particularly blacks, who were unemployed far above and paid far below the national rate. A few states, like

New York, were held up as models in the fight for EEO. However, at least half the states lacked EEO laws and/or regulatory commissions needed to administer them. Of course, representatives from these other states asserted—in fact boasted—that regulation was lacking because such laws were unnecessary (in their states).

Congress also recognized a need to protect age and sex, but a different course was plotted for these classes. Age was ultimately covered by a separate act, and the same fate was in store for sex. Shortly before the final senate vote, however, Senator Howard Smith from Virginia insisted that sex be included as a Title VII protected class.

Most observers believe Senator Smith wanted to sabotage Title VII; either to delay a vote or even to kill the Act. Of course, Congress enacted Title VII with sex as a protected class. However, the late decision left little legislative guidance for enforcement agencies and the courts. As a result, some issues that should have been resolved in the 1970s were still lingering in the 1980s. For example, as we will witness in Chapter 3, "hostile racial harassment" was resolved long before "hostile sexual harassment" was even recognized.

Two chapters are devoted to Title VII: this one, on boundary conditions for all Title VII classes, and Chapter 3, on class-specific issues. This chapter has six sections. Section I overviews the six dimensions. Sections II through V focus on adverse impact, disparate treatment, pattern or practice, and statutory defenses, respectively. Section VI focuses on compliance issues relating to adverse impact. Compliance in relation to disparate treatment, pattern or practice, and statutory defenses require the information in Chapter 3, and therefore, are discussed at the end of that chapter.

SECTION I
OVERVIEW OF THE TITLE VII STATUTE

A pictorial overview of the current status of Title VII is presented in Chart 2.1. Many core features of the original Act remain codified. However, the statute has been dramatically altered by three major events: (a) the **EEO Act of 1972**; (b) **Reorganization Plan #1** of 1978; and (c) the **Civil Rights Act of 1991**. No event has amended the **protected classes (Q1)**—they are and have always been race, color, religion, sex, and national origin. No other law protects more classes,[2] and no other law protects any one of these classes any better. The remaining five dimensions have been altered by one or more of the events cited above, and/or by other smaller amendments.

COVERED ENTITIES (Q2)

Title VII has always covered private entities. This coverage, based on the "Commerce" Clause in the Constitution, applies to individuals "affecting commerce," which is more encompassing than individuals "engaged in commerce" (a term used in the Fair Labor Standards Act). Thus covered private entities include people, partnerships, employment agencies, unions, and so forth.

The 1964 Act covered only private entities with 25 or more employees, and exempted educational institutions. The EEO Act of 1972 reduced the number of employees to 15, eliminated higher education exclusions except for religious schools, and, in fact, bettered that exclusion to cover all religious affiliated institutions. The Civil Rights Act of 1991 added coverage of overseas subsidiaries of American companies, a reversal of a 1991 Supreme Court ruling (*EEOC v. Arabian American Oil Co.*).

Most significantly, the EEO Act of 1972 extended Title VII coverage to state and local entities with 15 or more employees, and to most federal entities (i.e., military civilians, executive agencies, competitive jobs in Congress and the judiciary, the Postal Service and Postal Rate Commission, units of the Washington, D.C., Government, and the Library of Congress). And most recently, the Civil Rights Act of 1991 extended Title VII coverage to employees in Congress. Congress used its 14th Amendment powers to support coverage of state/local entities, and its 5th Amendment powers to support coverage of federal entities.

COVERED PRACTICES (Q3)

Different Title VII classes feature different illegal practices. For example, pregnancy discrimination is unique to sex, citizenship requirements are unique to national origin, and so forth. These class-specific practices will be addressed in Chapter 3. On a more general level Title VII has always covered a trilogy of practices, including: (a) terms, conditions, and privileges of employment; (b) segregation and classification; and (c) retaliation.

Terms and conditions are codified in Sec.703(a)(1), which makes it illegal to fail or refuse to:

> hire or to discharge any individual with respect to his compensation, terms, conditions, or privileges of employment because of such individual's race, color, religion, sex or national origin.

In other words, *terms and conditions* refers to most of the typical personnel decisions made in a company.

Segregation and classification is codified in Sec.703(a)(2), which makes it illegal to:

> limit, segregate, or classify employees or applicants for employment in any way which would deprive or tend to deprive any individual of employment opportunities or otherwise adversely affect his status as an employee because of such individual's race, color, religion, sex, or national origin.

Segregation and classification are usually associated with the pattern or practice of discrimination and with the continued adverse effects of those practices; most notably in race and sex discrimination.

The prohibition for **retaliation** is codified in Sec.704(a), which protects employees who challenge:

> any practice made an unlawful practice by this title, or because he has made a charge, testified, assisted or participated in any manner in an investigation, proceeding, or hearing under this title.

There are two types of retaliation; (a) for participation (e.g., filing an EEOC charge); and (b) for opposition (e.g., a good faith questioning of an employer's policies and practices).

ADMINISTRATIVE PROCEDURES (Q4)

Title VII administrative procedures include filing requirements for claimants, record-keeping requirements for employers, and EEOC policy-making decisions. Title VII has never been a simple administrative enterprise. The following discussion will therefore be divided into three categories: (a) filing procedures for nonfederal employees; (b) filing procedures for federal employees; and (c) record keeping and policy making.

Filing Procedures for Nonfederal Employees

Originally, the EEOC investigated and conciliated private claims (the only ones covered prior to 1972), but did not litigate. The Justice Department litigated, and initiated so-called Sec.707 pattern or practice suits. State and local coverage mandated by the EEO Act of 1972 altered the relationship between the EEOC and the Justice Department, and so did Reorganization Plan #1 of 1978.

The EEO Act of 1972 authorized EEOC investigation of all private and state/local claims, including Sec.707 pattern or practice claims, and litigation of private claims in the lower courts. The Justice Department assumed litigation responsibilities for state/local claims and representation of EEOC-sponsored litigation in the Supreme Court. The Reorganization Plan then relieved the EEOC of state and local Sec.707 suits in favor of the Justice Department. In other words, the Justice Department was initially responsible for private Sec.707 suits, had no Sec.707 duties whatsoever after the 1972 Act, and assumed state/local Sec.707 duties after the 1978 Reorganization.

The prerequisites for court action have remained intact, except for two surgical changes. **Nondeferral** claimants (in states lacking Fair Employment Practice Commissions, or FEPCs) have 180 days from notification of an event to file EEOC charges. The 1964 Act permitted only 90 days to file—the first surgical change. If the EEOC is tardy, a claimant can sue privately after 180 days have passed since filing. If the EEOC issues a right to sue notice, charges must be filed in federal district court within 90 days; increased from 30 days in the Civil Rights Act of 1991—the second surgical change.

In **deferral** states (with FEPCs), a claimant has 300 days to file with the EEOC, but must first file a state claim. The claimant may then file EEOC charges after 60 days regardless of state administrative actions. However, a plaintiff who permits a state court to rule on the charges can jeopardize a subsequent federal suit.

EEOC filing procedures can therefore serve as a barrier to federal court. The procedures were designed for three good reasons: (a) to permit the EEOC and FEPCs to resolve charges short of litigation; (b) to reserve the ultimate right of private access to federal court; and (c) to ensure that claims are filed and addressed in a timely manner. The barrier to court action is an unfortunate by-product.

To illustrate, in *Mohasco Corp. v. Silver* (1980), Silver filed EEOC charges 291 days after his termination notice. Because Silver worked in a deferral state, the EEOC deferred to the FEPC and reclaimed the case on day 357. The Supreme Court ruled that the 300-day filing period had expired before the claim was officially filed with the EEOC. In other words, Silver lost his right to sue—a result that could have been avoided had he filed his original claim on day 240 or earlier.

Thus with discrete acts such as discharge, demotion, or failure to promote, among others, the clock runs from the day of **notification**, unless it is officially tolled for procedural reasons. In cases of continuous violations (e.g., harassment), the clock does not stop. Employers should be wary of providing early notices and encouraging employees to hold their charges until after the date of enforcement (e.g., discharge more than 300 days after notification). Such a practice is illegal, and demonstrates a reckless disregard for the law.

Filing Procedures for Federal Employees

As noted in the preface, the main focus in this book is private and state/local entities. For present purposes, this a relief for both the author and the reader. The evolution of administration procedures for federal employees is a nightmare of options and multiple deadlines. The interested reader is directed to Bussey (1990). Basically, federal employees are subject to three types of procedures: (a) appeals before the Merit Systems Protection Board (MSPB); (b) EEOC filing procedures; and (c) MSPB appeals and/or EEOC filing (a so-called mixed case).

Policies and Record Keeping

Among other things, Carter's Reorganization abolished the Equal Opportunity Coordinating Council, which had consisted of the Directors and/or Secretaries of the EEOC, Civil Service Commission, Civil Rights Commission, and the Departments of Justice and Labor. The Coordinating Council had been created by Congress in the EEO Act of 1972 with the following mandate:

> The Council shall have the responsibility for developing and implementing agreements, policies and practices designed to maximize effort, promote efficiency, and eliminate conflict, competition, duplication and inconsistency among the operations, functions and jurisdictions of the various departments, agencies and branches of the Federal Government responsible for the implementation and enforcement of equal employment opportunity legislation, orders, and policies.

Thus the Coordinating Council was made responsible for record keeping and policy making (i.e., regulations and guidelines).

The record-keeping function is arduous. There are six different EEO forms, the most important being the **EEO-1** and **EEO-4** forms for private and state/local entities, respectively, with 100 or more employees. Records must be kept in accordance with key terms and conditions of employment broken down by key subgroups of employees.

Returning to the historical record, the Coordinating Council did not coordinate very well. In fact, the EEOC resisted early attempts to establish guidelines with Labor, Justice, and Civil Service. In fact, when the Council published its *Federal Executive Agency Guidelines* in 1976, they were not adopted by the EEOC. In 1977, the Council began developing the *Uniform Guidelines on Employee Selection Procedures*, a critical document that lays the foundation for discovery and treatment of adverse impact. Despite evidence of success, however, the Council's fate was sealed. In his message to Congress introducing Reorganization Plan No.1 in 1978, President Carter stated:

> By abolishing the Equal Employment Coordinating Council . . . the EEOC can give coherence and direction to the government's efforts by developing strong uniform enforcement standards to apply throughout the government; standardized data collection procedures. . . . Such direction has been absent in the Equal Employment Opportunity Coordinating Council.

With the Council dissolved, the EEOC was free to regulate without much competition. Most observers believe that the EEOC has been an effective policymaker. However, as we will witness later in this chapter and throughout the book, regulations and guidelines are not immune to invalidation by the courts. Fortunately, Title VII permits a **Sec.710 defense** for "good faith" adherence to guidelines and regulations.[3] The *Uniform Guidelines on Personnel Selection* will serve as a framework for the discussion on compliance issues in Section VI of this chapter.

REMEDIES (Q5)

Until 1991, **legal** relief was not a permissible Title VII remedy; all remedies were **equitable** and all awards were determined by judges. As specified in Sec.706(g), these legal remedies include injunction,

2-year back pay and/or benefit awards, reinstatement or front pay, affirmative action in cases of egregious violations (e.g., a pattern or practice of discrimination), and lawyer fees to prevailing plaintiffs other than the EEOC or the United States. It must be recognized that equitable relief is designed to restore lost rights. Thus if an excluded applicant finds work during the covered 2-year period the amount of back pay is limited to the difference between what was earned versus what would have been earned.

The Civil Rights Act of 1991 added legal relief in the form of compensatory and punitive damages, and codified expert fees in addition to previously permitted lawyer fees. Except in claims against the federal government, legal relief may be tried by jury. Also, the added damages apply only to intentional acts of discrimination; not to pure adverse impact. If a plaintiff is victorious, damages may be obtained ranging from $50,000 from employers with less than 100 employees, to $300,000 from employers with 500 or more employees. Punitive damages may not be obtained from federal, state, or local entities.

A final point to note is that in cases that would charge both adverse impact and intentional discrimination, the jury would decide the facts of both cases as well as the legal relief. Cases reviewed under Sec.1981 and Sec.1983 in Chapter 4 suggest that juries can be very generous with employer funds.

ATTACK/DEFENSE BALANCES (Q6)

As noted in Chapter 1, the two most common scenarios are adverse impact and disparate treatment. Title VII **adverse impact** is usually initiated with statistical evidence that a policy or practice screens out a disproportionate number of protected group members (e.g., blacks vs. whites or women vs. men). The employer is then burdened with a business necessity defense. A successful defense leaves the plaintiff with the option of proving that an alternative policy or practice is equally as valid, but has less adverse impact.

Disparate treatment comes in three forms. One form relies on presumptive evidence to establish an inference of illegal discrimination (e.g., I was qualified but not hired), answered by a facially plausible reason why the inference is wrong (e.g., the person hired was more qualified). The plaintiff must then provide persuasive evidence that the employer's stated reason is a pretext (e.g., that the person hired was less qualified). For reasons that will be evident later in the chapter, this scenario is termed "McDonnell-Burdine."

A second form of disparate treatment is the **pattern or practice** of discrimination, the so-called Sec.707 violation. Here, statistical evidence of segregation or classification can be used to establish a presumption of a violation and can be bolstered by examples of plaintiffs who were individually discriminated against. The defendant again answers with plausible alternatives in phase 2, and the plaintiff tries to prove pretext in phase 3.

The third form of disparate treatment is traditional and pre-dates Title VII. The plaintiff provides factual proof of discrimination in phase 1 and the defendant answers with factual proof to the contrary in phase 2. The plaintiff can then prove pretext in phase 3. A variation of this scenario is termed **mixed-motive**, where the plaintiff's factual proof of an illegal motive may be strong but the employer provides factual proof of legal motive (e.g., there is factual evidence of sexual harassment, but there is also factual evidence of poor job performance).

In addition to the various phase 2 defenses described above, an employer may argue that the adverse effect or the discriminatory treatment is protected by a **bona fide seniority system** (BFSS). Furthermore, if the discriminatory act is facial discrimination (e.g., no women allowed), the only valid defense is the **bona fide occupational qualification** (BFOQ). The employer must prove that the exclusion of an entire group is reasonably necessary for the job (e.g., that all or substantially all women, or men, cannot successfully perform the work). The BFOQ defense applies to facial discrimination based on sex, religion, and national origin; facial discrimination based on race or color is indefensible.

——— **BRIEF SUMMARY** ———

Title VII is the broadest of all EEO laws, fully protecting (**Q1**) the largest number of classes—race, color, religion, sex, and national origin. The statute covers (**Q2**) private, state/local, and federal entities for (**Q3**) all practices relating to nondiscrimination (i.e., not affirmative action). The administrative procedures (**Q4**) require EEOC charges prior to court charges, and in deferral states, state charges prior to EEOC charges. The remedies (**Q5**) are exhaustive, including equitable relief and capped legal relief. Finally, the attack/defense balances (**Q6**) include four scenarios, two statutory options for special circumstances (BFOQ & BFSS), plus the Sec.710 "good faith" defense.

SECTION II
ADVERSE IMPACT

Adverse impact is a unique product of Title VII case law. An analogy alluded to in Chapter 1 illustrates the attack. The 15th Amendment gave former slaves the right to vote. But the people in some states were not friendly to this prospect, and created facially neutral laws to remedy the amendment. For example, to cast a vote, a citizen had to own property, pay a poll tax, and so forth. In 1964 these badges of discrimination were outlawed by the 24th Amendment.

Analogously, after Title VII was enacted, some employers instituted requirements for job selection that were facially neutral, but they were as arbitrary to work as the poll tax was to voting. These requirements (e.g., a high school degree) were not related to job performance. Moreover, they had the same exclusionary impact on blacks as the poll tax. But unlike the voting issue, which required a constitutional amendment, these badges were struck down by the Supreme Court in *Griggs v. Duke Power* (1971).

GRIGGS V. DUKE POWER (1971)

Griggs v. Duke Power was a class action suit in the name of Willie Griggs, a black male excluded from the job of coal handler. Prior to Title VII, all coal handlers were white. After Title VII was enacted, the coal-handling job required a high school degree or a passing score on two IQ tests (the Wonderlic Personnel Test and Bennett Mechanical Comprehension Test); requirements that excluded significantly more blacks than whites. Griggs's charges were dismissed in the lower courts. For example, the 4th Circuit Court ruled that residual effects of pre-Title VII discrimination were "insulated from remedial action." The 4th Circuit also ruled that "absent a discriminatory purpose, the diploma and test requirements were proper."

The Supreme Court reversed. In a short but crisp unanimous ruling, Justice Burger stated:

> Under the Act, practices, procedures, and tests neutral on their face, and even neutral in terms of intent, cannot be maintained if they operate to "freeze" the status quo of prior discriminatory employment practices.

In other words, the Court viewed adverse impact as a way of maintaining the effects of past intentional discrimination. The Court outlined a three-phase scenario that became standard in adverse impact cases.

Phase 1: The Prima Facie Attack

Prima facie adverse impact requires statistical proof that a challenged criterion disproportionately screens out a higher percentage of one of two groups in the same class. The Uniform Guidelines advocate the 80% (or "four-fifths") rule. Or as stated in Sec.1607.4 of these Guidelines:

> A selection rate for any race, sex, or ethnic group which is less than four-fifths (4/5) (or eighty percent) of the rate for the group with the highest rate will generally be regarded by the Federal enforcement agencies as evidence of adverse impact.

For example, if 50 of 100 whites are hired (a selection ratio of 50%), the selection ratio for blacks should be 40% or higher (i.e., 4 out of every 10 applicants). This is not a quota rule because the challenged practice is illegal only if it is unrelated to job performance. Or as further stated in the Uniform Guidelines:

> When members of one race, sex or ethnic group characteristically obtain lower scores on a selection procedure than members of another group, and the differences in scores are not reflected in differences in measure of job performance, use of the selection procedure *may* unfairly deny opportunities to members of the group that obtains the lower scores. [emphasis added]

It should be noted that the 80% rule is a rule of thumb. Employers should examine differences in selection ratios in terms of statistical probabilities as they relate to smaller versus larger work forces.

The Supreme Court ruled that Griggs established adverse impact because the high school degree excluded nearly 3 times as many blacks as whites, and the two IQ tests excluded nearly 10 times as many blacks as whites. The Court also ruled that motive, as cited by the circuit court, is irrelevant. According to Justice Burger:

Congress directed the thrust of the Act to the consequences of employment practices, not simply the motivation.

Indeed, Title VII does not reference adverse impact. But it does speak
to standards that **adversely affect** job opportunities in Sec.703(a)(2)
on classification and segregation.

Phase 2: The Burden of Defense

Duke Power countered that its selection tests were "professionally
developed," citing Sec.703(h) in the statute, which states:

> nor shall it be an unlawful employment practice for an employer to give
> and to act upon the results of any *professionally developed* ability test pro-
> vided that such test . . . is not designed, intended or used to discriminate
> because of race, color, religion, sex, or national origin. [emphasis added]

The company may have understood this to mean that formal tests are
valid as long as they are professionally developed (the emphasized term).
The Court disagreed, stating:

> The touchstone is business necessity. If an employment practice which
> operates to exclude Negroes cannot be shown to be related to job perform-
> ance, the practice is prohibited.

This portion of the Griggs ruling is echoed in Sec.1607.9 of the
Uniform Guidelines, which states:

> Under no circumstances will the general reputation of a test of other
> selection procedures, its author or its publisher, or casual reports of
> validity be accepted in lieu of evidence of validity.

In short, adverse impact in phase 1 imposes a burden of persuasion in
phase 2. That burden is to prove job relatedness. Or as stated by Justice
Burger:

> Congress has placed on the employer the burden of showing that any
> given requirement must have a manifest relationship to the employment
> in question.

Phase 3: The Burden of Pretext

Griggs won the case in phase 2. Therefore, a pretext argument
was not necessary. Pretext was discussed, however, in the next case,

Albermarle Paper Co. v. Moody (1975). In Albermarle, the Supreme Court ruled that if the defendant is successful in phase 2:

> the employee may rebut the employer's showing with proof that the stated business necessity is a pretext for discrimination . . . by showing that less discriminatory alternatives to achievement of the employer's goal were available.

In other words, the plaintiff has to locate equally valid but less impactful criteria. The defendant does not have to prove that the choice of more impactful criteria was intentional, although this is an option. The Albermarle case will be discussed shortly.

OTHER TRADITIONAL ADVERSE IMPACT CASES

A key ingredient in Griggs was the use of formal tests. Obviously, formal tests are not the only means of producing adverse impact. But the emphasis in most Supreme Court adverse impacts cases since Griggs has been on formal tests. Other frequently cited cases in this tradition include the previously cited Albermarle case, and *Connecticut v. Teal* (1982). Another case usually cited with Albermarle and Teal is *Washington v. Davis* (1976), a Sec.1983 case.

Albermarle Paper Company v. Moody (1975)

Albermarle v. Moody contained Griggs-like circumstances, but the selection decision was promotion, not hiring. Unlike Duke Power, which based its defense on "professional development," Albermarle hired an industrial psychologist to statistically validate the formal tests[4] against a job-performance criterion. However, it was a hasty effort conducted shortly before trial. Ultimately, the Supreme Court cited four major defects in the study: (a) a general lack of quality, or "odd patchwork"; (b) unknown job-performance criteria based on "subjective supervisory rankings"; (c) a focus on top-of-the-line jobs in comparison to the "entering low-level jobs" that were being challenged; and (d) the validation sample, which included only "job-experienced white workers."

Any of these defects could have invalidated the study. As a result, the Albermarle Court treated poorly conducted professional validation no better than the Griggs Court treated absence of validation. The

Court, quoting from the then EEOC Guidelines (i.e., guidelines pre-dating the Uniform Guidelines), stated:

> Discriminatory tests are impermissible unless shown by professionally acceptable methods, to be "predictive or significantly correlated with important elements of work behavior which comprise or are relevant to the job or jobs for which the candidates are being evaluated."

The quoted portion from the EEOC Guidelines speaks to formal criterion validation, an issue to be discussed further in Section VI of this chapter.

Connecticut v. Teal (1982)

In *Connecticut v. Teal* (1982), provisional promotions for blacks were rescinded after they had failed a written test. The written test was part of a series of requirements (i.e., a multiple hurdle). The state advanced a **bottom-line** argument, asserting that when all hurdles were completed, a higher percentage of blacks (22.9%) than whites (13.5%) were promoted. But the selection rate for blacks on only the written test was 68% relative to whites. The state based its defense on a portion of the Uniform Guidelines stating that the EEOC:

> will not expect a user to evaluate the individual components for adverse impact, or to validate such individual components, and will not take enforcement action based upon adverse impact of any component of that process.

But the Supreme Court rejected this guidance, stating:

> It is clear that Congress never intended to give an employer license to discriminate against some employees on the basis of race or sex merely because he favorably treats other members of the employees' group.

Thus the State of Connecticut learned that good affirmative action numbers do not constitute a valid defense for individuous discrimination in a Title VII case. Though the state's affirmative action plan worked to produce ultimate goals favorable to blacks, the Supreme Court concluded that each individual has the same Title VII rights regardless of how well the class as a whole is treated.

Washington v. Davis (1976)

The fact that *Washington v. Davis* was a Sec.1983 case does not blemish its importance to Title VII. Indeed, the case established precedents for both statutes. Davis challenged recruitment practices in the Washington, D.C., Police Department, particularly the use of a test that disproportionately screened black applicants from police training school (Test 21 developed by the Civil Service Commission). The precedent for Sec.1983 was that adverse impact is not a viable attack under Sec.1983; plaintiffs must show a racially motivated purpose. This part of the case will be discussed in Chapter 4.

Nevertheless, the Court ruled that Test 21 (a measure of basic verbal skills) is valid because it predicts training school performance, and that training school is a necessary precursor for police work. Thus the Court permitted police (and fire) departments to use training in lieu of job performance to validate tests; a convenient route because training performance is easier to assess than job performance.[5]

TEMPORARY SETBACKS

The precedent established in Griggs, and broadened in Albermarle and Teal, clearly favored plaintiffs. Cases such as Davis favored defendants but did not alter the Griggs precedent. In what had become case law, differential effects of formal testing were sufficient to force business necessity defenses. Historically, Griggs-type cases involved **objective** formal tests easily identifiable as the cause of adverse impact. Before 1988, however, the requirement to identify these tests had never emerged as a Supreme Court issue.

This changed with *Watson v. Fort Worth Bank & Trust* (1988). Actually, at first blush, Watson presented as a further extension of plaintiff rights. But it served as a prelude to another case, *Wards Cove Packing Co. v. Atonio* (1989), which effectively reversed key elements of the Griggs ruling until the Civil Rights Act of 1991.

Watson v. Fort Worth Bank (1988)

Clara Watson, a black woman, was passed over for promotion to supervisor for the fourth time. Each time, a white employee was promoted.

The bank's promotional procedures were **subjective**. At trial, Watson pointed to statistical disparities, including absence of black upper level managers; only a single black supervisor (the position Watson wanted); higher salaries for white employees; and poorer performance ratings of black employees by white supervisors. The case was dismissed at the prima facie level in the lower courts, a common ruling in adverse impact attacks based on subjective issues (e.g., *Talley v. United States Postal Service,* 1983). Generally, plaintiffs challenging subjective decisions were forced to use disparate treatment, which offers a lighter burden of defense than adverse impact. The Supreme Court had never ruled on this issue.

The case was deemed critical by the American Psychological Association. Bersoff (1988), in an amicus curiae (friend-of-the-court) brief written on behalf of the American Psychological Association, offered three arguments favoring adverse impact evaluation for subjective decisions: (a) they are as amenable to validation as objective tests; (b) the bank had a history of using subjective decisions without concern for validity; and (c) if subjective decisions are immune to adverse impact, unscrupulous employers could use them exclusively to avoid the heavy burden of justifying business necessity.

The Supreme Court's ruling was complex. To begin with, Justice Kennedy sat out. The remaining eight justices formed three camps; O'Connor speaking for Rehnquist, White, and Scalia; Blackmun speaking for Brennan and Marshall; and Stevens speaking for himself. All eight justices ruled that subjective decisions *are* amenable to adverse impact evaluation; seemingly, a victory for adverse impact plaintiffs. However, O'Connor went further, expressing the following fear:

> Standardized tests . . . like those at issue in our previous disparate impact cases, can often be justified through formal "validation studies" . . . respondent warns, however, that "validating" subjective criteria in this way is impracticable.

In other words, O'Connor rejected Bersoff's arguments. She also asserted that "bare" bottom-line statistics would force a multitude of new adverse impact claims, and fearful employers would adopt quotas to protect themselves from having to justify business necessity.

Therefore, O'Connor asserted a need for a "fresh and somewhat closer examination" of adverse impact. More specifically, she made two proposals. First, citing traditional adverse impact cases in which challenged practices are invariably identified, O'Connor asserted that a statistical disparity should not be the only requirement in prima facie adverse impact. She proposed that:

> The plaintiff must begin by identifying the specific employment practice that is challenged.

Second, believing that a burden of **persuasion** should never shift to a defendant, O'Connor stated:

> Thus, when a plaintiff has made out a prima facie case of disparate impact, and when the defendant has met its burden of *producing* evidence that its employment practices are based on legitimate business reasons, the plaintiff must *"show that other tests or selection devices, without a similarly undesirable racial effect, would also serve the employer's legitimate interest in efficient and trustworthy workmanship."* [emphasis added]

There are two thoughts in this quote—both emphasized. The term **producing** is from the disparate treatment literature. It means that in lieu of demonstrating business necessity, the defendant can explain or articulate a nondiscriminatory reason for a selection decision. For example, the defendant can state: "our consultants advised us to use the test." The second part of the quote (the final lines) is taken directly from Albermarle, and expresses the traditional Griggs precedent for a phase 3 pretext argument.

Among the other camps, Stevens noted that the Court successfully ruled on the only issue it faced; applying adverse impact to subjective tests. The Blackmun camp, although agreeing with Stevens, wanted to dispute O'Connor's opinion.

Blackmun opposed O'Connor's first proposal (specific causes), but saved his venom for the second one (replacement of persuasion with production). He continuously referred to O'Connor's second proposal as an "echo" from the disparate treatment literature. Citing the same series of cases used by O'Connor, Blackmun stated:

> [These] cases make clear, however, that, contrary to the plurality's assertion . . . a plaintiff who successfully establishes this prima facie case shifts the burden of proof, not production to the defendant to establish that the employment practice in question is a business necessity.

On O'Connor's fear regarding validation of subjective tests relative to objective tests, Blackmun stated:

> While the formal validation techniques endorsed by the EEOC in its Uniform Guidelines may sometimes not be effective in measuring the job relatedness of subjective-selection processes, a variety of methods are available for establishing the link between these selection processes and job performance, just as they are for objective-selection devices.

Blackmun did *not* reject the APA brief; in fact, he footnoted it in connection with this quote. His point, however, was that lower courts had already accepted proofs of business necessity other than validation studies (e.g., nationwide studies, testimony from scholars, etc.). Blackmun cited a much publicized 5th Circuit case in which a business necessity defense succeeded without formal validation (*Davis v. Dallas*, 1985—a case the Supreme Court refused to review).

Wards Cove Packing Co. v. Atonio (1989)

Although the O'Connor opinion represented only a plurality of four, the Watson case proved to be the first act of a two-act play, the second act being Wards Cove. When the drama ended, the curtain temporarily fell on the Griggs precedent.

Wards Cove involved two salmon-packing companies in the Pacific Northwest, each with hiring-hall arrangements to select only minority packers during the salmon-catching season. To support this unskilled activity, the companies also hired, by different (subjective) means, skilled workers (e.g., engineers, mechanics, etc.). These workers were paid more, fed better, and so forth. Clearly, there was a statistical disparity between the two jobs. Eskimos and Filipinos were well represented in the unskilled positions, but virtually unrepresented in the skilled positions.

The plaintiffs charged both adverse impact and disparate treatment. The district court rejected both charges at the prima facie level, ruling in particular that subjective decisions were not amenable to adverse impact analysis. The 9th Circuit affirmed the disparate treatment ruling. However, citing Watson, the Court also ruled that: (a) subjective criteria are amenable to adverse impact analysis; (b) the plaintiffs had demonstrated adverse impact; and (c) a business necessity defense was therefore required.

With Justice Kennedy participating, he plus the Watson plurality of O'Connor, Rehnquist, Scalia, and White fashioned a 5 to 4 majority that turned O'Connor's Watson opinion into case law. In addition to the two proposals from O'Connor's Watson opinion, Justice White, the spokesperson, made a third ruling:

> The Court of Appeals erred in ruling that a comparison of the percent-
> age of cannery workers who are nonwhite and the percentage of noncan-
> nery workers who are white makes out a prima facie disparate-impact
> case.

That is, within a given work force, a statistical disparity between two
samples at two different jobs is not sufficient for prima facie discrimination; the sample in one job (unskilled) may not be qualified for the
other job (skilled). Continuing, White stated:

> The proper comparison [is] between the racial composition of [the
> at-issue jobs] and the racial composition of the qualified . . . popula-
> tion . . . that generally forms the proper basis for an initial inquiry in
> a disparate impact case.

Thus prima facie discrimination requires a comparison between minorities versus whites in a single (e.g., skilled) position. Of course,
virtually no minorities ever applied for the skilled positions, thus
rendering any such statistical comparison meaningless.

In the author's opinion, this third ruling is unprecedented. The
supporting cases cited by White were mainly Supreme Court rulings
on the **pattern or practice** of discrimination (e.g., *International Brotherhood of Teamsters v. United States,* 1977; *Hazelwood School District v.
United States,* 1977; *N.Y.C. v. Beazer,* 1979). As noted earlier, pattern or
practice is, technically speaking, not adverse impact.

Equally as surprising, the dissent also ignored the pattern or practice implications of Wards Cove. Thus Justice Blackmun, speaking for
Brennan and Marshall, summarized Stevens's solo dissent by stating:

> Today a bare majority of the court takes three major strides backwards
> in the battle against race discrimination. It reaches out to make last
> Term's plurality decision in Watson . . . the law, thereby upsetting the
> longstanding distribution of burdens of proof in Title VII disparate-
> impact cases. It bars the use of internal workforce comparisons in the
> making of a prima facie case of discrimination, even where the struc-
> ture of the industry in question renders any other statistical comparison
> meaningless. And it requires practice-by-practice statistical proof of
> causation, even where, as here, such proof would be impossible.

Justice Stevens, however, in both the text of his dissent and his footnotes, portrayed a history of discrimination in the salmon industry as
a chilling factor that discouraged applications from minorities. For
example, in footnote #4, Stevens states:

> Some characteristics of the Alaska salmon industry . . . bear an unsettling resemblance to aspects of a plantation economy.

The author has never practiced law; at least not in the courtroom. Nor would he wish to change clothes with any justices on the Supreme Court. Nevertheless, this is precisely the rationale courts have used in ruling against defendants in pattern or practice suits (e.g., Teamsters, 1977).

The pattern or practice implications for Wards Cove will be considered later. For present purposes, it is sufficient to note that the majority ruled that cross-job disparities cannot be used in adverse impact, and the minority disagreed. Pattern or practice aside, the O'Connor plurality in Watson and the majority ruling in Wards Cove are vulnerable to three other criticisms.

First, the Uniform Guidelines were misinterpreted by O'Connor and White to imply that formal validation is the only way to prove business necessity. It has certainly been necessary with formal tests (e.g., IQ tests), but has not been in lower court cases considering informal standards (e.g., credit information, arrest and/or conviction records, etc.). This issue will be discussed in Section VI of this chapter, and again in Chapter 3.

Second, as noted by Bersoff (1988), there is no difference in how subjective and objective tests are validated. For example, a criterion validity study uses the same statistical procedures for multiple choice tests, which are objective, and interview ratings, which are subjective. The method of validation is oblivious to this difference.

Third, because adverse impact plaintiffs invariably identify a challenged practice, this issue was never before ruled on. Therefore the requirement to specify the causes of adverse impact was not a reversal of prior precedent. But there is nothing in the 18-year span between Griggs and Wards Cove to imply a reflexive connection between specifying causes and eliminating the burden of business necessity. This was unquestionably a reversal of the Griggs precedent.

The Civil Rights Act of 1991

Congress agreed with the Blackmun minority in Wards Cove. Therefore, the Civil Rights Act of 1991 restores the business necessity defense to its pre-Wards Cove status. Or, as stated in Sec.105(A)(i) of the 1991 Act, an employer practice is deemed unlawful if adverse impact is demonstrated and:

the respondent fails to demonstrate that the challenged practice is job related for the position in question and consistent with business necessity.

However, Congress also agreed with Part 1 of O'Connor's opinion in Watson. Thus as stated in Sec.105(B)(i):

> the complaining party shall demonstrate that each particular challenged employment practice causes disparate impact, except that if the complaining party can demonstrate to the court that the elements of a respondent's decisionmaking process are not capable of separation for analysis, the decisionmaking process may be analyzed as one employment practice.

Putting (A) and (B) together—if the plaintiff establishes adverse impact and identifies its specific cause(s)—the pre-Wards Cove business necessity defense is required. However, if the "elements" cannot be separated, then the entire selection procedure is treated as a single cause. Of course, the courts must decide when the decision-making elements are inseparable.

This is clearly a compromise relative to the aborted Civil Rights Restoration Act of 1990. However, the bigger of O'Connor's two proposals in Watson was reversed. As for specifying causes of adverse impact, the reader is referred to Justice Stevens's words in Wards Cove:

> It is elementary that a plaintiff cannot recover upon proof of injury alone; rather the plaintiff must connect the injury to an act of the defendant in order to establish prima facie that the defendant is liable.

In other words, a statistical disparity standing alone is meaningless unless connected in some causal way to an action or policy by an employer. Although reasonable people are free to disagree, this principle of connection is also a key component in adverse impact against disabled people, as will be witnessed in Chapter 8. It does, however, put an extra pressure on subjective procedures that may be difficult to identify and isolate.

———— BRIEF SUMMARY ————

In traditional Title VII adverse impact scenarios, a burden of persuasion exists in all three phases. According to the Griggs-Albermarle tradition, statistical proof of adverse impact is required in phase 1, business necessity must be proven in phase 2, and pretext must be proven in phase 3. Albermarle reveals the importance of reliable and valid performance appraisal data in formal validity studies, and *Washington v. Davis* reveals the acceptable use of reliable and valid training appraisal data in lieu of job performance data for police and firefighters. Teal reveals a need to assess any impactful test, regardless of the bottom-line implications. As a result of the Civil Rights Act of 1991 the principle ruling in Wards Cove is reversed, meaning that the Watson ruling does extend adverse impact to subjective criteria. The new requirement, that the plaintiff establish a nexus to employer practices, mimics the reality in most prior adverse impact cases. The requirement may, however, make it more difficult to isolate causes of adverse impact when the challenged practices are subjective (e.g., unscored interviews).

SECTION III
TRADITIONAL ISSUES IN DISPARATE TREATMENT

Evidence of illegal motive can support adverse impact and evidence of adverse impact can support disparate treatment. However, just as adverse impact requires the statistics, disparate treatment requires the motive. Of course, motive is a private event that must be inferred from an employer's actions. The complicating factor is that negative actions (e.g., demotion) may be motivated by legitimate business reasons (e.g., ineptitude), illegal motives (e.g., racism), or both.

BACKGROUND ISSUES

If Title VII existed in prior centuries, many cases would have been easy to resolve. For example, the following ad, though fictitious, could have been appeared in a newspaper as recently as the Civil War era (and perhaps even more recently):

> Wanted—white male mathematics teacher for suburban elementary school. Must have good breeding, and be 100 percent white. Jews, Turks, and any other undesirables need not apply.

Obviously, the ad leaves little to infer. The discrimination is **facial** and the motive is clear.

Interestingly, blatant practices indefensible by Title VII standards currently exist in other cultures. For example, the following ad, excerpted from Cascio (1991), appeared in a Hong Kong newspaper in the early 1980s:

> Very obedient young woman required by *American Director* for position as Secretary/Personnel Assistant. Must be attractive and eager to submit to authority, have good typing and filing skills and be free to travel. Knowledge of Mandarin an advantage. Most important, she should enjoy following orders without question and cheerfully accept directions. Send handwritten resume on unlined paper and recent photo to G.P.O. box 6132, Hong Kong. (p. 29)

Clearly, the *American Director* would have placed a different ad in an American newspaper. Title VII disparate treatment cases do not generally contain such easy issues. Sometimes the illegal practice is crude, but more often it is subtle or naive.

A *Crude* employer may overtly mistreat an employee (verbally and/or physically), so that the discriminatory motive can be documented (e.g., witnesses, memos, etc.). A *Subtle* employer may avoid documentable displays, but demote or discharge poorly performing members of one group, while only reprimanding poorly performing members of another group. A *Naive* employer may use quotas and may be shocked to learn that bottom-line statistical balance among protected groups is not an adequate defense for individuous disparate treatment.

Key disparate treatment cases feature all three types of employer actions. A landmark case (*McDonnell Douglas Corp. v. Green,* 1973) tests subtlety, as do two follow-up cases (*Board of Trustees of Keene State College v. Sweeney,* 1978, & *U.S. Postal Service Board of Governors v. Aikens,* 1983). But two other follow-ups test naivety (*Furnco Construction Co. v. Waters,* 1978; *Texas Department of Community Affairs v. Burdine,* 1981), and a critical mixed-motive case tests crudeness (*Price Waterhouse v. Hopkins,* 1989).

McDONNELL DOUGLAS V. GREEN (1973)

Disparate treatment has a rich pre-Title VII history in union cases decided under the NLRA (National Labor Relations Act). However, these earlier cases relied on factual evidence of discriminatory motive (i.e., witnesses, documents, etc.). Factual evidence might snare the "crude" employer, but probably not the "subtle" employer. Aware of the distinction, the Supreme Court used *McDonnell Douglas v. Green* to create an easier attack. But at the same time, the Court created an easier defense. In essence, the McDonnell scenario (commonly termed the "McDonnell-Burdine" scenario) sets up a phase-3 pretext argument, where the plaintiff must provide a preponderance of factual evidence to counter a specific and productive phase-2 defense.

Percy Green, a black male, was a civil rights activist, which is legal behavior. When laid off in a reduction-in-force, Green and others engaged in demonstrations to protest alleged racial discrimination by the company. However, he committed illegal acts. During a "stall-in," cars were parked to prevent employees from entering the plant. During a "lock-in," an exit was padlocked to prevent employees from leaving the plant. Several weeks later, the company advertised for mechanics (Green's prior position). Green applied, but was not rehired.

Green filed two Title VII charges with the EEOC. One charge cited Sec.703(a)(1) (terms and conditions), and alleged racism as the reason for exclusion. The second charge cited Sec.704(a) (retaliation) and pointed to his participation in legitimate civil rights activities as the reason for exclusion. The EEOC ruled there was reasonable cause for retaliation, but not for terms and conditions related to racism.

The district court tried and dismissed the retaliation charge, but dismissed the racism charge without trial (because the EEOC failed to find reasonable cause). The 8th Circuit also dismissed on retaliation, but ruled that Green did not require an EEOC blessing to sue on racism. The 8th Circuit tried the racism charge and ruled in Green's favor in phase 1. But the company was ordered to *persuade* the court that failure to rehire Green was a *business necessity* (the phase-2 burden in Griggs). Thus the three-phase procedure for disparate treatment served as the agenda in this precedent-setting case.

Phase 1: The Prima Facie Attack

Justice Powell, speaking for a unanimous Court, stated:

> The case before us raises significant questions as to the proper order and nature of proof in actions under Title VII of the Civil Rights Act of 1964.

Powell affirmed that Green had established prima facie discrimination. But unlike the 8th Circuit, which had entertained factual evidence of discrimination in phase 1, the Supreme Court established a more lenient four-step prescription. According to Powell, these steps are:

(i) that he belongs to a racial majority; (ii) that he applied and was qualified for the job for which the employer was seeking applications; (iii) that, despite his qualifications, he was rejected; and (iv) that, after his rejection, the position remained open and the employer continued to seek applicants from persons of complainant's qualifications.

Green passed each step: (i) he was black; (ii) the company acknowledged his application and qualifications; (iii) he was not rehired; and (iv) the search continued after Green's exclusion.

Phase 2: A Productive Defense

The phase 1 attack illustrates **productive** evidence. There is no direct implication of a violation, only a presumption that the defendant must refute. For phase 2, Powell ruled that the persuasive business necessity defense required by the circuit court is an improper way to refute a simple presumption. Therefore, Powell established a productive defense to match the productive attack. Accordingly:

The burden then must shift to the employer to articulate some legitimate, nondiscriminatory reason for the employee's rejection.

The reader should recognize here the "echo" of disparate treatment alluded to by Blackmun in his plurality opinion in Watson.

The Court ruled that the company had successfully **articulated** "a legitimate nondiscriminatory reason"; that is, the exclusion of Green was for illegal protest behaviors, not racial discrimination.

Phase 3: Pretext

Powell remanded the case for consideration of pretext with clear instructions regarding potential pretext arguments. Accordingly:

Especially relevant to such a showing would be evidence that white employees involved in acts against petitioner of comparable seriousness to "stall-in" were nevertheless retained or rehired. . . . Other evidence . . . includes facts as to the petitioner's treatment of respondent during his prior term of employment; petitioner's reaction, if any, to respondent's legitimate civil rights actives; and petitioner's general policy and practice with respect to minority employment.

In other words, the burden on Green in phase 3 is **persuasive**, but can be accomplished indirectly or directly. An **indirect** showing would involve factual evidence that the employer's articulation is absurd (because whites who broke the law were rehired). A **direct** showing would involve factual evidence that the employer had a history of mistreating Green and/or black workers in general. Green lost on remand.

FOLLOW-UP CASES

The unanimity of the Green ruling proved deceptive. It took four more cases to codify the principles of disparate treatment, particularly the phase 2 burden on the defendant. These cases are *Furnco v. Waters,* 1978; *Board of Trustees v. Sweeney,* 1978; *Texas v. Burdine,* 1981, and *U.S. Postal Service v. Aikens,* 1983.

Furnco Construction Company v. Waters (1978)

Furnco, like Teal, dealt with an important Affirmative Action issue. It also spurred a series of debates because of a single word in the Court's ruling. Speaking for a unanimous Court on all issues relating to disparate treatment, Justice Rehnquist stated:

> The burden which shifts to the employer is merely that of *proving* that he based his employment decision on a legitimate consideration, and not an illegitimate one such as race. [emphasis added]

This ruling was virtually identical to *McDonnell v. Green,* except for the word *proving,* which provided a spark.

As for the case, Furnco was a construction company that hired its employees on a per-job basis. The employer used a voluntary affirmative action plan, but relied on construction-site supervisors to enforce it. Reflective of the fictitious "naive" employer described earlier, the company routinely achieved its affirmative action goals. But once achieved, its policies were relaxed. In response to what was essentially an affirmative action defense, Rehnquist stated:

> It is clear beyond a cavil that the obligation imposed by Title VII is to provide an equal opportunity for each applicant regardless of race, without regard to whether members of the applicant's race are already proportionately represented in the workforce.

In other words, affirmative action is as invalid a defense to individuous disparate treatment as it is to adverse impact.

Board of Trustees v. Sweeney (1978)

The issue created by the word *proving,* however, was burdensome. Was it a clarification of *McDonnell v. Green,* or was it a slip of the pen? Taken as clarification, it means the defendant must prove "absence of discriminatory motive" persuasively, not productively. In Sweeney, the charge was racial discrimination in promotion. The facts of the case were overshadowed by the Court's attempt to clarify its use of the word **articulate** in *McDonnell Douglas v. Green* versus **prove** in Furnco. Justice Rehnquist, speaking for Blackmun, Burger, Powell, and White, stated:

> While words such as "articulate," "show," and "prove" may have more or less similar meanings depending upon the *context* in which they are used, we think that there is a significant distinction between merely "articulating some legitimate, nondiscriminatory reason" and "proving absence of discriminatory motive." By reaffirming McDonnell Douglas analysis in Furnco Construction Co. v. Waters, supra, we made it clear that the former will suffice to meet the employee's prima facie case of discrimination. [emphasis added]

In other words, the "context" in Furnco rendered the word *prove* as nothing more than a slip of the pen. However, Justice Stevens, speaking for Brennan, Marshall, and Stewart, stated:

> In litigation, the only way a defendant can "articulate" the reason for his action is by adducing evidence that explains what he has done . . . If the Court intends to authorize a method of articulating a factual defense without proof, surely the Court should explain what it is.

In other words, Stevens was not convinced that a plaintiff in a phase 3 pretext argument could articulate a reason without providing some sort of proof.

Texas v. Burdine (1981)

Burdine had the same two elements as Furnco with respect to race and sex discrimination; disparate treatment and affirmative action. The 5th Circuit ruled that prima facie discrimination triggers the burden of persuasion. The 5th Circuit also ruled that the defendant must prove the plaintiff had inferior qualifications. On this affirmative action issue, the Court ruled:

> The views of the Court of Appeals can be read, we think, as requiring the employer to hire the minority or female applicant whenever that person's objective qualifications were equal to those of a white male applicant. But Title VII does not obligate an employer to accord this preference.

On the more general issue of the defendant's burden after a successful prima facie attack, the Court ruled:

> The defendant need not persuade the court that is was actually motivated by proffered reasons. . . . It is sufficient if the defendant's evidence raises a genuine issue of fact as to whether it discriminated against the plaintiff. . . . If the defendant carries this burden of production, the presumption raised by the prima facie case is rebutted. . . . The plaintiff retains the burden of persuasion.

This is a double affirmation of the principle ruling in *McDonnell v. Green*: (a) phase 2 carries a burden of production, not persuasion, and (b) the burden of persuasion belongs to the plaintiff at all times.

In discussing the burden of persuasion in phase 3, the Court noted that the plaintiff may succeed in a pretext argument by:

> persuading the court that a discriminatory reason more than likely motivated the employer or indirectly by showing that the employer's proffered explanation is unworthy of credence.

These two methods of proof were, of course, initially cited by Powell in his *McDonnell v. Green* ruling.

U.S. Postal v. Aikens (1983)

In view of prior rulings, Aikens involved a relatively simple issue. Aikens was a black male who was not promoted for an articulated reason (refusal to accept lateral transfers). The district court ruled that Aikens needed persuasive evidence of discriminatory intent in phase 1. Of course, this contradicted the Green precedent for the prima facie attack (presumptive evidence). Justice Rehnquist, speaking for a unanimous Court, ruled that Aikens had carried his burden in phase 1, and that the defendant had done likewise in phase 2. Thus the case was remanded for pretext. At the same time, the Court used the occasion to summarize the burdens in the three phases, stating clearly that presumptive evidence is required in phase 1, a burden of production is required in phase 2, and a burden of persuasion exists in phase 3.

THE MIXED-MOTIVE SCENARIO

In general, every case has two motives, one illegal and one legal. But in the McDonnell-Burdine scenario only one motive is true. In a mixed-motive case, both motives may be true. As noted earlier, the mixed-motive scenario is usually triggered by factual evidence of an illegal motive in phase 1. The defendant has two options: (a) directly refuting the discriminatory motive; and/or (b) providing factual evidence for a nondiscriminatory motive. The first option is disparate treatment as decided by pre-McDonnell-Burdine (NLRA) rules. It is the second option that defines the mixed-motive scenario.

Price Waterhouse v. Hopkins (1989)

The landmark mixed-motive case is *Price Waterhouse v. Hopkins* (1989). Interestingly, in Hopkins, a typical plurality of Brennan, Marshall, Blackmun, and Stevens was partially joined by White and O'Connor, leaving Kennedy, Rehnquist, and Scalia as an unlikely minority.

As for the case, Ann Hopkins, a senior manager at Price Waterhouse, was neither accepted nor rejected for promotion in a prior year. The next year, she was not even considered. Hopkins presented direct evidence of "crude" sex discrimination. The lower courts ruled that Hopkins's evidence was sufficient to indicate that an illegal motive played a substantial role in her exclusion, and required "clear and convincing" evidence that the legal motive was the only reason Hopkins was excluded. Or as stated in the Supreme Court Syllabus:

> Both courts held that an employer who allowed a discriminatory motive to play a part in an employment decision must prove by *clear and convincing evidence* that it would have made the same decision in the absence of discrimination, and that petitioner had not carried that burden. [emphasis added]

The term *clear and convincing* falls short of reasonable doubt (as in a criminal trial), but it is certainly stronger than **preponderance** of evidence (i.e., merely more believable than the plaintiff's evidence).

One thing was clear about the case—both sides had one. Hopkins documented numerous instances of crude sexual harassment. For example, one partner suggested that her flawed "interpersonal skills" could be "corrected by a soft-hued suit or a new shade of lipstick." Other partners stereotyped her as being "macho" and as having "overcompensated for being a woman." But the company presented evidence of a legal motive; Hopkins was brash and abrasive, particularly to staff and often to clients. Thus the company asserted that Hopkins's contrary behavior was the only reason she was not promoted.

Logically, the company's defense is untenable if the standard is clear and convincing evidence. Thus the company was saved when six justices asserted that only a preponderance of evidence favoring the legal motive is required.

However, this was the only issue agreed to by five or more justices. O'Connor argued for stronger evidence than the Brennan group would demand for a phase 1 attack (i.e., substantial evidence of an illegal motive as opposed to suggestive evidence), and White took issue with how the preponderance of evidence was to be presented in phase 2. Kennedy, Rehnquist, and Scalia saw no reason to depart from the McDonnell-Burdine scenario (i.e., the company should articulate its legal motive, leaving Hopkins the burden of proving pretext).

The Civil Rights Act of 1991

The bottom line in the Hopkins ruling was that the employer escaped liability. This was one of the rulings that triggered the aborted Civil Rights Restoration Act of 1990. The 1990 Act would have favored guilt if an illegal motive played any role in a selection decision. The Civil Rights Act of 1991 compromised on this issue.

Accordingly, a plaintiff can prevail on evidence of illegal discrimination as stated in Sec.107(a):

> Except as otherwise provided in this title, an unlawful employment practice is established when the complaining party demonstrates that race, color, religion, sex, or national origin was a motivating factor for any employment practice, even though other factors also motivated the practice.

But the award for the illegal behavior is:

> declaratory relief, injunctive relief . . . and attorney fees and costs directly attributable to [the illegal motive].

Otherwise, if the legal motive is determined to be the only reason the for the selection decision, the court shall *not* award:

> damages or issue an order requiring any admission, reinstatement, hiring, promotion, or payment.

Thus by the standards of the 1991 Act, Hopkins would be relieved for the effects of sex discrimination; more relief than supplied by the Supreme Court. Given the legal motive, however, Hopkins would not receive her promotion. On the other hand, Hopkins could pursue the added legal damages on the basis of a sexual harassment charge—a topic discussed in detail in Chapter 3.

——— **BRIEF SUMMARY** ———

The McDonnell-Burdine scenario is triggered with presumptive evidence indicating: (a) protection; (b) application and qualification; (c) exclusion; and (d) continuation of the search. This triggers a parallel burden of production for the defendant, followed by the only burden of persuasion in this scenario; the plaintiff must prove pretext via a preponderance of evidence. A different scenario emerges, however, if the defendant attacks with direct evidence of an illegal motive. The defendant can: (a) directly prove that the plaintiff is wrong; and/or (b) prove that a legal motive dictated the selection decision even though the illegal motive was true. The pretext argument remains unaltered relative to McDonnell-Burdine.

SECTION IV
THE PATTERN OR PRACTICE OF DISCRIMINATION

As noted earlier, the pattern or practice of discrimination (or simply *pattern*) is a form of disparate treatment. The employer shows a long-term trend that, by presumption, intentionally affects an entire class. Or, as defined in Black's Law Dictionary (1990):

a pattern or practice of resistance to the Act is more than isolated or accidental instance of conduct in violation of the Act; it means an intentional regular or repeated violation of the right granted by the Act.

Pattern suits are generally initiated for claimants by the Justice Department or EEOC; but not always. More importantly, the main presumptive factor is a bottom-line statistical disparity in the work force. Indeed, in *International Brotherhood of Teamsters v. United States* (1977), one of several major Supreme Court pattern cases, the Court suggested that bottom-line disparities are sufficient to make the prima facie case. Accordingly, a bottom-line disparity:

is often a telltale sign of purposeful discrimination; absent explanation, it is ordinarily to be expected that nondiscriminatory hiring practices will in time result in a work force more or less representative of the racial and ethnic composition of the . . . community from which the workers are hired.

In other words, a bottom-line statistical disparity sets up the presumption of illegal motive, much like the four-step prima facie procedure in the McDonnell-Burdine scenario.

Nevertheless, bottom-line statistics are rarely presented alone. Pattern suits are usually accompanied by individuous disparate treatment charges nested within the main pattern charge. In some cases, the court may evaluate 50 or more individual charges.

Unfortunately, because of a reliance on statistical disparities, pattern or practice is sometimes confused with adverse impact. Adding to this confusion is the general belief that the main danger of a pattern of discrimination truly *is* adverse impact. That is, the *effect* of past intentional discrimination is perpetuated by neutral factors. Thus the pattern of discrimination is a major reason courts order affirmative action in Title VII cases.

However, the pattern or practice itself is not adverse impact. Indeed, when pattern or practice and adverse impact occur together, they are analyzed as distinct and separable scenarios.

TWO LANDMARK CASES

Two landmark cases are *Teamsters v. United States* (1977) and *Hazelwood School District v. United States* (1977)—decided within the same 28-day period. Teamsters involved both pattern or practice and adverse impact. Hazelwood was a purer pattern case. Both cases involved lingering effects of pre-Title VII discrimination.

International Teamsters v. United States (1977)

In Teamsters, blacks and Hispanics were differentially classified in pre-Title VII days, a practice that continued beyond July 2, 1965 (the effective date of the original Act). Minority drivers were routinely assigned to lower paying (city) routes, whereas majority drivers had the lion's share of higher paying (distance) routes. There was also evidence of individuous disparate treatment. The Teamsters could not produce a reasonable nondiscriminatory explanation of why drivers of presumably equal ability were differentially classified. Thus they were virtually defenseless on the pattern charge.

However, the Teamsters beat the adverse impact charge. A bona fide seniority system (BFSS) in force prior to Title VII adversely perpetuated the effects of pre-Title VII discrimination. The ruling on this issue is germinal for the BFSS defense, and will be considered in Section V of this chapter.

Hazelwood v. United States (1977)

The Hazelwood school district had a history of discrimination in hiring pre-dating March 24, 1972 (the effective date of the EEO Act of 1972). For example, in 1970, only 0.6% of the teachers in the district were black. Based on its affirmative action plan, this percentage grew in subsequent years, but was still only 1.8% in 1972. The major issue was the relevant labor market for deciding what these percentages mean. In the Hazelwood district, a suburb of St. Louis, only 5.7% of the qualified teachers were black. But in the entire county (including St. Louis), this percentage was nearly 3 times higher (15.4%). Also, there were 55 individual charges of disparate treatment. In previewing the case, the Supreme Court outlined four issues (in terms of hiring) that have become standard in pattern cases.

(1) a history of alleged racial discriminatory practices; (2) statistical disparities in hiring; (3) the standardless and largely subjective hiring practices; and (4) specific instances of alleged discrimination against 55 unsuccessful applicants for teaching jobs.

As the for case itself, the district court ruled that the small percentage of black teachers matched the small percentage of black students.[6] The circuit court overruled, asserting that the small percentage of black teachers (1.8%) was significantly lower than the larger percentage available in the county (15.4%). The Supreme Court overruled the circuit court on two grounds.

First, the Supreme Court viewed the percentage available in the district (5.7%) as the relevant statistic; not the percentage available in the county (15.4%). Second, the Court preferred **applicant flow** data (i.e., percentage hired vs. percentage that applied) to **geographical** data. Based on applicant flow, the percentage of black teachers hired for new positions was higher than the percentage of those previously hired (i.e., 3.7% vs. 1.8%). Also, the percentage for new black hires (3.7%) was within the statistical limits of the percentage available in the district (5.7%). Thus the Supreme Court rejected the pattern charge at the prima facie level.

OTHER TRADITIONAL PATTERN CASES

Precedents established in Teamsters and Hazelwood have fueled the lower courts. Obviously, with lower court rulings, the illustrations are exhaustive. But among the many cases, two stand out; one as an example of combining pattern or practice and adverse impact (*United States v. County of Fairfax*, 1980), and one as an example of a purer pattern or practice case (*NAACP v. City of Evergreen*, 1982).

United States v. Fairfax (1980)

In Fairfax, the pattern case hinged two factors; (a) bottom-line disparities showing blacks and women disproportionately classified in "less desirable" jobs; and (b) multiple claims of individuous disparate treatment. Adverse impact hinged on a traditional factor; six employment tests that adversely impacted blacks (but not women). The 4th Circuit accepted the prima facie adverse impact charge, and remanded for consideration the validity of the six employment tests, five of which were never validated.

As in Teamsters, the pattern charge was treated independently of the impact charge. The district court rejected the prima facie charge based on geographical data. But as in Hazelwood, the 4th Circuit preferred the applicant flow data, which favored the prima facie charge. The 4th Circuit echoed Teamsters by stating:

> Of course, proof of a discriminatory motive is a necessary element of a disparate treatment case, but statistics can establish a prima facie case, even without a showing of specific instances of overt discrimination.

NAACP v. City of Evergreen (1982)

In Evergreen, the 11th Circuit ruled on a pattern suit filed on behalf of all adult black residents in the city. Showing a pattern of discrimination that pre-dated the turn of the century, the city lacked written job descriptions, uniform hiring and promotional practices, uniform wage schedules, and an affirmative action plan. These are precisely the "standardless" and "subjective" policies referred to in Teamsters. The plaintiffs won in district court, and the 11th Circuit merely clarified the remedies (i.e., declarative and injunctive relief).

WARDS COVE REVISITED

Taken together, these cases paint a different picture for pattern or practice versus adverse impact. Both focus on statistically significant disparities. However, adverse impact associates disparities with facially neutral tests, whereas pattern or practice associates disparities with long-term traditions.

The fact that motive is key to pattern or practice is codified in Sec.707 of Title VII, which states:

> Whenever the Attorney General has reasonable cause to believe that any person or group of persons is engaged in a pattern or practice of resistance to the full enjoyment of any of the rights secured by this title, and that the pattern or practice is of such a nature and is *intended* to deny the full exercise . . . the Attorney General may bring civil action.

Hindsight therefore suggests that Wards Cove and Teamsters are analogous cases. In other words, unskilled cannery workers (Wards Cove) are to lower paid drivers (Teamsters) what skilled noncannery workers (Wards Cove) are to higher paid drivers (Teamsters). The main difference is in merits. In Teamsters there was no difference in the abilities of the two classes of drivers, but this was precisely the arguable issue in Wards Cove. Perhaps Teamsters took the pattern route because the Justice Department prosecuted the case. The Wards Cove petitioners did not have this level of support.

Application of Teamsters to Wards Cove provides the following scenario. First, statistical disparity between cannery and noncannery jobs is presumptive for a prima facie pattern charge. Second, the employers resort to the productive defense that: (a) few of the minorities are qualified for the skilled positions; and (b) few ever apply. Third, faced with the ultimate burden of persuasion, a pretext argument by plaintiffs hinges on: (a) whether minority applicants are generally unqualified; and (b) whether they rarely apply because their applications are unwelcome.

Certainly, this analysis is in keeping with the end result of the majority ruling in Wards Cove, without having to impose a burden of persuasion based on "bare" bottom-line statistics. It is also in keeping with the two major assertions by Stevens: (a) a history of "plantation"-like abuse; and (b) the fact that every effect must be tied to a cause.

In contrast, the connection between Wards Cove and its precursor (*Watson v. Fort Worth*) is weak; subjectivity in selection. That is, the Wards Cove employers subjectively hired skilled workers; the Fort Worth Bank subjectively promoted employees. Otherwise, Wards Cove featured minorities versus whites for two *different* job categories, whereas Watson featured minorities versus whites within the *same* job category. In addition, Watson identified specific causes of adverse impact; the Wards Cove plaintiffs did not.

In short, the only true issues relating to prior Supreme Court precedents in Wards Cove were: (a) how to deal with subjective tests in true adverse impact cases; and (b) how to keep traditional pattern or practice suits from turning into adverse impact scenarios.

——— **BRIEF SUMMARY** ———

The pattern or practice of discrimination is a form of disparate treatment presumptively indicated by statistical evidence of segregation and/or classification. However, statistical discrepancies are invariably backed by evidence of individuous discrimination. More importantly, a successful pattern attack triggers the McDonnell-Burdine phase 2 defense; precisely what the Wards Cove majority wanted. Consequently, the author questions why the majority used Wards Cove as the occasion to address Griggs because Wards Cove addressed comparisons *between* jobs; not *within* jobs. Furthermore, Congress tied pattern or practice to segregation and classification, and its continuing effects; not to neutral tests that produce adverse impact irrespective of motive. Thus the adverse effect of pattern or practice is not the same as the adverse effect of neutral tests. The former continues a conscious, long-standing pattern, the latter may or may not involve ill motives.

SECTION V
STATUTORY ATTACKS AND DEFENSES

Among the two major statutory defenses,[7] the BFOQ (bona fide occupational qualification) is the only defense to facial discrimination based on sex, religion, and national origin (but never race or color), whereas the BFSS (bona fide seniority system) can be used to defend any charge. In general, the BFOQ is tough for the defendant to prove, whereas BFSS is tough for the plaintiff to buck.

BONA FIDE OCCUPATIONAL QUALIFICATION (BFOQ)

Facial discrimination can be justified only if it is reasonably necessary to exclude all or virtually all group members from a given job. Or as stated in part 1 of Sec.703(e), it is permissible to discriminate facially on the basis of:

> *religion, sex, or national origin* in those certain instances where religion, sex, or national origin is a bona fide occupational qualification *reasonably necessary* to the normal operation of the particular business or enterprise. [emphasis added]

The BFOQ defense resembles business necessity in adverse impact. In adverse impact, however, a facially neutral test is evaluated against *work*, not the *worker*. In *Dothard v. Rawlinson* (1977), a landmark BFOQ case, the Supreme Court heard arguments relating to both adverse impact and facial discrimination.

Dothard v. Rawlinson (1977)

In Dothard, women challenged an Alabama law requiring minimal height and weight standards for law enforcement officers on adverse impact grounds. These facially neutral standards screened out a disproportionate percentage of the women. During the trial, the Alabama Board of Corrections adopted "Administration Regulation 204," excluding all women from "contact positions" (i.e., guards) at its four all-male maximum security prisons. This regulation was facially discriminatory. The adverse impact issue is important in its own right and will be discussed in Chapter 3. On the facial discrimination/BFOQ issue, the Court ruled in favor of the defense, stating:

> The likelihood that inmates would assault a woman because she was a woman would thus directly undermine her capacity to provide the security that is the essence of a correctional counselor's responsibility.

In other words, being a male is **reasonably necessary** to preclude a major source of prisoner insurrection. It should be noted that the successful BFOQ defense in this case is the exception in sex discrimination cases, not the rule.

Other BFOQ Cases

Although the BFOQ defense statutorily applies to sex, religion, and national origin, sex is the only issue of the three that has been tried. National origin cases have simply not emerged and facial discrimination by religious entities is permitted by statutory exemptions (e.g., requiring Catholic teachers in Catholic schools). As we will witness in Chapter 6, the BFOQ defense is also critical to age discrimination.

Sec. 1604.2 of the EEOC *Guidelines on Discrimination Because of Sex* speaks to facial discrimination with warnings not to exclude women or men because of: (a) "assumptions" (e.g., higher turnover rates), (b) "stereotyped characterizations" (e.g., dexterity and aggressiveness), and/or (c) "preferences of co-workers." The EEOC stresses that the BFOQ will be narrowly construed, and despite the success of the Alabama Board of Corrections in Dothard, this has been the case.

For example, the courts have distinguished between reasonable necessity and convenience. Thus airlines cannot hire only female flight attendants because of passenger preference (e.g., *Diaz v. Pan American*, 1971) or preservation of a "sexy image" (e.g., *Wilson v. Southwest Airlines*, 1981). Generally, such factors are not essential to the critical function of airlines, which is to transport people.

The BFOQ defense has the best chance of succeeding in situations such as Dothard, where the key issue is workplace safety. For example, although airlines cannot exclude men because of passenger preference, they can exclude pregnant flight attendants for passenger safety (e.g., *Levin v. Delta Airlines, Inc.,* 1984). And although customer preference carries little weight for airlines, it becomes a reasonable necessity when the preference is for privacy. Thus female janitors cannot enter (and therefore not work in) all-male bathhouses when so demanded by male customers (*Brooks v. AFC Industries,* 1982); nor can females be hospital orderlies if male patients object to being touched by females in private places (*Jones v. Hinds General Hospital,* 1987). Obviously, the same is true for males who threaten female privacy.

This does not, however, make privacy the equal to safety. For example, despite the Dothard ruling, lower courts have struck down the BFOQ in an all-male prison when the issue is not prison safety, but rather prisoner privacy (e.g., *Gunther v. Iowa State Men's Reformatory*, 1980). Of course, a prison, unlike a bath house or a hospital, is not a business, and a prisoner is not a customer.

Finally, it is always possible to establish a BFOQ with a novel argument. For example, in *Torres v. Wisconsin Health & Social Services* (1988), the defendant, a state-run all-female reformatory, successfully argued that being female was a BFOQ because:

> giving women prisoners a living environment free from the presence of males in a position of authority was necessary to foster the goal of rehabilitation.

BONA FIDE SENIORITY SYSTEM (BFSS)

Statutory language covering exemption for the BFSS is relatively clear. As stated in Sec. 703(h):

> Notwithstanding any other provision of this title, it shall not be an unlawful employment practice for an employer to apply different standards of compensation, or different terms, conditions, or privileges of employment pursuant to a bona fide seniority or merit system, or a system which measures earnings by quantity or quality of production or to employees who work in different locations, provided that such differences are not the result of an intention to discriminate because of race, color, religion, sex, or national origin.

Thus if a seniority system is bona fide, the employer can legally promote, reclassify, discharge, and so forth, regardless of discriminatory effects or treatment. A seniority system is not bona fide if it is designed with the intention to discriminate.

Teamsters v. United States (1977)—Revisited

The landmark BFSS case, though not the first (see *Franks v. Bowman Transportation*, 1976), is the previously cited Teamsters case. Recall that prior to and after the effective date of Title VII, the Teamsters showed a pattern of discrimination against blacks and Hispanics. During both eras, the Teamsters also used separate but parallel seniority systems for city and distance drivers. The lower paid city drivers could transfer to the higher paid distance routes, but at the expense of accrued seniority. Thus two drivers could enter the company at the same time, and the city driver who transferred would have less accrued seniority than the distance driver in the higher paying position from day one.

The Supreme Court raised two major issues. The first, of course, was whether these seniority systems were bona fide. The Teamsters had little difficulty here. Clearly, if one job is more valued than another one, there is a legitimate business reason to provide separate and unequal benefits. Thus the seniority system was deemed bona fide.

The second issue concerned the victims of pattern discrimination pre versus post Title VII. The Supreme Court had no difficulty with those illegally classified after Title VII; the Court reaffirmed its earlier decision in *Franks v. Bowman,* and granted these drivers lost seniority time. However, blacks and Hispanics who were illegally classified prior to Title VII were granted nothing.

Thus the Supreme Court set a precedent in which a pre-Title VII seniority system could legally produce post-Title VII adverse effects, as long as the seniority system is bona fide. The fact that the seniority systems in Teamsters perpetuated the effects of pre-Title VII discriminatory policies, and indeed multiplied these effects, was deemed irrelevant. Blacks and Hispanics discriminated against prior to Title VII continued legally to suffer the adverse effects of pre-Title VII discrimination because the seniority system was deemed bona fide.

Other Cases

Plaintiffs have proven discriminatory motive behind the design of seniority systems (e.g., *United States v. Georgia Power Co.,* 1983). But this is the exception, not the rule. In *United Airlines Inc. v. Evans* (1977), the Supreme Court ruled that lost seniority time is not a "continuous violation" if the plaintiff does not file a timely charge. Evans was unlawfully discharged in 1968 and was rehired in 1973, but was not given accrued seniority for the time between the illegal discharge and the rehire. In *American Tobacco v. Patterson* (1982), the Supreme Court permitted perpetuation of pre-Title VII discrimination by a BFSS established after the effective date of Title VII. And in *Firefighters v. Stotts* (1984), the Supreme Court favored white firefighters challenging an affirmative action plan that reversed a "last-hired, first-fired procedure."

EEOC Guidance

The EEOC *Guidelines on Discrimination Because of Sex* provides the following example of a seniority system that is not bona fide:

A seniority system or line of progression which distinguishes between "light" and "heavy" jobs constitutes an unlawful employment practice if it operates as a disguised form of classification by sex, or creates unreasonable obstacles to the advancement by members of either sex into jobs which members of that sex would reasonably be expected to perform.

The author does not see why a crafty employer could not use "light" versus "heavy" jobs as a pretext, and escape the law. Thus if an employer can show: (a) that extra muscle is needed for "heavy" jobs; then (b) extra muscle could be rewarded with extra benefits; as long as (c) men and women have an equal opportunity to show they have the extra muscle. Of course, some women will qualify, but the group as a whole will do so at a lower rate then men. The bottom line is—how is one to know that the extra benefits are truly a function of the extra muscle?[8]

Civil Rights Act of 1991

Sec.112 of the Act of 1991 on "Expansion Of Right To Challenge Discriminatory Seniority Systems" states:

For purposes of this section, an unlawful employment practice occurs, with respect to a seniority system that has been adopted for an intentionally discriminatory purpose (whether or not that discriminatory purpose is apparent on the face of the seniority provision), when the seniority system is adopted, when an individual becomes subject to the seniority system, or when a person aggrieved is injured by the application of the seniority system or provision of the system.

It should be noted that Sec.112 is an addendum to Sec.706(e) in Title VII, which speaks to administrative procedures, not the BFSS (which is in Sec.703(h)). Thus it may apply to *United Airlines v. Evans,* where a plaintiff who was illegally discharged was prevented from filing EEOC charges because of a technicality. Otherwise, its language seems consistent with Sec.703(h).[9]

—— **BRIEF SUMMARY** ——

The BFOQ and BFSS are tradeoffs; the BFOQ provides strong protection for plaintiffs, the BFSS provides strong protection for defendants. Both will be reviewed again under various contexts in succeeding chapters. In the context of Title VII, the BFOQ is rarely applicable, despite the Dothard ruling. The general rule is that individuals must be given the opportunity to demonstrate their merits. Age cases add a different dimension to BFOQ that will be discussed in Chapter 6. As for the BFSS, the issue reduces to the history of the company. A plaintiff has to prove that the BFSS was part of a plan to perpetuate a pattern or practice of discrimination. Even in Teamsters, where pattern or practice was proven, the issue of whether the seniority system is bona fide was separated from the issue of whether it was illegal to segregate and classify drivers into higher paying versus lower paying jobs.

SECTION VI

IMPLICATIONS FOR COMPLIANCE ON ADVERSE IMPACT

The following discussion focuses on the Uniform Guidelines on Employee Selection Procedures (or the Guidelines) and their implications for adverse impact. Compliance issues related to disparate treatment, pattern or practice, BFOQ, and BFSS will be discussed at the end of Chapter 3. As a note of forewarning, many of the issues in the Guidelines are best addressed by trained professionals.

The Guidelines have been enforced by the EEOC since 1978. During this time there have been only minor revisions (in 1981). Key court rulings, however, have contradicted some of the guidance offered. The Guidelines are based on the older (1974) version of the *Standards for Educational and Psychological Tests*. There has been talk of revising the Guidelines since 1984, ostensibly to correct portions that no longer apply as well as to upgrade them in accordance with the 1985 *Standards for Educational and Psychological Tests* and the 1987 *Principles for the Validation and Use of Personnel Selection Procedures* (Society for Industrial and Organizational Psychology, 1987). As of this writing, however (October 1992), no revisions have been proposed.

The Guidelines contain 16 sections that address *General Principles* (Sec.1607.1 to 1607.13), *Technical Standards* for validity (Sec.1607.14), *Documentation* (Sec.1607.15), and *Definitions* of key terms used under the other three headings (Sec.1607.16). The following discussion focuses on *General Principles* and *Technical Standards,* as well as newer strategies for assessing validity.

FOCUS ON GENERAL PRINCIPLES
(SEC.1607.1-13)

The general principles in Sec.1607.1 to 1607.13 are a set of warnings and blessings based more on key court rulings than on Title VII statutory language. Some of the guidance is outdated, as noted above. But many of the principles are still relevant and should be adhered to unless and until the Guidelines are revised.

Purpose and Scope (1607.1, 1607.2, and 1607.13)

The purpose of the Guidelines is to create a uniform approach to the evaluation of tests and other procedures used to make employment selection decisions. The selection decisions include most of the terms and conditions of employment, but *not* recruitment. The Guidelines are neutral with respect to seniority systems. In general, the Guidelines apply to Title VII and E.O.11246, but not to ADEA and the Rehabilitation Act (and presumably the ADA). The reference to E.O.11246, however, does not imply heavy involvement in adverse impact cases by the OFCCP. As we will witness in Chapter 7, the OFCCP, which enforces E.O.11246, traditionally refers adverse impact cases to the EEOC.

The exemption for recruitment is designed to protect companies that affirmatively recruit minorities and women. Indeed, in accordance with 1981 amendments to the Guidelines, Sec.1607.13(A) states:

> The use of selection procedures which have been validated pursuant to these guidelines does not relieve users of any obligations they may have to undertake affirmative action to ensure equal employment opportunity. Nothing in these guidelines is intended to preclude the use of lawful selection procedures which assist in remedying the effects of prior discriminatory practices, or the achievement of affirmative action objectives.

Additionally, Sec.1607.13(B) encourages the "adoption and implementation of voluntary affirmative action programs by users who have no obligation under Federal law to adopt them."

However, as we will witness in Chapter 7, the Supreme Court has placed restrictions on **voluntary programs** that have the effect of producing **reverse discrimination**. Also, despite the Guidelines's hands-off policy on recruitment, **word-of-mouth** recruitment in walk-in situations has been subject to adverse impact analysis when this policy has created statistical disparity between the percentage of blacks versus whites that walk in (see *EEOC v. Kimbrough,* 1983).

Definition of Discrimination (Sec.1607.3)

The Guidelines define discrimination as any test or selection procedure that produces unjustifiable adverse impact. The Guidelines also advocate "alternative selection procedures." Accordingly:

> Where two or more selection procedures are available which serve the user's legitimate interest in efficient and trustworthy workmanship, and which are substantially equally valid for a given purpose, the user should use the procedure which has been demonstrated to have lesser adverse impact.

The reader will recognize this language from a number of Supreme Court rulings, most notably *Albermarle v. Moody* (1975).

It is critical to recognize when adverse impact is produced. For example, *Griggs v. Duke Power* focused on **applicant flow data**. More specifically, there was a statistical disparity between whites and blacks who applied for the same job (coal handler). In comparison, in Teamsters (1977), the statistical disparity was between bus drivers in two different job classifications. In general, **cross-job** disparities implicate segregation and classification, and therefore, the **pattern or practice** of discrimination.

In addition, disparities between actual employees in the work force versus potential employees in the **qualified labor pool** speaks to yet another issue, namely **underutilization**. For example, in *United Steelworkers v. Weber* (1979), Kaiser Aluminum hired less than 2% black workers (for skilled craft positions) in a city that was 39% black. The selection rate for whites was significantly higher. Kaiser had no overt policy of discrimination. Rather, the craft workers were supplied by a union that excluded blacks. Kaiser eliminated union involvement and adopted a voluntary affirmative action plan to increase the percentage of black craft workers (by providing in-house training opportunities). White employees challenged the plan (and lost); a critical **reverse discrimination** ruling to be discussed in Chapter 7.

Information on Adverse Impact (Sec.1607.4)

Covered entities are required to maintain records on selection decisions with regard to sex, race, and ethnicity. Private and state/local entities are required to complete EEO-1 and EEO-4 forms, respectively, if they employ 100 or more employees. The requirements for smaller entities are less exacting. An expanded discussion of documentation is provided in Sec.1607.15 of the Guidelines, which also details the documentation required when validity studies are conducted.

Sec.1607.4 also contains two general principles that require closer inspection. First, Sec.1607.4(C) contains the **bottom-line** rule that was struck down by the Supreme Court in *Connecticut v. Teal.* In general, the Guidelines are invoked only when a test or procedure produces adverse impact. However, the implication of the Teal ruling is that any impactful test must be justified regardless of the bottom-line percentages in the overall selection process.

Second, Sec.1607.4(D) contains the "four-fifths" or 80% rule, which —as noted earlier—is a rule of thumb. For example, a company with 16 applicants, 10 white and 6 black, breaks the rule if it selects 5 whites and 2 blacks (50% vs. 33%), but not 5 whites and 3 blacks (50% each), or 4 whites and 2 blacks (40% vs. 33%). The fact that one change (including one less white or one more black) would "fix" the numbers indicates that the 80% rule is more important for larger samples. In general, proper interpretation of statistical disparities can be complicated, and often requires outside expertise.

General Standards for Validity Studies (Sec.1607.5)

Sec.1607.5 contains four critical warnings, namely: (a) not to select on the basis of knowledge, skills, and abilities (KSAs) that can be quickly learned (on the job or in training); (b) that evidence sufficient to justify pass/fail selection may be insufficient to justify the ranking of applicants; (c) that cutoff scores should be consistent with normal expectations among workers;[10] and (d) that applicants may not be assessed for higher level jobs unless they are expected to progress to such jobs within a reasonable period of time. The latter is undoubtedly a reference to *Albermarle v. Moody* (1975), where the company attempted to validate two cognitive tests using a sample of workers who represented a much higher level job than the applicants were aspiring to.

Sec.1607.5 also permits companies to use nonvalidated tests on an **interim basis** if a technically feasible validity study is under way and is likely to be completed within a reasonable period of time. However, all completed validation studies must be periodically reevaluated for currency.

Alternatives to In-House Validation (Sec.1607.6-1607.10)

Adverse impact requires evidence of validity, but there are three alternatives for employers who do not wish to or cannot afford to conduct internal studies. First, Sec.1607.6 states:

> A user may choose to utilize alternative selection procedures in order to eliminate adverse impact or as part of an affirmative action program. . . . Such alternative procedures should eliminate the adverse impact in the total selection process, should be lawful and should be as job related as possible.

In other words, the employer may eliminate any test that produces adverse impact, but the employer has no choice but to eliminate the adverse impact, or to prove that the impactful test is valid.

Second, Sec.1607.7 permits validity studies by outside agents (i.e., transportability) if: (a) the study meets the technical standards in Sec.1607.14; (b) the jobs studied are "substantially the same" as those for which a test is being used; and (c) the study has evidence of fairness (i.e., validity for all groups, not just select groups).

Third, Sec.1607.8 encourages cooperative studies among employers, labor organizations, and employment agencies, but once again only if the technical standards in Sec.1607.14 are met. This offers a vehicle for companies with less funds and/or employees to combine their resources for the purpose of validating tests.

It should be noted, however, that Sec.1607.9.(A) warns that the reputation of a test is not a substitute for direct evidence of validity (i.e., the mistake made in Griggs). Also, Sec.1607.9.(B) asserts that professional supervision is "encouraged," but that the EEOC:

> will take into account the fact that a *thorough job analysis* was conducted and that careful development and use of a selection procedure in accordance with professional standards enhance the probability that the selection procedure is valid for the job. [emphasis added]

The "thorough job analysis" is particularly important for proving that different jobs are "substantially the same."

Remaining Principles (Sec.1607.10-1607.12)

The remaining principles are that (a) the Guidelines apply to employment agencies that design tests, and all agencies that administer tests must maintain records for documentation purposes (Sec.1607.10);

(b) the Guidelines do not apply to disparate treatment, but validated tests may not be used disparately to treat protected groups for whom the test has not been validated (Sec.1607.11); and (c) applicants should be retested where reasonable opportunities exist (Sec.1607.12).

FOCUS ON TECHNICAL STANDARDS (SEC.1607.14)

The technical standards apply to three historical types of validity: (a) criterion, (b) content, and (c) construct validity. By more recent standards, the Guidelines are somewhat outdated in this domain. Nevertheless, there are several critical points to note regarding validity in general, and the three types of validity in particular.

General Consideration

The "general consideration" is provided in Sec.1607.14(A), which speaks to the virtues of job analysis. Accordingly:

Any Validity study should be based upon review of information about the job for which the selection procedure is to be used. The review should include a *job analysis except as provided in section 14(B)(3)* below with respect to criterion-related validity. Any method of job analysis may be used if it provides the information required for the specific validation strategy used. [emphasis added]

This statement does not mean that job analysis is viable for only content and construct validity. It applies to criterion validity studies that use objective performance measures (e.g., production rate, error rate, absence, lateness, etc.). But for reasons beyond the scope of this book, most performance appraisal methods are subjective (i.e., rankings or ratings), and therefore require job analysis.[11] Also, as previously implied, job analysis can also facilitate the transportability of an outside criterion validity study.

Criterion Validity

Criterion validity has two forms: (a) predictive and (b) concurrent. Both forms use statistical correlations to compare predictors (selection tests) to criteria (job performance). Predictive **validity** measures the predictor now and the criterion later (i.e., it tests all applicants;

puts all applicants to work; assesses job performance at a later date; and compares test scores to performance scores). **Concurrent validity** samples the predictor and criterion measures from job incumbents usually, though not necessarily, at about the same time.

Ironically, the key to the continued importance of either form of criterion validity stems from the Guidelines references to content validity. For example, Sec.1607.C.(1) on "appropriateness of content validity studies" warns that:

> A selection procedure based on inferences about mental processes cannot be supported solely or primarily on the basis of content validity.

Practically speaking, this implies a need for criterion studies for any test of cognitive ability, aptitude, personality, and so forth. Construct validity studies are theoretically viable for inferred mental processes, but such studies are rarely used in the employment/litigation context.

Furthermore, Sec.1607.7.(C)(1) probably extends to virtually any inference based on tests that are far removed from the content of the job. There are thus implied warnings for interviews[12] and for certain forms of testing that are clearly not mental (e.g., biodata[13]).

In general, criterion validity studies must be **technically feasible**. That means:

> (1) An adequate sample of persons available for the study to achieve findings of statistical significance; (2) having or being able to obtain a sufficient range of scores on the selection procedure and job performance measures to produce validity results which can be expected to be representative of the results if the ranges normally expected were utilized; and (3) having or being able to devise unbiased, reliable and relevant measures of job performance or other criteria of employee adequacy.

In addition, where technically feasible, there must also be evidence of **fairness**. Sec.1607.B(8)(b) defines **unfairness** as:

> When members of one race, sex, or ethnic group characteristically obtain lower scores on a selection procedure than members of another group, and the differences in scores are not reflected in differences in a measure of job performance, use of the selection procedure may unfairly deny opportunities to members of the group that obtains the lower scores.

Thus the ideal is a criterion validity study that samples enough subjects whose scores vary widely on both the predictor and criterion, and that produces statistically significant correlations between tests and job performance for all subgroups in the available labor force.

Content Validity

Content validity, on the other hand, concerns whether the content of a test represents essential functions of the job. According to Sec. 1607.14(C)(4):

> If a test purports to sample a work behavior or to provide a sample of a work product, the manner and setting of the selection procedure and its level and complexity should closely approximate the work situation. The closer the content and the context of the selection procedure are to work samples or work behaviors, the stronger is the basis for showing content validity. As the content of the selection procedure less resembles a work behavior, or the setting and manner of administration of the selection procedure less resemble the work situation, or the result less resembles the work product, the greater the need for other evidence of validity.

Based on this guidance, the most content valid selection procedure is one that permits the applicant to do the job itself.

But short of performing the job, content validity is easier to demonstrate when essential job functions are directly demonstrable (e.g., a typing test for a secretary). However, job tasks can also be simulated. A good example is agility testing for police officers (e.g., carrying a weighted dummy a few hundred feet simulates carrying a victim away from a danger scene). Simulations are also possible for higher level managerial positions. For example, assessment centers have been used by AT&T and Fortune 100 companies to measure the abilities to communicate, lead, make decisions, and cooperate. But generally speaking, assessment centers do not rely solely on content validity.[14]

Thus the ideal in a content validity study is to have demonstrable essential job functions that are based on expert job analysis. Unlike criterion validity, which relies on statistical procedures, content validity relies entirely on expertise.

Construct Validity

By 1974 standards, construct validity refers to the degree to which a test measures an underlying construct (e.g., does an IQ test measure IQ?). According to Sec.1607.D.(1):

> Construct validity is a more complex strategy than either criterion-related or content validity. Construct validation is a relatively new and developing procedure in the employment field, and there is at present a lack of substantial literature extending the concept to employment practices. The user should be aware that the effort to obtain sufficient empirical support for construct validity is both an extensive and arduous effort involving a series of research studies which include criterion related validity studies and which may include content validity studies.

In other words, the EEOC advises avoiding construct validity study, a piece of advice that has been adhered to by employers.

But to illustrate, in one of the historical methods of assessing construct validity the researcher attempts to establish both **convergence** and **divergence**. For example, convergence means that a test of intelligence correlates with other validated measures of intelligence, whereas divergence means that the test of intelligence does not correlate with other validates measures of (say) personality.

On a more general level, construct validity is an important concept to researchers in industrial/organizational psychology, and it has taken a more encompassing meaning than that implied by the Guidelines (as we will witness shortly).

NEWER STRATEGIES FOR ASSESSING VALIDITY

Sec. 1607.5.(C) of the Guidelines cites the sources that were used in its creation. Accordingly:

> The provisions of these guidelines relating to validation of selection procedures are intended to be consistent with generally accepted professional standards for evaluating standardized tests and other selection procedures, such as those described in the Standards for Educational and Psychological Tests prepared by a joint committee of the American Psychological Association, the American Educational Research Association, and the National Council on Measurement in Education . . . and standard textbooks and journals in the field of personnel selection.

In addition, Sec. 1607.5(A) states that "New strategies for showing the validity of selection procedures will be evaluated as they become accepted by the psychological profession." As noted earlier, new strategies have been developed since 1978. Thus at least until newer guidelines are published, it is necessary to evaluate the Guidelines in light of advancements in the field as well in terms of court rulings.

The Principles

Newer strategies in the *Principles for the Validation and Use of Personnel Selection Procedures* (Society for Industrial and Organizational Psychology, 1987) downplay the distinction among criterion, content, and construct validity in favor of a research approach that considers *all* evidence of what a test measures as evidence of validity. In other words, the *Principles for the Validation and Use of Personnel Selection Procedures* consider all three historical types of validity as evidence of construct validity. In addition, since the Guidelines were originally published newer methods of assessing validity have been developed.

One new method, **meta analysis**, has been used to attack a major principle in the Guidelines, namely fairness. Recall that a test is **unfair** if it is valid for one group but not another. For example, in many criterion studies researchers have found higher correlations between predictor and criterion for whites than blacks. However, according to Schmidt and Hunter (1990), these prior findings are artifacts of differences in sample sizes between the white and black subgroups. Based on meta analysis studies, Schmidt and Hunter suggest that prior proclamations of unfairness are incorrect.

There are other new techniques in the field (e.g., confirmatory factor analysis). The findings generated with new techniques hold much promise for a newer conception of construct validity. However, in the author's opinion, what is acceptable to a journal editor or book publisher is not necessarily acceptable to a federal judge. In other words, employers should avoid these newer strategies until the courts have ruled on them. It would be particularly risky, for example, to argue that a test is fair based only on the results of a meta analysis.

A Realistic Strategy

Obviously, the employer cannot rely entirely on the Guidelines, if only because the courts have already ruled that some of its principles are not applicable. However, there are certain rules that are still applicable, and they should be followed. The most important of these are: (a) the use of job analysis to establish both essential job functions and requisite KSAs for these functions; (b) avoidance of adverse impact, if possible; (c) the use of criterion validity data where possible; and (d) the use of content validity where necessary. Job analysis will be discussed in greater detail in Chapter 8. For present purposes the more important issues are avoiding adverse impact, and performing criterion and content validity studies.

To avoid adverse impact, the employer should eliminate any test that produces it. That is, the employer should search for alternatives that do not produce adverse impact. However, the employer should not use **quotas** or **race norming**. Quota systems can lead to reverse discrimination, as we will witness in Chapter 7. Race norming (i.e., raising test scores without empirical justification) is clearly outlawed in the Civil Rights Act of 1991.

On the other hand, where there is adverse impact there must be evidence of validity. Furthermore, where it is **technically feasible** to conduct a criterion validity study, it should be done. This does not mean that content validity will suffice if criterion validity is not technically feasible. Again, the Guidelines make it clear that certain tests can be validated using only criterion validity (e.g., tests used to make inferences about mental processes).

The Guidelines also make it clear that not all tests and procedures that produce adverse impact require a criterion validity study. As noted by Justice Blackmun in his 1988 criticism of O'Connor's opinion in *Watson v. Fort Worth,* there are numerous lower court cases in which business necessity has been factually proven without appealing to criterion validity. These are narrow rulings, however, and should be carefully scrutinized before being applied.

For example, a criterion validity study would *not* be needed to exclude from a security guard position a felon previously convicted of armed robbery (see *Hyland v. Fukada,* 1978). It follows from this type of ruling that some suspect tests can be linked to certain jobs with job analysis data, research, and expert testimony. The case providing the most guidance on this issue is *Davis v. Dallas* (1985), the case cited by Justice Blackmun in *Watson v. Fort Worth* (1988) in his response to O'Connor's "fresh look" at adverse impact.

In Davis, the 5th Circuit upheld a policy of screening out individuals with a history of reckless driving convictions for the job of police officer. The case involved other tests that were also upheld (college course credits and recent marijuana use). The defense was based on extensive factual documentation. For example, for reckless driving there was both expert witness testimony and documented data from the research literature indicating that past driving habits are the best predictor of future driving habits.

The critical issues in Davis were twofold. First, testimony and research indicated that all three tests spoke to essential job functions and to KSAs necessary for these job functions (e.g., course work teaches people how to interact with members of the community; illegal drug use indicates reckless disregard for the law; and driving skill is necessary for several essential functions). Second, it would have been impossible—predictively or concurrently—to validate any of these tests without endangering the public. Thus the expert testimony and research spoke essentially to content validity.

On a more general level many important tests could not withstand a strict requirement for criterion validity studies. Teachers need teaching certificates; college professors need advanced degrees; engineers need engineering degrees; and so forth. Thus there are many circumstances in which content validity must suffice.

──────── CHAPTER SUMMARY ────────

Title VII is the broadest of all EEO statutes, protecting **(Q1)** race, color, religion, sex, and national origin, and covering **(Q2)** private, state/local, and federal entities. The covered practices **(Q3)** focus on non-discrimination, not affirmative action. Title VII claims must satisfy EEOC administrative procedural requirements **(Q4)**, and can produce both equitable and legal remedies **(Q5)**. The major attack/defense balances **(Q6)** include adverse impact and three different versions of disparate treatment (McDonnell-Burdine, direct motive, and pattern or practice). Title VII also incorporates a statutory defense for BFOQ for sex, religion, and national origin (but not race or color), and a BFSS defense to any charge. Critically, to avoid adverse impact complications, employers need to understand the *Uniform Guidelines on Personnel Selection*. Some of the guidance is out of date. However, the courts still use the Guidelines, and it is particularly important to understand where criterion validity studies are required and where content validity will suffice.

NOTES

1. The standard source for the legislative history of any statute is the *Congressional Record*. However, there are better sources. Usually, legislative history is discussed in key court cases or in books written near the time of enactment. For Title VII, the best source the author has found is a book by Sovern (1966).

2. Part I of E.O.11246 on affirmative action in federal agencies lists seven classes; the five Title VII classes plus age and disability. However, the Title VII classes are not really "protected." Rather, minorities and female groups within some of these classes are "preferred."

3. The *Uniform Guidelines on Personnel Selection* are only one set of guidelines enforced by the EEOC. The EEOC enforces many other guidelines, including those for discrimination based on sex, national origin, and religion.

4. Albermarle Paper Company used the same two tests as Duke Power.

5. The use of training data in formal validation studies applies to recruitment of police and firefighters because training is a natural step in the progression from recruitment to hiring. An excellent discussion of this issue, and in general FEP cases related to training, is presented by Russell (1984).

6. In essence, the argument here is that black students need black teachers as role models. The argument was rejected in Hazelwood and later again in an important reverse discrimination case discussed in Chapter 7.

7. Technically speaking, undue hardship for failure to reasonably accommodate a sincerely held religious belief is also a statutory defense incorporated into Title VII in the EEO Act of 1972. This defense will be discussed in Chapter 3.

8. This is not an unusual complaint. In general, many women distrust job evaluation procedures because men do the evaluating. This is an important issue in what is known as comparable pay for comparable work (or jobs of "comparable worth"). Comparable worth will be discussed in Chapter 5 on the Equal Pay Act.

9. This is a tough call. The *Congressional Record* is not that illuminating on this issue (at least to the author), and—based on personal discussions—it is not clear to personnel lawyers either.

10. The issue of cutoff scores is discussed in relation to legal, psychometric, and professional issues by Cascio, Alexander, and Barrett (1988).

11. The role of job analysis (and other factors) in performance appraisal and formal test validation in case law is reviewed by Field and Holley (1983).

12. In general, interviews should be structured. An excellent discussion of the role of structured interviews in job selection is provided by Arvey (1979). A more recent discussion is provided by Harris (1989). An excellent practical guide to structuring interviews is provided by Levine (1983).

13. For example, Cascio (1976) reported criterion validity coefficients between .75 and .80 for prediction of turnover between white versus black workers.

14. Assessment center methodology is the product of mainly one person—D. W. Bray. An easy-to-digest article on assessment center methodology was written by Bray (1982) for the *American Psychologist*. Bray's article describes how the assessment center methodology was studied using criterion validity principles.

Protected Class Issues in Title VII (Part II)

CHART 3.1. TITLE VII

Q1	Q2	Q3	Q4	Q5	Q6
Race	Federal	Terms, conditions, & privileges	EEOC filing procedures	Injunction	Adverse impact
Color	State/local*			Back pay	Disparate treatment
Religion	Private*	Segregation & classification	180 days in nondeferral states	Reinstatement	
Sex	*15 or more employees for each day, 20 or more weeks in current or prior year	Retaliation	300 days in deferral states	Front pay	Pattern/practice
National origin		Religious accommodation		Legal fees	Mixed motive
				Compensatory & punitive damages (capped)	Statutory defenses: BFOQ BFSS
					Undue hardship in religious accommodation

(Q1): What classes of people are protected (or have rights)?
(Q2): What business entities are covered (or have duties)?
(Q3): What employment practices are covered?
(Q4): Is the law administered, and if so, how?
(Q5): What are the penalties (or remedies) for breaking the law?
(Q6): What are the attacks and defenses used in litigation?

Chapter 2 outlined the six dimensions for Title VII and focused on **attack/defense balances (Q6)** irrespective of the **protected classes (Q1)**. The organizational principle of this chapter is protected class, the goal being to sample **covered practices (Q3)** for race and color (Section I), religion (Section II), national origin (Section III), and sex (Section IV), and to complete the discussion of compliance (Section V).

As one might imagine, Title VII is dominated by race[1] and sex[2] issues. By circumstance, many of the critical race issues were cited in Chapter 2. Therefore, race will serve as a background for summarizing personel practices that have produced EEO problems in the workplace. The major issues in religion and national origin are unique to those classes, and will be discussed relatively briefly. More than half of the chapter will be devoted to sex discrimination, which has more unique or sex- dominated scenarios than any other class.

SECTION I
RACE DISCRIMINATION

Race features discrimination based on every term, condition, or privilege of employment, segregation and classification, and retaliation. Race also features reverse discrimination, a topic reserved for Chapter 7.[3] The following discussion briefly overviews race discrimination in: (a) recruitment, (b) screening, (c) segregation and classification, (d) promotion, and (e) discharge.

RECRUITMENT

Advertisement used to be a major source of race and sex discrimination. However, ads have produced few recruitment violations in recent years.[4] Most current violations involve agents other than the employer. For example, in *EEOC v. Kimbrough* (1983), a word-of-mouth referral system yielded significantly more applications from whites than blacks and therefore triggered adverse impact. Word-of-mouth referral is cited by both the EEOC and OFCCP as a major factor that perpetuates the pattern of discrimination. Companies that rely on walk-in applications are most apt to suffer from word-of-mouth effects.

By and large, however, most recruitment violations are a product of union and employment agency activities. For example, in *United Steelworkers v. Weber* (1979), Kaiser Aluminum hired its skilled craft workers directly from a union guilty of a pattern or practice of discrimination against blacks. In *Peques v. Mississippi* (1983) state employers relied on a state referral agency, within which agent interviewers were guilty of a pattern or practice of discrimination (they referred blacks and women mainly for lower paying jobs).

In addition, there is the example of *Furnco v. Waters* (1978) discussed in Chapter 2. In Furnco, the employer commissioned a supervisor to recruit and select construction workers. The supervisor carried out the affirmative action goals of the employer, but when these goals were reached, he injected his own values.

These cases merely illustrate the problem; many others could be cited. The main point is that recruitment is the first step in job entry,[5] and violations can occur because of informal procedures and/or subjective decisions by the employer or other agents inside or outside of the company. The word-of-mouth illustration aside, the frequent violation is disparate treatment, often in the form of the pattern or practice of discrimination.

SCREENING

Companies with large applicant pools are apt to screen with formal tests (e.g., *Griggs v. Duke Power*, 1971; *Connecticut v. Teal*, 1981). The term *test*, remember, includes any basis for screening. Thus IQ tests, interviews, and high school degrees are all tests. Formal tests (e.g., IQ tests) receive more emphasis than other tests because of the major Supreme Court rulings. But other tests have long been featured items in lower court rulings.

Employers should be wary of background information obtained from application blanks and background checks; particularly arrest records. The germinal case is *Gregory v. Litton* (1970), where the company screened out applicants with multiple arrests for violations other than minor misdemeanors. Gregory was offered, and accepted employment as a sheet metal mechanic. But based on information on in his "Preliminary Security Information" form, the offer was rescinded. Gregory had been arrested 14 times but never convicted. A California district court struck down this test and the 9th Circuit affirmed.

Between the district and circuit court rulings in Gregory, the 8th Circuit tried a public safety case (*Carter v. Gallagher,* 1971). The city of Minneapolis excluded applicants (for firefighting) with a history of jail time for misdemeanors or felonies. The court did not rule, however, as the parties themselves agreed that a felony or misdemeanor does not "per se constitute an absolute bar to employment."

The 8th Circuit also tried *Green v. Missouri Pacific Railroad Company* (1975). The company ("MoPac") responded to the Gregory ruling by rescinding its arrest policy. However, MoPac continued to screen on the basis of convictions. Green's application blank indicated a prior conviction for refusing military service. MoPac could not prove business necessity for this exclusion. Indeed, a consulting psychologist for MoPac testified that ex-offenders should be treated on a case-by-case basis; that to do otherwise would increase the recidivism rate. The court also cited *Butts v. Nichols* (1974), where an Iowa law similar to MoPac's was struck down via the 14th Amendment.

Exclusion based on credit information is also suspect. The worst offender is wage garnishment, which produces adverse impact against blacks. For example, in *Johnson v. Pike* (1971), the company asserted that wage garnishment is tedious and costly. A California district court rejected this argument, ruling that an employee's performance record is the only basis for a business necessity defense. In a subsequent case (*Wallace v. Debron,* 1974), the 8th Circuit ruled that garnishment poses "artificial, arbitrary, and unnecessary racial barriers to employment"; the very essence of adverse impact theory.

SEGREGATION AND CLASSIFICATION

Segregation and classification is the main historical source of the pattern or practice of discrimination against blacks and women. These issues will be addressed in detail in Chapters 5 (Equal Pay Act) and 7 (affirmative action). For present purposes, the Teamsters (1977) and Weber (1979) cases illustrate the problem. In Teamsters, there was an overt, pre-Title VII practice of differentially classifying minority versus majority drivers. In Weber, Kaiser Aluminum unwittingly accepted skilled workers from a discriminatory union.

These cases also illustrate violations related to benefits and training. Discrimination in benefits is almost always a residual effect of the pattern of discrimination. In post-Title VII years, there have been few instances in which blacks receive one set of benefits and whites another (although this is a major issue in sex discrimination). In race discrimination there is no arguable issue, because facial discrimination is indefensible. However, there are residual effects of facial discrimination from the prior era, as illustrated in Teamsters, where minority drivers seeking higher paying jobs lost seniority accrued in their prior (lower paying) jobs.

Training can be a conduit to segregation. Unions, for example, have a history of differential assignment of blacks versus whites to training for higher versus lower quality jobs. For example, in Weber the unions provided training for skills required by Kaiser Aluminum.

PROMOTION

Promotion decisions can involve both adverse impact and disparate treatment. Large-scale promotion often uses formal tests that screen out minorities (*Albermarle v. Moody*, 1975), whereas small-scale promotion usually involves subjective decisions indicative of disparate treatment. *Watson v. Fort Worth* (1988), therefore, is a landmark ruling for cases traditionally decided by disparate treatment attack/defense balances. As a result of Watson, subjective tests are now subject to adverse impact scrutiny. Of course, the effect of the Watson ruling was blocked in Wards Cove (1989) and unblocked in the Civil Rights Act of 1991. Thus the true effect of the Watson ruling remains to be seen.

DISCHARGE

Finally, discharge is usually a disparate treatment issue; but not always. For example, the background information cited earlier (convictions, credit, etc.) could emerge for job incumbents. This occurred, for example, with wage garnishment in *Wallace v. Debron* (1974). In addition, in reductions in force (RIFs), employers may use impactful criteria. However, RIFs are more likely to impact age, as will be witnessed in Chapter 6.

Disparate treatment scenarios for discharge are quite variable. However, two scenarios stand out. First, in *McDonald v. Santa Fe* (1976), a combined Title VII/Sec.1981 suit, two whites and one black stole from the company, but only the two whites were discharged. This was a clear-cut violation, probably induced by a false fear of affirmative action sanctions. There is nothing in affirmative action or any other EEO law that legalizes disparate treatment against white employees.

The second scenario involves constructive discharge. The conditions of work are often so deplorable that the employee quits before being terminated. A term used for the offense is *hostile environment,* or *hostile harassment. Constructive discharge* is the term used for quitting as a result of hostile harassment. As noted in the overview to Chapter 1, hostile racial harassment was judicially defeated in the 1970s before hostile sexual harassment was even recognized as an offense. The germinal case was *Rogers v. EEOC* (1971).

In Rogers, an Hispanic woman suffered hostile harassment but no tangible employment consequence (i.e., she was not fired or demoted). The 5th Circuit ruled that terms and conditions of employment is:

> an expansive concept which sweeps within its protective ambit the practice of creating a work environment heavily charged with ethnic or racial discrimination. . . . One can readily envision working environments so heavily polluted with discrimination as to destroy completely the emotional and psychological stability of minority group workers.

The Rogers ruling has achieved landmark status as an important precursor to issues in hostile sexual harassment. Nevertheless, it would be a mistake to infer that racial harassment is a dead issue. As recently as 1987, the Supreme Court struck down a union's refusal to process racial harassment grievances (*Goodman v. Lukens Steel*). Moreover, harassment has emerged in both religion and national origin cases, although with much less frequency than in race or sex.

───────── **BRIEF SUMMARY** ─────────

Title VII protects all races and colors. Minority issues involve all terms, conditions, and privileges of employment, whereas majority issues involve mainly reverse discrimination. Adverse impact is used for all screens, including history of arrest and conviction, credit information, and even word-of-mouth referral. Disparate treatment is normally reserved for subjective procedures, particularly by agents other than the employer. However, the Civil Rights Act of 1991 breaths life into the 1988 Watson ruling, and adverse impact cases attacking subjective procedures is a relevant issue for the future. In general, minorities (and women) are historical victims of segregation and classification, both within companies and by outside agents. Segregation and classification has implications for both Title VII and affirmative action. For present purposes, it is sufficient to recognize that Title VII is designed to impose remedies for identifiable victims of identifiable violations, whereas affirmative action is designed to redistribute opportunities for underutilized minorities (and women) who have been discriminated against as a group though not necessarily as individuals. The issue of reverse discrimination for both minorities and women is reserved for Chapter 7.

SECTION II
DISCRIMINATION BASED ON RELIGION

As laymen we have images of facial discrimination against religion. In part this stems from the history of our nation, which is founded on the premise of religious freedom. It also stems from personal experiences of religious harassment. Cases involving animus toward religion are the exception, however, not the rule. There are instances of religious harassment (e.g., *Compston v. Borden*, 1976), but the dominant issues relate to three other sources: (a) religious accommodation; (b) First Amendment challenges; and (c) conscientious religious objections to unionism (and union dues).

AN OVERVIEW OF THE MAJOR ISSUES

Religious Accommodation

As noted in Chapter 2, the original Act exempted religiously affiliated educational institutions (Sec.703(e)). The EEO Act of 1972 added Sec.702, broadening this exemption to all religiously affiliated corporations. The EEO Act also added Sec.701(j), giving religion its unique EEO flavor. In the typical Sec.701(j) case, an employer has a neutral work policy (e.g., work on Saturday) that conflicts with a sincerely held religious belief. The employer must reasonably accommodate this belief, unless doing so imposes **undue hardship**. Aside from the general requirement in all statutes for posting notices, this is the only affirmative requirement in Title VII.

First Amendment Issues

The "Establishment" clause in the First Amendment states:

Congress shall make no law respecting an establishment of religion, or prohibiting the free exercise thereof.

There have been two types of First Amendment challenges: (a) by employers challenging the constitutionality of reasonable accommodation in Sec.701(j); and (b) by employees challenging privileges granted to religiously affiliated institutions in Sec.702.

Conscientious Objection

Finally, prior to 1980 conscientious objections to unions and union dues were treated within the framework of reasonable accommodation. In 1980, however, Congress amended the NLRA (National Labor Relations Act), permitting sincere objectors to pay the equivalent of union dues to a restricted list of "nonreligious, nonlabor organization" tax-exempt charitable funds.

FOCUS ON REASONABLE ACCOMMODATION

The historical record reveals that in 1966 the EEOC issued Guidelines absolving employers from accommodating religious employees. However, the EEOC reversed itself in 1967 and Congress followed this lead in 1972. Accordingly, Sec.701(j) defines "religion" as follows:

> The term "religion" includes all aspects of religious observance and practice, as well as belief, unless an employer demonstrates that he is unable to reasonably accommodate to an employee's or prospective employee's religious observance or practice without undue hardship on the conduct of the employer's business.

Missing from this definition is the concept of religious "belief." For this purpose, courts have relied on prior non-EEO Supreme Court rulings. For example, in *United States v. Seeger* (1965) (regarding conscientious objection to military service) the Supreme Court created the following test for a "sincere and meaningful" religious belief:

> A sincere and meaningful belief which occupies in the life of its possessor a place parallel to that filled by the God of those admittedly qualifying for the draft exemption.

The courts have successfully integrated this definition with the reasonable accommodation requirement. For example, an employee can have a sincerely held Christian belief, but leaving work early to prepare for a Christmas play does not constitute a practice or observance central to this belief (*Wessling v. Kroeger,* 1982). Also, a religious employer cannot impose religious rules in a company that has a clear secular mission (*EEOC v. Townley Engineering,* 1988).

What the courts have wrestled with is the relationship between reasonable accommodation and undue hardship. Although the reasonable accommodation scenario fits easily into adverse impact theory, the language of Sec.701(j) dictates a different scenario. The plaintiff must first provide prima facie evidence of discrimination based on a three-step procedure. These steps are best summarized in *Brener v. Diagnostic Center Hospital* (1982) and are as follows:

(1) he or she has a bona fide religious belief that conflicts with an employment requirement; (2) he or she informed the employer of this belief; (3) he or she was disciplined for failure to comply with the conflicting employment requirement.

A successful prima facie attack then forces a statutory defense; undue hardship. The germinal ruling was provided by the Supreme Court in *Trans World Airlines, Inc. v. Hardison* (1977). Precedents established in Hardison were further clarified by the 5th Circuit in *Brener v. Diagnostic Center Hospital* (1982), and by the Supreme Court in *Ansonia Board of Education v. Philbrook* (1986).

Hardison was a member of a "Saturday" religion (Worldwide Church of God) and a clerk in a company with a Saturday work policy. A collectively bargained seniority system dictated a pecking order for exclusion from Saturday work. Hardison, lacking sufficient seniority, notified his employer of his need for accommodation. The employer tried to engineer voluntary swaps with senior employees, but none would cooperate. Hardison suggested a number of alternatives, not one of which was acceptable to the company (e.g., ordering supervisors to perform his duties or paying for a replacement). One Saturday Hardison observed his Sabbath and was discharged.

The Court's ruling covered two major issues. First, the seniority system prescribed the pecking order, and the system was deemed bona fide (i.e., protected by Sec.703(h)). Consequently, the company could not violate the rights and privileges of senior personnel. Second, the Court ruled that payment for a temporary replacement would impose undue hardship on the company because it would involve extra (or more than *de minimis*) costs. Or, in the words of the Court:

to require TWA to bear more than a de minimis cost in order to give Hardison Saturdays off is an undue hardship.

In *Brener v. Diagnostic Center Hospital* (1982), the 5th Circuit clarified the employee's role in seeking reasonable accommodation. Brener, a pharmacist, requested accommodation for the Jewish (Saturday) Sabbath and major Jewish holidays. Initially, the employer accommodated him by ordering other employees to swap shifts. But when complaints emerged, Brener was ordered to arrange his own swaps. He failed to do so, and provided no assistance in identifying other accommodations. Like Hardison, he stayed home one Saturday, and was discharged.

The court ruled that the hospital had acted in good faith in trying to accommodate Brener, but that Brener, in turn, did not reciprocate. Thus in addition to the requirement of informing the employer of a need for accommodation, the 5th Circuit established that an employee must also actively assist in the effort to find one.

Finally, in *Ansonia v. Philbrook* (1986), the Supreme Court clarified the employer's responsibility when faced with a range of proposals from an otherwise cooperative employee. The Philbrook ruling contradicted an important 1980 guideline by the EEOC. Accordingly:

> when there is more than one means of accommodation which would not cause undue hardship, the employer or labor organization must offer the alternative which least disadvantages the individual with respect to his or her employment opportunities.

As for the case itself, Philbrook, a teacher, requested six days per year leave for religious observance. He was permitted three days for this purpose, and another three for "necessary personal business." However, a union agreement listed the conditions for using personal days and religious observance was not on the list. The school board offered Philbrook the alternative of three days of unpaid leave. Philbrook made counteroffers (e.g., allowing him to pay for a substitute). Based on EEOC Guidelines, the lower court ruled that the school board failed to demonstrate undue hardship in relation to Philbrook's proposals. The Supreme Court overruled, stating:

> We find no basis in either the statute or its legislative history for requiring an employer to choose any particular reasonable accommodation. By its very terms, the statute directs that any reasonable accommodation by the employer is sufficient to meet its accommodation obligation.

In other words, the school board made its reasonable accommodation and was under no other obligations. The Court, however, remanded the case for evaluation of pretext (i.e., why the union did not include religious observance in the list for personal days).

Since Hardison, employers have won those cases where religious beliefs have confronted union requirements. For example, in *Yott v. North American Rockwell* (1979), the 9th Circuit rejected the alternative of staying at a union job at lower pay. In *Turpin v. Missouri-Kansas-Texas Railroad Co.* (1984), the 5th Circuit ruled that flexible work schedules, favored in the 1980 EEOC Guidelines, were invalid in the face of a collective bargaining agreement prohibiting this policy.

Following Hardison, employers have also won where accommodations involved more than *de minimis* costs. For example, in Yott, the employee offered to transfer outside of the bargaining unit. This was deemed an undue hardship because the employer would have to absorb extra training costs. In *Howard v. Haverty* (1980), the 5th Circuit followed the *de minimis* principle where financial costs were not evident. The court accepted as an undue hardship defense factual evidence that temporary replacements reduce business efficiency.

However, plaintiffs have won some cases, particularly when the employer has exerted no effort to accommodate (e.g., *Wangness v. Watertown School District,* 1982; *Protos v. Volkswagen of America,* 1986). This is the inverse of the Brener ruling (where the employee exerted no effort). Additionally, plaintiffs have won when accommodations have required no extra costs, real or otherwise. For example, in *Redmond v. GAF* (1978), the 7th Circuit ruled it would not be undue hardship for the company to obtain temporary replacement for an unskilled position. In *Cook v. Lindsay Olive Growers* (1990), the 9th Circuit ruled likewise regarding temporary transfer to a lower paying position.

Hindsight predicts the outcomes of most of these cases. Nevertheless, there remain a cadre of cases where rulings are not easily predicted by precedents. For example, in *Smith v. Pyro Mining* (1987), a mechanic's sincere belief regarding (Sunday) Sabbath did, of course, require accommodation. However, the 6th Circuit found it unreasonable to require self-generated swaps (as in Brener) because the employee considered asking others to work on Sundays a sin. And in *United States v. Board of Education for School Dist. of Philadelphia,* (1990), the 3rd Circuit held that the right to wear religious garb, though generally preserved, violates religious neutrality when done in a public school classroom.

FOCUS ON FIRST AMENDMENT CASES

Religious Accommodation Cases

In general, First Amendment rulings have followed the 1971 Supreme Court precedent in *Lemon v. Kurtzman* (regarding state aid to church-related schools). In Lemon, the Court specified a three-step test for a First Amendment violation. Specifically, (a) the statute cannot serve a nonsecular purpose; (b) its primary effect cannot be to advance religion; and (c) it cannot create excessive entanglements between church and state.

The germinal Sec.701(j) case is *Cummins v. Parker Seal* (1975), which involved a scenario similar to Hardison and to Brener. In defending its failure to accommodate Cummins, the employer asserted:

> reasonable accommodation . . . fosters religion by requiring employers to defer to their employee's religious idiosyncrasies.

In an equally divided ruling, Sec.701(j) was deemed constitutional by the 6th Circuit because it serves "pragmatic, neutral purposes" and requires "no financial support" for religious institutions. The dissenting opinion was that Sec.701(j) benefits only religion.

Subsequent rulings did not exactly clarify the issue. For example, in *Yott v. North American Rockwell* (1979), the 9th Circuit ruled that Sec.701(j) contradicted the Establishment clause, but ruled in favor of the defendant on other (previously discussed) grounds. The 3rd Circuit did likewise in *Gavin v. People's Natural Gas* (1979). Both circuits, however, have upheld Sec.701(j) in more recent rulings; the 9th Circuit in *Tooley v. Martin Marietta* (1981) and *International Association v. Boeing* (1987), and the 3rd Circuit in *Protos v. Volkswagen* (1986).

Although the Supreme Court has not ruled on this issue directly, it vacated and remanded Cummins in light of its Hardison ruling, and declined to review the Yott case. Considering that the Supreme Court has issued two landmark reasonable accommodation rulings (Hardison and Philbrook), the clear inference is that the Court deems Sec.701(j) constitutional.

The skeptical reader might note that the Supreme Court struck down a Connecticut state law that *guaranteed* employees the right not to work on their chosen Sabbath (*Estate of Thornton v. Caldor*, 1985). Although this ruling would seem to counter the affirmations of Sec.701(j) just cited, it is clear that the Court was not making a general statement against accommodation. Indeed, its ruling supported the principle that the accommodation-hardship relationship needs to be evaluated on a case-by-case basis. Or in the words of the Court:

> the statute allows for no consideration as to whether the employer has made reasonable accommodation proposals.

Nonaccommodation Cases

The key Sec.702 ruling was made recently by the Supreme Court in *Corporation of Presiding Bishop etc. v. Amos* (1987). However, the 5th Circuit had decided two critical preliminary issues in *McClure v. Salvation Army* (1972) and *EEOC v. Mississippi College* (1980).

In McClure, a female minister claimed sex discrimination in pay and benefits relative to male ministers, and that she had suffered retaliatory discharge. The 5th Circuit refused to encroach on the church/minister relationship, fearing a violation of religious freedom guaranteed by the First Amendment. However, the 5th Circuit did encroach in Mississippi College. The college was exempt for *religious* discrimination as the Salvation Army was in McClure, but unlike McClure, discrimination charges involved a faculty position, not the church/minister relationship. In the words of the court:

> The language and the legislative history of Sec.702 compel the conclusion that Congress did not intend that a religious organization be exempted from liability for discriminating against its employees on the basis of race, color, sex or national origin.

Similar rulings were subsequently rendered by (again) the 5th Circuit (*EEOC v. Southwestern Baptist Theological Seminary,* 1981), and the 9th Circuit (*EEOC v. Pacific Press Publishing Association,* 1981). Thus the McClure-Mississippi precedent is that institutions exempt as a function of Sec.702 may discriminate based on religion for any job, and may discriminate for any reason for the job of church minister.

The McClure-Mississippi precedent, though important, does not directly speak to the core issue: Is Sec.702 Constitutional? This issue was decided by the Supreme Court in Amos, where a building engineer was employed at a nonprofit gymnasium closely affiliated with the Mormon Church. The engineer and others were discharged because they did not qualify as church members. The lower court had ruled for Amos, asserting that the defendant had failed step 2 of the Lemon test (i.e., advancement of religion). The Supreme Court overruled, stating:

> A law is not unconstitutional simply because it allows churches to advance religion, which is their very purpose. . . . We do not see how any advancement of religion achieved by the Gymnasium can be fairly attributed to the Government, as opposed to the Church.

The Court also ruled in favor of the defendant in steps 1 (nonsecular purpose) and 3 (unnecessary church/state entanglements).

A Postscript to First Amendment Cases

On June 25, 1992, the Supreme Court ruled on a non-EEO case challenging the Lemon test. The issue involved public school benedictions that invoke a deity. According to the September 24, 1991 edition of *United States Law Week,* the Justice Department favored abandoning the Lemon test, and five of the current Supreme Court justices were on record as having similar sentiments. Abandonment of the Lemon test could have reopened questions regarding the constitutionality of Sections 701(j) and 702. However, the Court did not revoke the Lemon test as suggested in the *Law Week* article.

RELIGIOUS OBJECTIONS TO UNIONS

Although employees invariably lose cases when accommodations contradict union agreements, they usually win cases based on religious objections to unions and dues. Prior to 1980, such cases were treated in the Hardison tradition. The EEOC Guidelines of 1967 (not modified until after Hardison) protected the rights of conscientious objectors. The Guidelines asserted that the objecting employee should not be forced to join the union, and that in lieu of union dues alternative payments may be made to charitable organizations.

Prior to 1980, the 9th Circuit ruled on three cases based on the Hardison precedent and the EEOC Guidelines. In *Burns v. Southern Pacific* (1978), the union claimed undue hardship based on extra (i.e., more than *de minimis*) administrative work that substitutions would entail. In *Anderson v. General Dynamics* (1978), the employer claimed undue hardship would ensue because union workers would be offended. The court accepted neither argument, mainly because both were based on assumptions unsupported by actual evidence.

The third case, *Yott v. North American Rockwell* (1979), was discussed previously. Yott's basic gripe was his opposition to unions. Recall that the court rejected Yott's proposals to stay at the union position at a lower salary or transfer to a job outside the union. The accommodation offered by the company was for Yott to pay the equivalent of union dues to his own church. Yott refused. The 9th Circuit, however, found the accommodation reasonable.

Ironically, the offer to Yott is illegal by post-1980 standards. The previously alluded to amendment to NLRA (known as Sec. 19) stipulates that the alternative-payment accommodation must be made, but employees must choose from a pre-agreed-upon list of *nonreligious* and nonlabor tax-exempt charities. When enacted, the main legal issue was the relationship between Sec. 19 and Sec. 701(j). Once again, it was the 9th Circuit that made the major rulings.

In *Tooley v. Martin Marietta* (1981), the 9th Circuit affirmed the alternative-payment accommodation in Sec. 19, and reaffirmed the accommodation in *International Association v. Boeing* (1987). The constitutionality of Sec. 702 was also questioned (and upheld) in both cases. Basically, in Tooley, the court established that Sec. 19 parallels rather than supersedes Title VII. This ruling was predictable, considering that from an employer or union standpoint the 9th Circuit had previously supported a more objectionable accommodation in Yott (i.e., contributions to one's own church).

——— **BRIEF SUMMARY** ———

Religious discrimination evokes images of facial discrimination, but case law has not featured this issue. Central to most religion cases is the reasonable accommodation requirement. When neutral factors conflict with sincerely held beliefs the employer must reasonably accommodate the belief unless doing so imposes undue hardship. The employee must express the need for accommodation, cooperate in identifying accommodations, and accept any accommodation that overcomes the neutral barrier. The employer is not required to experience more than a *de minimis* cost, either in terms of money or work efficiency. Employers usually win reasonable accommodation cases, unless they: (a) exert no effort to accommodate; (b) claim less than *de minimis* hardships; or (c) attack its constitutionality. The constitutionality of Sec. 701(j) and 702 have been established, and reasonable accommodation has been extended to protect religious convictions opposing unions and union dues.

SECTION III
DISCRIMINATION BASED ON NATIONAL ORIGIN

National origin shares some issues with other protected classes, most notably harassment (e.g., *Carriddi v. K. C. Chiefs,* 1977). Like religion, however, most national origin cases are unique. Critically, there is a major gap in Title VII coverage. This gap affords other laws nearly as much influence on national origin as Title VII. These other laws include Sec.1983, the NLRA, the FLSA (Fair Labor Standards Act), and the IRCA (Immigration Reform and Control Act).

TITLE VII COVERAGE

The gap in Title VII is that it does not protect employment discrimination based on U.S. citizenship, unless U.S. citizenship is a pretext for discrimination. Title VII does, however, speak strongly to two other issues, namely language fluency and speak-English policies.

The Citizenship Gap

In its original guidelines on national origin discrimination (1972), the EEOC asserted that:

> Because discrimination based on citizenship has the effect of discriminating on the basis of national origin, a lawfully immigrated alien . . . may not be discriminated against on the basis of his citizenship.

The validity of this Guideline was challenged in *Espinoza v. Farrah* (1973), a dominant Supreme Court case. Farrah, a clothing manufacturer, excluded Cecillia Espinoza, a "lawfully immigrated (Mexican) alien," only because she was not a U.S. citizen. Pretext was never an issue. All Farrah employees were U.S. citizens; 96% of them were Mexican American; and an Hispanic was hired after Espinoza was excluded. The district court, paying deference to EEOC guidance, favored Espinoza. But the circuit court overruled, and the Supreme Court affirmed, stating:

Aliens are protected from illegal discrimination under the Act, but nothing in the Act makes it illegal to discriminate on the basis of citizenship or alienage.

Thus any employer, in any business, and for any reason, may exclude on the basis of citizenship unless, of course, such exclusion is pretext (e.g., excluding Hispanic aliens, but not European aliens).

The Court also affirmed the right of federal agencies to require U.S. citizenship, and provided the currently applicable definition of national origin. As reflected in Sec.1606.1, of the EEOC Guidelines, national origin refers to:

an individual's, or his or her ancestor's place of origin; or because an individual has the physical, cultural or linguistic characteristics of a national origin group.

Fluency-in-English Requirements

Fluency is addressed in Sec.1606.6(1) of the EEOC Guidelines, which states:

The Commission has found that the use of the following selection procedures may be discriminatory. . . . Fluency-in-English requirements, such as denying employment opportunities because of an individual's foreign accent or inability to communicate in English.

The Guideline is not as instructive as it appears. For example, one can communicate well in English, and do so with an accent (e.g., Henry Kissinger). When separated, defendants have the advantage in "communication" cases and plaintiffs have the advantage in "accent" cases. When combined, traditional Title VII considerations prevail.

The defendant's advantage in communication cases is illustrated in *Meja v. N. Y. Sheraton* (1978) and *Stephen v. P.G.A. Sheraton* (1989). In Meja, a female Dominican national with poor language skills was internally trained for promotion from chambermaid to cashier, but was not promoted because of language deficiencies. A New York district court accepted the defendant's articulation based on direct observation of Meja's general deficiencies during her testimony. In Stephen, a black Haitian was discharged from his job as purchasing clerk. The 11th Circuit accepted documented evidence that Stephen had made a number of costly mistakes directly attributable to the his "inability to speak and understand English."

The plaintiff's advantage in accent cases is illustrated in *Berke v. Ohio Public Welfare* (1980) and *Carino v. University of Oklahoma* (1984). In Berke, a woman with a master's degree and above average command of the English language was denied two positions she was seemingly qualified for. The 10th Circuit attributed the exclusion to Berke's thick Polish accent. The 10th Circuit did likewise in Carino, where a Filipino male, deemed competent enough to assume interim duties as supervisor in a dental lab, was not considered for the permanent position.

In cases where communication and accent are not clearly separable, the outcome is more difficult to predict. For example, in *Kureshy v. C.U.N.Y.* (1980), a New York district court upheld a college's failure to tenure a dark skinned Indian Muslim. Although both communication and accent were raised as issues, the deciding factor was that Kureshy was treated like hundreds of other tenure applicants before him. In contrast, in *Loiseau v. Dept. of Human Resources* (1983), an Oregon district court ruled in favor of a black, French-speaking West Indian who was seemingly qualified for, but was twice denied, promotion. As in Kureshy, the issue of communication and accent were raised. However, unlike Kureshy, where there was a uniform, time-honored system for tenure, Loiseau was evaluated on a "Promotional Merit Rating" test that was entirely subjective and easily contrived.

Speak-English-Only Rules

The final Title VII issue pits a 5th Circuit ruling against EEOC guidance. In *Garcia v. Gloor* (1980), the company discharged Gloor for multiple violations of a speak-English-only policy. Employees were required to speak English while working (unless speaking to Spanish-speaking customers), but were permitted to speak Spanish on their own time (e.g., on breaks; when working outside away from customers).

This case was tried shortly before publication of the 1980 update of the EEOC Guidelines. The EEOC supported Gloor with testimony. Gloor asserted that the policy is arbitrary, and that speaking Spanish is a source of ancestral pride. The company argued that the policy is necessary for supervisory reasons. The 5th Circuit rejected the relevancy of whether the policy was arbitrary or necessary. Instead, the court cited its prior ruling in *Willingham v. Macon* (1975), a sex discrimination case to be discussed later. In Macon, the court ruled that hair length was a mutable characteristic that does not impede employment opportunity. In Gloor, the court stated:

> To a person who speaks only one tongue . . . language might well be an immutable characteristic. . . . However, the language a person who is multi-lingual elects to speak at a particular time is by definition a matter of choice.

Despite the ruling, the EEOC Guidelines devote an entire section (1606.7) to speak-English-only rules. Sec.1606.7 emphasizes that an English-only policy creates "an atmosphere of inferiority" when applied at all times. The EEOC stresses that business necessity must be demonstrated even when applied selectively (i.e., during work, but not on breaks). However, the EEOC has ruled that the policy can be justified for safety reasons (EEOC Decision 83-7, 1983). It is unclear what weight this guidance would receive if an employer refused to establish business necessity. Clearly, the 5th Circuit treats the issue as a matter of choice for multilingual employees. And for those who are unilingual and cannot speak English, the issue reverts to the fluency questions raised in cases such as Meja and Stephen.

NON-TITLE VII INFLUENCES

The 5th and 14th Amendments

It is clear that discrimination based on citizenship is illegal under the **Equal Protection** Clause of the 14th Amendment (i.e., "under the color of state law"). Thus the Supreme Court struck down an Arizona law requiring 15 years of residency for lawful aliens to be eligible for welfare benefits (*Graham v. Richardson,* 1971). In the EEO context, the Supreme Court ruled against New York City for discharging four legal aliens for not becoming citizens (*Sugarman v. Dougall,* 1973). The Court also ruled against the Connecticut Bar Association for denying a Dutch citizen access to the state bar exam (In Re Griffiths, 1973).

However, discrimination based on citizenship is legal under the color of federal law. In *Matthews v. Diaz* (1976), also a non-EEO case, the plaintiffs challenged a provision in the Social Security Act using the **Due Process** Clause of the 5th Amendment. The challenged provision requires a 5-year residency for Medicare supplemental insurance eligibility. The Supreme Court upheld the provision, stating:

> The fact that all persons, aliens and citizens alike, are protected by the Due Process Clause does not lead to the further conclusions that aliens are entitled to enjoy all the advantages of citizenship.

In commenting on its prior rulings based on the 14th Amendment, the Court stated:

> it is the business of the political branches of the Federal Government, rather than that of either the States or the Federal Judiciary, to regulate the conditions of entry and residence of aliens.

In other words, Congress can legislate freely in this arena.

Other Federal Statutes

The provisions of the FLSA and NLRA apply to both lawful aliens and citizens. Thus it is illegal to pay lawful aliens a less than minimum wage, and it is illegal to prevent them from engaging in normal union activities. More important, though, are the anti-discrimination provisions of the IRCA (1986) as amended in 1990. The main purpose of IRCA is to control the flow of illegal aliens. Employers must verify that all employees are properly authorized to work in the United States, under threat of civil and criminal penalties.

Of course, without additional provisions, employers could avoid liability by simply excluding all aliens; a legal practice within the boundaries of Title VII. Therefore, IRCA contains anti-discrimination provisions. Basically, an employer with more than four employees is prohibited from denying the terms, conditions, or privileges of employment to any individual based on national origin, citizenship, and/or intention to become a citizen. In the 1990 amendment, these protections were extended to seasonal agricultural workers. At the same time, the verification responsibility was softened and the penalties for discrimination were hardened.

In general, IRCA is administered by the Justice Department, which uses a special counsel to investigate claims and administrative law judges to decide cases. It is important to note that IRCA defers to Title VII on common issues. Thus IRCA does not cover discrimination already covered by Title VII, and the Special counsel may not investigate cases already under EEOC jurisdiction.

─────── **BRIEF SUMMARY** ───────

Title VII permits nonpretextual discrimination based on citizenship, as does the Due Process Clause of the 5th Amendment. However discrimination based on citizenship is prohibited by the 14th Amendment, FLSA, NLRA, and IRCA. Title VII prohibitions against fluency and English-only policies apply to lawful aliens, as do the other general provisions of the Act (e.g., harassment). In Title VII fluency cases, the employer has the advantage when exclusion is based on communication, but the plaintiff has the advantage when exclusion is based on accent; cases that mix communication and accent are more difficult to predict. English-only policies are permitted in the interest of business efficiency and safety. However, the issue of "inferiority," as addressed in the EEOC Guidelines, remains unclear. The employer would be wise to avoid an English-only policy unless it is truly a business necessity.

SECTION IV
Sex Discrimination

Discrimination based on sex spans the entire spectrum of terms and conditions. In fact, much of the race-by-practice overview provided in Section I of this chapter could have been provided using sex discrimination examples. However, sex discrimination contains seven issues that are either sex-specific or sex-dominant. These include state protective laws, height/weight criteria, pregnancy benefits, fetal protection, sex-plus discrimination, benefits unrelated to pregnancy, and two forms of sexual harassment.

STATE PROTECTION LAWS

During the Civil War era, factory and plant managers abused women (and children), demanding unreasonable work for pitiful wages. For protective purposes, state laws were enacted to limit such things as, for example, hours of work, lifting of weight, or type of work. The 1938 FLSA and its subsequent amendments eliminated some of these excesses. Nevertheless, in the early days of Title VII companies continued to use state protective laws as pretexts for excluding women from reasonably good jobs. By Title VII standards, such exclusionary practices constitute **facial discrimination** and of course require a BFOQ defense.

The constitutional basis for federal jurisdiction in such cases is in the "Supremacy" clause in Article VI, which states:

The laws of the United States dealing with matters within its jurisdiction are supreme and the Judges in every state shall be bound thereby, anything in the Constitution or laws of any state to the contrary notwithstanding.

The last relevant Supreme Court ruling was in *Muller v. Oregon* (1908), where a state law limiting women to a 10-hour factory shift was upheld. Consequently, in more recent times the lower courts faced Title VII challenges similar to Muller but with an outdated precedent.

Most of the major cases in this arena occurred within the same time frame. Two cases stand out: *Weeks v. Southern Bell Telephone* (1969) and *Rosenfeld v. Southern Pacific Co.* (1971). Other similar cases include *Schaeffer v. San Diego Yellow Cabs* (1972), *Koeber v. Westinghouse Electric* (1973), and *Williams v. General Foods* (1974).

The Weeks and Rosenfeld cases considered the same issue; can employers use state protection to facially discriminate against women? Weeks was excluded from the position of Switchman based on a Georgia law proscribing weight lifting in excess of 30 pounds. Rosenfeld was excluded from the position of agent-telegrapher based on a California law proscribing weight lifting in excess of 25 pounds.

Weeks was decided prior to Rosenfeld at the circuit court level, but Rosenfeld was more influential. In Rosenfeld, a state court struck down the state law. A state court in Georgia did likewise in response to the California court while the Weeks case was in circuit court. In any event, both companies were stripped of state protection, and forced into a **BFOQ** defense. The 5th Circuit (Weeks) and the 9th Circuit (Rosenfeld) rejected the BFOQ argument because individual women were denied the opportunity to prove they could lift the necessary weight. According to the 9th Circuit, there was no evidence that:

all or substantially all women would be unable to perform safely and effectively the duties of the job involved.

There was another interesting factor in these cases. In Rosenfeld, the company argued **good faith**, because its policy was based on the (then) written EEOC Guidelines that seemingly supported the state protective laws. However, the court did not accept this argument because the company had not written the EEOC for a ruling. Moreover, the EEOC had provided amicus support to Weeks based upon its Guidelines on sex stereotyping.

Following the Weeks and Rosenfeld rulings, the EEOC altered its recommendations in its 1972 Guidelines, stating:

> Many states have enacted laws . . . with respect to employment of fe-
> males. Among these laws are those which prohibit . . . females . . . in jobs
> requiring the lifting or carrying of weights exceeding certain prescribed
> limits, during certain hours of the night, for more than a specified
> number of hours. . . . The Commission has found that such laws and
> regulations do not take into account the capacities, preferences, and
> abilities of individual females.

In retrospect, invalidation of the state law is an important precedent
but no surprise. An equally important precedent, however, concerns
the good faith ruling in Rosenfeld. Clearly, state laws (or EEOC Guidelines) cannot be used to **willfully** discriminate. A company is more vulnerable if it knows or believes a state law is illegal, even if the law has
not been revoked.

To further illustrate, in *Schaeffer v. San Diego Yellow Cabs* (1972),
women were denied overtime work because the previously cited California law also limited maximum work hours. The case was decided much
like Rosenfeld and Weeks. However, in Schaeffer the company admitted its awareness of the Rosenfeld decision and, nevertheless,
continued its policy. As a result, its case for good faith was weak and
all applicable Title VII remedies were awarded. In contrast, where
companies have shown good faith in their reliance on state laws,
remedies have been limited to nonmonetary relief (e.g., *Alaniz v.
California Processors, Inc.*, 1986).

HEIGHT AND WEIGHT REQUIREMENTS

Protective laws are facially discriminatory because they exclude all
women. The BFOQ defense did not succeed in Weeks or Rosenfeld
because employers could not demonstrate that virtually all women
were incapable of meeting a given standard. A similar issue exists with
height and weight standards. They are not facial; they are **neutral**.
They do not exclude all women; they produce **adverse** impact. Nevertheless, the business necessity defense in height/weight is fundamen-
tally the same as the BFOQ defense in state protection. For such tests
to be valid, it must be demonstrated that virtually all "short" and
"light" people, regardless of class, cannot do the work.

As noted in Chapter 2, the germinal case is *Dothard v. Rawlinson*
(1977). Recall that a state law imposed height and weight standards
for law officers, and that the law was rescinded while the case was pending. Stripped of its law, the state faced a business necessity defense

that it could not win. The state argued that the height and weight standards were necessary because law enforcement jobs required strength. The Supreme Court ruled that all individuals, regardless of height or weight, should be given the opportunity to demonstrate their strength.

In subsequent cases featuring neutral requirements, the lower courts have routinely followed Dothard. For example, in *Horace v. Pontiac* (1980), the defendant argued that height (5'8" or taller) is required for police officers to fend off and/or gain respect from criminals. The 6th Circuit rejected this argument, citing superior means for assessing this capability. But in *Boyd v. Ozark Airlines* (1977), the defendant successfully established that height (5'7" or taller) is necessary to operate instruments properly in the cockpit.

Currently, many airlines have a minimal height requirement for flight attendants (5'2"). The airlines contend that minimal height is required to reach the overhead compartments. This policy adversely impacts women, particularly Asians and possibly Hispanics. Thus it is likely that a myriad of these cases will play at the various district and circuit courts in the near future. Based on the precedents in Dothard, the ruling is likely to be that all applicants, regardless of height, must be afforded the opportunity to demonstrate their ability or inability to reach the overhead compartments.

PREGNANCY AND FRINGE BENEFITS

The focus here is on selected fringe benefits denied *only* to pregnant women. Of course, since men are never pregnant, men and women literally receive identical coverage in most instances. Rulings in this arena were dominated by several Supreme Court cases until 1978. In 1978, Congress, reacting negatively to one such ruling (*General Electric v. Gilbert*, 1976), passed the **Pregnancy Discrimination Act**. Currently, any policy that discriminates against pregnant women does so **facially**, and requires a **BFOQ** defense.

Early 14th Amendment Cases

The early Supreme Court cases were 14th Amendment challenges to forced maternity leave (*Cleveland Board of Ed. v. LaFleur*, 1974), exclusionary insurance policies (*Geduldig v. Aiello*, 1974), and exclusionary unemployment benefits (*Turner v. Department of Employment Security of Utah*, 1975). Two of these cases resulted in favorable rulings for pregnant woman. In LaFleur, women were unilaterally forced into pregnancy leave without pay for a 6-7 month interval spanning pre- and post-delivery. In Turner, a state law denied unemployment benefits to women from 12 weeks prior to 6 weeks after delivery. The LaFleur Court struck down the forced leave policy because of its presumption that all pregnant women are incapable of working during a period of pre and post pregnancy (a familiar tune). The Turner Court did likewise because the Utah state law implied the same presumption.

But in Geduldig, the Supreme Court upheld a state insurance policy excluding pregnancy from disability coverage. The Court stated:

> Absent a showing that distinctions involving pregnancy are mere pretexts designed to effect an individuous discrimination against the members of one sex or the other, lawmakers are Constitutionally free to include or exclude pregnancy from the coverage . . . on any reasonable basis, just as with respect to any other physical condition.

In other words, the Geduldig Court felt that men and women had identical coverage. Thus barring pretext, insurance companies are free to create their own unique lists of covered and uncovered disabilities.

At first blush the Geduldig and Turner rulings seem contradictory, because both involved insurance-type benefits. The key issue in Turner, however (as well as in LaFleur), was the presumption, without case-by-case consideration, that all women are incapacitated during intervals of pre- and post-pregnancy. In Geduldig, the policy did not concern the pregnant woman's ability to work, but instead, whether pregnancy itself should be included/excluded as a coverable illness.

Title VII Rulings Preceding the Pregnancy Act

The pregnancy/benefits issue emerged in Title VII in *General Electric v. Gilbert* (1976). In circumstances quite similar to Geduldig (but with a private insurer), the plaintiffs tried to force a business necessity defense with adverse impact. Adverse impact is not available in 14th Amendment cases. In Gilbert, the plaintiffs based their charge on a portion of the 1972 EEOC Guidelines that states:

> Disabilities caused or contributed to by pregnancy . . . for all job-related purposes . . . should be treated as such under any health or temporary disability insurance or sick leave plan available in connection with employment.

However, the Court rejected this interpretation. Using its Geduldig precedent, the policy was deemed **facially neutral**, but the Court denied that adverse impact was demonstrated. Therefore, the phase 2 business necessity defense was not required. The Court stated:

> an employer who has no disability benefits program at all does not violate Title VII even though the "underinclusion" of risks impacts, as a result of pregnancy-related disabilities, more heavily upon one gender than upon the other.

In other words, if no employee was entitled to disability benefits (a legal policy), pregnancy benefits would be a special privilege. Viewed this way, men could actually charge reverse discrimination.

The Gilbert ruling triggered the Pregnancy Discrimination Act (PDA), but not before another Supreme Court ruling (*Nashville Gas v. Satty*, 1977). In Satty, the company permitted unpaid maternity leave but imposed a loss-of-seniority penalty for taking the leave. The company granted sick pay without seniority penalty for medical leaves other than pregnancy. Thus only pregnant women faced lost seniority. Moreover, it is conceivable that the policy was a pretext for discouraging pregnancy.

But the plaintiffs filed adverse impact charges only. The Court ruled that both the leave and penalty were facially neutral and that the penalty did produce differential effects. But the Court treated sick leave in the same way it had previously treated insurance coverage in Gilbert. On remanding the case, the Court literally urged the plaintiffs to make a phase 3 pretext charge. However, the need for a pretext case was neutered by the PDA.

The Pregnancy Discrimination Act of 1978 (PDA)

The PDA inserted Sec.701(k) into Title VII, which, in part, states:

> The terms "because of sex" or "on the basis of sex" include, but are not limited to, because of or on the basis of pregnancy, childbirth or related medical conditions; and women affected by pregnancy, childbirth, or related medical conditions shall be treated the same for all employment related purposes, including receipt of benefits under fringe benefit programs, as other persons not so affected but similar in their ability or inability to work.

In other words, the Act defines virtually any discrimination based on pregnancy as **facial**, not neutral. Sec.701(k) also protects the rights of women who seek abortions, covers abortion as a disability when obtained because of potential danger to the mother, and covers as a disability medical complications to an otherwise uncovered abortion.

Subsequently, the EEOC modified its Guidelines to reflect Congressional intention. In a succession of question and answer illustrations, the EEOC demonstrated the "sameness" principle. That is, the PDA demands that pregnancy be treated the same as any other illness. Thus a company can force unpaid leave on pregnant mothers, but only if all other illnesses are treated likewise. The same holds for insurance coverage and, for that matter, any other term, condition, or privilege of employment. A company cannot, however, reduce prior benefits in order to comply with the Act.

Thereafter, in a Title VII test of the PDA (*Newport News Shipbuilding & Dry Dock v. EEOC,* 1983), the company provided superior pregnancy benefits for female employees relative to female spouses of male employees. Citing the PDA, the Court struck down the policy, stating:

> Although Gilbert concluded that an otherwise inclusive plan that singled out pregnancy-related benefits for exclusion was non-discriminatory on its *face,* because only women can become pregnant, Congress has unequivocally rejected that reasoning.

In other words, the Court recognized not only the Act, but also that any differential based on pregnancy is facially discriminatory.

But in an interesting twist, the Supreme Court recently upheld a state protective law favoring pregnant women. In *California Federal Savings and Loan Association v. Guerra* (1987), the state law provided superior benefits (i.e., extended unpaid maternity leave with reduced risk of job loss) to pregnant women; a policy not automatically available to men. The Supreme Court supported the 9th Circuit ruling, which had previously noted that Congressional Intention in the PDA was:

> to construct a floor beneath which pregnancy disability benefits may not drop—not a ceiling above which they may not rise.

FETAL PROTECTION

At issue here is **facial discrimination** based on fetal protection. Historically, few EEO issues have been as complex. Most of the significant cases in this arena were tried after the PDA. The implications of the

Act, however, so seemingly clear for fringe benefits, were not as clear for fetal protection. Indeed, this issue was clarified only recently by the Supreme Court's ruling in *International Union et al. v. Johnson Controls, Inc.* (1991). But in order to understand this ruling and its clarifying effects, it is necessary to understand the years of confusion that preceded it.

Throughout the history of Title VII, no federal court ever denied that facial discrimination mandates a BFOQ defense. However, as witnessed in the prior section, Congressional intention regarding the definition of facial discrimination has been misinterpreted even by the Supreme Court. In fetal cases, where all decisions prior to Johnson Controls were made by lower courts, confusion existed regarding not only the definition of facial discrimination, but the BFOQ defense as well. Unfortunately for the lower courts, the time period between successive Supreme Court rulings on Title VII BFOQ was 14 years (between *Dothard v. Rawlinson* in 1977 and *International Union et al. v. Johnson Controls* in 1991). In its recent ruling the Supreme Court amplified its Dothard ruling, stating:

> more was at stake than the "individual woman's decision to weigh and accept the risks of employment." We found sex to be a BFOQ inasmuch as the employment of a female guard would create real risks of safety to others if violence broke out because the guard was a woman.

Thus to reiterate a point made in Chapter 2, prison guard safety was not the basis for the successful BFOQ defense; it was prison safety.

Fetal Protection as a Secondary Issue

Beginning at about the time of the Dothard ruling, a number of cases emerged involving the airlines. The central issue was the grounding of pregnant women for purposes of passenger safety. The various airlines established nearly identical policies. What the lower courts could not decide definitively was whether the appropriate defense is business necessity or BFOQ.

To illustrate, in an early case (*Condit v. United Airlines,* 1977), the 4th Circuit affirmed a district court ruling that entertained only the BFOQ defense. But in a later case requiring more extensive analysis (*Burwell v. Eastern Airlines,* 1980), the same court entertained only the business necessity defense. On the other hand, the 5th Circuit (*Levin v. Delta Airlines,* 1984) and the 9th Circuit (*Harriss v. Pan Am World*

Airways, 1980) considered both defenses concurrently. In fact, in the Levin case, the 5th Circuit stated:

> For present purposes, the distinction between a business necessity defense and a BFOQ defense is largely irrelevant. If Delta's pregnancy policy can be shown to reduce substantially the risks attending air travel, its policy should be upheld against Title VII challenge.

Interestingly, all four rulings supported the grounding of pregnant flight attendants at some point in pregnancy. Furthermore, regardless of the theories behind them these rulings would likely satisfy current BFOQ scrutiny. But, as we will witness shortly, this legacy of confusion regarding the appropriate attack/defense scenario ultimately produced incorrect rulings in fetal protection cases.

Each of the airline cases focused on passenger safety; not flight attendant safety. Fetal protection was a secondary issue in one of these cases (*Burwell v. Eastern Airlines,* 1980), and also, in a district court ruling (In Re *National Airlines v. National Airlines,* 1977). On the secondary fetal issue, the ruling from both courts was clear. In the National Airlines case, a Florida district court ruled:

> the question of harm to the fetus is basically a decision to be made not by this court, but by the mother of the fetus.

In the Burwell ruling, the 4th Circuit stated:

> If this personal compassion can be attributed to corporate policy it is commendable, but in the area of civil rights, personal risk decisions not affecting business operations are best left to individuals who are the targets of discrimination.

Therefore, the National and Burwell rulings provided a seemingly solid precedent for cases focusing on fetal protection as a primary issue. The precedent should have been that fetal protection is a private matter, having no place in either a business necessity or BFOQ defense. However, subsequent rulings ignored the precedent.

Fetal Protection as a Primary Issue

The 4th Circuit, which played the Burwell tune, was the first court to alter the music. The 4th Circuit decided two cases in which fetal protection was the primary issue. In both cases, the business necessity defense was the only one evaluated.

In *Wright v. Olin* (1982), the defendant, a paper company, excluded fertile women from jobs requiring contact with toxic agents. The 4th Circuit gave theoretical consideration to three scenarios. The court rejected traditional disparate treatment theory immediately, and opted for business necessity over BFOQ, reasoning:

> While the "facial neutrality" of Olin's fetal policy vulnerability program might be subject to logical dispute, the dispute would involve semantic quibbling having no relevance to the underlying substantive principle that gave rise to this theory.

And the court, not wishing to "quibble," deemed the policy **facially neutral**. Moreover, the Court accepted as a business necessity defense scientific evidence indicating the danger of toxic agents to (as yet) unconceived fetuses. Thus in contrast to its Burwell ruling, fetal safety was now in the hands of the employer, rather than the *"individuals who are the targets of discrimination."* To justify this apparent reversal, the 4th Circuit reasoned:

> Viewing this problem in this focused way in attempting to divine probable legislative intent, we believe the safety of unborn children is more appropriately analogized to the safety of personal service customers of the business.

In other words, unborn children were viewed as customers (or visitors), and their protection was deemed a legitimate business concern. Of course, actual fetuses were not accorded such status in the Burwell ruling. In the Court's defense it could be argued that in Burwell, fetal protection was easy to dismiss because passenger safety concerns had already dictated the grounding of pregnant women.

The 4th Circuit then proceeded to outline a pretext argument against a successful business necessity defense, namely:

> By showing an "acceptable alternative" that would accomplish the protective purpose "equally well with lesser differential impact," the evidence would at least negate prima facie proof of business necessity of the specific program by having demonstrated an "unnecessary" degree of overkill in it.

This pretext argument served as the central feature in *Zuniga v. Kleberg County Hospital* (1982), a case decided by the 4th Circuit at about the same time as Olin. In Zuniga, the hospital's first ever female X-ray technician was discharged immediately upon announcement of her pregnancy. As in Olin, the hospital presented evidence of threat to the fetus. But rather than focusing on the merits of the case (as in Olin), the Court focused on the hospital's voluntary leave policy, which the hospital did not invoke in this instance. In fact, this was the first applicable instance that failed to trigger the policy. Therefore, Zuniga won on pretext.

The 4th Circuit's hold on fetal cases was broken in *Hayes v. Shelby Memorial Hospital* (1984). As in Olin, a pregnant X-ray technician was fired without consideration of alternative assignment. The 11th Circuit added further to the growing confusion. As in Olin, the court rejected outright the traditional disparate treatment theory. The court noted that the Olin ruling used pre-PDA logic in entertaining adverse impact theory. The court expressed its preference for facial discrimination (and a BFOQ defense), but being "fair" to the hospital, the court also entertained adverse impact. Relative to both the PDA and the 4th Circuit Olin ruling, both 11th Circuit rulings seemed questionable.

In its **BFOQ** ruling, the 11th Circuit citing the PDA, stated that the presumption of facial discrimination:

> may be rebutted . . . if the employer can show that although its policy applies only to women, the policy is neutral in the sense that it effectively and equally protects the offspring of all employees.

The novelty here was that a BFOQ defense failed to focus on ability of pregnant women to do the work. Instead, danger to the fetus, the same rationale used by the 4th Circuit for business necessity in Olin and Zuniga, was construed as the appropriate defense.

For **adverse impact**, the 11th Circuit ruled differently than the 4th Circuit, focusing on whether pregnancy prevents a woman from effectively doing her work (i.e., job relatedness). The court stated:

> For example, Hayes can perform her job as an X-ray technician as well while pregnant as she could beforehand.

Based on the Supreme Court's Dothard ruling, this analysis should have been used by the 11th Circuit for BFOQ, not adverse impact.

Nevertheless, the bottom-line ruling in Hayes was the same as in Zuniga in both evaluations. In its BFOQ evaluation, the 11th Circuit rejected the evidence of danger to the fetus. In its adverse impact evaluation, the 11th Circuit rejected the hospital's business necessity defense (threat of lawsuit). The court also ruled that the hospital would have lost a pretext challenge. In its "Conclusion," the court prescribed the following three-step procedure for deciding fetal protection cases:

> (1) that a substantial risk of harm exists; (2) that the risk is borne only by members of one sex; and (3) the employee fails to show that there are acceptable alternative policies that would have a lesser impact on the affected sex.

The Johnson Controls Ruling

In the case that triggered the recent Supreme Court review (*International Union et al. v. Johnson Controls, Inc.* 1989), the 7th Circuit, like the 11th Circuit, considered both the BFOQ and business necessity defenses. The defendant, a battery maker, had a policy of warning fertile women of the dangers of lead toxicity. The warnings went unheeded by eight women. Basing its ruling on scientific and federal agency documentation, the company upgraded its policy from a warning to screening fertile women from entry to high-lead jobs and positions promotable to high-lead jobs. In a divided decision, the 7th Circuit accepted the policy under both the business necessity and BFOQ defenses.

In its BFOQ ruling, the 7th Circuit cited Dothard for its emphasis on worker safety; a misinterpretation. The ruling itself was a first—no circuit court had ever upheld BFOQ in a fetal protection case. For business necessity, the 7th Circuit used the three-step prescription by the 11th Circuit in Hayes. The EEOC issued an immediate policy statement to its field agents to, in effect, ignore both rulings. Of course, the Supreme Court accepted the case. In the interim, the 6th Circuit reversed a similar ruling that excluded fertile women from foundry jobs involving exposure to lead (*Grant v. General Motors,* 1990).

In its ruling, the Supreme Court was unanimous regarding the most important issue. Using the PDA as the basis, all fetal protection policies were deemed **facially discriminatory**, thus requiring the **BFOQ** defense—and nothing else. Thus the 7th Circuit's logic in its adverse impact ruling (i.e, the three-step procedure) was deemed incorrect. In the words of the Court:

> the absence of a malevolent motive does not convert a facially discriminatory policy into a neutral policy with a discriminatory effect.

Moreover, the 7th Circuit did misinterpret Dothard in assuming that worker safety was the primary consideration; it was workplace safety. Regarding fetal safety, the Court agreed that parents maintain the right of determination, much as originally expressed in both the Burwell and National Airlines rulings.

A final consideration was lawsuits by affected children, an issue raised in several lower court rulings. The Court noted that such torts rely on state legislation, and:

> When it is impossible for an employer to comply with both state and federal requirements, this Court has ruled that federal law pre-empts that of the States.

In other words, the Court ruling itself was insulation against such suits.

There were dissents on some of the issues. For example, Justices White, Rehnquist, and Kennedy disagreed with the presumption that "the BFOQ defense is so narrow that it could never justify a sex-specific fetal protection policy." Justice Scalia argued that the Court underestimated the implications of litigation costs as a legitimate business concern. It is possible that these issues not have reached final resolution—but it is unlikely that fetal protection will ever again be the subject of an adverse impact evaluation.

SEX-PLUS DISCRIMINATION

The following scenario may be playing at a police station or department store in your neighborhood. Mrs. Smith, a female mother of two, while being interviewed for a position, is asked: "Does your husband approve of this work?" Or, "How does work affect your duties as a wife and mother?" On the other hand, Mr. Smith, husband to Mrs. Smith, while interviewing for the same position, is not queried with respect to his wife's thoughts or his familial duties. This scenario constitutes disparate treatment in the form of "sex plus" discrimination. Mrs. Smith is being discriminated against not because she is a woman, but because she is a woman *plus* other neutral things (parent and spouse).

At first blush, the "Smith" scenario may seem the same in principle as *General Electric v. Gilbert* (1976). Pregnancy, however, is not neutral, it is facial; only women can get pregnant. Also, it required an Act of

Congress to induce the Supreme Court to interpret the pregnancy-benefits scenario properly. But on the issue of sex-plus marriage, the Supreme Court laid down a clear and convincing precedent in its first and only attempt (*Phillips v. Martin Marietta*, 1971).

The Phillips Precedent

In Phillips, women made up 70% to 80% of the applicants and hires for manufacturing positions. However, the company accepted no applications from mothers of preschool children. At the same time, fathers of preschoolers were not excluded. Because the percentage of workers favored women overall, the lower court saw "no question of bias against women." But a unanimous Supreme Court disagreed, and ruled:

> The Court of Appeals . . . erred . . . permitting one hiring policy for women and another for men—each having pre-school-age children.

However, the Court also suggested, without ruling, that future cases can evaluate female parental duties as a BFOQ. This suggestion elicited a strong dissent from Justice Marshall, who stated:

> the Court has fallen into the trap of assuming that the Act permits ancient canards about the proper role of women to be a basis for discrimination . . . the 1964 Civil Rights Act intended to prevent employers from refusing "to hire an individual based on stereotyped characterizations of the sexes."

Interestingly, both the concurrence and the dissent formed legal precedent in the 1972 version of EEOC Guidelines. Written shortly after the Phillips ruling, the EEOC echoed the concurrence, but also, respecting Justice Marshall's dissent, cast "no opinion" on the BFOQ suggestion. Since the Phillips case no case has featured the duties of mothering as a BFOQ.

Marriage and Family Issues

Most sex-plus cases after Phillips entertained either marriage and family issues as in Phillips, or grooming and dress code issues. Most marriage and family cases used the Phillips precedent to rule against the companies. For example, in a case following closely on the heels of Phillips (*Sprogis v. United Air Lines*, 1971), the 7th Circuit evaluated a "no marriage" policy applied to female "stewardesses," but not to male "stewards." The airline attempted a BFOQ defense asserting (a) stewardess and steward jobs are different; (b) sex is a valid criterion for stewardess; and (c) additional criteria for women are justified. Citing the Phillips case, the Court ignored this logic and struck down the no-marriage policy, asserting it "must stand upon its own feet." This ruling guided similar rulings at the district court level (e.g., *Laffey v. Northwest Airlines*, 1973; *Inda v. United Airlines*, 1973). Also, in a nonairline case involving a marriage and family issue, the 6th Circuit ruled against demotion based on pregnancy out of wedlock (*Jacobs v. Martin Sweets*, 1977).

Because of complications, however, other airline cases did not follow the Phillips precedent. These were holdovers (because of delays and remands) from pre-Title VII days, when airlines employed all-female attendant crews. Two of these cases were evaluated in rapid succession by the 5th Circuit (*Stroud v. Delta*, 1977, & *EEOC v. Delta*, 1978). Simply stated, there were no male stewards who could have been treated differently than the female stewardesses. However, married men in non-attendant positions were permitted to work. In the Stroud case, the Court acknowledged that in a mixed-attendant job category the Phillips precedent would hold, stating:

> Any question as to whether discrimination against married women might per se be removed from the ambit of the statute was settled by Phillips v. Martin Marietta.

But the court ruled that men "were simply not involved in the policy."

The Stroud charge was discrimination in terms, conditions, and privileges of employment. In the subsequent case, the EEOC took a different position, asserting discrimination based on classification and segregation. The EEOC asserted that the no-marriage policy cast:

> a stereotype into which the male would not have been forced if Delta had to employ any male flight attendant.

But the court was not convinced, and echoed its Stroud ruling.

The reader should not downplay these rulings because flight crews are now mixed. The implication is that sex-plus is not a viable charge if a work force is all female or all male; a possibility in any era for de facto reasons (e.g., an all-female nursing crew at a hospital).[6]

Grooming and Dress Codes

The sex-plus issues other than marriage and family involved novel complaints and rulings. For example, in the mid-1970s, many of the circuit courts entertained charges from males that policies restricting hair length (and/or facial hair) constitute sex-plus discrimination. Such cases were evaluated by the 2nd (*Longo v. Carlisle DeCoppet & Co.*, 1976), 4th (*Earwood v. Continental Southeastern Lines*, 1976), 5th (*Willingham v. Macon Telegraph Publishing Co.*, 1975), 6th (*Barker v. Taft Broadcasting Co.*, 1976), 8th (*Knott v. Missouri Pacific Railway Co.*, 1975), 9th (*Baker v. California Land Title Co.*, 1974) and D.C. (*Dodge v. Giant Food*, 1973) Circuits. The charges were invariably dismissed for reasons best summarized by the 5th Circuit, which, in Macon, stated:

> Distinctions in employment practices between men and women on the basis of something other than immutable characteristics or legally protected rights do not inhibit employment opportunities in violation of the Civil Rights Act.

In other words, women cannot (easily) change their sex, and they do have a constitutional right to be married and have children (in and out of wedlock). Hair length is mutable, and "does not inhibit employment opportunities" for men.

The courts have ruled, however, that some easily mutable characteristics do restrict employment for females by perpetuating sex stereotypes. In *Carrol v. Tallman* (1979), a bank required color-coded attire for female employees, but not males. As in the aforementioned grooming cases, the lower court had previously ruled that dress codes do not "prevent employment opportunity." But the 7th Circuit overruled. In a more recent case, an Ohio district court ruled against a retail store that required female (but not male) sales clerks to wear smocks (*O'Donnell v. Burlington Coat Factory Warehouse*, 1987). In the words of the court, the:

> "smock requirement" perpetuated sexual stereotypes by encouraging (a) natural tendency to assume that uniformed women had lesser professional status than their colleagues attired in normal business clothes.

In short, two things are clear regarding sex-plus discrimination. First, a mixed work force is required, and second, the Phillips precedent is easiest to apply when the "pluses" are marriage and parenting. The precedent can apply to grooming and dress codes, but only if they imply restrictions on employment (by way of sex stereotyping). The dress code issue is particularly complex because an employer certainly has a right to enforce one. However, it must apply to each sex in comparable fashion (see *Fountain v. Safeway Stores,* 1977).

BENEFITS IN GENERAL

The issue here is sex discrimination in benefits to women independently of facial or neutral add-ons. Legal action in this arena has been as decisive, if not more so, than in any other arena of EEO law. It is essentially a three-case issue with a single modifying event. In all three cases, the Supreme Court left no doubt regarding how such issues would be decided.

In the germinal case (*Los Angeles Department of Water & Power v. Manhart,* 1978), the city required higher pension fund contributions from women (by about 14%) based on mortality tables revealing that they, on the average, live longer than men. Before the case was decided, California enacted a state law striking down the policy. The law, however, did not speak to remedies for retroactive violations. A 6-2 majority upheld the California law (Justice Brennan did not participate), ruling that "but for" sex, the policy would not have existed. However, a 7-1 majority also ruled that retroactive return of excess contributions (ordered previously by the district court) was not appropriate because of the drastic impact such relief would have on the fund.

In the second case (*Arizona Governing Committee v. Norris,* 1983), the state offered a menu of policies, all requiring equal contributions. However, based on mortality tables, each plan paid out less money to women at retirement. The Supreme Court struck down this policy, and, as in Manhart, ruled against retroactive relief.

In the final case (*Florida v. Long,* 1988), the differential pay-out policy existed in three of the four available retirement plans. The state altered the policy immediately after the Norris ruling, and the lower courts granted retroactive relief to affected women. But, in keeping with its rulings in Manhart and Norris, the Supreme Court reversed on retroactive relief.

In short, although both the pay-in and pay-out policies in Manhart and Norris were clearly struck down, victims of these policies prior to the effective dates of the rulings were never afforded equitable monetary relief.

The modifying event was the **Retirement Equity Act** of 1984, which amended the Employee Retirement Income Security Act (ERISA) of 1974. The amendment strengthened the Supreme Court's rulings in Manhart and Norris by closing loopholes affecting female employees. Most notably, it allows all employees a 5-year leave of absence without loss of pension eligibility, and treats a one-year maternity leave as no break in service for pension benefits. The implication of the one-year rule is obvious. The 5-year rule permits a woman (or male) to leave work, raise a child to school age, and retain pension eligibility.

SEXUAL HARASSMENT

Even though harassment is not unique to sex, there are four good reasons to treat harassment as a sex-related topic. First, harassment is sex-dominated. Second, many behaviors that are harassing are sex-specific (touching, fondling, intercourse, etc.). Third, one whole arena known as "quid pro quo" harassment is unique to sex. Finally, even in the common ("hostile environment") arena, clear precedents from prior cases were delayed in their application to sex.

The two types of sexual harassment alluded to above are illustrated in Sec.1604.11 of EEOC Guidelines. According to the EEOC, the following three examples illustrate sexual harassment:

(1) submission to such conduct is made either explicitly or implicitly a term of condition of an individual's employment. (2) submission to or rejection of such conduct by an individual is used as the basis for employment decisions affecting such individual. (3) such conduct has the purpose or effect of unreasonably interfering with an individual's work performance or creating an intimidating, hostile or offensive working environment.

Examples 1 and 2 illustrate "quid pro quo" (i.e., something for something) harassment; where an employment consequence such as promotion is made contingent on sexual favors (e.g., do this or else). Example 3 illustrates "hostile environment" theory; where there is evidence of harassing behaviors, but no connection to a tangible employment consequence or economic harm.

Early District Court Rulings

The early sexual harassment cases spawned unfriendly rulings at the district court level. Among these, *Barnes v. Train* (1974) was the first case tried, but *Corne v. Bausch & Lomb* (1975) was the first one reported. Together with *Miller v. Bank of America* (1976) and *Tompkins v. Public Service Electric & Gas* (1976), these rulings initially denied the viability of sexual harassment as a Title VII charge. By current standards, Corne was a hostile environment case in which the plaintiff resigned (i.e., constructive discharge), whereas Barnes, Tompkins, and Miller were quid pro quo cases in which the plaintiffs were terminated.

To illustrate the mood of these courts, in Corne, two females charged their supervisor with repeated acts of sexual abuse. Despite amicus support from the EEOC, an Arizona district court dismissed the case without ruling on merits. The court ruled that the supervisor's behavior served no employer policy, and provided no benefit to the company. Therefore, the issue of harassment was deemed irrelevant. The Court suggested that the supervisor's conduct was "nothing more than a personal proclivity, peculiarity or mannerism," and that he was merely "satisfying a personal urge." The court also concluded:

> It would be ludicrous to hold that the sort of activity involved here was contemplated by the Act because to do so would mean that if the conduct complained of was directed equally to males, there would be no basis for suit.

In other words, there is no differential "mistreatment" if men and women are equally abused. As "ludicrous" as this statement may sound, the legality of nondifferential abuse has been consistently supported.

The quotes from Corne are typical of the era. In *Barnes v. Train,* where the plaintiff was inundated with repeated unwelcomed requests for sexual favors, the D.C. District Court asserted that Barnes:

> was discriminated against, not because she was a woman, but because she refused to engage in a sexual affair with her supervisor.

In Tompkins, where refusal of sexual favors lead to demotion and ultimate termination, a New Jersey district court ruled that the aim of Title VII is:

> to make careers open to talents irrespective of race or sex. It is not intended to provide a federal tort remedy for what amounts to physical attack motivated by sexual desire . . . which happened to occur in a corporate corridor rather than a back alley.

And in Miller, where the unwelcoming plaintiff was also terminated, a California district court expressed the following fear regarding the implications of such cases:

> And who is to say what degree of sexual cooperation would found a Title VII claim? It is conceivable . . . that flirtations of the smallest order would give rise to liability.

Circuit Court Reversals: Establishment of Quid Pro Quo

The first finding for a plaintiff was in *Williams v. Saxbe* (1976). However, as a district court case cited and basically ignored in other district court rulings (e.g., Miller), its influence was limited. A more germinal ruling was rendered by the D.C. Circuit in *Barnes v. Costle* (1977), the appeal case for *Barnes v. Train* (1974). The D.C. Circuit overruled the lower court in Barnes. Subsequently, the 3rd Circuit overruled the lower court in Tompkins (1977), as did the 9th Circuit in Miller (1979).

In the *Barnes v. Costle* ruling, the D.C. Circuit suggested two criteria for prima facie discrimination in quid pro quo cases: (a) disparate treatment of women versus men (the "ludicrous" issue in the lower court ruling in Corne), and (b) a tangible employment consequence.

The court illustrated the need for disparate treatment by suggesting that men and women equally mistreated by a bisexual supervisor would have no case. But in this particular case, the Court ruled that Barnes was mistreated only because she was a woman. Using sex-plus logic from *Phillips v. Martin Marietta* (1971), Barnes was deemed a victim of sex-plus subordination because male subordinates were unlikely targets. Thus Barnes was disparately mistreated.

But the court also required evidence of a tangible employment consequence, which Barnes had. The court believed she was retaliated against (via abolishment of her job) because she refused sexual favors. And, in the words of the court:

> It is much too late in the day to contend that Title VII does not outlaw *terms of employment* for women which differ appreciably from those set for men, and which are not genuinely and reasonably related to performance on the job. [emphasis added]

Another factor in this, and all sexual harassment cases, is the liability of the employer when his agent (e.g., a supervisor) commits an illegal act. Implicating the employer is critical because only he can provide the Title VII awards (back pay, declarative relief, etc.). The supervisor may be liable for compensatory and punitive damages in a personal civil suit, but personal damage awards are not available in Title VII. Judge MacKinnon, in his concurrence with the Barnes ruling, suggested **respondeat superior** as the mechanism of implication. According to this doctrine, the employer is responsible for his agents if he knew or should have known of illegal behavior, and failed to take prompt corrective action.

In *Heelan v. Johns-Mansville* (1978), where the plaintiff was also abused and then terminated, a Colorado district court articulated the following three criteria for a prima facie quid pro quo case:

> (1) submission to sexual advances of a superior was a term or condition of employment, (2) this fact substantially affected the plaintiff's employment, and (3) employees of the opposite sex were not affected in the same way by these actions.

The court also seconded the principle of respondeat superior.

However, in its updated Guidelines (1980) the EEOC refuted respondeat superior, asserting instead "strict liability." According to Sec. 1604.11(d) of the Guidelines, the employer:

> is responsible for its acts and those of its agents and supervisory employees regardless of whether . . . the employer knew or should have known of their occurrence.

In a subsequent case germinal to both hostile environment theory and quid pro quo harassment (*Bundy v. Jackson*, 1981), the D.C. Circuit clarified its prior burdens of proof in the quid pro quo case. Although written in terms of a promotional consequence (which the Bundy case involved), these burdens are as follows:

> the plaintiff must show (1) that she was a victim of a *pattern* of sexual harassment attributable to her *employer* . . . and (2) that she applied for and was denied a promotion for which she was technically eligible and of which she had a reasonable expectation. If the prima facie case is made out, the employer may rebut it by showing, by *clear and convincing evidence,* that he had legitimate nondiscriminatory reasons for denying the claimant the promotion. [emphasis added]

Three things should be noted. First, *pattern* means continual, long-term abuse. As a general rule, isolated incidents of innuendo, flirtation, and so forth do not meet this standard.

Second, regarding the liability of the employer, the court endorsed the interpretation of the EEOC in Sec.1604.11(d) of updated Guidelines, thus rejecting respondeat superior.

Third, the court examined the McDonnell-Burdine prescription for prima facie evidence in a disparate treatment case and deemed it unfair to the plaintiff. The plaintiff would have to establish a step 4 (that a search continued after a qualified and protected applicant was excluded[7]), and the employer's burden would be simply to articulate an alternative (e.g., the other candidate is better). The plaintiff would then be burdened with presenting a preponderance of direct evidence supporting pretext. The court felt that the plaintiff deserved some kind of advantage for having presented direct evidence of a pattern of harassment to begin with.

Thus the attack/defense balance in the aforementioned quote represents a combination of processes described in Chapter 3. The prima facie attack involves persuasive evidence of sexual harassment (as in *Price Waterhouse v. Hopkins,* 1989), and also, productive evidence of qualification and likelihood of promotion (i.e., somewhat stiffer than McDonnell-Burdine). The plaintiff who is successful at the prima facie level then burdens the defense to answer with direct evidence. Clearly, a simple production (as in McDonnell-Burdine) is insufficient. But given the recent ruling in Price Waterhouse, the Supreme Court (which has never ruled on a quid pro quo case), would likely alter the standard of the defendant's evidence in phase 2 from clarity to preponderance.

Subsequently, the courts have accepted some of the prescriptions of the D.C. Circuit in quid pro quo cases (and/or quid pro quo components of cases involving both quid pro quo and hostile environment claims). The courts have favored "strict liability" over "respondeat superior" in quid pro quo cases (e.g., *Henson v. City of Dundee,* 1982; *Katz v. Dole,* 1983; *Horn v. Duke Homes,* 1985; *Huddleston v. Roger Dean Chevrolet,* 1988; *Carrero v. N.Y.C. Housing Authority,* 1989), but—as we will witness shortly—not in hostile environment cases. Or, as stated by the 11th Circuit in *Henson v. Dundee:*

> In the classic quid pro quo case an employer is strictly liable for the conduct of its supervisors, while in the work environment case the plaintiff

must prove that higher management knew or should have known of the sexual harassment before the employer may be held liable.

The rationale is that in a quid pro quo case the supervisor is acting through the authority of his employer, whereas in hostile environment cases he is acting outside of this authority.

The courts have also accepted the D.C. Circuit's two basic steps in making the prima facie case: (a) proof of a pattern of unwelcomed sexual advances; and (b) an employment consequence resulting from refusal to grant favors (such as discharge, failure to promote, failure to train, etc.). However, the courts have typically followed the original **McDonnell-Burdine** prescription rather than the D.C. Circuit's unique modification (see especially *Jones v. Flagship Intern.*, 1986; *Waltman v. International Paper Co.*, 1989). In short, the burden of proving the connection between a pattern of harassment and retaliation for refusal is basically on the plaintiff.

Hostile Environment Harassment

Hostile environment reduces to a pattern of harassment with no tangible evidence of a negative employment consequence (e.g., no termination or economic harm). As noted earlier, this issue was decided in favor of plaintiffs in *Rogers v. EEOC* (1971), a racial harassment case. But the transfer of the Rogers precedent to sexual harassment required a battle that ultimately forced a Supreme Court ruling in *Meritor v. Vinson* (1986).

The germinal case in this battle was none other than *Bundy v. Jackson* (1981). We have already considered the quid pro quo aspects of this case. Regarding hostile environment, Bundy was repeatedly abused by two of her supervisors over a 2-year period, with no tangible employment consequence during that interval. On the critical issue of hostile environment and "conditions of employment," the court stated:

> Bundy's claim . . . is that "conditions of employment" include the psychological and emotional work environment—that the sexually stereotyped insults and demeaning propositions to which she was indisputably subjected and caused her anxiety and debilitation.

In ruling on this issue, the court relied almost exclusively on *Rogers v. EEOC* (1971). The Rogers ruling, in tandem with EEOC Guidelines created between the Barnes and Bundy cases, motivated the D.C. Circuit's conclusion that women in hostile environments face a "cruel trilemma" to: (a) "endure the harassment"; (b) "oppose it with little hope of success"; or (c) "leave the job with little hope of legal relief." Therefore the Court ruled that a hostile environment makes "endurance of sexual intimidation" a condition of employment. The court also adopted "strict liability" as opposed to respondeat superior.

In *Henson v. City of Dundee* (1982), also a combination of quid pro quo and hostile environment, the 11th Circuit formalized a five-step procedure for prima facie evidence of a hostile environment. First, the employee must belong to a protected class (e.g., all humans). Second, the employee must be subject to "unwelcome" advances (stay tuned). Third, harassment must be based on sex (the "ludicrous" issue first raised in Corne). Fourth, the harassment "must be sufficiently pervasive so as to alter the conditions of employment and create an abusive working environment" (a paraphrase of example #3 from the EEOC Guidelines). And fifth, the plaintiff must show "that the employer knew or should have known of the harassment in question and failed to take prompt action" (respondeat superior).

In Meritor, the Supreme Court addressed a number of issues regarding these steps—particularly unwelcomeness, terms and conditions, and strict liability versus respondeat superior. The facts of this case were rather remarkable. Michelle Vinson had sexual intercourse on 40 to 50 occasions with Sidney Taylor, a bank vice president, and Vinson's supervisor. According to Vinson, early advances were rebuffed and many later advances were accepted because she feared losing her job. Taylor was also charged with public fondling and forcible rape. Vinson was ultimately discharged for excessive use of the sick leave policy—after she took an indefinite leave.

The district court ruled that Vinson failed to establish prima facie evidence of hostile environment harassment, asserting (a) the relationship between Vinson and Taylor was voluntary; (b) it was not a condition of employment; and (c) the employer was not responsible because a formal complaint was never filed. The D.C. Circuit reversed, ruling that (a) the advances were unwelcome; (b) an employment consequence is not needed to break the terms and conditions of employment; and (c) the employer has strict liability. The Supreme Court seconded two of the three.

On the first assertion of the circuit court, the Supreme Court, citing Sec.1604.11(a) of the updated Guidelines, stated:

> The Graveman of any sexual harassment claim is that the alleged sexual
> advances were "unwelcome" . . . the District Court in this case erron-
> eously focused on "voluntariness."

In other words, as in the "cruel trilemma," an individual can voluntarily
engage in behaviors that are unwelcomed because of fear of reprisals.

On the second assertion, the Court, citing Rogers, supported the
D.C. Circuit's transfer of racial harassment logic to sexual harassment.
In the words of the Court:

> the language of Title VII is not limited to "economic" or "tangible" dis-
> crimination. The phrase "terms, conditions, or privileges of employment"
> evinces a Congressional intent "to strike at the entire spectrum of dis-
> parate treatment of men and women" in employment.

But on the third assertion, the Court disputed the D.C. Circuit's
ruling, as well as Sec.1604.11(c) of the Guidelines with the following
doubled-edged statement:

> Congress' decision to define "employer" to include any "agent" of an em-
> ployer . . . surely evinces an intent to place some limits on the acts of
> employees for which employers under Title VII are to be held responsible.
> For this reason, we hold that the Court of Appeals erred in concluding
> that employers are always automatically liable for sexual harassment by
> their supervisors. . . . For the same reason, absence of notice to an em-
> ployer does not necessarily insulate the employer from liability.

In other words, the employer is never automatically liable, but then
again, he is never automatically not liable.

Thus the Supreme Court seconded all of the common elements in
cases such as Rogers, Bundy, and Henson, but placed a question mark
on employer liability. The lower courts, however, have interpreted
Meritor to imply that hostile environment requires respondeat superior, whereas quid pro quo requires strict liability. This viewpoint is
best represented by the First Circuit in *Lipsett v. University of Puerto
Rico* (1988). Although Lipsett was a Title IX and Sec. 1983 case, the First
Circuit used logic typical of Title VII cases. On hostile environment,
the Court echoed the principles of respondeat superior as follows:

> We hold therefore, following Meritor, that . . . an educational institu-
> tion is liable upon a finding of hostile environment sexual harassment
> perpetrated by its supervisors upon employees if an official representing

that institution knew, or in the exercise of reasonable care, should have known, of the harassment's occurrence, unless that official can show that he or she took appropriate steps to halt it.

Regarding quid pro quo cases, the Court noted that in Meritor the Supreme Court did not address the issue of employer liability, but "implicitly" supported the traditional belief that the employer is (strictly) liable for the acts of the supervisor "whether or not it knew, should have known, or approved of the supervisor's actions."

Other Related Issues

We have not exhausted all sexual harassment issues. For example, sexual favoritism is a quid pro quo scenario in which one employee is not promoted because of sexual favors granted by the employee who is promoted. In *King v. Palmer* (1985), the D.C. Circuit modified the McDonnell-Burdine prescriptions so that after the protected employee applies but is not promoted, she (or he) must provide direct evidence of a sexual relationship between the decision maker and the successful applicant. To meet this standard, the lower court had required factual evidence of "consummation" (as have other courts —e.g., *Toscano v. Nimmo,* 1983). But the D.C. Circuit ruled that documentation of a close relationship is sufficient.

Other issues include the culpability of the male homosexual who harasses the male employee. As one would expect, this is prohibited (e.g., *Joyner v. AAA Cooper Trans.,* 1983). In general, the male and female are both protected as long as harassment is a "but for" issue. Again, if the male and female are equally abused—there is no case.

The reader should also recognize that Title VII is not the exclusive remedy for sexual harassment. Indeed, this may explain why the early rulings were so negative. Judges probably felt that the other avenues, particularly private and/or state torts and criminal charges, are more appropriate (see *Continental Can Co. v. Minnesota,* 1980). Also, an issue to be expanded in Chapter 5 is the amenability of sexual harassment to Sec.1983—when the employer operates under the "color of state law."

Finally, as this section was written, the Senate "tried" Anita Hill v. Clarence Thomas. Judge Thomas, of course, has replaced Justice Marshall on the Supreme Court. What is striking, regardless of one's viewpoint, is that many observers wondered why Professor Hill did not sue a decade earlier. Some cited the "battered woman" syndrome, a viable reason, as represented by the D.C. Circuit's "trilemma." But additionally, who would know better the fate of a pre-Meritor hostile harassment case than an EEOC attorney? In the author's opinion, it is sad that Hill v. Thomas was *not* a trial. Congress is proud of its reversals of judicial misinterpretations. Based on the Senate's performance, our country should be relieved that courts conduct trials. The author is undecided about the facts of Hill v. Thomas because they were not revealed in their totality. Nevertheless, the public should not confuse a Congressional hearing with a judicial trial.

———— BRIEF SUMMARY ————

Clearly, any "but for" sex policy is facial discrimination and requires a BFOQ defense. This includes state protective legislation (now passe), pregnancy discrimination, fetal protection, any pay-in or pay-out requirements for any employee benefit. Height/weight requirements produce adverse impact and require a business necessity defense, but one that is more similar to the BFOQ defense than the Griggs defense (i.e., proving that all or virtually all people of a certain height or weight cannot do a job). Sex-plus is a disparate treatment issue, but if a prima facie attack is accepted there is virtually no productive argument to explain away why one group is being differently treated than the other. Finally, among all the sex-related issues, the most current one is harassment; also a disparate treatment scenario. Quid pro quo harassment has been recognized for years, but hostile environment harassment is still fresh and will undoubtedly generate new case law for years to come.

SECTION V
IMPLICATIONS FOR COMPLIANCE

From the perspective of compliance, Title VII is a race/sex statute. That is, employers who establish policies for preventing illegal adverse impact and disparate treatment are also prepared for religion and national origin, except for their unique circumstances. The following discussion focuses briefly on compliance issues relating to individuous disparate treatment, the pattern or practice of discrimination, facial discrimination, and seniority systems.

INDIVIDUOUS DISPARATE TREATMENT

Title VII has a standard maxim for individuous disparate treatment —treat everyone the same.[8] Also, while adverse impact is more of an issue for large-scale screening, hiring, promotion, transfer, and layoff, individuous disparate treatment is more of an issue for small-scale promotion, discharge, and general mistreatment of workers. It is critical to understand the sources of intentional discrimination as well as employer duties with respect agents inside and outside of the company.

Pretext: The Major Issue

Subtle practices can exist by design, but they can also occur without conscious awareness. An employer can easily fall into traps. A good example is supplied by what could have happened, but did not, in *McDonnell Douglas v. Green*. Green and his cohorts committed illegal acts against the company, and it is certainly legal to discipline such misconduct. However, the company won the case because all employees guilty of these acts received the same treatment. In other words, the company did not rehire whites who had committed illegal acts, and it did not exclude blacks who did not commit illegal acts.

On a more general level, pretext can be both antisocial and political. Socially, it is dishonest to refuse an appointment because of excuses (e.g., too much work to do) when the true reason is a lack of interest. Politically, it is dishonest to enforce jaywalking for disfavored citizens, and ignore the violation for favored citizens. Translated into work ethics, one should not use mechanisms that hide true motives, and one should not use selection prerogatives as weapons for dealing with nonbusiness issues. The search for excuses to discipline and/or ways to treat disfavored workers differentially will invariably leave a trail of factual evidence for a pretext charge.

Agents Other Than the Boss

The employer has a double duty; to set fair policies, and to accept responsibility for employees and other agents. The employer is generally responsible for disparate treatment by others; especially when an illegal act triggers a selection decision such as discharge, or failure to promote. Also, the employer must be aware of discriminatory practices conducted by unions, employment agencies, or any other outside agents affecting the interests of the company.

Focus on Harassment

Thus quid pro quo harassment implicates the employer regardless of what the employer knows. The hostile harassment charge, on the other hand, requires factual evidence of employer awareness.

The employer, however, should not wait for clues. A good policy for all forms of discrimination is to establish an internal mechanism for complaints, with built-in safeguards against the fear of reprisal. This policy should be enforced with training that emphasizes: (a) the definition of harassment and other common illegal acts; and (b) that harassment and other violations will not be tolerated. Being naive with respect to even the most subtle form of harassment (e.g., silly jokes, pranks, etc.) is a fuse under which there is a powder keg.

Employees who have problems with forced physical involvement may need more than simple knowledge and precaution. These employees may have psychological problems that require counseling or therapy. Some of the violations witnessed in the sexual harassment section are criminal and therefore have implications for remedies beyond those prescribed in Title VII. Since the *Hill v. Thomas* affair, a number of good books have been written on sexual harassment; on how to recognize it and how correct it. Among them, the author is particularly impressed by Catherine MacKinnon's chapter in Eskenazi and Gallen (1992). MacKinnon is a long-time contributor to the sexual harassment literature. In fact, her contributions have been quoted in several court rulings. Also, the Eskenazi and Gallen book is written from the perspective of the victim, which is precisely the perspective lacking among those who commit harassment or who turn their backs on it.

PATTERN OR PRACTICE

Pattern or practice is invariably the effect, and segregation and classification is invariably the cause. The effects of discrimination can be very long lasting. For example, blacks are still suffering both emotionally and economically from the effects of slavery, and women are still suffering from the effects of stereotyping and paternalistic attitudes

that pre-date the Civil War. There are two major types of pattern or practice violation.

First, a company may unwittingly continue the effects of past discrimination. Ignorance is no excuse, particularly because this more
subtle form can be traced by examining cross-job statistical data.
Segregation and classification for de facto reasons occur when one
group tends to occupy certain positions in society at large. For
example, nursing has traditionally been a "female" profession. As we
will witness in Chapter 5, market force is a legitimate reason to pay
differential wages even where there is internal evidence that "female"
jobs are worth more than the salary that is offered. However, within the
work force, segregation of groups by jobs is suspect and must be
investigated for cause. As we will witness in Chapter 7, in certain cases,
segregation, even at the involuntary level, must be corrected with
affirmative action.

Second, the company that consciously preserves a history of intentional discrimination is committing the worst violation possible. It is
an egregious act that can yield the harshest of penalties even from the
most conservative of judges. For example, the author believes that
Duke Power was lucky. The company had shown a long-standing, consciously designed pattern of discrimination. Indeed, the discriminatory tests were probably used because adverse impact on blacks was
a desirable outcome. Under current standards, Duke Power would
have faced more than just an adverse impact attack. Also, the company
would have received the harshest of remedies now available in the
Civil Rights Act of 1991.

FACIAL DISCRIMINATION

The advice here is basic—avoid facial discrimination unless it is
mandated. For example, in Chapter 6 we will witness that it is legal
and necessary to retire certain people in certain jobs at certain ages.
Those are federal mandates. Laws and regulations at the state level
should be scrutinized for consistency with federal law. When facial
discrimination is not mandated, which is the norm, the only safe
practice is to provide each person the same opportunity to qualify or
disqualify, and to refrain from alternative methods (e.g., neutral and
adversely impactful criteria designed to accomplish the goal of facial
discrimination).

Of course, there is no defense to facial discrimination for race and color. Students often inquire about certain exceptions; for example, an actor portraying a white character. Technically speaking, this is not facial discrimination. Indeed, black actors have portrayed white characters and vice versa. A black actor who applies for the role of George Washington or a white actor who applies for the role of George Washington Carver can be excluded for business necessity reasons (i.e., the portrayal needs to be realistic). What would be facial (and unnecessary) is an ad specifying that whites or blacks need not apply.

SENIORITY SYSTEMS

Seniority is a time-honored American tradition that clearly predates Title VII. Unfortunately, it was time-honored in an era that tolerated racial and sexual discrimination. Thus bona fide systems are protected in Title VII, even though they may perpetuate the effects of past discrimination. Moreover, as we will witness in Chapter 7, the effects of bona fide seniority systems are safeguarded, practically speaking, even from the requirements of affirmative action. As noted in Chapter 2, it is not clear (at least to the author) what effect, if any, the Civil Rights Act of 1991 has on bona fide seniority systems. But it is clear that the employer has a duty to ensure that seniority systems are not designed with illegal motives, regardless of how the system is created. Obviously, such an act is as egregious and as punishable as the pattern or practice of discrimination.

——— CHAPTER SUMMARY ———

Title VII protects race, color, religion, sex, and national origin; but race and color are really one class, and most of the critical issues involve race and sex. Adverse impact is a dominant issue in race cases, but race covers the full spectrum of violations, and adverse impact can affect any other class. Sex has a history of unique or dominant issues, many of which have been resolved. The resolved issues are protective legislation, pregnancy discrimination, height/weight criteria, any discrimination in benefits, and to a large extent, sex-plus discrimination. The BFOQ will probably continue to be an issue and sexual harassment is likely to be a dominant issue. Employers need to know the religious accommodation rules and related First Amendment issues. Employers also need to know the various laws relating to citizenship requirements, and Title VII's treatment of specific issues such as communication and speak-English rules. On a more general level, disparate treatment requires an understanding of pretext, the effects of other agents, and a focus on harassment. Regarding other issues, pattern or practice is the worst violation possible, BFOQ should be avoided unless facial discrimination is federally mandated, and seniority systems should be investigated for motive.

NOTES

1. In other words, using the 20th century definition, race and color are treated as the same class.

2. Technically speaking, what the statute terms "sex discrimination" is more tastefully referred to as "gender discrimination." However, it would be difficult to buck case law and literary traditions, so the label "sex discrimination" will be used.

3. Reverse discrimination is a major issue in sex as well as race discrimination. It is reserved for Chapter 7 for two reasons: (a) its close connection to affirmative action, the main topic of Chapter 7; and (b) its reliance on the 14th Amendment (as well as Title VII), a central topic in Chapter 4.

4. However, as we will witness in Chapter 6, advertisement is still a potentially fertile ground for age discrimination (e.g., "wanted: recent college grad").

5. Job entry violations can also occur in promotion via internal advertising, word of mouth, unions, and employment agencies.

6. Indeed, wage disparity for "male" versus "female" jobs is the central feature for "comparable worth," an issue to be discussed in Chapter 5.

7. In general, step 4 of the McDonnell-Burdine prima facie attack is difficult to establish in a discharge case because an employee may not be replaced, at least not immediately. This is particularly true in reductions-in-force. Thus discharge cases often require modification of the four-step attack (replacement of steps 3 and 4 with factual evidence), an issue particularly relevant to age discrimination, as we will witness in Chapter 6.

8. The exclusive application of this principle to disparate treatment must be emphasized. It does not apply to neutral requirements. This is illustrated by adverse impact in general and religious accommodation in particular. More importantly, as we will witness in Chapter 8, it becomes a dominant issue in disability discrimination, because disabled people must be treated differently in order to have equal employment opportunity and equal access to public transportation and facilities.

Civil Rights Statutes From
the Reconstruction Era

CHART 4.1. SEC.1981

Q1	Q2	Q3	Q4	Q5	Q6
Race By 19th century standards; includes ethnic groups and illegal aliens *but not sex*	Private entities Any number of employees	Provides same provisions as Title VII	Direct access to court subject to state statutes of limitation	Equitable and uncapped legal relief	Only intentional discrimination Respondeat superior applies

(Q1): What classes of people are protected (or have rights)?
(Q2): What business entities are covered (or have duties)?
(Q3): What employment practices are covered?
(Q4): Is the law administered, and if so, how?
(Q5): What are the penalties (or remedies) for breaking the law?
(Q6): What are the attacks and defenses used in litigation?

The 13th Amendment to the Constitution was ratified in 1865 to outlaw slavery. According to Part 1 of the 13th Amendment:

> Neither slavery nor involuntary servitude, except as a punishment for crime whereof the party shall have been duly convicted, shall exist within the United States, or any place subject to their jurisdiction.

125

Part 2 of the 13th Amendment authorized Congress to enforce Part 1 with appropriate legislation, which Congress did in Sections 1 and 2 of the Civil Rights Act of 1866.

The 14th Amendment was ratified in 1868. Part 1 (of 5 Parts) contains the critical **Equal Protection** clause. Accordingly:

> All persons born or naturalized in the United States, and subject to the jurisdiction thereof, are citizens of the United States and of the State wherein they reside. No State shall make or enforce any law which shall abridge the privileges or immunities of citizens of the United States; nor shall any State deprive any person of life, liberty, or property without due process of law; nor deny to any person within its jurisdiction the equal protection of the laws.

Part 5 of the 14th Amendment authorizes Congress to enforce the 14th Amendment, a power that includes overriding sovereign state immunity.

Sections 1 and 2 of the Civil Rights Act of 1866 were subsequently re-enacted as Sec.1981 and Sec.1982 in the Civil Rights Act of 1871. At the same time, Congress enacted three other statutes; Sec.1983, 1985, and 1986. In general, Sec.1981 and 1982 enforce the 13th Amendment, Sec.1983 enforces the 14th Amendment, and Sec.1985 and 1986 enforce both Amendments. A sixth statute, Sec.1987, details the duties of marshals and magistrates to enforce the other five statutes. Collectively, Sec.1981 through 1987 were codified as *42 USCS* in 1874.

In the modern era, a seventh statute, Sec.1988, was added in 1976 for attorney fees. Sec.1988 significantly increased the number of lawsuits, enough so that some Senators and Congressmen dubbed Sec.1988 "LIRA" (lawyers income retirement act) or "LISA" (lawyers income security act). Sec.1988 was further amended in the Civil Rights Act of 1991 to cover expert fees. Thus seven statutes are currently codified under *42 USCS.* The two critical statutes for EEO purposes are Sec.1981 and Sec.1983. Sec.1985 and Sec.1986 have not greatly affected EEO, at least thus far. However, Sec.1982 a non-EEO statute, is critical to EEO because of its companionship to Sec.1981.

Sec.1981 is depicted in Chart 4.1. The statute **protects (Q1)** race and ethnicity by the 19th century standards, and the only realistically **covered entities (Q2)** are private sector employers. However, unlike Title VII, there is no minimal employee number. The **covered practices (Q3)** are the same as in Title VII, and there are no **administrative procedures**

(Q4). Sec.1981 permits both equitable and uncapped legal **remedies (Q5)**, and the only **attack (Q6)** is intentional discrimination.

Sec.1983 is depicted in Chart 4.2. For EEO purposes, Sec.1983 **protects (Q1)** each Title VII class, **covers (Q2)** state and local entities, and **covers (Q3)** each Title VII practice. Like Sec.1981, there are no **administrative procedures (Q4)**, there are uncapped equitable and legal **remedies (Q5)** (subject to 11th Amendment constraints), and the only **attack (Q6)** is intentional discrimination.

CHART 4.2. SEC.1983

Q1	Q2	Q3	Q4	Q5	Q6
Race Color Religion Sex National origin, including illegal aliens	Under color of state law Includes mainly state and local entities	Same as Title VII Designed to protect federal laws	Direct access to court subject to state statutes of limitation	Equitable uncapped legal relief against individuals but not officials	Only intentional discrimination Respondeat superior does not apply

(Q1): What classes of people are protected (or have rights)?
(Q2): What business entities are covered (or have duties)?
(Q3): What employment practices are covered?
(Q4): Is the law administered, and if so, how?
(Q5): What are the penalties (or remedies) for breaking the law?
(Q6): What are the attacks and defenses used in litigation?

Therefore, Sec.1981 and 1983 address Title VII gaps. These include: (a) the minimum employee requirement (there is none); (b) administration procedures (there are none); and (c) uncapped damage awards. This Chapter contains four Sections. Sections I and II cover Sec.1981 and 1983, respectively, and Section III briefly addresses Sec.1985 and 1986. Because there are no unique compliance issues relative to those already discussed for Title VII, Section IV evaluates the gaps in Title VII in light of new provisions in the Civil Rights Act of 1991.

SECTION I
SEC.1981

In its entirety, Sec.1981 reads as follows:

All persons within the jurisdiction of the United States shall have the same right in every State and Territory to make and enforce contracts, to sue, be parties, give evidence, and to the full and equal benefit of all laws and proceedings for the security of persons and property as is enjoyed by *white citizens,* and shall be subject to like punishment, pains, penalties, licenses, and exactions of every kind, and to no other. [emphasis added]

As regards EEO, Sec.1981 and 1983 are distinctively different with respect to their **protected classes (Q1)** and **covered entities (Q2)**, but share many principles with respect to **covered practices (Q3), administrative procedures (Q4)**, and to a lesser degree, **remedies (Q5)** and **attack/defense balances (Q6)**.

PROTECTED CLASS (Q1)

The protected class is the 19th century concept of racial discrimination. However, the statutory reference to "white citizens" raises the question of whether whites are protected. Sex, disability, and age are not protected because they are clearly unrelated to race. But the first two words of the statute ("all persons") provide protections for lawful aliens who belong to the protected racial groups; a protection not afforded by Title VII.

Protection of "white citizens" was the major issue in *McDonald v. Santa Fe* (1976), where three employees stole from the company; two white and one black. As noted in Chapter 2, the two white employees were discharged but the black employee was not. The company argued that Sec.1981 does not apply to whites, a proposal favored by both lower courts. However, the Supreme Court overruled.

By 19th century standards, race is more than a black versus white issue. Sec.1981 overlaps with but does not provide blanket protection for national origin and religion. However, two recent Supreme Court rulings indicate that some national origins and/or religions are protected. Thus in *St. Francis College v. Al-Khazraji* (1987), an Iraqi-born U.S. Citizen used Sec.1981 to challenge a no-tenure decision. In *Shaare*

Tefila Congregation v. Cobb (1987), a companion case, a Jewish congregation used Sec.1982 to challenge desecration of its synagogue. The district courts saw no discrimination in either case because the plaintiffs and defendants were all Caucasian. The Supreme Court overruled these decisions for reasons best illustrated by the following quote (from Shaare Tefila):

> As Saint Francis makes clear, the question before us is not whether Jews are considered to be a separate race by today's standards, but whether, at the time . . . Jews constituted a group of people that Congress intended to protect. It is evident from the legislative history . . . reviewed in Saint Francis College . . . that Jews and Arabs were among the peoples then considered to be distinct races and hence within the protection of the statute.

COVERED ENTITIES (Q2)

Practically speaking, Sec.1981 does not apply to state, local, or federal entities. Exclusion of state and local entities is dictated more by Sec.1983 than by 1981, as we will witness later. Exclusion of federal entities stems from a Supreme Court ruling in *Brown v. General Services Administration* (1976). However, coverage of private entities independently of *governmental* action was the result of two Supreme Court rulings (*Jones v. Alfred Mayer,* 1968, & *Runyon v. McCrary,* 1976).

Historically, Sec.1982 had been applied like a 5th or 14th Amendment statute. That is, by circumstance, private sector cases had always entailed governmental action. Purely private action was first considered in *Jones v. Alfred Mayer* (1968), a Sec.1982 challenge to refusal of property sale to blacks. The issue was not a first, as the Supreme Court struck down refusal of property sale to blacks in *Hurd v. Hodge* (1948). But as the Mayer Court noted:

> It is true that a dictum in Hurd said that Sec.1982 was directed only toward "governmental action" . . . but neither Hurd nor any other case before or since has presented that precise issue for adjudication in this Court. Today we face that issue for the **first time**.

The "first time" issue, of course, is whether Sec.1982 covers discrimination unconnected to "governmental action." The two lower courts upheld Hurd. But the Supreme Court overruled, stating:

We hold that Sec.1982 bars all racial discrimination, private as well as public, in the sale or rental of property, and that the statute, thus construed, is a valid exercise of the power of Congress to enforce the Thirteenth Amendment.

Justice White dissented, asserting that Sec.1981 and Sec.1982 became 14th Amendment statutes (requiring state governmental action) when they were reenacted in 1871. White believed other statutes (e.g., federal fair housing laws) to be better suited for purely private actions. His expressed fear was that the Mayer ruling could impact other unrelated issues (e.g., freedom of association in private clubs).

The Supreme Court then applied Mayer to Sec.1981 in *Runyon v. McCrary* (1976) by striking down racial bars by private schools (Sec.1982 applies only to property rights). Justice White, dissenting together with Justice Rehnquist, asserted that the right to make and enforce contracts only holds for "willing second parties"; an interpretation that would permit any person to refuse to "contract" with any other person. However, the other seven justices viewed the actions of the private schools as "a classic violation of Sec.1981."

COVERED PRACTICES (Q3)

This is the most relevant but complicated dimension. The covered practices in Sec.1981 may be viewed in terms of four separate historical phases. First, the Mayer ruling paved the way for Sec.1981 EEO cases. Second, precedents established in these scenarios were dealt a crushing but temporary reversal by the Supreme Court's ruling in *Patterson v. McLean* (1989). Third, a number of post-Patterson cases in the lower courts were decided using Patterson rules. And fourth, the Civil Rights Act of 1991 reversed Patterson.

Post-Mayer EEO Rulings

Between the Mayer and Runyon rulings a number of circuit courts adopted the Mayer precedent in Sec.1981 EEO cases—including the 8th Circuit (in *Brady v. Bristol-Meyers*, 1972), which had deemed Sec.1982 inapplicable to "pure" private actions at lower court level in *Jones v. Alfred Mayer*. But now, pursuant to the Mayer ruling, the 8th Circuit reversed its stance, stating:

It would seem more accordant with reason that Sec.1981 receive a similar interpretation . . . than to view it as being circumscribed by doctrinal limitations wholly jettisoned in a case dealing with its companion statute. We therefore conclude that Sec.1981 extends beyond State action and reaches private racially discriminatory practices.

Prior to Patterson, the circuits applied Sec.1981 to Title VII terms and conditions of employment, including hiring (*Waters v. Wisconsin Steel,* 1970 [7th Circuit]); union segregation (*Young v. ITT,* 1971, & *Macklin v. Spector Freight,* 1973 [D.C. Circuit]); subjectivity in hiring and promotion (*Brown v. Gaston,* 1972 [4th Circuit]); retaliatory discharge (*Caldwell v. National Brewing,* 1971 [5th Circuit]); and discharge for cause (*Sanders v. Dobbs House,* 1970 [5th Circuit]).

After Runyon and prior to Patterson there were a number of Sec.1981 challenges to hostile racial harassment (e.g., *Taylor v. Jones,* 1981; *Johnson v. Bunny Bread,* 1982; *Vaughan v. Pool Offshore,* 1982; *Erebia v. Chrysler Products,* 1985; *Leonard v. City of Frankfort Electric & Water,* 1985). These rulings dealt with the same fundamental issues previously discussed in Title VII hostile harassment cases, most notably: (a) the pervasiveness of the harassing acts, and (b) respondeat superior. And as it turned out, harassment was a major issue in *Patterson v. McLean.*

Patterson v. McLean (1989)

The Patterson charges were racial harassment and promotional bias. A North Carolina district court ruled that harassment is not covered by Sec.1981, and that a prima facie promotion charge requires proof that the nonpromoted applicant is superior to the promoted applicant. The 4th Circuit affirmed, and the Supreme Court conducted two reviews.

In 1988, the Supreme Court suspended rulings on merits pending a ruling on whether the *Runyon v. McCrary* (1976) ruling should be reversed. With the addition of Justices O'Connor, Scalia, and Kennedy, the Court now had five justices willing to question again whether Sec.1981 (and therefore, Sec.1982) applies to purely private discrimination. Runyon was not reversed—but only because of respect for stare decisis. Justices Blackmun, Brennan, Marshall, and Stevens objected to the fact that the question of overruling Runyon was even raised.

In its 1989 review, the Court distinguished between "making" and "enforcing" contracts versus "terms, conditions, and privileges" of employment (i.e., Sec.1981 language vs. Title VII language). Justice

Kennedy, speaking for O'Connor, Rehnquist, Scalia, and White, made a "common sense" ruling. He defined *enforcement* as "protection of a legal process" (the right to sue). To illustrate, in *Goodman v. Lukens Steel* (1987), two unions failed to challenge discriminatory discharge of black employees. The unions, therefore, failed to protect (or **enforce**) a legal right to challenge discrimination.

But the more sweeping implications were reserved for **making** the contract. According to Kennedy, this concept:

> extends only to the formation of the contract, but not to the problems that may arise later from the conditions of continuing employment.

Thus Kennedy linked "making" to hiring, and distinguished hiring from other "postformation" consequences of "continuing employment." He ruled that promotion makes a contract if:

> [it] raises the level of an opportunity for a new and distinct relation between the employee and employer.

Thus the new position has to differ substantially from the old position in order to constitute a "new contract" (e.g., from hourly to salary).

Kennedy conceded, however, that if the plaintiff could satisfy the "new contract" test, she would *not* have to prove greater qualifications than the successfully promoted candidate. Rather, traditional disparate treatment standards for prima facie discrimination would suffice.

Post-Patterson Rulings

Obviously, many lower court precedents were erased, particularly with respect to **postformational** issues such as discharge and harassment. The 8th Circuit ruled that discharge was still viable under Sec.1981 (*Hicks v. Brown Group,* 1990), but other circuits disagreed (*Lavender v. V & B Transmission,* 1990 [5th circuit]; *McKnight v. General Motors,* 1990 [7th circuit]; *Overby v. Chevron,* 1989 [9th Circuit]).

The McKnight ruling was particularly painful. McKnight won a Title VII/Sec.1981 discharge case in district court. The Sec.1981 award included $600,000 for legal damages. McKnight kept the Title VII remedies, but lost the $600,000. And in a post-Patterson harassment case, the 5th Circuit pulled a slight McKnight in *Carroll v. General Accident Insurance* (1990). Carroll was awarded $32,500 in back pay (Title VII), and $231,800 in Sec.1981 legal damages. Of course, Carroll kept the back pay, but the insurance company kept the damages.

The Civil Rights Restoration Act of 1991

Obviously, the Patterson rulings devalued the victories in Mayer and Runyon, as well as in numerous lower court precedents. In the words of Justice Brennan, speaking for Blackmun, Marshall, and Stevens:

> What the Court declines to snatch away with one hand, it takes with the other. Though the Court today reaffirms Sec.1981's applicability to private conduct, it simultaneously gives this landmark civil rights statute a needlessly cramped interpretation.

But Patterson was reversed in the Civil Rights Act of 1991, and without compromises relative to the aborted Restoration Act of 1990. The Act of 1991 defines "making and enforcing as contract" as:

> the making, performance, modification, and termination of contracts, and the enjoyment of all benefits, privileges, terms and conditions of the contractual relationship.

Thus the range of covered practices in Sec.1981 mimics terms and conditions of employment in Title VII.

ADMINISTRATIVE PROCEDURES (Q4)

The absence of administrative procedures is common to all constitutional claims. Thus Sec.1981 and Sec.1983 are interchangeable in this dimension. The critical point for both statutes is that direct access to federal court does not imply hassle-free claims. There are four potential problems.

Problem 1: Statute of Limitations

Having no precedent for time limits in constitutional claims, the Supreme Court, in *Johnson v. Railway Express Agency* (1976), ruled that the "controlling period" is the most "appropriate one provided by state law." In *Board of Regents v. Tomanio* (1980) the Supreme Court ruled that the "appropriate" limit is defined by "state law governing an analogous cause of action." But ironically, in *Burnett v. Grattan* (1984), the Supreme Court overruled what seemed "analogous" to EEO, favoring a 3-year limit for general civil actions as opposed to a 6-month limit for state employment discrimination cases. In the words of the Court:

> borrowing an administrative statute of limitations ignores the dominant characteristics of civil rights actions: they belong in court.

In other words, Title VII-type administrative procedures are designed to promote conciliation, whereas pure constitutional common law procedures are designed to promote litigation.

Then, in *Goodman v. Lukens* (1987), the Supreme Court favored a 2-year Pennsylvania limit for personal injury versus a 6-year limit for contracts. In other words, even though Sec.1981 explicitly references the making of contracts, the Court reasoned that contract disputes are not usually racial; reasoning that would also apply to Sec.1983. On the other hand, racial bias is "a fundamental injury to the individual rights of a person."

In short, an *appropriate* state law on limits generally fits one or all of the following three conditions: (a) it governs limits for all state court actions; (b) it is designed to facilitate court action, not administrative resolution; and/or (c) its coverage includes personal injury cases (which are pure civil actions).

Problem 2: Multiple Claims and "Appropriate" Limits

Independently of limits, faithful claimants can suffer unfriendly side effects in *multiple* claims. The landmark example is *Johnson v. Railway Express* (1976), where a timely Title VII suit was filed, and Johnson received a right-to-sue notice 17 months later (beyond the 180 days allotted to the EEOC). Johnson's 30-day limit to exercise his Title VII right-to-sue was extended because of difficulty in finding counsel. Once filed (3-plus years after initial charges), a Sec.1981 claim was added to the suit. The Title VII charges were tried and disallowed, but his Sec.1981 charges were dismissed without trial.

During EEOC processing, the state's one-year limit (for torts) had expired. Johnson assumed that his Sec.1981 charges were tolled pending EEOC resolution. The Supreme Court ruled otherwise. Justice Blackmun, speaking for five others, ruled that Johnson should have gone to court on the Sec.1981 claim and asked for a delay pending outcome of the EEOC procedures. Blackmun also stated:

petitioner has slept on his Sec.1981 rights. The fact that his slumber may have been induced by faith in the adequacy of his Title VII remedy is of little relevance inasmuch as the two remedies are truly independent.

Justice Marshall,[1] speaking for Brennan and Douglas, dissented, asserting that a Sec.1981 trial prior to a complete EEOC investigation could result in unnecessary litigation—which is probably true.

Problem 3: Res Judicata

In 1790, Congress enacted a statute on "res judicata," also known as **claim preclusion**. The statute defines res judicata to mean that:

> judicial proceedings of any court of any such State . . . shall have the same full faith and credit in every court within the United States . . . as they have by law or usage in courts of such State.

Since constitutional claims (like Title VII) permit prior state court action, res judicata can provide unfriendly side effects.

The landmark case is *Kremer v. Chemical Construction* (1982), a pure Title VII case. Kremer suffered negative rulings from the New York State FEPC, an appeals board, and, most importantly, the state court of appeals. Kremer then exercised his EEOC right-to-sue notice. The lower courts dismissed on grounds of res judicata, and these rulings were affirmed by the Supreme Court. Of course, Kremer could have opted for federal court prior to action in the state appeals court.

The same issue emerged shortly thereafter in *Davis v. U.S. Steel Supply* (1982). The 3rd Circuit echoed Kremer in a case where a state court overruled an FEPC. In *Brown v. St. Louis* (1982), the 8th Circuit invoked res judicata even though a constitutional claim was not invoked in state court. And in *Migra v. Warren City* (1984) the Supreme Court favored summary dismissal even though the state court had not ruled on a federal claim. Migra believed she could litigate one claim at the state level and another claim at the federal level. She moved for dismissal of the federal claim in state court, and that was sufficient for the res judicata ruling by the Supreme Court.

Problem 4: Collateral Estoppel

Res judicata applies to final civil rulings in courts of law. It does not apply to rulings of administrative law judges (ALJs). But a companion principle, "collateral estoppel," often referred to as **issue preclusion**, does. According to Black's Law Dictionary (1990), collateral estoppel applies if an issue resolved in noncourt procedures provides the "essential equivalent of judicial proceeding." The landmark case is *University of Tennessee v. Elliot* (1986).

Elliot claimed that his firing for cause was racially motivated. He requested an administrative hearing (based on a state law). He also filed charges under Title VII, Sections 1981, 1983, and 1985. The ALJ, a university official, dismissed on racial motivation but ruled that discharge was too severe a penalty. After an unsuccessful administrative appeal (to another university official), Elliot eschewed judgment in state court and pursued his federal claims—thinking he had that right.

The district ruled that the ALJ's findings for racial motivation precluded both the Title VII and constitutional charges. The circuit court overruled on both counts. The Supreme Court ruled that Title VII is insulated from administrative rulings—EEOC or otherwise (as we already know). However, the Court applied collateral estoppel to the constitutional claims. Justice Stevens, speaking for Brennan and Blackmun (Marshall took no part), dissented, echoing what is undoubtedly a true message to all employees considering constitutional claims:

> litigants apprised of this decision will presumably forgo state administrative determinations for the same reason they currently forgo state judicial review of those determinations—to protect their entitlement to a federal forum.

REMEDIES (Q5)

Title VII specifies statutory remedies, whereas constitutional claims such as in Sec.1981 and Sec.1983 rely on **common law**. Common law remedies include equitable relief, with back pay awards that can exceed the 2-year Title VII limits. But the major attraction is **uncapped** damage awards. In general, compensatory damages require physical or mental suffering, and punitive damages require willful misconduct by the employer. These damages are separable. For example, in *Erebia v. Chrysler Plastic* (1985), a pre-Patterson racial harassment case, the plaintiff did not prove pain and suffering but did prove willful misconduct (he took the harassment as a joke).

The reversal of Patterson is critical, therefore, because it is easier to demonstrate pain and suffering and/or intentional misconduct in harassment and discharge than in hiring and promotion (see *Lindsey v. Angelica Corp.*, 1981; *Croker v. Boeing,* 1979).

ATTACK/DEFENSE BALANCES (Q6)

Finally, a major pre-1991 difference between Title VII and constitutional claims *was* the jury trial for legal damages. A jury verdict binds on merits, but a judge can adjust damage awards. A jury's ruling on a Title VII issue in a combined Title VII/constitutional case is also binding. Procedurally, jury trials[2] do not use distinct phases. Evidence is presented as in ordinary civil trials, and the judge instructs the jury of the various burdens. Indeed, failure to instruct the jury properly was a major challenged issue in Patterson. The attack/defense balances in all constitutional claims require proof of intent and therefore prohibit adverse impact.

Impermissibility of Adverse Impact

The inapplicability of adverse impact stems from *Washington v. Davis* (1976), a Sec.1983 case discussed in Chapter 2. This suit was filed prior to the EEO Act of 1972 (before Title VII was applicable to state employers). The main ingredient in the ruling is summarized by Justice White, who, for six others, ruled that adverse impact:

> is not the constitutional rule. We have never held that the constitutional standard for adjudicating claims of individuous racial discrimination is identical to the standards applicable under Title VII, and we decline to do so today.

The Supreme Court ruled similarly in *Arlington v. Metro* (1977) and *Personnel Administrator v. Feeney* (1979). In Metro, however, the Court also ruled adverse impact can be used to prove motive if an employer can foresee the impactful consequences of a test.

Disparate Treatment

Applicability of the McDonnell-Burdine attack/defense balance to constitutional claims was never in doubt until the lower court ruling in Patterson. In the one bright spot for plaintiffs in Patterson, Justice Kennedy ruled:

A plaintiff must prove purposeful discrimination. . . . We have developed, in analogous areas of civil rights laws, a carefully designed framework of proof to determine, in the context of disparate treatment, the ultimate issue whether the defendant intentionally discriminated against the plaintiff . . . this scheme . . . should apply to claims of racial discrimination under Sec.1981.

In other words, today's treatment of intent is applicable to yesterday's laws, as long as there is a common issue.

Other Title VII-Type Scenarios

Pattern or practice is a pre-Title VII common law tradition, a fact recognized by the Supreme Court in *General Building Constructors v. Pennsylvania* (1982). In Constructors, a union responsible for feeding construction engineers to a trade association had a long history of excluding blacks. The union also ran a discriminatory apprenticeship program. A key issue in this case was **respondeat superior**; which, as we will witness later, does not apply to Sec.1983. The union was found guilty, but not the trade association, because of its lack of awareness of discriminatory union behavior. In the words of the Court:

It would anomalous to hold that Sec.1981 could be violated only by intentional discrimination and then to find this requirement satisfied by proof . . . that the defendants merely failed to ensure that the plaintiffs enjoyed employment opportunities equivalent to that of whites.

Regarding other Title VII scenarios, BFOQ is moot in Sec.1981 because the only protected class is race. However, even if BFOQ applied to race, it is doubtful that it could be deemed a pre-Title VII common law tradition. In contrast, the BFSS is a pre-Title VII common law tradition (see *Brown v. Bd. of Regents of the Univ. of Nebraska*, 1986). But it must be noted that the 11th Circuit ruled that the plaintiff must be forewarned that the BFSS defense will be used (*Jackson v. Seaboard*, 1982).

——— **BRIEF SUMMARY** ———

Sec.1981 Protects (**Q1**) blacks, whites, certain ethnic groups, lawful aliens, but not sex, age, or disability, nor religion and national origin by 20th century standards. Coverage extends to private entities (**Q2**) independently of the number of employees, and independently of governmental involvement.

The covered practices (Q3) were temporarily limited by the Supreme Court's ruling in *Patterson v. McLean,* but Patterson was reversed in the Civil Rights Act of 1991. Thus Sec.1981 again covers the Title VII terms and conditions. The administrative procedures *(Q4)* are the same as in any constitutional claim; there are none, but a plaintiff must use appropriate state limits for filing in federal district court. Also, the claimant must be aware of the unfriendly side effects of claim preclusion (res judicata), issue preclusion (collateral estoppel), and multiple claims. The equitable and legal remedies (Q5) are slightly stronger than the amended Title VII (i.e., more than 2-year back pay awards and uncapped damages), and the attack/defense balances (Q6) are consistent pre-Title VII common law principles (i.e., adverse impact is out; McDonnell-Burdine and pattern or practice are in; BFOQ is moot; and BFSS is permitted, but with advanced warning to plaintiffs).

SECTION II
SEC.1983

As enforcement for the 14th Amendment, Sec.1983 addressed a more general mission than the 13th Amendment: to combat the insurrection of the Ku Klux Klan. Indeed, Sec.1983 is one of two "Ku Klux Klan Acts" (the other being Sec.1985). Sec.1983 did nothing directly to the Klan. Rather, it forced *state and local governments,* and all others acting under **color of state law,** to uphold *federal laws.* In other words, one reason the Klan was free to reign was that state and local governments did not uphold federal laws outlawing their activities. Sec.1983 states:

> Every *person* who, *under the color of any statute,* ordinance, regulation, custom or usage, of any *State* or Territory, subjects or causes to be subjected, *any citizen* of the United States *or other person* within the jurisdiction thereof to the *deprivation* of any rights, privileges, or immunities secured by the *Constitution and laws,* shall be liable to the party injured in an action at law, suit in equity, or other *proper proceeding for redress.* [emphasis added]

As noted in Chapter 1, the **protected classes (Q1)** and **covered practices (Q3)** transcend EEO. For example, invasion of privacy by state or local officials (a 4th Amendment violation) is a Sec.1983 offense regardless of who is invaded. There are exceptions relevant to EEO. For example, Sec.1983 has been held inapplicable to age (*McCroan v. Bailey* 1982; *Zombro v. Baltimore City Police,* 1989) and disability (*Ruth v. Alvin Independent School District,* 1982) because courts have ruled that

ADEA and the Rehabilitation Act are exclusive EEO remedies for these classes.

EEO aside, Sec.1983 applies to society's most controversial practices, including desegregation (*Brown v. Board of Education,* 1954) and abortion (*Roe v. Wade,* 1973). The application of Sec.1983 to affirmative action, a major EEO issue (e.g., *Regents v. Bakke,* 1978), will be explored in Chapter 7. It is critical to understand that Sec.1981 *provides* rights (as does Title VII), whereas Sec.1983 *protects* rights. It is the application of this protection to *all* federal laws (see *Maine v. Thiboutot,* 1979) that makes the 14th Amendment one of the most powerful protectors of all human rights, along with the 5th Amendment, which provides parallel protections against unlawful federal government actions.

However, the state governmental action requirement restricts the **covered entities (Q2)**. It is possible for a private entity to operate under the color of state law. For example, in *Burton v. Wilmington Parking Authority* (1961), the Supreme Court struck down refusal to serve black customers by a private restaurant that rented municipal parking facilities. But these cases are not common and not particularly germane to EEO issues. The critical issues relate to complex rules for state and municipal governments and agencies that, obviously, do operate under the color of state law.

Among the remaining three dimensions, relative to Sec.1981, there are no unique Sec.1983 issues regarding **administrative procedures (Q4)**, and the framework for **remedies (Q5)** and **attack/defense balances (Q6)** are similar to Sec.1981. Thus Sec.1983 permits equitable and legal remedies and the various judicial scenarios witnessed earlier. However, unique rules apply to the most likely targets of a Sec.1983 claim. These rules create unique variations in how remedies are pursued against state entities, municipal entities, and state laws.

STATE ENTITIES

In one of the earliest Supreme Court cases (*Chisholm v. Georgia,* 1793), a citizen from South Carolina recouped inheritance money from the Georgia state treasury. Enraged, Congress initiated, and the states ratified, the 11th Amendment. The 11th Amendment speaks to **sovereign state immunity** as follows:

> The judicial power of the United States shall not be construed to extend to any suit in law or equity, commenced or prosecuted against one of

the United States by Citizens of another state, or by Citizens or Subjects of any Foreign state.

The language of the amendment is deceptive. The gift of sovereign (or absolute) immunity from suit is only a half-truth. In addition, the amendment has been interpreted to protect states from insiders as well as outsiders. The main concern, of course, is for the state treasury.

Obviously, if states were totally immune to federal laws the 14th Amendment would be meaningless. But we have already witnessed 14th Amendment control of state laws discriminating against women (*Turner v. Dept. of Employment Security of Utah,* 1975) and lawful aliens (*Graham v. Richardson,* 1971; In Re Griffiths, 1973). So the real issue concerns *when* sovereign immunity is applicable.

Absolute Immunity

This story can be shortened considerably by review of a recent Supreme Court case—*Will v. Michigan State Police* (1989). Will charged the Michigan State Police with discrimination, contending that his promotion was denied because his brother was a student activist. He also lodged an **official capacity** suit against the head of his department. Both charges were upheld by the state civil service commission and the state claims court. The state appeals court overruled the charge against the state, however, and the state supreme court overruled the charge against the official. The U.S. Supreme Court affirmed both of these rulings. Justice White, speaking for Rehnquist, Kennedy, O'Connor, and Scalia, stated:

> Section 1983 provides a federal forum to remedy many deprivations of civil liberties, but it does not provide a forum for litigants who seek a remedy against a State for alleged deprivations of civil liberties. The Eleventh Amendment bars such suits unless the State has waived its immunity, or unless Congress has exercised its undoubted power under Part 5 of the Fourteenth Amendment to override that immunity.

In other words, the state, and the director in his **official capacity**, do not constitute "persons" within the meaning of Sec.1983. Thus they cannot be sued unless immunity is waived or Congress overrides it.

A state is not likely to waive its immunity, and there are some states with laws prohibiting waiver (see *Alabama v. Pugh,* 1978). More importantly, the Will Court expressed its unwillingness to treat states and officials as "persons" under Sec.1983 unless given clear statutory direction by Congress via Part 5 of the 14th Amendment.

Obviously, Congress has used its Part 5 powers before, as in the EEO Act of 1972, which extended Title VII coverage to state entities (upheld by the Supreme Court in *Fitzpatrick v. Bitzer,* 1976), and again in 1976 when Sec.1988 was enacted to provide lawyer fees (upheld by the Supreme Court in *Hutto v. Finney,* 1978). But the Court has consistently denied personage to states or state officials in Sec.1983 (see also *Quern v. Jordan,* 1979).

Ironically, Part 5 of the 14th Amendment empowered Congress to create Sec.1983. In fact, the minority in the Will Court (Brennan, Blackmun, Marshall, and Stevens) used this fact to argue that Congress had already provided the clear message that the majority was searching for. Obviously, unless Congress writes a statute declaring states as Sec.1983 "persons," states and state officials are likely to maintain their nonpersonage.

The "Fiction" of Ex Parte Young

Will made an elementary error—he should have also sued the director in his **personal capacity**. He might have lost on merits, but the merits would have been tried. Some officials have an easier defense in personal capacity suits (e.g., judges, legislators, and prosecutors), but nobody is absolutely immune. The precedent that permits personal capacity suits against state officials, however, is almost laughable. It is commonly termed the "fiction" of Ex Parte Young.

In *Ex Parte Young* (1908), a state attorney general refused to heed a federal injunction. The Supreme Court ruled that in such failure to uphold the federal Constitution the individual is not acting for the state and, therefore, is not immune. Or in the words of the Court:

> The [state] act to be enforced is alleged to be unconstitutional; and if it be so, the use of the name of the state to enforce an unconstitutional act to the injury of complainants is a proceeding without the authority of, and one which does not affect, the state in its sovereign or governmental capacity. It is simply an illegal act upon the part of a state official in attempting by the use of the name of the state, to enforce a legislative enactment which is void because it is unconstitutional.

This is an inherent contradiction. If illegal action is defined as not being state action, then Sec.1983 is inapplicable because the action could not have occurred under the color of state law. But the true fiction of Ex Parte Young is that the 11th Amendment is being upheld and therefore the state treasury is being saved.

In *Edelman v. Jordan* (1974), involving wrongful denial of welfare benefits, the Supreme Court interpreted Ex Parte Young as follows:

> A federal court's remedial power, consistent with the Eleventh Amendment, is necessarily limited to *prospective* injunctive relief . . . and may not include a retroactive award . . . of funds from the state treasury. [emphasis added]

In other words, back pay and damages for plaintiffs are **retrospective** and violate the 11th Amendment, whereas injunctive relief for future corrective purposes is **prospective** and does not violate the 11th Amendment. Another term commonly used by courts for prospective relief is *ancillary* relief.

The fiction, therefore, rests in the belief that prospective (or ancillary) injunctions are free of charge, which is actually a fantasy. For example, an injunction ordering school desegregation cost the state of Michigan six million dollars (*Milikin v. Bradley*, 1974). This same ancillary cost is extracted when courts invalidate state laws that deny benefits, because these benefits now have to be paid (e.g., *Graham v. Richardson*, 1971).

Interestingly, Ex Parte Young does not generalize to abuse of *state* laws by *state* officials (*Pennhurst v. Halderman*, 1981). Despite its perfect parallel to abuse of *federal* laws by *state* officials, the Supreme Court did not accept the argument.

It is also "fictitious" to believe that Ex Parte Young and Edelman do not offer a direct route to the state treasury. In *Hutto v. Finney* (1978), the Supreme Court ruled that the state pay attorney fees because a prison had not heeded two prior lower court injunctions to improve prison conditions. In the words of the Court:

> A criminal contempt prosecution for . . . may result in a jail term or a fine. . . . Civil contempt may also be punished by a remedial fine, which compensates the party who won the injunction. . . . If a state agency refuses to adhere to a court order, a financial penalty may be the most effective means of insuring compliance.

In other words, sending officials to jail would not improve the prison environment, but the threat of attorney fees (and perhaps other fines) might. The Court ruled, in effect, that such fees and fines are "ancillary" to the already ancillary prospective costs.

Qualified Immunity

In *Kentucky v. Graham* (1985), state police rampaged after the murder of a fellow officer. The plaintiffs lodged *personal capacity* charges against the rampagers, and sued the state, *not* the rampagers, for attorney fees. The personal capacity charges were settled in the plaintiff's favor, but attorney fees from the state were denied. The plaintiffs mistook the Hutto ruling to imply that attorney fees from the state were viable in any personal capacity victory. But a unanimous Supreme Court ruled that attorney fees were tied to victory against the state (which Hutto had achieved). Graham was not awarded fees from the state because the state was not charged with any illegal actions.

Comparison of *Kentucky v. Graham* to *Ex Parte Young* reveals the difference between qualified immunity and no immunity. In *Ex Parte Young*, the attorney general was doing state bidding; he was not acting with malicious intent. The federal government was trying to enjoin the state, not the attorney general personally. However, an illegal act must be committed by people, and some acts are in bad faith. As established in *Scheuer v. Rhodes* (1974), state officials enjoy **qualified**, or "good faith" immunity for "discretionary acts performed in the course of official conduct." Judges, legislators, and prosecutors enjoy absolute immunity for all discretionary acts. But nobody is immune for illegal acts committed beyond the boundaries of their official job descriptions. Thus the rampagers in *Graham v. Kentucky* were personally liable for damages.

The action does not have to be rampaging. For example, in *Forrester v. White* (1988), the district court ruled that a state judge was guilty of sex discrimination in demoting and then discharging a female probation officer (a typical EEO scenario). The circuit court viewed the judge's actions as discretionary, and overruled. The Supreme Court ruled that the judge was acting in a nondiscretionary administrative capacity, and therefore, was not immune. Using the "functional" approach, the Court stated:

> Immunity is justified and defined by the functions it protects and serves, not by the person to whom it attaches.

The *Forrester v. White* ruling was recently affirmed by the Supreme Court in *Hafer v. Melo* (1991), also a discriminatory discharge claim.

The newly appointed Auditor General of Pennsylvania was not protected in her personal capacity based on *Will v. Michigan Department of State Police*, (1989). According to Justice O'Connor, speaking for a unanimous Court:

> The claims considered in Will were official-capacity claims, and the phrase "acting in their official capacities" is best understood as a reference to the capacity in which the state officer is sued, not the capacity in which the officer inflicts the alleged injury. . . . Officers sued in their personal capacity come to the Court as individuals and thus fit comfortably with the statutory term "person."

Thus any state official can be sued for behavior that is not in accordance with the job the official is supposed to do.

Returning to *Will v. Michigan*—if Will's charges had merit, he could have successfully sued his supervisor. But the State of Michigan would have had only one responsibility; to correct any policies or customs that might have produced or contributed to such illegal actions.

MUNICIPAL ENTITIES

Obviously, personal capacity also applies to local (or municipal) officials. However, 11th Amendment immunity does not. Therefore, in suits against local school boards, police, city managers, and so forth, the plaintiff invariably attempts to extract remedies from both officials and the municipalities. Historically, 11th Amendment immunity was applicable to municipal governments. Sovereign municipal immunity was reversed, however, and the conditions for implicating the municipality apart from its officials were refined.

Early Rulings

In *Monroe v. Papes* (1961), an illegal breaking and entering case, the Supreme Court ruled that municipalities are not "persons" within the meaning of Sec.1983. This ruling was subsequently reversed in *Monell v. New York City* (1978), an official capacity, EEO suit.

Monell was a class action suit against a city, a mayor, two major departments, and two department heads. As in *Cleveland Board of Education v. LaFleur* (1974) discussed in Chapter 3, the two departments forced early pregnancy leave as a "matter of official policy." The plaintiffs requested injunctive relief and back pay. The policy was altered prior to trial, mooting the need for injunctive relief. The lower courts, in keeping with *Monroe v. Papes,* denied "retrospective" back pay. The Supreme Court reversed the lower courts and the *Monroe v. Papes* precedent.

Four reasons were given for reversing Monroe. First, the Court admitted to misinterpreting congressional meaning behind Sec.1983 in *Monroe v. Papes.* Second, the Court had routinely treated school boards as "persons," both pre- and post-Monroe, and saw a need for a single policy for all municipal agencies. Third, the court asserted logical reasons for municipalities to "arrange their affairs" to ensure constitutional rights. Finally, the Court felt that Congress had recognized municipal liability in Sec.1988 (on lawyer fees) and did not require a clear statement for municipal personage as was subsequently requested for state personage in *Will v. Michigan.*

However, the Monell Court denounced **respondeat superior** (acceptable in both Title VII and Sec.1981 cases) as a basis for determining municipal liability. Accepted instead was evidence of a causal connection between the constitutionally illegal act and: (a) policy statements, ordinances, regulations, or decisions officially adopted by departmental officers; or (b) deprivations pursuant to "governmental customs."

In *Owen v. City of Independence* (1980), a police chief was discharged without due process. He sued the city manager, city council, and the city. He wanted injunctive relief, back pay, and attorney fees. The lower courts agreed that constitutional violations had occurred, but ruled that the officials were blameless because they "acted in good faith and without malice." The Supreme Court overruled, stating:

> there is no tradition of immunity for municipal corporations, and neither history nor policy support a construction of Sec.1983 that would justify the qualified immunity accorded the city of Independence by the Court of Appeals. We hold therefore, that the municipality may not assert the good faith of its officials as a defense to liability under Sec.1983.

Thus good faith, acceptable for discretionary acts of state officials, does not apply to discretionary acts of municipal officials.

And in *City of Newport v. Fact Concerts* (1981), the Supreme Court ruled on compensatory and punitive damages under post-Monell rules. Seven high-ranking city officials prevented the plaintiffs from substituting a rock group ("Blood, Sweat, and Tears") for a cancelled jazz act.

The jury awarded compensatory ($72,910) and punitive ($275,000) damages against the officials and the city, the latter calling for $75,000 from the officials and $200,000 from the city. The Court struck down the punitive damages against the city, stating:

> we find that considerations of history and policy do not support exposing a municipality to punitive damages for bad-faith actions of its officials.

Thus municipal liability extends to equitable relief and compensatory damages, but not punitive damages. Of course, personal liability can include punitive damages.

More Recent Rulings

Punitive damages aside, the Monell, Owen, and Newport rulings distort the true difficulty involved in causally connecting a municipality to the illegal acts of its officials. These three cases involved easy rulings. In Monell there was an identifiable official municipal policy, and in both Owen and Newport, high municipal officials were clearly guilty of committing the illegal acts. But when officials are not so high ranking, implicating the municipality is practically impossible. Ironically, this precedent was initiated in *Pembaur v. Cincinnati* (1986), another seemingly easy ruling.

In Pembaur, a physician under grand jury investigation refused entry into his clinic to deputy sheriffs tasked with serving subpoenas to two of the physician's employees. On a direct order from the county prosecutor, city police chopped down the clinic door (a 4th Amendment violation). The district court ruled that the police were not acting under official policy as defined in Monell, and the circuit court added that a single official decision was not sufficient to force municipal liability. But a Supreme Court majority of seven ruled that official policy is executed when an official with **final policy-making authority** makes even a single illegal discretionary decision.

Although this sounds like a victory for plaintiffs, Justice O'Connor, in a concurring opinion, suggested that municipal liability be limited to situations where discretionary decisions are traced to a "final policy-maker" (as in Pembaur). She also suggested that state law, not federal law or fact-finding, serve as the basis for identifying the final policy-maker. Justice Brennan, who wrote the majority ruling, also wrote a plurality opinion stating the obvious—that O'Connor's rules would limit municipal liability to the acts of only the "highest" officials. Brennan also asserted that **fact-finding** is more appropriate than state law for discovering final policy-making authority.

The debate continued in *City of St. Louis v. Praprotnik* (1988), where a city-employed architect suffered a retaliatory discharge by his immediate supervisors. The lower courts exonerated the supervisors and implicated the city. Justice O'Connor, announcing for a majority of eight, echoed her concurring opinion in Pembaur, and ruled that the plaintiff failed to trace the illegal discharge to a final policymaker. Justice Brennan, speaking for Marshall and Blackmun, agreed with the overall ruling, but echoed his concurring opinion in Pembaur.

Brennan also noted that the rules for determining final policy-making authority were left undecided for a second time. However, despite the Supreme Court's failure to resolve the O'Connor versus Brennan debate, the lower courts have followed O'Connor's rules. Consider, for example, *Carrero v. N.Y.C. Housing Authority* (1989), a sexual harassment case combining Title VII and Sec.1983 charges.

Carrero lodged both hostile environment and quid pro quo charges. The offender was an EEO officer who both verbally and physically abused Carrero (hostile harassment), and restricted her training opportunities (quid pro quo). Carrero received Title VII relief (injunction, back pay, and lawyer fees). But her Sec.1983 efforts to implicate a much higher ranking official—the district director—failed. There was evidence sufficient to connect the director via respondeat superior, but respondeat superior does not apply in Sec.1983. In liberating the district director (and hence, the municipality) from Sec.1983 liability, the 2nd Circuit quoting from Monell, stated: "Municipalities and their entities may be held liable under Sec.1983 only when the deprivation of rights is caused pursuant to":

> a policy statement, ordinance, regulation, or decision officially adopted and promulgated by that body's officers.

The Court also echoed direct quotes from both Pembaur and Praprotnik illustrating O'Connor's rules, ruling that "although Peterson [the EEO officer] exercised some discretion in training and evaluating Carrero":

> discretion in the exercise of particular functions does not, without more, give rise to municipal liability based on the exercise of that discretion [from Pembaur] . . . mere failure to investigate the basis of a subordinates discretionary decisions does not amount to a delegation of policymaking authority. [from Praprotnik]

In short, Title VII and Sec.1981 differ from Sec.1983 regarding the causal connection between higher level and lower level officials. Based on O'Connor's rules, heeded in Carrero, the Sec.1983 plaintiff, for all intents and purposes, has to show that the lower level official was acting on orders, or on the basis of a commonly held **custom**.

Implicating the municipality is not easier for "customs" relative to "policymakers." For example, in *City of Canton v. Harris* (1989), the plaintiff received poor emergency medical care while in custody because the police were not properly trained. The "official policy" in the city charter did call for proper training, but by "custom" such training was not provided. The Supreme Court unanimously ruled that the negligence in failure to train would have to pass a **deliberate indifference** test in order for the municipality to be implicated. In short, someone with final policy-making authority would intentionally have to ignore the training need in a provable way.

Actually, the deliberate indifference test is a prophecy from an earlier ruling (*Oklahoma City v. Tuttle*, 1985) in which the Supreme Court spoke of "gross negligence amounting to deliberate indifference." A number of lower court rulings combined the language of Tuttle with terms used by O'Connor in Pembaur (e.g., "deliberate" or "conscious" choices) well before the Praprotnik case. The most interesting of these rulings from the EEO perspective is *Lipsett v. University of Puerto Rico* (1988), a combined Title VII, Title IX, and Sec.1983 case.

Lipsett, who was completing her medical residency requirement, charged both hostile harassment (by male residents) and quid pro quo harassment (discriminatory discharge). Although the University enjoyed sovereign immunity, the suit included charges against the head official in his personal capacity. There was clearly an "atmosphere" of discrimination against women. The head official (the chancellor of the campus) would probably have been implicated under respondeat superior. However, according to the 1st Circuit his actions did not pass the deliberate indifference test.

Attempts to Circumvent the Rules

Our review of municipal entities reveals tough standards for both the municipality and the claimant. The municipality must adhere to a standard the state can ignore, and the claimant must establish a higher municipal responsibility than respondeat superior. Two recent cases illustrate attempts to circumvent these standards, one on each side.

In *Howlett v. Rose* (1990), a student charged the school board and its head official with illegally breaking into and entering his parked car. Because Florida state law extends sovereign immunity to municipalities, the Florida Supreme Court moved to dismiss the case without prejudice. But the U.S. Supreme Court, in a unanimous ruling, asserted that Sec.1983 cannot be nullified simply on the basis of state common law. According to the Supreme Court, refusal by a state court to entertain a Sec.1983 case violates the Supremacy Clause of the Constitution.

In *Jett v. Dallas* (1989), the plaintiff tried to use Sec.1981 to impose respondeat superior on traditionally construed Sec.1983 entities and officials. A coach/teacher prevailed in district court against his principal and the school board for retaliatory discharge and reassignment based on respondeat superior. His awards were substantial. However, the Supreme Court exonerated the school board (the principal panicked and settled privately), asserting that Sec.1983 provides exclusive remedies for 14th Amendment violations. Thus it makes no sense to use Sec.1981 in typical Sec.1983 scenarios. Even when permitted, Sec.1983 remedies still apply.

FIGHTING STATE LAWS

As defined in Chapter 1, and as witnessed in Chapter 3, state laws that contradict federal laws may be declared unconstitutional via the Supremacy Clause of the Constitution. This is a critical issue for the discussion of reverse discrimination suits in Chapter 7. For present purposes, the issue can be framed in the context of a current non-EEO debate—the right to an abortion.

The issue is not whether abortion is, per se, legal or illegal, but rather the justification a state must use to enact laws restricting abortions. For most laws, the state needs only a *rational basis*. In accordance with 14th Amendment traditions, that means a reasonable relationship between a statute and a legitimate governmental objective. Prior to the monumental 1973 *Roe v. Wade* opinion (authored by Justice Blackmun), challenges to state abortion laws were reviewed under the rational basis standard, which is basically easy for a state to justify.

The essence of Justice Blackmun's opinion in Roe was that abortion is a **fundamental right**, much like the freedom of speech. By 14th

Amendment traditions, a law that threatens a fundamental right requires a **strict scrutiny** justification, where the state must have a **compelling interest** for enacting the statute, and the statute must prescribe solutions that are **narrowly tailored** to the interest (i.e., no other alternatives). By ruling that abortion is a fundamental right, Justice Blackmun made it virtually impossible for states to prevent abortion during the early months of pregnancy. What the Supreme Court decided on June 29, 1992, is that the fundamental right to abortion is still valid, but a state can legislate certain restrictions (e.g., time constraints, parental approval, etc.).

The relationship of *Roe v. Wade* to reverse discrimination is elementary. When states or municipalities engage in affirmative action designed to benefit minorities and women, white employees may argue that a fundamental right (equal protection) is threatened. Indeed, the strict scrutiny analysis is a dominant feature of 14th Amendment reverse discrimination challenges, and the principles of strict scrutiny have been slowly incorporated into Title VII reverse discrimination cases. The rational basis versus strict scrutiny issue has also emerged in age discrimination cases, as we will witness in Chapter 6.

—— BRIEF SUMMARY ——

A key distinction between Sec.1981 and Sec.1983 is that Sec.1981 provides rights (like Title VII) whereas Sec.1983 protects rights. In particular, Sec.1983 obliges state and local governments to uphold federal laws. Thus Sec.1983 offers protections (**Q1**) for covered practices (**Q3**) that transcend traditional EEO boundaries. The covered entities (**Q2**), practically speaking, are limited to states and municipalities. The administrative procedures (**Q4**) (or lack thereof) are precisely parallel between Sec.1981 and Sec.1983. But due to 11th Amendment immunity, remedies (**Q5**) against states require a waiver, and state officials must be sued in their personal capacities (and in some cases, only for nondiscretional acts). Municipal officials do not enjoy sovereign immunity. However, they enjoy a qualified immunity because attack/defense balances (**Q6**) in Sec.1983 require a higher standard than respondeat superior. The official must practically be caught in the Act or show a deliberate indifference to customary policies. Finally, for litigation that attacks state laws, the state must pass a stiff defense (strict scrutiny) if the law threatens a fundamental right, but a much easier defense (rational basis) for nonfundamental rights.

SECTION III
A BRIEF REVIEW OF SEC.1985 AND SEC.1986

Unlike Sec.1983, which focuses on state enforcement of federal laws, Sec.1985 focuses on **conspiracy**, making it a federal offense. Sec.1986, A companion statute, punishes failure to prevent conspiracy. Sec.1985 has three Parts, one of which, Sec.1985(3), is relevant in modern times. The essential features of Sec.1985(3) are as follows:

> If two or more persons in any state or territory *conspire* or go into disguise on the highway, or on the premises . . . for the purpose of depriving . . . *equal protection* of the [federal] laws or of *equal privileges* and immunities under the laws . . . the party so injured or deprived may have an action for the recovery of damages . . . against any one or more of the conspirators. [emphasis added]

The statute has been interpreted to have both 13th and 14th Amendment implications. Other factors, however, restrict it from being as broad as this characterization would seem to imply.

Historically, Sec.1985(3) never had its intended effect in its own era. The first Supreme Court ruling occurred at a time, 11 years after enactment, when most officials were fed up with reconstruction. Thus in *United States v. Harris* (1882), where 20 whites lynched a black citizen, the Court ruled that private conspiracies were not covered. A similar ruling was rendered in *Baldwin v. Franks* (1887), where lawful Chinese aliens were run out of a California town. Then, after a 65-year dormancy, the Supreme Court again rejected private conspiracies in *Collins v. Hardyman* (1952) (involving a political club).

However, the Court reversed these rulings in *Griffin v. Breckenridge* (1971), where a group of whites stopped and assaulted a group of blacks on a Mississippi highway. The defendants argued that they mistook the blacks for civil rights workers, and that their conspiracy was not within the color of state law. The Court, in a unanimous ruling, responded:

> To read any such requirement into Sec.1985(3) would thus deprive that section of all independent action.

Therefore, Griffin established that purely private conspiracies apply to race within the meaning of the 13th Amendment.

The issue of sex as a protected class emerged in an EEO case in *Great American v. Novotny* (1979). The plaintiff was a white male victim of a retaliatory discharge. He had attempted to advocate the cases of females in the company who were victimized by sexual discrimination. The issue at the circuit court level was whether two or more officials within the same company could promote a conspiracy under the meaning of the statute. The 3rd Circuit affirmed this notion, but the Supreme Court reversed and remanded on other issues.

The Supreme Court spelled out three conditions under which the Act applies: (a) conspiracy; (b) deprivation of a federal right (e.g., "equal protection" or "equal privileges"); and (c) class-based "animus." The lower court issue was not directly resolved. Instead, the Court ruled that although race was protected in Griffin, sex, which is not protected in the 13th Amendment, requires state action (Novotny was a private case). The Court also ruled that Sec.1983(5) could not be used in lieu of Title VII (to avoid its administrative procedures).

Thus although Sec.1985(3) is a potential sleeper, its application to EEO under current conditions is limited by two obvious restrictions. First, it applies only to conspiracy, which has not been a common EEO complaint. Second, potentially applicable situations (such as Novotny) are precluded when statutes such as Title VII can provide a remedy. In addition, because the Supreme Court did not rule on the lower court issue in Novotny, it is not clear whether conspiracy by two or more members of a single company would be upheld.

A potentially good EEO case did exist in *University of Tennessee v. Elliot* (1986). The plaintiff had grounds for conspiracy between the state and the institution because two university officials were permitted to serve as ALJs. This could have also tested, at the Supreme Court level, whether two officials from within the same "company" could conspire within the meaning of the statute. However, the very issue that could have been tested served as the basis for dismissal of the case on grounds of collateral estoppel.

SECTION IV
EVALUATION OF SEC.1981 AND SEC.1983

There are no compliance issues in Sec.1981 and Sec.1983, at least from an employer's perspective, that are unique relative to Title VII. Basically these statutes are Title VII gap-fillers. The relevant issue therefore is how well these gaps are filled—particularly in light of expanded Title VII remedies in the Civil Rights Act of 1991.

SEC.1981

Prior to the Patterson ruling, the advantages of Sec.1981 relative to Title VII were **coverage (Q2)** of private sector "mom and pop" shops (with less than 15 employees), **direct access (Q4)** to federal court, and jury trials with **legal remedies (Q5)**. On the other hand, the **covered practices (Q4)** were, at best, the same as Title VII, and Title VII had decided edges in protecting a wider range of **classes (Q1)** and providing a wider range of judicial **attacks (Q6)**. The Patterson ruling provided only a temporary setback. However, expansion of Title VII remedies casts a new light on the relationship between Title VII and Sec.1981.

A main attraction of Sec.1981, legal relief, is now available in Title VII. Plaintiffs can still use Sec.1981 to reap awards over and above the Title VII ceilings, and even back pay awards beyond 2 years. Also, Sec.1981 may be used by the tardy plaintiff who sleeps on Title VII EEOC procedures, but who wakes up in time to satisfy the generally longer statutes of limitation in Sec.1981 (and Sec.1983). However, the sweetening of Title VII will probably focus attention away from juries and damages to choices relating to administrative procedures in Title VII versus the administration-free route in Sec.1981.

That choice is not that simple. EEOC procedures can benefit a claimant by providing: (a) feedback on the merits of a case; (b) a conciliatory remedy from a strong federal commission; and (c) federal payment of investigatory and conciliatory costs. On the other hand, an EEOC investigation can forewarn a defendant of the issues it will likely face in court. Thus the decision to choose one versus the other, or both, will require considerable forethought.

SEC.1983

Most students of EEO find Sec.1983 more difficult to understand than Sec.1981. It is easy to get lost in the broad scope of 14th Amendment applications beyond EEO **classes (Q1)** and employment **practices (Q3)**. However, it is necessary to understand the scope of the 14th Amendment in order to recognize its applications to EEO. From the perspective of Sec.1983, EEO is just another way for state action to contradict federal law. Indeed, EEO is not necessarily the only Sec.1983 issue in the workplace. For example, state employees, regardless of class protections in any other statute, have a valid Sec.1983 claim if they are discharged for exercising their 1st Amendment right to free speech in the workplace.

Thus in assessing Sec.1983, the **protected classes (Q1)** and **covered practices (Q3)** overlap with Title VII for reasons having nothing to do with EEO. The critical factor is that Sec.1983 provides an alternative to Title VII for EEO violations in state and local **governmental agencies (Q2)** that Sec.1981 does not address. Within this context, Sec.1983 has been an important tool. We have already witnessed the power of Sec.1983 and/or the 14th Amendment to remedy (a) state protective laws discriminating against women; (b) facial discrimination in pregnancy policies; (c) restrictions against lawful aliens; (d) sexual harassment; (e) discriminatory discharge; and more. And we will also witness its power in reverse discrimination cases in Chapter 7.

Among the remaining dimensions, there is no fundamental difference between Sec.1983 and 1981 on **administrative procedures (Q4)**, and the only difference in **attack/defense balances (Q6)** (inapplicability of respondeat superior) makes certain charges (e.g., harassment) more viable under Title VII. Thus the broadening of Title VII provides some of the same thoughts discussed above regarding tardiness, namely EEOC intervention versus direct access to court, and damages in personal capacity suits. Otherwise, the main advantage of Sec.1983 is time honored; it is a strong vehicle to challenge laws that threaten fundamental rights.

——— CHAPTER SUMMARY ———

Sec.1981 protects **(Q1)** the 19th century definition of race, and lawful aliens. It covers **(Q2)** private employers (no minimum), and its practices **(Q3)** are the same as Title VII. There are procedural side effects but no administrative procedures **(Q4)**. The remedies **(Q5)** include compensatory and punitive damages. Judicially **(Q6)**, however, motive must be proven (i.e., no adverse impact) and all Title VII disparate treatment scenarios are permitted (including respondeat superior). Sec.1983 offers the same protection **(Q1)** and coverage **(Q3)** as Title VII, and provides the same administrative procedures **(Q4)** as Sec.1981, but its covered entities (Q2) must connect to state enforcement of federal laws. State and local entities, because of their total and/or qualified immunities, enjoy advantages relative to Sec.1981 entities in both remedies (Q5) and mode of attack (Q6). The individual is vulnerable, but the state and "official" officials are not. Also, respondeat superior may not be used as a vehicle for attacking any individual not directly involved in a discriminatory action. Sec.1985 is a limited statute, and Sec.1986 requires a Sec.1985 victory. The most distinctive dimensional feature of Sec.1985 is coverage (Q3) of only one act; conspiracy. In addition, there is an interaction between the protected classes (Q1) and covered entities (Q2), such that race (the 19th century version) is protected in the private sector, but the other classes must be protected within the meaning of Sec.1983. The administrative procedures (Q4) are the same as Sec.1981 and 1983, and the remedies (Q5) and attack modes (Q6) follow from Sec.1981 in private cases and Sec.1983 in state law cases.

NOTES

1. Based on rulings surveyed in Chapters 2 and 3, the reader may be surprised to see a disagreement between Blackmun versus Marshall and Brennan. Justice Blackmun, though a "liberal" over the past dozen years, was a Nixon appointee who, in earlier years, tended to follow the dictates of another Nixon appointee—Chief Justice Burger.

2. Jury trials are procedurally different than nonjury trials. These differences are most clearly seen in age discrimination cases, and will be discussed in Chapter 6.

The Equal Pay Act

CHART 5.1. THE EQUAL PAY ACT

Q1	Q2	Q3	Q4	Q5	Q6
Sex only	Private, state/local & federal entities Engaged in commerce or production of goods Only 2 employees required Unions may not cause violation	Unequal wages for job of equal skill, effort, responsibility, & working conditions	EEOC procedures or direct access to federal court EEOC uses Sec.17 or Sec.16(c) Direct access uses Sec.16(b)	Sec.17 for injunction and back pay Sec.16(b) or (c) for back pay and liquidated damages Lawyer fees	Proof of unequal pay for equal work Seniority, merit, quantity/quality, or factor other than sex defenses Jury can decide merits; judge decides damages

(Q1): What classes of people are protected (or have rights)?
(Q2): What business entities are covered (or have duties)?
(Q3): What employment practices are covered?
(Q4): Is the law administered, and if so, how?
(Q5): What are the penalties (or remedies) for breaking the law?
(Q6): What are the attacks and defenses used in litigation?

The Equal Pay Act (EPA) is depicted in Chart 5.1. EPA[1] **protects (Q1)** only sex and **covers (Q3)** only wage discrimination. The **covered entities (Q2)** basically mimic Title VII, except that only two employees are required (one from each sex). The EEOC **administers (Q4)** the

157

Act, and can sponsor lawsuits. A claimant can also obtain direct access, as long as the EEOC has not filed suit before a direct-access claim reaches federal court. EPA suits may be filed within 2 years, or 3 years if a violation is deemed willful. The **remedies (Q5)** include injunction, 2- or 3-year back pay awards, liquidated damages, and lawyer fees, and the **attack/defense balances (Q6)** are statutorily determined, with persuasive burdens in each of the three phases.

By itself, EPA offers five alternatives relative to the pre-1991 version of Title VII: (a) the two-employee requirement; (b) longer limits for filing; (c) direct access to federal court; (d) 3-year back pay awards; and (e) liquidated damages. Of course, wage disparity is also covered in Title VII. However, the key issue for a plaintiff is not whether to use EPA versus Title VII, but rather, how best to combine these statutes to achieve the best remedies. As we will witness below, plaintiffs who use only EPA or Title VII (i.e., "pure" claims) cannot reap the full range of possible remedies.

The chapter contains six sections. Section I overviews the social and legislative history behind the EPA, and the statute itself. Section II focuses on pure EPA cases, and Section III on the advantages of combined EPA + Title VII claims. Section IV addresses critical residual issues for EPA, and Section V evaluates a related Title VII issue termed *comparable worth*. Finally, Section VI addresses the continued usefulness of EPA in light of the Civil Rights Act of 1991, and a single but critical issue of compliance—**job evaluation**.

SECTION I
THE HISTORY OF THE EPA AND ITS CURRENT STATUS

THE HISTORICAL RECORD

In the pre-Civil War era, an archaic view of women as wives and mothers kept most women at home. After the Civil War, the industrial revolution created a need for cheap labor. Women and children provided most of that labor. Initially, state protective laws did prevent factory owners from abusing women and children. But by 1900 these laws were outdated and served mainly to segregate and classify women in such ways as to restrict employment opportunities and wages.

Women's rights groups were particularly upset with the Supreme Court's ruling in *Muller v. Oregon* (1908) (upholding Oregon's law on maximum working hours for women). One group, the National Consumer's League, lobbied state legislatures protesting the "ceiling" in hours and the "floor" in wages (see Babcock, Freedman, Norton, & Ross, 1975, p. 41). By 1920, more than a dozen states responded with minimum wage laws for women. However, the Supreme Court struck down this concept in *Adkins v. Children's Hospital* (1923).

The Fair Labor Standards Act of 1938 (FLSA) provided some relief by establishing minimum wages and overtime pay for men and women. The wage law eliminated ultracheap labor in blue-collar jobs, and the overtime law (time and a half) made it unprofitable to extend the work week. However, women were still segregated and classified into lower paying jobs.

Women had a stronger advocate in World War II. The National War Labor Board, established in 1942, deemed that women should receive the same wages for jobs previously held by departing servicemen. To bolster its effort, the Board conducted job evaluations within federally contracted companies. These evaluations focused on: (a) equal pay for similar jobs; and (b) equal pay for dissimilar but comparable jobs. Despite the clear demonstration by women of their equal abilities (and government sponsored documentaries and testimonials), the country returned to its pre-1942 status quo after World War II. A similar cycle occurred before and after the Korean War.

By the late 1950s, women were holding approximately 40% of all jobs. To federal legislators, it was clear that an equal wage law was needed. But there was a snag. Some legislators wanted to rekindle the wartime policy of equal pay for comparable work. Indeed, the 1962 version of the House and Senate bills, representing the views of the Kennedy administration, precluded an employer from paying:

> a rate less than the rate at which he pays wages to any employee of the opposite sex for work of *comparable* character on jobs the performance of which requires *comparable skills,* except where such payment is made pursuant to a *seniority or merit* increase system which does not discriminate on the basis of sex. [emphasis added]

It was Congresswoman St. George (among others) who objected and countered with an amendment calling for "equal work on jobs . . . which require equal skill." These EPA bills died in their respective House and Senate committees in 1962, to be rekindled in 1963.

The early House versions in 1963 used the "equal work" language from the St. George amendment. However, the bill was still narrow, containing a single criterion for equal work (skill), and only two defenses (seniority and merit). Based on testimony from professionals in the field, Congress added three equal work criteria (effort, responsibility, and working conditions), and two defenses (quantity and quality of work, and factors other than sex).

Special note should be taken of **factors other than sex** (FOS). Professionals who testified before Congress wanted the FOS defense to protect time-honored personnel practices such as job evaluation and bona fide training programs. However, the FOS defense has become a vehicle for both pretextual as well as legitimate practices. For example, while they were still legal, state protective laws provided a defensible FOS because women were legally prohibited from performing essential features of many blue-collar jobs (e.g., heavy lifting). In more recent times, employers have attempted to use FOS to hide other shady practices. In general, regardless of whether the personnel selection system is sound or unsound, once a plaintiff has established a prima facie case, the burden is on the defendant to prove that the FOS is representative of a sex-blind practice.

Of course, in addition to the relevant social and legislative history of the EPA, there was a major post-EPA event; Title VII. The final Title VII vote occurred 2 days after the effective date of EPA. Because wage discrimination was projected as a covered Title VII practice, some legislators feared that the statutory burdens in the EPA would be neutralized. Thus at the 11th hour, Sec.703(h) in Title VII was appended with the **Bennett Amendment**. According to this amendment:

> It shall not be an unlawful employment practice under this title for any employer to differentiate upon the basis of sex in determining the amount of wages or compensation paid or to be paid to employees of such employer if such differentiation is authorized by the provisions of Section 6(d) of the Fair Labor Standards Act of 1938, as amended [by EPA].

The Bennett Amendment was designed to incorporate the four defenses in EPA into Title VII wage discrimination cases. However, because of the amendment's ambiguous language, debates emerged regarding a different issue: Does the Bennett Amendment open up for Title VII scrutiny the historical **comparable worth** issue rejected by Congress in 1963? As we will witness in Section V of this chapter, the amendment did indeed open up the question, but the ultimate answer has not been to the liking of comparable worth proponents.

THE EPA STATUTE

The logic of EPA is expressed in EPA-specific language incorporated into Sec.6(d)(1) in the FLSA. That language explicitly addresses the **protected class (Q1), covered practices (Q3),** and **attacks and defenses (Q6)** as underlined below. Accordingly:

> No employer having employees subject to any provisions of this section shall discriminate, within any establishment in which such employees are employed, between employees *on the basis of sex* by *paying wages* to employees in such establishment at a rate less than the rate at which he pays wages to employees of the opposite sex in such establishment for equal work on jobs the performance of which requires *equal skill, effort, and responsibility, and which are performed under similar working conditions, except where such payment is made pursuant to (i) a seniority system; (ii) merit system; (iii) a system which measures earning by quantity or quality of production; or (iv) a differential based on any other factor than sex:* Provided, that an employer who is paying a wage rate differential in violation of the subsection shall not, in order to comply with the provisions of this subsection, reduce the wage rate of any employee. [emphasis added]

The **covered entities (Q2), administrative procedures (Q5),** and **remedies (Q5)** are inferred from other portions in the FLSA.

Protected Class (Q1)

The protected class is the simplest dimension—the Act protects sex. And although most claimants are women, the Act protects both sexes (e.g., *Hodgson v. Pet,* 1974; *Board of Regents of Nebraska v. Dawes,* 1976).

Covered Entities (Q2)

Although seemingly a quibble, Title VII references individuals "affecting commerce," whereas FLSA references employees and enterprises "engaged in commerce" or in producing "goods for commerce." The permutations and combinations of FLSA coverage are quite complex, and the interested reader is directed to Sections 1620.1 through 1620.9 of the EEOC EPA Regulations. For present purposes, it is sufficient to know that Title VII is broader than EPA, because a person not engaged in commerce or in producing goods can nevertheless "affect" commerce.

A noteworthy feature of EPA, however, is stated in Sec.6(d)(2) as follows:

No labor organization, or its agents, representing employees of an employer having employees subject to any provisions of [EPA] shall cause or attempt to cause such an employer to discriminate against an employee in violation of [EPA].

Thus unions, generally exempt from FLSA coverage, are prohibited from influencing an employer to violate EPA.

Despite these complications, EPA covers most of the same employers as Title VII. EPA has covered private entities since its inception. Selected public entities were added in 1966, and much broader federal, state, and local coverage was provided in 1974.

Covered Practices (Q3)

The EPA motto is **equal pay for equal work**; not equal or comparable pay for comparable work (or jobs of "comparable worth"). Comparable worth, as we will witness later, is a pure Title VII issue. The EPA covers only wage discrimination, and its coverage applies to jobs similar in **skill** (experience, training, education, and ability); **effort** (physical and mental exertion); **responsibility** (accountability and supervisory duties); and **working conditions** (surroundings and hazards). Jobs need not be exactly equal, only "substantially equal" with respect to each criterion (e.g., *Shultz v. Wheaton*, 1970). A 1977 amendment covers retaliation.

Administrative Procedures (Q4) and Remedies (Q5)

Originally, the Department of Labor (DOL) administered all private claims (the only ones permitted). In 1974, the DOL added state/local claims and the Civil Service Commission (CSC) took on federal claims. Reorganization Plan #1 (1978) then transferred all control to the EEOC. Because of the FLSA roots, the EEOC does not administer EPA as it does Title VII. For example, the EEOC must investigate and conciliate Title VII claims; in EPA, conciliation is only an option. In addition, there are four distinct FLSA suits. One suit—Sec.16(a)—is of minor importance, being for criminal penalties only.

The three critical suits are inherently tied to two different sets of remedies. The EEOC may initiate a **Sec.17** suit for injunction and 2-year back pay awards, or a **Sec.16(c)** suit for 2 or 3 years of back pay and liquidated damages (double the back pay award). Alternatively, claimants may directly access the court in a **Sec.16(b)** suit for the same remedies offered in Sec.16(c), plus lawyer fees. In general, interest on back pay is available when liquidated damages are statutorily precluded or not awarded by the court. It should also be noted that class actions require written consent (i.e., they are "opt in" actions, whereas Title VII class actions are "opt out").

In general, jury trials have not been a major factor in EPA case law. They are not permitted in Sec.17 because FLSA tradition considers these suits equitable (i.e., primarily for injunction). And although jury trials are permitted in Sec.16(b) and Sec.16(c), juries can only decide the merits of the wage disparity case (i.e., whether the plaintiff deserves back pay). In other words, liquidated damages are always at the discretion of the court (i.e., a judge).

The key issues for remedies, therefore, are twofold. First, because a single EPA suit cannot result in the full array of EPA awards (i.e., injunction, back pay, and liquidated damages), the sensible strategy is to use Title VII to obtain injunctions and EPA to obtain back pay and damages. Second, the requirement for liquidated damages has evolved. As we will witness later, the current standard is that the employee must prove that the employer knew a violation was committed, or acted in reckless disregard for the statute. This standard replaces an early FLSA standard that punished the employer for simply having reason to know EPA applied, and a later standard developed within EPA case law that focused on a reasonable basis for the employer to believe that the statute was being violated.

Attack/Defense Balances (Q6)

EPA plaintiffs must prove that jobs pay sex-based disparate wages despite substantial equality in *each* of the four statutory criteria: skill, effort, responsibility, and working conditions. The defendant must then prove that wage disparity is based on *only one* of the four statutory defenses: seniority, merit, quantity or quality, or any factor other than sex. Pretext is characterized by the same considerations witnessed in disparate treatment Title VII cases.

─────── BRIEF SUMMARY ───────

EPA protects (Q1) sex-based wage disparity (Q3) for jobs with substantial equality in skill, effort, responsibility, and working conditions. The covered entities (Q2) basically, though not totally, mimic Title VII, and only two employees are required to make a case. The EEOC administers (Q4) the Act, and Remedies (Q5) are tied to lawsuits. The EEOC may sponsor Sec.17 suits for injunction and back pay, or Sec.16(c) suits for back pay and liquidated damages. Alternatively, claimants may file Sec.16(b) suits for back pay, liquidated damages, and lawyer fees. The attack/defense balances (Q6) are fixed. The plaintiff must prove that the jobs are substantially equal, and the defense must prove that wage disparity is a function of seniority, merit, quantity and quality of work, or any factor other than sex. To avoid a third year of back pay and liquidated damages, the employee must prove the employer knew there was a violation, or showed a reckless disregard for the statute.

SECTION II
"PURE" EPA CASES

Prior to Carter's 1978 reorganization, most EPA plaintiffs were named Shultz, Hodgson, Brennan, or Marshall—all Secretaries of Labor. Furthermore, the overwhelming majority of DOL suits used Sec.17 (for injunction and back pay), and most suits during this era (although not all) did not combine EPA with Title VII. It should be noted, however, that the liquidated damages option in Sec.16(b) was not available until 1974, and it is not clear how the DOL and the EEOC would have or could have combined in an EPA + Title VII suit prior to President Carter's Reorganization Plan. Also, it is difficult to assess how frequently the DOL advised plaintiffs to use Sec.16(b) and how frequently they were advised to file additional EEOC Title VII charges. These are reasonable conjectures because some of the best examples of how to combine EPA and Title VII properly occurred during the DOL era.

To its credit, the DOL tested each of the four components of substantial equality, as well as each of the four statutory defenses. Furthermore, the DOL reaped large class-action awards. These cases did not pay out large back pay awards on a per-head basis (maybe about $600 to $700 per victim), but given the sizes of some of the classes (often 1,000 to 1,500), the payouts were in the million dollar range; certainly enough to induce other companies to comply with the statute.

There was only one Supreme Court ruling on a pure EPA case (*Corning v. Brennan*, 1974) during this era, but it served to cement prior rulings and pave the way for all future rulings. For purposes of exposition, the DOL effort will be segmented into four categories: early lower court rulings, subsequent critical lower court rulings prior to Corning, the

Corning ruling itself, and cases initiated by the DOL but completed by the EEOC.

EARLY LOWER COURT RULINGS

Three early circuit court rulings established critical EPA precedents; *Shultz v. Wheaton Glass* (1970), *Shultz v. First Victoria National Bank* (1969), and *Hodgson v. Brookhaven General Hospital* (1970). Two of these cases (Wheaton and First Victoria) illustrate classic historical patterns of discrimination; the third case (Brookhaven) was a signal of more subtle things to come.

Shultz v. Wheaton Glass Company (1970)

Wheaton had a history of employing only male "selector-packers." In 1956, the company hired female selector-packers because of a shortage of males. Fearing a permanent threat to males, the union added two provisions to its collective bargaining agreement: (a) females were prohibited from lifting cartons weighing in excess of 35 pounds; and (b) they could not replace male selector-packers except for retirement, vacancy, resignation, or dismissal for cause. Obviously, neither provision was facially neutral. However, there was nothing to prohibit facial discrimination in 1956.

The EPA charge was that male selector-packers were paid 10% more per hour than female selector-packers for equal work. The rebuttals were: (a) prohibited activity (heavy lifting) constituted extra effort because it was 18% of the male's job; and (b) males had to show "flexibility" by occasionally filling another job ("snap-up boy"). The district court rejected the charges at the prima facie level.

The 3rd Circuit disagreed, ruling that flexibility was irrelevant because snap-up boys were paid about the same wages as female selector-packers. The court also noted that females were not permitted to show their flexibility. However, the court did not challenge facial discrimination (i.e., why females were not permitted to show their flexibility). The ultimate ruling hinged on extra effort (i.e., heavy lifting). According to the court:

> Differences in job classifications were in general expected to be beyond the coverage of the Equal Pay Act. This was because in the case of genuine job classifications the differences in work necessarily would be *substantial*

and the differences in compensation therefore would be based on the differences in work which justified them. Congress never intended, however, that an *artificially created job classification* which did not *substantially* differ from the genuine one could provide an escape for an employer from the operation of the Equal Pay Act. This would be too wide a door through which the content of the Act would disappear. [emphasis added]

In other words, two jobs, though not identical, can be "substantially equal" in skill, effort, responsibility, and working conditions, and non-substantial differences in work requirements should not be "artificially" hidden by job classifications. Every court since Wheaton has adopted the "substantially equal" standard for equal work.

Shultz v. First Victoria National Bank (1969)

In *Shultz v. First Victoria* (1969), the 5th Circuit recognized what was essentially a scam. A bank used as a pretext a DOL regulation exempting "bona fide training programs" as a legitimate factor other than sex. According to the regulation (Sec.800.148):

> Employees employed under a bona fide training program may, in the furtherance of their training, be assigned from time to time to various types of work in the establishment. At such times, the employee in training status may be performing equal work with non-trainees of the opposite sex whose wages or wage rates may be unequal to those of the trainees. Under these circumstances, provided the rate paid to the employee in training status is paid regardless of sex, under the training program, the differential can be shown to be attributable to a factor other than sex.

Thus John, a trainee, can be paid more than Mary, a non-trainee, for equal work—as long as John and Jane (another trainee) are paid equally. It does not say, however, that John, Mary, and Jane have the same right to be trained.

The facts in First Victoria were that the bank paid its male and female tellers disparate wages. The bank answered with FOS; that males were enrolled in "executive training programs." But the training programs were fictitious. There were no written plans, no rotational sequences, no formal instruction, and no systematic scheme for advancement. In fact, the "trained" employees did not know they were "trainees." Thus the 5th Circuit defined these training programs as nothing more than a "post-event justification."

Hodgson v. Brookhaven General Hospital (1970)

Wheaton and First Victoria were easy verdicts. Both were crude vestiges of the bygone era. On the other hand, subtle variations of the Brookhaven theme are still playing in hospitals and other businesses throughout the country.

In Brookhaven, male "orderlies" were paid more than female "nurse's aides." The hospital used three rebuttals: (a) orderlies did "extra work" (e.g., lifting heavy patients, moving TV sets, etc.); (b) one task performed mainly by orderlies required extra skill (catheterizations); and (c) because of patient preferences, orderlies performed "private" duties for male patients assigned to nurse's aides.

The 5th Circuit did not decide the preference issue, but concluded instead that the extra "private" duties were insubstantial. The Court ruled likewise on the extra skill issue, treating it much like "snap-up" work was treated by the Wheaton Court. But on the issue of extra lifting, the Court applied a "three-pronged test":

> Jobs do not entail equal effort, even though they entail most of the same routine duties, if the more highly paid job involves additional tasks which require (a) extra effort, (b) consume a significant amount of time, and (c) are of an economic value commensurate with the pay differential.

The 5th Circuit used this test in a subsequent case (*Hodgson v. Behrens Drug*, 1973), where its ruling was conclusive, and ended the case. In Brookhaven, however, the 5th Circuit remanded and instructed the district court to do the pronging (this will be discussed later in the chapter).

CRITICAL LOWER COURT FOLLOW-UPS

These germinal rulings were a precursor to many subsequent rulings, including the Supreme Court's ruling in *Corning v. Brennan* (1974). But between Brookhaven and Corning, there was a flurry of activity related to the earlier scenarios, particularly First Victoria and Brookhaven.

After First Victoria

There were other scam training cases similar to First Victoria. For example, the 8th Circuit struck down a bank training program in *Hodgson v. Security National Bank of Sioux City* (1972), and the 4th Circuit struck down a sales training program in *Hodgson v. Fairmount*

Supply (1972). But the most important case in this series was *Hodgson v. Behrens Drug Company* (1973)–where training actually occurred.

In Behrens Drug, the 5th Circuit, which had ruled in First Victoria, evaluated a training program that had no women trainees. The company, pleading FOS, asserted: (a) their program was designed with "good faith and without fraud"; (b) invalidation of such a program would serve to "discriminate against small companies"; and (c) trainees performed "extra work." The 5th Circuit struck down each defense. Thus the Court struck down the "good faith" assertion, stating:

> A bona fide training program to constitute a valid exception to the Equal Pay Act must represent more than an honest effort; such a program must have substance and significance independent of the trainee's regular job.

Of course, the "good faith" argument is viable, but only to determine whether a guilty defendant committed a willful act.

The Court rejected outright the assertion regarding discrimination against small companies. In the words of the Court:

> all "training programs" which exclude females, whether originated by large companies or small, carry a stigma of suspect validity.

Finally, the Court struck down the "extra work" argument based on the three-pronged test it had previously used in *Hodgson v. Brookhaven General Hospital* (1970).

After Brookhaven

When we left *Hodgson v. Brookhaven,* the 5th Circuit had used its three-prong test as a basis for remand. On remand, the district court favored the female "nurse aides." The hospital appealed, and the 5th Circuit affirmed the remand ruling in Brookhaven #2. In this second appeal, the 5th Circuit used the standard rationale for affirmation– the lower court's findings were deemed "not clearly erroneous."

Normally, remands are not that critical–the lower courts usually get the message or the parties settle. But in Brookhaven #1, the 5th Circuit provided no message. According to one source (Babcock et al., 1975), the Court had sufficient evidence for a decisive ruling. Certainly, the three-pronged test resulted in a decisive ruling in the Behrens Drug case. But by remanding indecisively in Brookhaven, the 5th Circuit set itself up for an embarrassment.

Specifically, in a case nearly identical in substance to Brookhaven (*Hodgson v. Golden Isles Convalescent Homes,* 1972), a district court ruling favoring the hospital was also upheld by the 5th Circuit because the findings were deemed not clearly erroneous. This ruling occurred one month before Brookhaven #2. There is no clear-cut reason why the ultimate rulings in Brookhaven and Golden Isles should have been different. As in Brookhaven, the Golden Isles issue was male orderlies versus female aides. And once again, the males did the heavy lifting and most of the catheterizations. In other words, in these two cases, the 5th Circuit ended up affirming opposite conclusions—not on the merits of the cases, which were similar, but because neither of these opposite conclusions were clearly erroneous.

Other Critical Cases

The aforementioned cases illustrate the essence of the DOL era. The DOL attacked arbitrary job classifications as FOS pretexts for wage discrimination. There were other important cases prior to the Supreme Court's ruling in Corning.

In *Hodgson v. Daisy Manufacturing Co.* (1971), the 8th Circuit cut through a pretext case in which male jobs did, in fact, require extra effort. Males performing "heavy" duty tasks exerted greater physical effort than females performing "light" duty tasks. However, the 8th Circuit accepted the counter assertion that the light duty tasks required greater mental effort.

In *Hodgson v. Miller Brewing Co.* (1972), the 5th Circuit ruled on physical segregation within the "establishment"; that is, males working in one place and females working in another. The Court ruled that female technicians in one lab performed the same work as male technicians in another lab. In *Brennan v. City Department Stores* (1973), the 5th Circuit rendered a similar ruling for a male "tailor" and female "seamstress" working in different clothing departments.

In *Brennan v. J. M. Fields* (1973), the 5th Circuit upped the ante in its Miller Brewing and City Department precedents. Finding wage discrimination in 3 of 66 stores in Fields's chain of stores, the court upheld an injunction against all of the stores.

And in *Hodgson v. Pet* (1974), the DOL won a case that had the traditional trappings of illegal segregation. Here, however, male "bartenders" working the day shift made substantially less money than female "barmaids" working the night shift.

CORNING GLASS WORKS V. BRENNAN (1974)

The Supreme Court established at least one precedent in Corning (for working conditions). However, its greater function was to affirm major lower court rulings, and establish the validity of congressional intention behind the EPA.

Until the mid-1920s, all of Corning's inspectors were female and each worked daytime shifts. The company then created a night shift. However, state protective laws in both New York and Pennsylvania prevented females from working at night. Males applying for night work demanded and received higher wages than the all-female day crews. The wage difference was codified when the plant was unionized in 1944. After EPA was enacted, the union agreed to fair and unrestricted application for the higher paid night work (in 1966). In 1969, the wage difference for day versus night work was abolished. However, the incumbent male employees kept higher wages, although all new male and female workers received equal but lower wages (a so-called red circle effect).

It should be noted that red circling is legal when not a pretext for discrimination. For example, an employee no longer capable of higher level work may be transferred to lower level work at the higher level salary (e.g., *Salazar v. Marathon Oil,* 1980). In effect, the employee is credited with seniority, regardless of sex.

Returning to Corning, the EPA charge was for female victims of wage disparity prior to the 1966 and 1969 union agreements. Separate suits were filed in New York and Pennsylvania. The Supreme Court reviewed the case because the two suits resulted in opposite rulings. The New York District Court and the 2nd Circuit found for the plaintiffs, and the Pennsylvania District Court and the 3rd Circuit found for the defendants. The Supreme Court upheld the 2nd Circuit.

The company rebutted the prima facie attack, asserting that the night shift had different working conditions. The Court disagreed, ruling that the "surroundings" and "hazards" were no different across shifts (a precedent). The burden was therefore on the company to use one of the four statutory defenses. It chose FOS, asserting that night work justifies higher wages. The Court rejected the defense. In the words of Justice Marshall, speaking for a 5-3 majority:

> The question remains whether . . . the higher rate paid for night inspection . . . was in fact intended to serve as compensation for night work, or rather constituted an additional payment based on sex. We agree

that the record amply supports the District Court's conclusion that Corning had not sustained its burden of proof.

The Court also ruled that the 1966 and 1969 agreements failed to correct EPA violations. The 1966 agreement left many prior victims and the 1969 agreement imposed the wrong solution. Wage discrimination, as codified in EPA, can only be corrected by raising the lower wage.

Ironically, Corning was defeated in part by its own contribution to the legislative history of EPA in 1963. Justice Marshall cited testimony by a Corning representative urging Congress to expand beyond skill in defining equal work. Accordingly:

> Job evaluation is an accepted and tested method of attaining equity in wage relationship. A great part of the industry is committed to job evaluation by past practice and by contractual agreement as the basis for wage administration. "Skill" alone as a criterion, fails to recognize the other aspects of the job situation that affect job *worth*. We sincerely hope that this committee in passing legislation to eliminate wage differences based on sex alone, will recognize in its language the general role of job evaluations in establishing an equitable rate relationship. [emphasis added]

This quote would elicit approval from many professionals in the field. Indeed, industrial psychologists have used this logic to justify not only equal pay for "substantially equal work," but also comparable pay for comparable worth. The counterargument, as we will witness later, is that market conditions should determine worth.

TRANSITION CASES

After the Corning ruling, DOL cases continued to expand on the issues of segregation and classification. For example, in *Brennan v. Goose Creek Independent School District* (1975), the statutory concept of "establishment" was expanded beyond the single physical "plant." The 5th Circuit deemed that all district schools were "one establishment" because of frequent interschool transfers by employees. Secretary Marshall (Secretary Brennan's successor) extended Goose Creek in two subsequent cases (*Marshall v. Building Maintenance Corp.* 1978, & *Marshall v. Dallas Independent School District,* 1979). However, it was during the Marshall's tenure that control passed from the DOL to the EEOC.

The initial task of the EEOC was to complete a number of circuit court appeals initiated by the DOL at the district court level. Four of these cases are particularly noteworthy, including *EEOC v. Aetna* (1980), *EEOC v. Universal Underwriters* (1981), *EEOC v. Liggett & Myers* (1982), and *EEOC v. Kansas Medical Center* (1983).

EEOC v. Aetna (1980)

EEOC v. Aetna, or the saga of "Barratt, Garrett, and Archer," set a precedent for **bona fide merit systems**, one of the four statutory defenses. Aetna used two merit systems, one for already employed (or internal) underwriters, and one for incoming (or external) underwriters. Garrett, a male, was hired at a higher salary than Barratt (the female plaintiff). Barratt and Garrett performed the same job. Barratt had received significant raises based on merit. But when Garrett was fired for poor performance and Barratt learned of Garrett's salary, she complained. Due mainly to conciliatory efforts by the DOL, this claim was settled in Barratt's favor—out of court.

Enter Archer—Garrett's replacement. Upon entry, Archer received a substantially higher salary than Barratt (and Garrett). Barratt again complained, but Aetna stood its ground. According to Aetna, Barratt was brought to Garrett's salary level based on an internal merit system. But Archer received a higher entering salary because of an external merit system (based on information gleaned from application data and subjective interviews). The 4th Circuit agreed with Aetna. On the pay differential between Barratt and Archer, the Court ruled:

> sex bias was not the cause of the pay differential, the explanation being rather that Archer was measured by one sex-blind standard applicable to new hires, while Barratt was measured by another sex-blind standard applicable to existing employees.

EEOC v. Universal (1981)

EEOC v. Universal illustrates a legitimate **bona fide training program**. During a period of rapid expansion to the point of industry leadership, Universal created a "fast track" training program. Thus the company had two promotional tracks (the other being the traditional "slow" track). Virtually all slow trackers were female, and virtually all fast trackers were male. The EPA charge was that during fast-track training, the two tracks provided disparate wages for substantially equal work. The 8th Circuit ruled in favor of the company because it was able to demonstrate that the fast track required additional skill, effort, and responsibility.

EEOC v. Liggett & Myers (1982)

In *EEOC v. Liggett,* males and females had the same job title, namely "production supervisor." The case was prosecuted on behalf of three female supervisors who were disparately paid. Liggett did not dispute the claim, but instead asserted that all supervisor salaries were determined by a uniform sex-blind procedure. Specifically, a constant amount was added to the salary of every new supervisor at the point of promotion. But the 4th Circuit found for the plaintiffs because the company could not explain the prepromotion disparities.

This case is important for another reason. It was the first ruling in which a circuit court resolved actual dollar figures in a back pay dispute. As noted by the Court, in all prior cases:

> Either the defendant prevailed . . . so that there was no . . . back pay award . . . or neither party challenged the exact amount.

EEOC v. Central Kansas Medical (1983)

Finally, *EEOC v. Central Kansas Medical* is a throwback to Wheaton Glass and Brookhaven Hospital. The medical center segregated females versus males performing substantially equal work into different shifts. The males were paid more. They were called "janitors" and worked the night shift, and the females were called "housekeepers" and worked the day shift. Prior to 1974, there was no choice-of-shift option. The 10th Circuit found for the plaintiffs.

—————— BRIEF SUMMARY ——————

The DOL can be credited for its focus on pretextual classification schemes to cover up jobs substantially equal in skill, effort, responsibility, and working conditions. Thus cases like Wheaton addressed skill, effort, and responsibility, and cases like Corning addressed working conditions. Each defense was tested, but none more than the elusive "factor other than sex" (FOS). Furthermore, the DOL did not completely eschew the Sec.16(c) suit for liquidated damages (e.g., *Hodgson v. Miller*). However, as we will witness shortly, DOL cases did not extract the full amount by current standards.

SECTION III
The Combination of EPA and Title VII

Technically, EPA can combine with Sec.1983, the Age Act, and the disability laws. However, except for side effects (e.g., a jury hearing an age case may influence a judge's ruling on EPA liquidated damages), these statutes present independent remedies. But with Title VII there is interdependence. The following discussion addresses the source of interdependence, the potential awards that could have been reaped in past cases, and examples of awards that have been reaped in successful EPA + Title VII cases.

THE SOURCE OF INTERDEPENDENCE

Obviously, EPA and Title VII both cover sex-based wage discrimination. Furthermore, this dual coverage was envisioned by Congress in the Bennett Amendment. The Bennett Amendment (1964) was not a prophecy; Congress could not foresee in 1964 that in 1975 the Supreme Court would create a disparate treatment scenario with lighter judicial burdens than EPA. All Congress wanted to do was ensure that all sex-based wage discrimination cases used the EPA burdens, regardless of how the charge was made. All courts have accepted this premise.

The DOL, and then later the EEOC, accepted this premise also. In 1986 the revised EEOC EPA Regulations codified two important principles. First, Sec.1627(a) of the Regulations states:

> In situations where the jurisdictional prerequisites of both the EPA and Title VII . . . are satisfied, any violation of the Equal Pay Act is also a violation of Title VII. However, Title VII covers types of wage discrimination not actionable under the EPA. Therefore, an act or practice of an employer or labor organization that is not a violation of the EPA may nevertheless be a violation of Title VII.

In other words a winning claim in EPA also wins in Title VII, as long as the entity is covered by both statutes. Obviously, because Title VII is more extensive than EPA, the reverse is not true.

Second, Sec.1627(b) of the Regulations practically begs plaintiffs to use Title VII for injunctions and EPA for other remedies. Accordingly:

> Recovery for the same period of time may be had under both the EPA and Title VII so long as the same individual does not receive duplicative

relief for the same wrong. Relief is computed to give each individual the highest benefit which entitlement under either statute would provide (e.g., liquidated damages may be available under the EPA but not under Title VII). Relief may be computed under one statute for one or more periods of the violation and under the other statute for other periods of the violation.

These other remedies are back pay awards and liquidated damages.

UNCLAIMED REMEDIES

The list of cases where plaintiffs could have reaped more than they asked for is exhaustive; particularly those cases where wage discrimination coexisted with non-EPA Title VII violations. Therefore the following sample of cases is selective.

Thus in *EEOC v. Universal* (1981), one of the aforementioned DOL cases inherited by the EEOC, Universal proved it had a bona fide training program. However, the company was never burdened to explain why most men received "fast" training and most women received "slow" training. Indeed, as stated by the 8th Circuit:

> We note that the EEOC brought this action under the Equal Pay Act, not under Title VII. . . . Thus, we do not decide whether UUIC discriminated on the basis of sex under the *provisions of Title VII.* [emphasis added]

Similarly, the 5th Circuit was cognizant of Title VII violations in both Brookhaven and Golden Isles (i.e., male "orderlies" vs. female "nurse's aides"). In Golden Isles, the Court stated:

> We do not here decide whether the job of orderly should be open to females, or whether the job of nurse's aide should be open to males. Those questions are to be resolved in actions under Title VII. . . . Courts must be cautious not to apply improperly one Congressional act to achieve a purpose for which another was intended. *We here decline, nevertheless, to sanction the concept that only males can perform the work of an orderly.* [emphasis added]

The reader should not conclude that unclaimed remedies are a unique feature of the DOL era. For example, in *Waters v. Turner Insurance* (1989), the company employed both "inside" and "outside" sales agents. Female insiders were paid less than male outsiders. Waters issued a pure EPA claim that cited: (a) less pay for substantially equal work; and (b) barriers barring women from the higher paying jobs. The wage discrimination charge was defeated on its merits. But on the second charge the 11th Circuit stated:

> She asserts that an employer should not be able to avoid Equal Pay Act liability by prohibiting qualified females from performing duties that males perform. This very argument establishes that Waters' claim is essentially one that is based on sex discrimination under Title VII [emphasis added]

Finally, there are even recent examples of pure Title VII wage discrimination claims. Thus in *Gibbs v. Pierce County* (1986), female "records supervisors" received 27% less in wages than males previously holding the same job, and males currently working as "records specialists" (a substantially equal job). The plaintiffs won back pay and injunction. But given the facts of the case, the plaintiffs possibly could have also prevailed on EPA liquidated damages.

EXAMPLES OF CLAIMED REMEDIES

Once again, the list of applicable cases is exhaustive and the sampling must be selective. For illustration purposes, therefore, two of the cases are older and a third case is of more recent vintage.

Thompson v. Sawyer (1982)

Thompson v. Sawyer was an 8-year ordeal because of the death of the original trial judge. The judge had rendered some but not all of the required rulings. The replacement judge ordered a retrial, and the motions and rulings preceding and following retrial prolonged the case. Ultimately, the case was appealed to the D.C. Circuit Court.

Sawyer focused on discrimination in a federal agency, the GPO (Government Printing Office). In 1974, all 279 "bookbinders" were males and all 325 "bindery" workers were females. Bookbinding was classified as a "craft" worthy of higher wages than "bindery" work. There were four different grades of bindery jobs; each using different equipment. The EPA charge was that all bindery jobs were substantially equal to bookbinding. The Title VII charges were pattern of discrimination and illegal classification.

The critical issue in the EPA charge was a DOL regulation regarding work on different machines (Sec.800.128). Accordingly:

> Performance of jobs on different machines or equipment would not necessarily result in a determination that the work so performed is unequal within the meaning of the statute if the equal pay provisions otherwise apply.

The D.C. Circuit affirmed the district court's ruling that only the grade-4 bindery job (the highest female classification) was equal to bookbinding. This ruling was based on job evaluation data comparing the grade-4 and bookbinding machines. The EPA award for the grade-4 bindery workers was 3 years of back pay and liquidated damages.

The lower court ruled in favor of all bindery grades on the pattern charge, but not on the classification charge. The D.C. Circuit overruled, favoring all grades on both charges. The classification issue was critical, as it formed the basis for a more substantial charge; exclusion from training for promotional purposes. All bindery workers received 2-year Title VII back pay awards, **including** the grade-4 workers who had won the EPA awards. Explaining the additional award for the grade-4 workers, the D.C. Circuit stated:

> Although the Smyth operators will receive back pay under the Equal Pay Act, this additional [Title VII] back pay award did not give them duplicate recovery. The wrong of denying them promotions was separate from the the wrong of paying them inadequately for their work as Smyth operators, and they are entitled to compensation for both.

All bindery workers also benefited from an injunction ordered at the lower court level, and affirmed (though slightly modified) by the D.C. Circuit. Normally, if employees are denied promotion the selection decision is reversed; if possible. However, in view of the large number of bindery workers who were potentially excluded, the Court, to ensure compliance, ordered front pay for all of them for as much time as needed for promotion of half of them (i.e., many years).

Of course, the GPO exhausted a number of defenses, one of which is particularly revealing. In the words of the D.C. Circuit:

> In this appeal, the GPO contends that traditional industry patterns of classification and training are a differential based on a factor other than sex, and hence a defense to the Equal Pay Act charge.

In other words, the GPO pleaded helplessness to the fact-of-life historical injustice to women in the trade (by unions and others), and used this plea as an FOS. The Court's response was:

> the "traditions" of paying women less than men, or of assigning different labeling to female and male jobs, no matter how hoary, are not defenses to the Equal Pay Act. To hold otherwise would protect the most egregious forms of discrimination, merely because, like Faulkner's Dilsey, they have endured.

Laffey v. Northwest Airlines, Inc. (1984)

The original charges in *Laffey v. Northwest Airlines* were lodged in 1970. The 1984 case was the third (and final) appeal heard by the D.C. Circuit. The second and third appeals were followed by denials of certiorari by the Supreme Court. Also, in a totally separate suit (*Northwest Airlines v. Transport Workers*, 1981), the airline tried to displace its remedial duties onto the Transport Workers Union, a ploy struck down by the Supreme Court. The airline had a lot to lose and never gave up.

The facts of the case were that male "pursers" and female "stewardesses" performed equal work for unequal pay, and unequal benefits as well (e.g., males received laundry money and better sleeping accommodations). Both were EPA and Title VII violations resulting in back pay, liquidated damages, and attorney fees. Furthermore, because events prior to 1970 were deemed illegal and causal with respect to the plaintiffs' lower salaries after 1970, wage differences from as early as 1965 were figured into the back pay calculations.

Additional Title VII violations for facial discrimination were remedied with injunctive relief. The illegal practices included such things as granting males higher ranking regardless of seniority, or permitting males but not females to wear eyeglasses.

In the 14-year history of the case, the airline used defenses based on four different landmark Supreme Court rulings: (a) a BFSS defense for pattern of discrimination (Teamsters, 1977); (b) a "comparable worth" claim that one of two substantially equal jobs is less valuable to the company (*County of Washington v. Gunther*, 1981); (c) justification of extra benefits based upon pregnancy rulings (*General Electric v. Gilbert*, 1976–after Gilbert was struck down); and finally, (d) heavy penalties would destroy the airline much as returned benefits would destroy a pension system (*LA v. Manhart*, 1978).

In a last-gasp effort to save liquidated damages, the airline argued that willfulness required "evil" intent. The D.C. Circuit rendered its own precedent on willfulness, affirming the validity of "good faith" and "reasonable grounds," and asserting that:

> "Good faith" must be established affirmatively . . . it is not enough that it appear that the employer probably did not act in bad faith.

Of course, the D.C. Circuit's willfulness precedent was subsequently superseded by the reckless disregard standard in *Trans World Airlines v. Thurston* (1985). The airline, however, had clearly shown its reckless disregard for the law on several occasions over a 14-year period.

McKee v. Bi-State Development Agency (1986)

McKee v. Bi-State Development Agency was begun and concluded in the modern era. It is one of the more unusual cases in the literature. It was also a pure wage discrimination case using EPA + Title VII. The unusual feature was that at the district court level, a jury decided the EPA charges and favored McKee, but a judge decided the Title VII charges and favored Bi-State. The jury used EPA burdens, but the judge used McDonnell-Burdine. The judge allowed the EPA back pay and associated lawyer fees. But McKee did not receive EPA liquidated damages, injunction, and lawyer fees for the Title VII portion of the case.

The 8th Circuit reversed. Based on its review of prior interpretations of the Bennett Amendment, and seeking "harmony" between EPA and Title VII, the court ruled that:

> The district court's finding that Bi-State acted in good faith cannot be reconciled with the jury verdict of discrimination due to sex. . . . We conclude that these findings of the district court are clearly erroneous.

Equating an EPA victory with a Title VII victory, the court granted McKee her Title VII injunction, lost Title VII lawyer fees, and EPA liquidated damages.

A POSTSCRIPT TO EPA + TITLE VII

In general, the EPA-Title VII combination will obviously work for strong wage discrimination charges, and for strong non-EPA-Title VII charges packaged with strong EPA charges. However, weaker charges present caveats, particularly for ill-advised plaintiffs.

This is illustrated by what could have happened to McKee. McKee permitted her claim to be bifurcated, thus separating the consequences for lawyer fees contingent upon winning both parts of the case. Ultimately, she won both parts (i.e., the jury's EPA ruling was upheld and the judge's Title VII ruling was overruled). However, a substantial portion of her back pay award would have been canceled by lawyer fees had the 8th Circuit not overruled.

The plaintiffs in *EEOC v. Madison School District* (1987) were not so lucky. The EEOC litigated a pure EPA charge under Section 16(c), and two plaintiffs were allowed to intervene with individual Title VII charges. The case featured an EPA violation; female coaches of female teams were paid less than male coaches of male teams. The jobs were deemed substantially equal by the district court, and the plaintiffs won a back pay award but not liquidated damages. The court also ruled for the plaintiffs on one of two separate Title VII charges.

Prior to the appeal, the school district and the plaintiffs settled on an injunctive remedy for the Title VII case won by the plaintiffs. However, the EEOC appealed the EPA ruling (to capture liquidated damages), and the plaintiffs appealed the other Title VII charge (hoping to capture compensatory and punitive damages, which were not permitted in Title VII at the time). The EEOC won its appeal, but the plaintiffs lost theirs—and more. The plaintiffs were charged with all but a small portion of the lawyer fees. The 7th Circuit ruled that the EPA victory was paid for by government funds and that there was no Title VII victory to justify Title VII costs. The only Title VII victory had occurred at the district court level, and that issue had been settled previously by conciliation.

Clearly, the lower court had mistakenly permitted the plaintiffs to intervene on an EEOC-sponsored EPA suit, and the plaintiffs mistakenly believed they had nothing to lose.

——— **BRIEF SUMMARY** ———

The issues speak for themselves. The primary intention of the Bennett Amendment was to ensure that EPA burdens were used in Title VII cases, an interpretation recently codified in the EEOC EPA Regulations. Many of the DOL cases cited in Section II, therefore, could have addressed issues beyond EPA and could have reaped additional remedies even within EPA. Certainly this is illustrated by the Sawyer, Laffey, and McKee rulings. However, also indicated in McKee as well as in Madison, is that plaintiffs need good legal advice to ensure they do not jeopardize what is otherwise, a good deal.

SECTION IV
RESIDUAL EPA ISSUES

The Bennett Amendment is strong as it relates to the combination of EPA + Title VII in wage discrimination per se. But there some residual issues. One of these is the aforementioned standard of willfulness for liquidated damages. A second issue concerns secondary or fringe considerations.

LIQUIDATED DAMAGES IN EPA CASES

Liquidated damages is one of the oldest principles in FLSA. Historically, a victory in a wage and overtime FLSA case usually carried additional damages as a punishment for the crime. However, the easy standard from FLSA has been superseded in both the EPA and the Age Act (which also has FLSA connections). As noted in the overview in Section I, there have been three standards, ranging from light, to moderate, to heavy.

Coleman v. Jiffy June (1971): The Light Standard

In Jiffy June, an employer, following the advice of his lawyer, miscomputed overtime wages for his employees (he actually changed their rate of pay). The facts of the case are not that important. What is important is that 5th Circuit defined a violation as willful when:

> there is substantial evidence . . . to support a finding that the employer knew or suspected that his actions might violate the FLSA. Stated most simply, we think the test should be: Did the employer know the FLSA was *in the picture*? [emphasis added]

Consistent with FLSA traditions, this standard is difficult to defend, because willfulness is implied by merely knowing that a statute applies to a violated covered practice (i.e., is "in the picture").

Laffey v. Northwest (1976): The Moderate Standard

The Laffey case has already been reviewed in detail, enough so as to recognize that the airline was guilty of willful violations regardless of the standard used. Prior to Laffey, however, courts had routinely applied the Jiffy June standard. The Laffey Court was the first to apply a stronger standard. More specifically, the employer could argue:

> that his failure to comply was in good faith and also was predicated on reasonable grounds for a belief that he was in compliance.

Thus an employer could establish reasonable grounds even if it was known that EPA was "in the picture." The Laffey standard is practically a verbatim application of a DOL regulation (acting "without a reasonable basis for believing he was complying with the statute").

TWA v. Thurston (1985): The Heavy Standard

Thurston was a BFOQ age case lost by Trans World Airlines. The facts of the case will be reserved for the next chapter. In determining the standard for willfulness, the Supreme Court rejected the Jiffy June standard. Extracting language from criminal rather than civil cases, Justice Powell, speaking for a unanimous Court, adopted language used by the 8th Circuit in the lower court ruling, stating:

> a violation is "willful" [if] the employer either knew or showed a reckless disregard for the matter of whether its conduct was prohibited by the ADEA.

Thus if the employer knows an action is a violation and commits it anyway, or does not know but shows what can best be described as deliberate "indifference" to the requirements of a statute (a term extracted by Powell from prior criminal cases), the act is willful.

The Thurston case did not directly cite EPA and did not cite the Laffey standard. However, in a subsequent pure FLSA case (*McLaughlin v. Richland Shoe Company,* 1988), the Supreme Court addressed and directly refuted the Laffey standard. Speaking for a majority of six, Justice Stevens, citing Laffey, stated:

> This proposal differs from Jiffy June because it would apparently make the issue in most cases turn on whether the employer sought legal advice concerning its pay practices. It would, however, permit a finding of willfulness to be based on nothing more than *negligence,* or perhaps, on a completely good-faith but incorrect assumption that a pay plan complied with the FLSA in all respects. [emphasis added]

In other words, "reckless disregard" is more than "negligence," as is deliberate "indifference" (Powell's term from Thurston). As important, if there was any doubt that the Thurston ruling applies to EPA, it was eliminated even in the dissent. The dissenting justices (Marshall, Brennan, and Blackmun) were only concerned with application of the Thurston standard to pure FLSA cases, not ADEA nor EPA.

A Postscript

In the author's mind it is not clear that circuit courts have fully integrated the meaning ascribed by Powell and Stevens. The 7th Circuit applied Thurston in an EPA case between Thurston and Richland (*Peters v. City of Shreveport*, 1987). However, in *McKee v. Bi-State* (1986), which was post-Thurston, the 8th Circuit applied the Laffey standard. Obviously, the 8th Circuit felt that reckless disregard applies only to ADEA; it was the 8th Circuit that the Supreme Court paraphrased in establishing the Thurston precedent. Moreover, after Richland, the 9th Circuit applied Laffey in *EEOC v. White & Son* (1989). However, the facts of this case (wage discrimination topped by retaliatory discharge) would easily justify reckless disregard.

The language in both Thurston (1985) and Richland (1988) could not be clearer. It is an either-or standard: either the employer knowingly commits a violation, or acts deliberately and indifferently to a statute. The fact that this standard applies to EPA was relatively clear in Thurston and absolutely clear in Richland. Indeed, it is also clear in the Civil Rights Act of 1991, meaning that Thurston probably is approved by both the Supreme Court and Congress as the standard for all punitive damages (of which liquidated damages are an example).

FRINGE ISSUES

Although a violation of the EPA is clearly a violation of Title VII by Bennett Amendment standards, there are two scenarios that call the amendment into question: (a) the implications of a Title VII disparate treatment victory for determining willfulness in EPA; and (b) mixed-motive.

Intentional Discrimination Versus Willfulness

This issue can be dispensed with quickly. By Jiffy June standards, a combined EPA + Title VII victory implied willfulness in EPA if Title

VII disparate treatment was proven for a non-EPA violation. Indeed, this may have been why the 9th Circuit was loose with its Laffey language in *EEOC v. White* (1989), because the Laffey standard for willfulness and the McDonnell-Burdine standard for intent are comparable. But the McDonnell-Burdine standard does not equate to the Thurston standard, a point that was obvious in the 7th Circuit ruling in *Peters v. City of Shreveport* (1987).

An example will suffice. If an employer illegally segregates and classifies workers (clearly a Title VII disparate treatment violation), the wage discrimination impact of that segregation must still be separated and subject to reckless disregard scrutiny. The employer could have been aware of the illegal segregation/classification without recognizing its adverse impact on wage discrimination.

Mixed-Motive Scenarios

By the EPA definition of wage disparity, adverse impact is usually irrelevant; wage disparity is clearly disparate treatment. However, as just noted, other factors can effect wage disparity (i.e., segregation and classification). These other factors are usually illegal (as in the above example). But when they are legal, they create a mixed-motive scenario. The 7th Circuit has evaluated two such cases.

In the previously cited *Peters v. Shreveport* (1987) case, the fundamental issue was the validity of an original DOL regulation. Specifically, Sec.800.142 stated:

> The exception of factor other than sex under the Equal Pay Act is met if, and only if, sex provides *no part* of the basis for the wage differential. [emphasis added]

Taken literally, an FOS is voided if sex is *in part* responsible for wage discrimination. The Title VII standard, both pre- and post-1991, is of course that sex must be the *determining* (or but for) cause. The 7th Circuit affirmed the Title VII standard as an FOS defense.

The facts were that most females were "police communication officers" (PCOs) and most males were "fire communication officers" (FCOs). These jobs were substantially equal, but FCOs were paid more because of a state law mandating that FCOs receive 25% more pay than firemen (a legal motive). In other words, a state law adversely impacted female wages. However, in addition there was also independent evidence of sex discrimination (the illegal motive).

The district court favored the defendants on the Title VII charges because the legal motive was deemed the "but for" factor for the higher FCO wage. However, the court did not accept the state law as a legitimate FOS, ruling that sex discrimination was *in part* responsible for the lower PCO wages. On appeal, the 7th Circuit requested an amicus brief from the EEOC explaining why Sec.800.142 was omitted in the 1986 EPA Regulations. The EEOC in effect pleaded oversight, and supported the original DOL regulation. However, the 7th Circuit rejected both the original regulation and the EEOC brief in favor of the Title VII *but for* standard. According to the court:

> A fundamental precept of our system of justice is that it is unfair to impose liability for a result which would in any event have occurred absent the defendant's wrongdoing; in other words, the defendant's wrongful conduct must be a "but for" cause of the complained of result.

Subsequently, in *Fallon v. State of Illinois* (1989), male VSOs (Veteran Service Officers) were paid more than female VSOAs (Veteran Service Officer Associates) for substantially equal work because an Illinois statute demanded wartime experience for the VSO position (i.e., adverse impact by the law on VSOA wages). The district court favored the plaintiffs on the EPA charge, ruling that the law does not set lower limits for VSOAs. In addition, the court, relying on the previously cited EEOC EPA Regulations (i.e., an EPA violation equals a Title VII violation), favored the plaintiffs.

The 7th Circuit overruled, finding that the Illinois law was facially neutral and sex-blind. In other words, the state law was a legitimate FOS despite its adverse impact. The Court also made it clear that neither the Bennett Amendment nor the EEOC regulations could be stretched to issues beyond pure wage discrimination.

─── BRIEF SUMMARY ───

The history of the willfulness standard reveals that it was mild throughout the early days of FLSA and the early days of the EPA. A moderate standard was established by the D.C. Circuit in Laffey, but a heavier standard was established by the Supreme Court in Thurston. The heavier standard (knowledge of violation or reckless disregard) was later affirmed in Richland, where it was generalized to all FLSA cases. A direct effect of tightening the willfulness standard in EPA was to sever any automatic connection between intentional discrimination by McDonnell-Burdine standards and willful discrimination in EPA. Further countering the automatic EPA/Title VII connection is that wage discrimination that results from legal adverse impact follows the "but for" standard in Title VII mixed-motive cases.

SECTION V
COMPARABLE WORTH

Most sources estimate that females earn between 60 and 70 cents on the dollar relative to males. This wage difference is only partially explained by unequal pay as a function of illegal segregation and classification. Irrespective of causes, females are crowded into poorer paying jobs (e.g., teaching, nursing, clerical, etc.). Proponents of comparable worth believe that (a) so-called female jobs are worth more than prevailing market rates; and that (b) many of these jobs pay less only because they are crowded by females.

Comparable worth was a viable concept during World War II and in early versions of the 1962 EPA bills. Of course, the final Act made it clear that EPA covers only equal work. However, in 1981 the Supreme Court opened the door to Title VII comparable worth claims in *County of Washington (in Oregon) v. Gunther.* Since Gunther, many such cases have been tried in the lower courts—with negative results.

BACKGROUND CONSIDERATIONS

"Equal work" is a simple dichotomy; two jobs are substantially equal or substantially unequal. "Comparable worth," on the other hand, represents a continuum of *value* to the company. The real issue is not equal pay for comparable work (as implied in the aborted 1962 version of the EPA bill), but rather, comparable pay for comparable work.

To illustrate, imagine a standard job (i.e., any job in the company) assigned an arbitrary value of 100, and a standard wage. According to comparable worth theory, any other job valued at 100 should yield the standard wage. Furthermore, a job valued at 75 should yield 25% less than the standard wage; a job valued at 125 should yield 25% more than the standard wage; and so on. Thus equal pay does not begin to capture the continuum of possibilities in comparable worth.

According to Mahoney (1983), comparable worth may be viewed from three perspectives; social philosophy, administrative practice, and economics. Social philosophy, as the name would suggest, is a general principle by which we compare people. However, administrative practice and economics generally reduce to internal versus external worth. Both concepts are illustrated in *American Federation of State, County, and Municipal Employees (AFSCME) v. State of Washington* (1985).

To determine internal worth, the state used a job evaluation procedure in which point values were assigned to jobs based on skill (280 points), mental effort (140), accountability (160), and working conditions (20). To determine external worth, the state surveyed other employers to learn the prevailing market rates for various jobs. The state found that jobs with 70% or more females were underpaid relative to their internal worth, whereas jobs with 70% or more males were not. However, the state also found that these "female" jobs were paid at about the going market rate. The state ignored the internal data and based its wages on the external data.

In general, comparable worth proponents are not satisfied with either standard. They claim that internal worth determinations are biased because males do the point counting, and external worth determinations are biased because they merely reflect discriminatory practices responsible for the wage gap.

COMPARABLE WORTH CASE LAW

Comparable worth may be conceptualized as the adverse impact of past societal injustice, much like state laws impact wages for similar jobs (e.g., Peters, 1987; *Fallon v. State of Illinois,* 1988). In other words, comparable worth follows from mixed-motive themes. Ironically, the comparable worth argument has been used (unsuccessfully) for the reverse purpose. Recall that in *Laffey v. Northwest,* it was argued that females were paid less because their jobs were worth less to the airline. Similar arguments had been made in other cases (e.g., *Gibbs v. Pierce County,* 1986). Nevertheless, the true issue in comparable worth is whether Title VII can support a charge of wage discrimination based on past discrimination in society and by employers.

Pre-Gunther

At least two noteworthy decisions pre-date the Supreme Court's ruling in Gunther; *Molthan v. Temple University* (1977) and *Lemons v. Denver* (1980). In Molthan, a Pennsylvania district court ruled against female faculty physicians on EPA charges and simply transferred its EPA ruling to Title VII, stating:

> Implicit in my decision . . . is the conclusion that the differentiation which
> Molthan complains was "authorized" . . . by the Equal Pay Act. It follows
> that the complained-of differentiation cannot be an unlawful employ-
> ment practice under Title VII.

Lemons, however, involved no EPA issues. The City surveyed the community for wages in "key classes" of employees. Nurses in two of these classes ("Graduate" and "Practical") objected. Based upon their self-perceived worth (they were paid less than gardeners), the nurses sued in order to receive a higher classification ("General Administrative"). The 10th Circuit rejected the claim, stating:

> The equal pay for "comparable work" concept had been rejected by
> Congress in favor of "equal work" in 1962. The Bennett Amendment
> is generally considered to have the equal pay/equal work concept apply
> to Title VII in the same way as it applies in the Equal Pay Act.

In other words, the Lemons Court stated what the Molthan Court only implied—that the Bennett Amendment limits Title VII wage cases to discrimination based on EPA principles.

County of Washington v. Gunther (1981)

In Gunther, the County closed a female prison. Four discharged female guards claimed: (a) they had been disparately paid under EPA; and (b) part of the pay differential was discriminatory under Title VII. The district court found for the county on EPA, but disallowed the Title VII claim for reasons cited by the Lemons Court. The 9th Circuit affirmed on EPA, but ruled that the plaintiffs were entitled to sue under Title VII. In the Supreme Court ruling, Justice Brennan, speaking for Blackmun, Marshall, Stevens, and White, stated that the only issue was whether the Bennett Amendment:

> restricts Title VII's prohibition of sex-based wage discrimination to
> claims of equal pay for equal work.

In short, Gunther only decided whether the Bennett Amendment limits Title VII wage cases to equal pay for equal work. And, with the support of an amicus brief from the EEOC, the Court permitted comparable worth claims. In supporting his ruling, Justice Brennan stated:

if an employer used a transparently sex-biased system for wage determination, women holding jobs not equal to those held by men would be denied the right to prove that the system is pretext for discrimination.

In dissent, Justice Rehnquist, speaking for Burger, Powell, and Stewart, cited the 1962 congressional debates alluded to earlier in the chapter. Pointing in particular to the St. George Amendment, Rehnquist concluded that "Congress clearly rejected the entire notion of 'comparable worth.'"

Post-Gunther Cases

The Gunther ruling did not validate comparable worth; it only provided the *opportunity* for a prima facie Title VII attack. And, thus far, plaintiffs have not made it past the prima facie phase. The most notable rulings have been by the 9th Circuit—the same court that rendered the ruling ultimately affirmed by the Supreme Court in Gunther.

In *Spaulding v. University of Washington* (1984), nursing faculty filed Sec.1983, EPA, and Title VII charges against the university. The Sec.1983 charges were denied on grounds of immunity (there were no individual capacity charges), and the EPA charges were denied because evidence of intradepartmental male versus female discrepancies were lacking, and the interdepartmental jobs were deemed unequal. The 9th Circuit was therefore left with a pure Title VII comparable worth case.

The court, citing the need for additional evidence from which to infer "animus," ruled that the mere existence of incomparable worth statistics was insufficient for prima facie disparate treatment. The court also rejected prima facie adverse impact resulting from facially neutral "market prices," because this factor did not represent a "specific employment practice."

Recall that in the *AFSCME v. Washington* (1985) case cited earlier, the state based salaries on external market surveys despite internal evidence of inequity. The district court accepted the adverse impact argument rejected in Spaulding (neutral market forces), and ordered back pay and injunction. This created much excitement among comparable worth proponents. However, the 9th Circuit overruled, and also rejected a disparate treatment charge, stating:

While the Washington legislature may have the discretion to enact a comparable worth plan if it chooses to do so, Title VII does not obligate it to eliminate an economic inequity it did not create.

The critical point is that simply knowing about inequity does not equate to intentional discrimination.

Similar rulings have been rendered by other circuits. Thus in *American Nurses v. Illinois* (1986), a case similar to AFSCME, the 7th Circuit rejected a Sec.1983 appeal, ruling that it required the same level of proof as in Title VII disparate treatment. The Court affirmed that knowledge does not equal intent in Title VII disparate treatment, and also, rejected an adverse impact argument based on market forces.

And in *International Union v. Michigan* (1989), the plaintiffs refrained from using the term *comparable worth* but the 6th Circuit recognized it as such nevertheless. The state conducted an internal job evaluation study combining the key position principle in Lemons with the point principle in AFSCME. The state, as in AFSCME, opted for market forces, and the 6th Circuit echoed the rulings of the 9th and 7th Circuits in the aforementioned cases.

There is one exception to the flow of comparable worth cases. In *Bartlett v. Berlitz* (1983), two female language instructors successfully used Title VII to circumvent the **establishment** rule in EPA. Having many establishments, Berlitz escaped EPA liability for paying directors unequal wages in different establishments (for equal work). The 9th Circuit, which rejected two of the comparable worth claims cited above, accepted that Title VII can apply to this situation where EPA cannot. Nevertheless, the victory was small; the Berlitz theme, after all, is not comparable worth.

BRIEF SUMMARY

It seems relatively clear that Gunther was a false signal to comparable worth proponents, opening a door that only provided a legal basis for closure. A comparable worth adverse impact claim is negated, because the only viable culprit (market forces) is not viewed as a specific employment practice. And although disparate treatment theory is still viable, the plaintiff must directly prove that but for the fact that the underpaid jobs are crowded by females, market forces would not dictate wages. This seems difficult if not impossible because the agencies in such cases (usually state or local) establish "good faith" (and spend much money) by commissioning comparable worth studies to begin with.

SECTION VI
Usefulness of and Compliance With the Equal Pay Act

EPA is not as well known relative to Title VII and the other EEO statutes. But its value exceeds its limited purpose; to remedy sex-based wage discrimination. The causes of sex-based wage discrimination are historically important and currently relevant. The statute is still useful for its limited purpose, and EPA cases emphasize the importance of yet another issue of compliance; job evaluation.

CONTINUED USEFULNESS OF EPA

Because its partner, Title VII, now has stronger remedies, the EPA + Title VII combination is less attractive for pure sex-based wage discrimination. The full compliment of remedies (injunction, back pay, damages, and lawyer fees) is now available within a single Title VII suit. Thus for a pure EPA case, the only remaining advantage concerns small businesses with less than 15 employees.

On the other hand, cases such as *Thompson v. Sawyer* (1982) suggest that a sex-based wage charge using EPA plus a nonwage Title VII violation could net the post-1991 legal remedies and the traditional EPA liquidated damages. Clearly, EPA and Title VII are still independent remedies. Therefore it may be possible to exceed the damage limits in the Civil Rights Act of 1991.

Therefore, because few valid EPA claims carry only wage discrimination implications, EPA maintains its usefulness for most purposes and, if anything, the EPA + Title VII combination may be enhanced by the new remedies available in Title VII.

COMPLIANCE

The relationship between job evaluation and comparable worth is discussed in Treiman and Hartmann (1981). The legal advice in this report is outdated. Clearly, comparable worth has suffered the same fate as the perpetuation of pre-Title VII discrimination by bona fide seniority systems. Thus as in Teamsters (1977), where a BFSS legally perpetuated pre-Title VII classification in city versus distance driving, the failure to establish prima facie discrimination based on comparable worth data permits continued impact of the historical classification of lower paying "female" jobs versus higher paying "male" jobs. However, this does not negatively implicate **job evaluation** per se.

Job evaluation data can uncover unknown sources of segregation and classification within a company. More specifically, if internal and external inequity coexist, it is difficult to explain why a job crowded by females pays less money than the going market rate, whereas a job crowded by males does not. Certainly, it would be better for the employer to ask this question before the EEOC does.

Furthermore, although an employer may base wages on any nondiscriminatory factor deemed valuable to the company, it makes sense to have a structured pay system. The gist of the comparable worth argument is that females are unsatisfied making less money for what they perceive as a more valuable contribution to the company. Within jobs rated equal by external standards, and for males and females alike, it would follow that any individual would be unsatisfied with less than a fair wage, particularly if another individual is making a higher wage for a less valued contribution.

In the final analysis it is difficult to argue against market forces, as long as these forces are not conspiratory. Certainly, the courts have deemed that external equity outweighs internal equity, unless males and females are receiving differential wages for substantially equal work. It is easy, however, to argue against internal equity procedures controlled by white male point counters. The common sense solution is to represent all classes of people in the job evaluation process.

It also makes sense to study crowding. Some instances of crowding are legitimate. For example, some women are second wage earners, and as such, are likely to take a lower paying job that has good family medical coverage. But it would be discriminatory for human resources managers to base selection decisions on the assumption that all or most women are second wage earners.

─────── **CHAPTER SUMMARY** ───────

EPA protects **(Q1)** sex-based wage disparity **(Q3)** for substantially equal work for most of the same entities **(Q2)** as Title VII, plus smaller businesses with less than 15 employees. The EEOC administers **(Q4)** the Act for selective remedies **(Q5)**, and the attacks and defenses **(Q6)** are persuasive. The full compliment of remedies (injunction, back pay, liquidated damages, and lawyer fees) requires EPA + Title VII charges. The continued value of the combination case is questionable in pure EPA situations given the expanded remedies in Title VII. The combination remains viable, however, and is perhaps enhanced when EPA violations are combined with non-EPA Title VII violations. The acceptable meaning of the Bennett Amendment is that sex-based wage discrimination requires the same attack (proof of inequality based on skill, effort, responsibility, and working conditions) and defense (seniority, merit, quantity/quality of work, and FOS) regardless of whether the claimant uses EPA and/or Title VII. However, the courts have refused to accept a "comparable worth" extension of the Bennett Amendment via Title VII. Basically, market forces are not considered a job practice and therefore cannot support an adverse impact argument. Market forces can, however, serve as a legitimate productive defense to disparate treatment charges. Nevertheless, job evaluation, the stimulus to comparable worth cases, remains a viable practice for companies to detect unknown patterns of discrimination, and to structure equitable pay systems.

NOTE

1. It is grammatical to say "the Equal Pay Act," and therefore "the EPA." However, it is common to speak of simply "EPA" when the acronym is used, much like one speaks of "Title VII" rather than "the Title VII."

Age Discrimination in Employment Act

CHART 6.1. ADEA

Q1	Q2	Q3	Q4	Q5	Q6
Age minimum = 40; no maximum; not a dichotomy

Exemptions for tenure/age 70; BFEs/age 65; police & fire; policymakers; apprentices | Private, state, local, & federal as in Title VII

20 employees 25 in unions | Terms, conditions, & privileges

Segregation & classification

Retaliation

Emphasis on benefits and waiver of rights | EEOC controls for 60 days

Thereafter, direct access

Must be filed with EEOC by day 300 | Injunction

Back pay

Lawyer fees

Reinstatement (or front pay)

Liquidated damages for private and state/local plaintiffs | Disparate treatment

Adverse impact

Pattern/practice

Good cause, RFOA, BFBP, BFSS, & BFOQ

Juries for private & state/local plaintiffs |

(Q1): What classes of people are protected (or have rights)?
(Q2): What business entities are covered (or have duties)?
(Q3): What employment practices are covered?
(Q4): Is the law administered, and if so, how?
(Q5): What are the penalties (or remedies) for breaking the law?
(Q6): What are the attacks and defenses used in litigation?

The Age Discrimination in Employment Act (ADEA) is depicted in Chart 6.1. Technically, ADEA[1] is a 1967 amendment to the Fair Labor Standards Act (FLSA). However, ADEA is better viewed as a self-sufficient

194

statute with strong outside influences. ADEA has one unique dimension; its **protected class (Q1)** (age 40 and over). Otherwise, Title VII dominates three of the five remaining dimensions and combines with FLSA to influence the other two dimensions.

The dimensions dominated by Title VII include the **covered entities (Q2), covered practices (Q3)**, and **attack/defense balances (Q6)**. The covered entities mimic Title VII, but with slightly larger employee numbers. The covered practices include the Title VII trilogy (terms, conditions, and privileges; segregation and classification; and retaliation), but with added emphasis on age-specific privileges such as retirement benefits. And the attack/defense balances include adverse impact disparate treatment, and statutory defenses from Title VII, but also statutory defenses unique to ADEA (bona fide benefit plan, good cause, and reasonable factors other than age).

The **administrative procedures (Q4)** and **remedies (Q5)** are more hybrid in nature. The administrative procedures contain both FLSA and Title VII filing principles, but there are age-specific provisions to speed up ADEA claims. And the remedies borrow from both FLSA (e.g., liquidated damages) and Title VII (e.g., affirmative relief in the form of reinstatement or front pay), but juries can rule on both back pay and liquidated damages, and the filing procedures and remedies are not connected to each other as they are in FLSA.

This chapter contains seven Sections. Section I briefly overviews the evolution of the ADEA statute, and the remaining Sections focus on the protected class (Section II), covered entities and covered practices (Section III), administrative procedures and remedies (Section IV), attacks/defense balances from Title VII case law (Section V), the five statutory defenses (Section VI), and compliance (Section VII).

SECTION I
EVOLUTION OF THE ADEA STATUTE

Congress debated age discrimination issues in the early 1950s, but no action was taken until 1964. During the Title VII debates serious consideration was given to including age as a Title VII protected class. However, there was disagreement regarding whether Title VII or FLSA should provide the statutory model. Therefore Congress directed the Secretary of Labor to study age discrimination for the purpose of creating an independent statute.

THE SECRETARY'S STUDY

There were two other reasons why Congress deferred on age in 1964. First, unlike racial discrimination, which was perceived as intentional, age discrimination was perceived as a coincidental by-product of false beliefs and stereotypes. Second, congressional leaders wanted factual information on the impact of age discrimination on older workers and on the economy. The Secretary of Labor's findings are reflected in Sec.2 of the original Act, which provides the following four motives for the statute:

1. in the face of rising productivity and affluence, older workers find themselves disadvantaged in their efforts to retain employment, and especially regain employment when displaced from jobs;
2. the setting of arbitrary age limits regardless of potential for job performance has become a common practice, and certain otherwise desirable practices may work to the disadvantage of older persons;
3. the incidence of unemployment, especially long-term unemployment with resultant deterioration of skill, morale, and employer acceptability, is, relative to the younger ages, high among older workers; their numbers are great and growing; and their employment problems grave;
4. the existence in industries affecting commerce of arbitrary discrimination in employment because of age, burden commerce and the free flow of goods in commerce.

AMENDMENTS TO ADEA

Since 1967 several age-related crises have emerged. As a result there have been several amendments. The broadest amendments were written in 1974 and 1990. In 1974, Congress, motivated by a parallel amendment to Title VII (in the EEO Act of 1972), extended coverage of ADEA (and EPA) to state/local and federal entities. In 1990 Congress wrote the "Older Workers Benefit Protection Act" to reverse the effects of a Supreme Court ruling on benefits and to provide special coverage for the waiver of ADEA rights and privileges.

Amendments written in 1978, 1984, and 1987 were more surgical. Thus the ceiling age was raised in 1978 from 65 to 70, and eliminated entirely in 1987. The 1978 and 1987 amendments also created and/or extended exemptions for tenured faculty and high-level employees. Other notable amendments extended ADEA coverage to overseas subsidiaries of American companies, and exempted from ADEA protection high-level state and local officials.

In addition, the Reorganization Plan of 1978 transferred administrative control of ADEA from the Department of Labor (DOL) and Civil Service to the EEOC. And in 1986 ADEA incorporated core features of the Employee Retirement Income Security Act (ERISA) as well as amendments to the Internal Revenue Code. Among other things, these latter amendments guaranteed contributions to pension plans for employees working past age 65.

The most recent amendment to ADEA was written in the Civil Rights Act of 1991. Previously, Title VII and ADEA claimants had only 30 days to exercise a right-to-sue notice from the EEOC. The Civil Rights Act of 1991 raised that limit to 90 days for both statutes.

——— BRIEF SUMMARY ———

ADEA can be described as a self-sufficient statute built on issues uniquely related to age discrimination, plus principles borrowed from Title VII and FLSA. The issues investigated by the Secretary of Labor formed the basis for the statute, but ADEA has continued to evolve. The initial delay in enacting ADEA was probably beneficial to older workers. In 1967, Congress borrowed many strong features from Title VII and FLSA, while excluding many Title VII and FLSA restrictions. As a result, ADEA has more administrative options and remedies than FLSA or the pre-1991 version of Title VII. Had Congress incorporated age as a protected Title VII class, or as a protected class in FLSA, older workers might have experienced years of judicial and congressional fidgeting, much like women experienced during the early years of Title VII.

SECTION II
THE PROTECTED CLASS (Q1)

ADEA has a floor age of 40 and no ceiling age. But this is merely a starting point. Age is not a dichotomous class, and there are five major exemptions to the provisions of ADEA.

DEFINITION OF THE CLASS

ADEA cannot be evaded by arbitrarily replacing older protected employees (say 65 years of age) with much younger protected employees (say 40 to 50 years of age). Furthermore, replacement of younger employees with older employees is also challengeable. Both points are captured by the 1st Circuit in *Loeb v. Textron, Inc.* (1979). On point #1, the Loeb Court focused on the critical issue in age discrimination, **age difference**. Accordingly:

> In an age case, the probative value of evidence as to the age of complainant's replacement obviously will depend on complainant's own age and the age *difference*. Replacement of a 60 year old by a 35 year old or even a 45 year old within the protected class would be more suggestive of discrimination than replacement of a 45 year old by a 42 year old within the protected class or by a 39 year old outside it. [emphasis added]

On point #2 the Loeb Court focused on the possibility of hiring or promoting the older worker as a **pretext**. Accordingly:

> Replacement by someone older would suggest no age discrimination but would not disprove it conclusively. The older replacement could have been hired, for example, to ward off a threatened discrimination suit.

Both points from Loeb are codified in Sec.1625.2 of the 1981 EEOC ADEA Regulations. Accordingly:

> It is unlawful . . . for an employer to discriminate in hiring or in any other way giving preference because of age between individuals within the [covered age range]. Thus, if two people apply for the same position, and one is 42 and the other 52, the employer may not lawfully turn down either one on the basis of age, but must make such decision on the basis of some other factor.

In other words, except for exemptions and statutory defenses, age cannot be the factor responsible for excluding a protected employee, regardless of whether the employee is replaced, and regardless of the age of the replacement.

THE FIVE EXEMPTIONS

The five exemptions include: (a) forced retirement of tenured faculty at age 70; (b) forced retirement of bona fide executives at age 65; (c) state and local laws specifying mandatory hiring and retirement ages for firefighters and law enforcement officers; (d) exceptions to the definition of the term *employee*; and (e) exclusion of older workers from apprentice trainee programs. Clearly, these exemptions permit facial discrimination where otherwise a statutory BFOQ defense would be required.

Tenured Faculty in Higher Education (Sec.12(d))

Sec.12(d) permits colleges and universities to involuntarily discharge tenured faculty. For those unfamiliar with tenure systems, tenured faculty are traditionally blessed with lifetime employment unless it can be proven: (a) they are incompetent, (b) they display moral turpitude, or (c) the institution is failing financially. Sec.12(d) mitigates this guarantee by permitting forced retirement of a faculty member at 70 if he or she:

> is serving under a contract of unlimited tenure (or a similar arrangement providing for unlimited tenure) at an institution of higher education.

Sec.12(d) is a 1987 update of a 1978 amendment. It should be noted that the exemption was created and modified in concert with the National Academy of Sciences, the American Council of Education, the Association of American Universities, and the National Association of State Universities and Land Grant Colleges. In other words, it was not an invasion of academia by the federal government.

Bona Fide Executives (Sec.12(e))

Sec.12(c) is broader than Sec.12(d), permitting involuntary retirement at age 65 if:

> for the 2-year period immediately before retirement, [he or she] is employed in a bona fide executive or a *high policymaking* position, if such employee is entitled to an immediate nonforfeitable annual retirement benefit from pension . . . [of] at least $44,000. [emphasis added]

The key is "high policymaking position." According to Sec.1625.12(e) of the EEOC regulations, high policymakers include:

> individuals who have little or no line authority but whose position and responsibility are such that they play a significant role in the develop-

ment of corporate policy and effectively recommend the implementation thereof.

For example, the 6th Circuit ruled that a college president was a bona fide executive even though he described himself as a "mere administrator with some measure of discretionary power" (*EEOC v. Board of Trustees of Wayne Community College,* 1983). On the other hand, the 2nd Circuit ruled that a chief labor counsel was not a bona fide executive despite his "high salary and title" (*Whittlesey v. Union Carbide,* 1984).

More recently, the Washington, D.C., district court ruled that a defendant must factually prove that a plaintiff is a bona fide executive in order to claim the exemption (*Passer v. American Chemical Society,* 1990). According to the Passer Court:

> the burden is on the defendant to show that a particular employee falls within the exemption. Thus, plaintiff not need assert in his complaint that he was not a bona fide executive.

This ruling, however, did not help Passer, the head of an education division, as the defendant succeeded in carrying that burden.

Firefighters and Law Enforcement Officers (Sec.4(i))

Sec.4(i) contains a 1987 exemption allowing states and municipalities to legislate hiring and discharge ages in two major areas of public safety; firefighting and law enforcement. Accordingly:

> It shall not be unlawful for an employer which is a State, political subdivision of a state, or . . . if such action is taken—(1) with respect to the employment of an individual as a firefighter or as a law enforcement officer [if] the individual has attained the age . . . in effect under applicable state or local law on March 3, 1983. and (2) pursuant to a bona fide hiring or retirement plan that is not a subterfuge to evade the purposes of the Act.

The Sec.4(i) exemption corrected a disparity between federal and state/local safety personnel. For example, in *Johnson v. Baltimore* (1985), a city law mandated involuntary retirement for firefighters at age 55; clearly, a facially discriminatory law. The city of Baltimore asserted that since federal firefighters and law officers can be legally retired at age 55, Congress had established age 55 as a BFOQ. But in a unanimous ruling, favoring firefighters Justice Marshall noted that the federal cutoff age was not related to occupational factors. Instead, Congress chose age 55 only to "maintain the image of a 'young man's service.' "

Exemptions to the Term *Employee* (Sec.11(f))

Sec.11(f) is a 1984 amendment that excludes four types of *persons* from the definition of *employee,* including:

> [1] any person elected to public office in any State or political subdivision . . . [2] any person chosen by such officer to be on such officer's personal staff . . . [3] an appointee on the *policy-making level* . . . [4] an immediate advisor with respect to the exercise of the Constitutional or legal powers of the office. [numbering and emphasis added]

Most claims have been by appointed state judges, who have disputed whether they are at "policy-making level." The issue emerged rather quickly and was resolved rather quickly.

Thus the 1st Circuit (*EEOC v. Massachusetts,* 1988) and 8th Circuit (*Gregory v. Ashcroft,* 1990) supported state laws requiring appointed judges to retire at age 70, but the 2nd Circuit (*EEOC v. Vermont,* 1990) was "unpersuaded" by 1st and 8th Circuit rulings. In the Massachusetts case, the 1st circuit concluded that:

> Policymaking is indisputably a part of the function of judging. . . . Moreover, the substantive interest identified by the phrase on the "policy-making level" is closely aligned with "exercise of discretion" and "exercise of judgment."

But in the Vermont case, the 2nd Circuit ruled that: (a) Congress had not explicitly exempted judges from the definition of *employee;* (b) ADEA mandates that all older employees be evaluated on "merit"; and (c) the State of Vermont was using an appeals process in which the law can be overridden based upon individual merit.

The Supreme Court resolved the issue in favor of state laws in *Gregory v. Ashcroft* (1991). Speaking for a majority of seven on most of the substantive issues, Justice O'Connor ruled that a state has a rational basis for defining appointed judges as being at the policy-making level. The two oldest justices (Blackmun and Marshall) dissented from this part of the ruling.

Apprenticeship

Finally, apprenticeship training is a **regulatory** exemption based on a DOL regulation (Sec.860.106) adopted by the EEOC (Sec.1625.13). Sec.1625.13 is based on Sec.9 in ADEA, which permits the EEOC to establish "reasonable exemptions." The regulation states:

> Age limitations for apprenticeship . . . were not intended to be affected by the Act. Entry . . . has traditionally been limited to youths under specified ages. This is in recognition . . . that apprenticeship is an extension of the educational process to prepare young men and women for skilled employment. Accordingly, the . . . Act will not be applied to bona fide apprenticeship programs.

The apprenticeship issue was litigated twice—by the same New York district court (*Quinn v. N.Y. State Gas & Electric,* 1983 & 1985).

Quinn #1 struck down Sec.1625.13, and the EEOC offered to rescind the regulation. But in Quinn #2, Quinn #1 was reversed because the employer had demonstrated **good faith** in the regulation. The employer also modified the training policy after Quinn #1, thereby eliminating the need for an injunction. Although the court did not rule directly on whether the regulation is lawful, it did *not* grant attorney fees to the plaintiff because "he [was] not a prevailing party." Since Quinn #2, several EEOC news releases have been issued in support of Sec.1625.13, including a release in 1987 by the then EEOC Director, Clarence Thomas. Therefore, it would appear that the Sec.1625.13 exemption is lawful.

-------- **BRIEF SUMMARY** --------

At first blush, an age category (**Q1**) is established (from 40 to infinity) that has an either/or property. However, as the Loeb decision suggests, except for exemption or statutory defense, age may not be the reason for exclusion regardless of who serves as the replacement. Among the four *statutory* exemptions, the exemption for tenured faculty seems airtight, as does the exemption for state/local laws that create hiring and retiring ages for firefighters and police officers. In addition, the lower courts have clarified what constitutes a "bona fide executive," and the Supreme Court has made it clear that appointed judges are at the policy-making level. The exemption for apprentice trainees is *regulatory,* but appears strong enough to have withstood judicial scrutiny.

SECTION III
COVERED ENTITIES (Q2) AND COVERED PRACTICES (Q3)

Much of the statutory language for the covered entities and covered practices is taken verbatim from Title VII. The FLSA makes no contribution to these dimensions. However, there are critical age-related influences.

COVERED ENTITIES (Q2)

In 1967 ADEA covered only private employers with 25 or more employees based on the **Commerce** Clause of the Constitution (the same basis as Title VII). The 1974 amendments extended coverage to the federal and state/local entities and at the same time reduced the employee number for private and state/local entities from 25 to 20. ADEA also covers employment agencies and unions with 25 or more members, and overseas subsidiaries of American companies.

Like Title VII, ADEA covers federal entities in a separate section of the statute (Sec.15). Thus what is not written in Sec.15 of ADEA does not apply to federal employers. For example, the five exemptions for protected class coverage apply only to private and state/local employers. And as we will witness in Section IV of this chapter, Sec.15 provides weaker remedies for federal employees than Sec.7 does for private or state/local employees.

On balance, entity-related litigation has not been substantial. Aside from an unsuccessful 11th Amendment challenge to the application of ADEA to state entities (*EEOC v. Wyoming*, 1983), the more intriguing cases have involved overseas subsidiaries of American companies and application of the 20-employee rule to state entities.

Overseas Subsidiaries of American Companies

This is one area where ADEA has led Title VII. Recall from Chapter 2 that in *EEOC v. Aramco* (1991), the Supreme Court did not extend Title VII coverage to overseas subsidiaries, a ruling reversed by Congress in the Civil Rights Act of 1991. For Congress, it was a return trip. In *Cleary v. U.S. Lines* (1984), the 3rd Circuit upheld a discharge of an older European operative. The Court demanded "more affirmative evidence of congressional intent," which Congress provided in 1984. This 1984 amendment was subsequently upheld by the D.C. Circuit in *Ralis v. Radio Free Europe* (1985).

The motive for overseas coverage is transparent; to prevent companies from assigning older workers to places beyond the reach of ADEA. For example, in *Goodman v. Heublein* (1981), an older employee was transferred overseas because of his objections to not receiving a stateside promotion.

The 20-Employee Rule for State/Local Entities

This issue reflects a minor difference in how ADEA and Title VII define terms and phrases. The definitions of *person, employer, employment agency,* and so forth are contained in Sec.11 in ADEA. With exceptions for unique age-related terms (e.g., *firefighters*), Sec.11 borrows heavily from Title VII. The most important definitions for present purposes are for "person" and "employer." In ADEA, private "person(s)" are defined as in Title VII. Accordingly:

> The term "person" means one or more individuals, partnerships, associations, labor organizations, corporations, business trusts, legal representatives, or any organized groups of persons.

However, where Title VII defines state/local entities as "person(s)," ADEA defines them as "employer(s)." Accordingly, Sec.11(b) of ADEA defines its "employer(s)" as follows:

> [A] The term employer means a person engaged in an industry affecting commerce who has *twenty or more employees* . . . The term also means (1) any agent of such person, and . . . [B] (2) a State or political subdivision of a state and any agency or instrumentality of a state or a political subdivision of a state, and any interstate agency. [emphasis and lettering added]

Segment [A] is excerpted from the Sec.701(b) Title VII definition of *employer*. Segment [B] reflects the 1974 extension of ADEA coverage to state and local entities. Clearly, private and state/local entities are covered, as they are in Title VII.

Interestingly, in *Kelly v. Wauconda Park District* (1986), Kelly tried to use the [A] versus [B] distinction to his advantage. He was a grounds keeper in a small park district with an all-voluntary, unpaid commission, and less than 20 paid employees. The district court dismissed Kelly's charge of discriminatory discharge because of the 20-employee rule. On appeal, Kelly asserted that:

by setting state and political subdivisions in a separate sentence, Congress unambiguously indicated that government employers were a separate category of employees not subject to the twenty-employee minimum.

The EEOC supported Kelly in an amicus brief stating that FLSA "provides a better parallel for interpreting ADEA" than Title VII. However, the 7th Circuit disagreed, ruling that:

> the legislative histories of both the ADEA and Title VII amendments indicate that Congress' main purpose in amending the statutes was to put public and private employers on the same footing.

EMPLOYMENT PRACTICES (Q3)

Sections 4(a)(1), 4(a)(2), and 4(a)(3) in ADEA use Title VII language from Sections 703(a)(1), 703(a)(2), and 704(a) to cover: (a) terms, conditions, or privileges; (b) segregation and classification; and (c) retaliation, respectively. ADEA also borrows the EPA clause for wage discrimination. However, ADEA uses age-specific language for health benefits and, more importantly, separation benefits.

Three critical separation issues were addressed in Titles I and II of the "Older Workers Benefit Protection Act" (OWBPA), a broad 1990 amendment to ADEA. They include: (a) bona fide benefit plans; (b) early retirement; and (c) voluntary waivers. The main purpose of Title I was to reverse the Supreme Court's ruling in *Public Employees Retirement System of Ohio v. Betts* (1989). The Betts ruling implicated both bona fide benefit plans and early retirement. Title II added structure to voluntary waivers, an issue closely related to benefit plans and early retirement.

Bona Fide Benefit Plans (BFBPs)

The facts of the Betts case were that the state of Ohio had established a benefit plan in pre-ADEA times (1933). But the plan was altered in 1976 so that disabled employees under 60 could elect disability benefits, whereas those over 60 were forced to accept age-and-service retirement benefits; clearly, a facially discriminatory policy. The policy hurt Betts who, as a disabled employee over age 60, was forced to accept retirement benefits worth only $158.50 per month. Had she been under 60, she would have received disability payments worth

$355 per month. The lower court ruled that the 1976 alteration of the plan was a "subterfuge to evade the purposes of [ADEA]." This ruling was based on an EEOC regulation (Sec.1625.10) stating:

> benefit levels for older workers may be reduced to the extent necessary to achieve approximate equivalency in cost for older and younger workers.

Had the regulation been valid, Betts would have won because there was no differential cost for the higher paying benefit. But the Supreme Court invalidated Sec.1625.10, and deemed the Ohio plan bona fide even though the it was altered after the effective date of ADEA (i.e., *post*-ADEA).

Previously, the Supreme Court had addressed "subterfuge" in *pre*-ADEA benefit plans (*United Air Lines v. McMann,* 1977). At that time, Sec.4(f)(2) of ADEA made it legal to discriminate based on age:

> To observe . . . a bona fide seniority system or a bona fide benefit plan . . . which is not a *subterfuge* to evade the purposes of this Act, except that no such benefit plan shall excuse the failure to hire any individual, *and no such seniority system or employee benefit plan shall require or permit the involuntary retirement of any individual . . . because of the age of such individual.* [emphasis added]

The initial segment (including the term *subterfuge*) represents the pre-McMann definition of the bona fide seniority system (BFSS) and bona fide benefit plan (BFBP). That is, a system or plan is bona fide as long it is not a "subterfuge(s)" to evade ADEA.

McMann had charged "subterfuge" because the airline's pre-ADEA benefit plan was tied to mandatory retirement at age 60. The Supreme Court ruled there can be no subterfuge in a plan that pre-dates ADEA. The lengthier emphasized portion above represents a 1978 congressional amendment that was designed to reverse the McMann ruling.

In Betts, however, the Supreme Court focused on the term *subterfuge*, which Congress did not remove from Sec.4(f)(2) in the 1978 amendments. Regarding the EEOC regulation cited earlier, Justice Kennedy, speaking for six others, stated that it was "contrary to the plain language of [ADEA]." Regarding McMann, Kennedy felt that the court's 1977 definition of "subterfuge" still applied. The McMann Court had ruled that subterfuge is an employer motive a plaintiff must prove. The EEOC regulation had put that burden on the defendant to prove differential cost. Therefore, the Betts ruling reduced to a burden on the plaintiff to provide factual evidence of "subterfuge," regardless of whether a plan was written pre or post ADEA.

Justice Marshall, speaking for Brennan, dissented, stating that the majority ruling:

> immunizes virtually all employee benefit programs from liability under [ADEA]. . . . Henceforth, liability will not attach under the ADEA even if an employer is unable to put forth any justification for denying older worker the benefits younger ones receive.

The bottom line is that Congress supported the lower Betts Court, and its interpretation of the EEOC regulation. Thus Title I of the OWBPA adds a new term to the definitions in Sec.11(f). Accordingly:

> The term "compensation, terms, conditions, or privileges of employment" encompasses all employee benefits, including such benefits pursuant to a bona fide employee benefit plan.

Addressing the Betts ruling directly, Congress rewrote major portions of Sec.4(f)(2) eliminating the term *subterfuge*. Accordingly, it is still permissible to discriminate in benefits based on age:

> To observe . . . a bona fide seniority system that is not intended to evade the purposes of this chapter except that no seniority system require or permit the involuntary retirement of any individual.

Congress also codified the Sec.1625.10 of the EEOC Regulations in Sec.4(f)(2) as follows:

> (i) where, for each benefit or benefit package, the actual amount of payment made or cost incurred on behalf of an older worker is not less than that made or incurred on behalf of a younger worker, as permissible under *section 1625* . . . or (ii) that is a voluntary *early retirement* incentive plan consistent with the relevant purposes of this Act. [emphasis added]

Thus it is now clear that age-based discrimination in benefit plans (or seniority systems) requires factual evidence of actuarial cost differences for older versus younger employees.

Early Retirement

Early retirement became a featured issue when, during RIFs (reductions in force), several companies provided severance pay for employees under age 55, and early retirement in lieu of severance pay for eligible workers over age 55 (e.g., *EEOC v. Westinghouse*, 1983; *EEOC v. Bordens* (1984). Bordens, for example, argued that the early retirees received a more valuable benefit than severance. But the 9th Circuit ruled that the plaintiffs were entitled to severance and early retirement and were therefore losing a benefit. The Bordens and Westinghouse policies are illegal under pre- or post-Betts rules.

But in a subsequent Westinghouse RIF (in a different state), the company gave all their employees a choice between retirement benefits versus severance pay (*EEOC v. Westinghouse*, 1990, usually referenced as "Westinghouse II"). Most older employees had more to lose by choosing severance pay, and thus chose retirement. The 3rd Circuit deemed the policy a "subterfuge," but the Supreme Court vacated the ruling based on Betts. Because the plaintiffs had no factual evidence of subterfuge, the original 3rd Circuit ruling was reversed (although a dissenting 3rd Circuit judge felt there was plenty of evidence of subterfuge).

But by reversing Betts, Title I of the OWBPA also reverses Westinghouse II. In complex language written in Sec.103(4)(C) of the Act, severance pay is defined as "supplemental unemployment compensation." Employers are permitted to offer early retirement, and they are also permitted to offset severance pay with other forms of supplemental compensation. However, they cannot exclude employees from severance based on age for any reason. Unfortunately for the Westinghouse II plaintiffs, Title I of the OWBPA was not retroactive.

Waivers

Title II of the OWBPA addresses "Waiver of Rights or Claims," another issue for older workers facing termination. For example, in *Ackerman v. Diamond Shamrock* (1982), Ackerman was told of his impending discharge and that his job was being divided between two other employees. He accepted early retirement in exchange for enhanced benefits, and waived his ADEA rights. He then charged coercion, but the 6th Circuit ruled that the waiver agreement was in accord with "ordinary contract principles." The 6th Circuit ruled similarly in a subsequent case (*Runyon v. NCR*, 1986). Thus prior to 1990, the voluntary waiver was treated like any other contract.

But Title II of the OWBPA establishes more stringent standards. Codified as Sec.7(f)(1)(A) through 7(f)(1)(H), Title II stipulates that a waiver agreement must: (a) be clearly written and easily understood; (b) cite ADEA; (c) ignore rights effective after the date of waiver; (d) be in exchange for benefits of increased value; (e) advise employees in writing to seek counsel; (f) provide 21 days for individuals (45 days for groups) to make a decision; and (g) be revokable within 7 days of signing. Additionally, Sec.7(f)(1)(H) states that if the agreement contains or implicates an exit incentive (e.g., enhanced early retirement), the employee must be provided with extensive information regarding who is and who is not eligible for the incentive.

———— BRIEF SUMMARY ————

The covered entities (Q2) are the same as in Title VII, although the required number of employees is slightly higher for private and state/local employers (20 employees) and unions (25 members). Overseas subsidiaries are also covered. The covered practices (Q3) include terms, conditions, and privileges; segregation and classification; and retaliation, with extra emphasis on factors relating to discharge. Thus Title I of the OWBPA dictates that older workers are entitled to the same benefits as younger workers for the same costs to the employer. Title I also prevents differential application of severance based on age. Title II of the OWBPA establishes eight criteria that address an offer of early retirement in exchange for added benefits.

SECTION IV
ADMINISTRATIVE PROCEDURES (Q4) AND REMEDIES (Q5)

These are the hybrid dimensions, with influences from both FLSA and Title VII. For **administrative procedures (Q4)**, FLSA contributes only the 2- and 3-year filing limits for federal lawsuits. But for **remedies (Q5)** FLSA has a more dominant influence than Title VII.

ADMINISTRATIVE PROCEDURES (Q4)

Technically, the FLSA lawsuits discussed in Chapter 5 (Sec.16(b), 16(c), & 17) are applicable, but only in name. And normally the FLSA filing limits are not as important as the Title VII limits. An ADEA claimant must first file EEOC charges as in Title VII. The Title VII filing limits for deferral states (300 days) and nondeferral states (180 days) apply. Also, in order for the EEOC to sponsor a suit there must be good faith conciliation (not necessary in FLSA). In order to control the suit, however, the EEOC must file in court within 60 days. Because the EEOC is not likely to finish an investigation and conciliation in 60 days, particularly in deferral states, the claimant, practically speaking, has a choice between direct access and EEOC intervention.

There are three other things to note. First, class action suits obey opt-in rules as in FLSA, but these rules are relaxed so that only one plaintiff needs to meet the EEOC filing criteria. Second, in deferral states, the state and EEOC charges do not have to be filed successively. Finally, these rules, as with Title VII, are far more complex for federal entities. The reader interested in federal procedures is directed to Bussey (1990).

There have been two major areas of litigation in the private and state/local sectors: (a) EEOC conciliatory efforts; and (b) EEOC filing requirements. Filing is the more dominant issue, particularly in deferral states.

EEOC Conciliatory Efforts

As noted in Chapter 5, although conciliation is optional in FLSA it is as mandatory in ADEA as in Title VII. More specifically, Sec.7(b) in ADEA states:

> the EEOC shall attempt to eliminate the discriminatory practice . . . and to effect voluntary compliance . . . through informal methods of conciliation, conference, and persuasion.

Thus in an early DOL suit (*Brennan v. Ace Hardware,* 1974), the 8th Circuit dismissed an ADEA claim because:

> Two personal meetings and one telephone call did not constitute substantial compliance with the requirement . . . that voluntary compliance through informal methods of conciliation, conference, and persuasion be sought prior to instituting legal action.

A similarly weak effort was reviewed by the 10th Circuit in *Marshall v. Sun Oil* (1979). But the Sun Oil Court took less drastic action—the ADEA case was stayed for completion of the conciliatory process.

The good faith conciliatory requirement is the reason why the EEOC needs more than 60 days to complete an investigation. Even the

180 days permitted in Title VII investigations can be problematic. For example, in the Sun Oil case cited above, the 10th Circuit based its ADEA ruling on its own precedent in *EEOC v. Zia* (1978), a Title VII case.

EEOC Filing Procedures

The Title VII filing requirements are illustrated by Supreme Court ruling in *Mohasco v. Silver* (1980). As discussed in Chapter 2, Silver filed EEOC charges 293 days after the alleged violation. Because Title VII requires **sequential** procedures beginning with state charges, the EEOC filed the state charges for Mohasco and the claim was returned to the EEOC 60 days later (on day 353). The Supreme Court ruled that Silver had not officially filed his EEOC charges within the 300-day limit for deferral states.

The ADEA procedures are illustrated in *Oscar Mayer v. Evans* (1979), a Supreme Court ruling preceding Mohasco. Evans received permission from the DOL to bypass state filing procedures; a contradiction to ADEA statutory requirements. The DOL accepted Evans's petition about 3 months after the alleged violation. Evans waited for the EEOC to finish its conciliatory efforts (about a year), and sued. The case was dismissed by the lower courts on two grounds: (a) Evans did not file state charges; and (b) a statute of limitations dictated by state law (120 days) had long since expired.

The Supreme Court affirmed that state filing procedures are mandatory in deferral states. Focusing on language common to Sec.706(c) of Title VII and Sec.14(b) of ADEA, Justice Brennan, speaking for majority of eight, stated:

> Since the ADEA and Title VII share a common purpose, the elimination of discrimination in the workplace; since the language of Sec.14(b) is almost in haec verba with Sec.706(c), and since the legislative history of Sec.14(b) indicates that its source was Sec.706(c), we may properly conclude that Congress intended that the construction of Sec.14(b) should follow that of Sec.706(c).

Next, Brennan ruled that limits mandated by state law are irrelevant to ADEA suits. Because Evans filed his DOL charges within the 300-day ADEA limit for deferral states, he was permitted, more than 3 years after the alleged violation, to file deferral state charges, wait 60 days, and proceed with his federal suit.

The Evans ruling is magnified by Silver's mistake. The difference between Title VII and ADEA procedures in deferral states is only 60 days. A Title VII claimant retains the right to sue if deferral state charges are filed by day 240 (i.e., enough time for the state to have its 60 days). The Evans ruling dictates that an ADEA claimant may petition the EEOC as late as day 300, regardless of when it petitions the state. Otherwise, the key to maintaining a federal right to sue in ADEA or Title VII is "commencement." Thus as further noted by Brennan in *Oscar Mayer v. Evans:*

> By its terms, then, the section [Sec.14(b)] requires only that state proceedings be commenced 60 days before federal litigation is instituted. Besides *commencement,* no other obligation is placed upon the ADEA grievant. [emphasis added]

After the Evans and Mohasco rulings, the lower courts faced several challenges referencing state law statutes of limitation. For example, in *Davis v. Calgon* (1980), Davis filed deferral state ADEA charges on day 213, and EEOC charges on day 223. Calgon argued that the 300 day federal limit applies only when the state claim is filed within a shorter limit legislated by state law. The 3rd Circuit disagreed. Similar rulings were rendered in *Cicone v. Textron* (1981), *Goodman v. Heublein* (1981), and *Anderson v. Illinois Tool Works* (1985).

A ruling similar to Evans was rendered by the 6th Circuit in *Jones v. Airco* (1982), a Title VII case. Jones filed EEOC charges 228 days after the alleged violation. The EEOC deferred to the state on day 231, and the state returned the claim to the EEOC on day 259. The district court dismissed the claim because EEOC charges were not filed within a shorter limit legislated by state law. The 6th Circuit overruled. Applying Brennan's ADEA ruling to Title VII, the Court stated:

> Nothing whatsoever in the section requires the respondent to *commence* those [EEOC] proceedings within the allotted time under state law to preserve the right of action.

Finally, it should be noted that "commencement" also applies in nondeferral states, where the federal EEOC filing limit is only 180 days. In *Vance v. Whirlpool* (1983), Vance commenced his federal claim by filing EEOC charges within the 180-day federal limit. However, Vance filed a direct access suit before the EEOC finished its investigation. The 4th Circuit ruled that EEOC filing procedures are mandatory. But instead of dismissing the case, the Court retraced to the point of commencement and ordered Vance to complete the necessary steps.

REMEDIES (Q5)

ADEA incorporates the four major remedies from FLSA: injunction, back pay, liquidated damages, and attorney fees. Of course, damages were not available in the pre-1991 version of Title VII. But unlike the Equal Pay Act, private and state/local ADEA claimants can obtain liquidated damages and injunctions in a single suit. Also, private and state/local claimants are entitled to jury trials. Federal employees are not entitled to either liquidated damages or jury trials, but all claimants are entitled to affirmative relief (i.e., reinstatement or front pay). Front pay is more important to ADEA than Title VII because older workers have fewer remaining working years and/or fewer reemployment options. Conceivably, an over-60 employee may obtain front pay up to a court-determined age of retirement (say 70) (see *Whittlesey v. Union Carbide,* 1984).

The remedies available for private and state/local employees are written into Sec.7(b) of the statute as follows:

> Amounts owing to a person as a result of a violation of this Act shall be deemed to be unpaid minimum wages . . . for purposes of sections 16 and 17 of [FLSA as amended]. . . . *Provided.* That liquidated damages shall be payable only in cases of willful violations of the Act. In any action . . . the court shall have jurisdiction to grant such legal or equitable relief as may be appropriate to effecting the purposes of this Act including without limitation judgments compelling employment, reinstatement or promotion, or enforcing the liability for amounts deemed to be unpaid minimum wages. [italics in original, underlining added]

In comparison, Sec.15(b), for federal employees, states:

> Except as otherwise provided in this subsection, the [EEOC] is authorized to enforce the provisions of subsection (a) through appropriate remedies, including reinstatement or hiring of employees with or without backpay, as will effectuate the policies of this section.

Clearly, there are common remedies between Sec.7(c) and Sec.15(b), but liquidated damages is *not* one of them.

The major litigated issues for remedies have been: (a) the willfulness criterion for liquidated damages; (b) legal relief for nonfederal employees; and (c) legal relief for federal employees.

The Willfulness Criterion for Liquidated Damages

Willfulness was discussed for Equal Pay Act claims in Chapter 5. The Equal Pay rules apply to ADEA. Indeed, as noted in Chapter 5, the current standards for both statutes are dictated by the Supreme Court's ruling in an ADEA case (*TWA v. Thurston,* 1985). To force liquidated damages, the employee has the burden of proving the employer knew there was a violation or acted in reckless disregard for the statute. Of course, the burden on the employee has increased over time from proving: (a) the employer knew the statute applies; to (b) having reasonable grounds for believing there was a violation; to (c) the current standard of knowledge or reckless disregard.

Legal Relief for Private and State/Local Plaintiffs

Generally, **legal relief** is a code term for jury trials. The history behind the jury trial issue is quite interesting. In response to circuit court rulings that, in two cases, permitted jury trials (*Rogers v. Exxon,* 1977; *Pons v. Lorillard,* 1977), but in a third case did not (*Morelock v. NCR Corp.,* 1976), Senator Kennedy proposed a bill to permit jury trials in ADEA suits seeking liquidated damages. Between Kennedy's proposal and Congress's final amendment, the Supreme Court reviewed *Lorillard v. Pons* (1978). The Court favored jury trials in nonfederal claims seeking *any* monetary relief (i.e., not just liquidated damages). Justice Marshall, speaking for a unanimous Court, equated legal relief with the 7th Amendment right to a jury trial.

Then, less than 4 months after the Lorillard ruling, Congress amended ADEA by adding Sec.7(c)(2). Accordingly:

> a person shall be entitled to a trial by jury of any issue in any such action for recovery of amounts owing as a result of a violation of this Act regardless of whether equitable relief is sought by any party in such action.

Note that Congress was more generous to plaintiffs relative to Kennedy's initial proposal (which limited jury trials to claimants seeking liquidated damages).

Interestingly, Justice Marshall's ruling in Lorillard reads much like the 5th Circuit's ruling in *Wirtz v. Jones* (1965), a pure FLSA case. In Jones, the 5th circuit distinguished between "equity jurisdiction" versus "actions at law." The Court ruled that FLSA provides equitable and legal relief (and hence jury trials) in Sec.16(b) claims, but only equitable relief (and hence no jury trials) in Sec.17 claims. Of course, in the Equal Pay Act, this FLSA ruling is negated by an EPA provision that the court must rule on liquidated damages.

Legal Relief for Federal Plaintiffs

The rules are different in the federal sector, where the 7th Amendment does not apply. By common law, charges against the federal government do not command juries and damages unless federal immunity is waived by Congress. However, the statutory language for federal entities in Sec.15(c) parallels the language used for private and state/local entities in Sec.7(b). Accordingly:

> Any persons aggrieved may bring a civil action in any Federal district court or competent jurisdiction for such *legal* or equitable relief as will effectuate the purposes of this Act. [emphasis added]

In other words, Sec.15(c) provides legal relief for federal entities just as Sec.7(b) provides legal relief for nonfederal entities.

Nevertheless, in *Lehman v. Nakshian* (1981), the Supreme Court did not equate legal relief in Sec.15(c) with waiver of federal immunity. Five justices (led by Stewart) questioned why Congress would create an explicit jury right for nonfederal entities in Sec.7 without doing likewise in Sec.15. Four dissenters (led by Brennan) argued that Congress did not address federal entities because the Lorillard case that spurred the congressional amendment implicated only nonfederal entities. But the trump card was Sec.15(f), which explicitly divorces federal entities from the remainder of the ADEA statute. Sec.15(f) was also a 1978 amendment.

——— BRIEF SUMMARY ———

Administrative procedures (**Q4**) follow mainly from Title VII. But unlike Title VII, the EEOC has only 60 days to conciliate (vs. 180 days in Title VII). Thus the ADEA claimant, practically speaking, can choose between direct access to federal court versus EEOC conciliation. Also, in deferral states, the claimant can file state and EEOC charges **simultaneously** and as late as day 300 (Title VII charges must be sequential and by day 240). The Remedies (**Q5**) include injunction, back pay, lawyer fees, liquidated damages, and affirmative relief. Front pay is a particularly important form of affirmative relief in age cases because older employees may have fewer remaining working years and/or fewer alternatives for other work. Finally, **legal relief** implies jury trials for any private or state/local claim, but damages and juries are not permitted for federal employees. The concept of liquidated damages follows from principles discussed in Chapter 5; the employee must prove the employer had knowledge of an ADEA violation, or acted in reckless disregard for the statute.

SECTION V
ATTACK/DEFENSE BALANCES (Q6)
BASED ON TITLE VII CASE LAW

The courts have evaluated adverse impact and pattern or practice charges, but ADEA is mainly a disparate treatment statute. The following discussion will focus briefly on adverse impact and pattern or practice, and then more extensively on adaptation of the McDonnell-Burdine scenario to age-specific issues.

ADVERSE IMPACT

Employers have been quick to react to the realities of case law. Practically speaking, adverse impact is a smoking gun. The business necessity defense is difficult to make because the employer has to persuade the court (or a jury) that exclusion of older workers improves the business. The only alternative is to concede discrimination and use a statutory defense, which is also difficult. Among the adverse impact cases in the literature, some are naive blunders and others combine adverse impact with disparate treatment.

Pure Adverse Impact Cases

In what may be the oldest adverse impact case in ADEA (*Hodgson v. Approved Personnel Services*, 1975), the 4th Circuit evaluated more than 50 newspaper advertisements that impacted older people (e.g., "recent college graduate"), as well as other Title VII groups. As noted in Chapter 3, advertisers have refrained from impacting the Title VII groups in recent years. References to age-related factors are easy to make, however, and obviously should be avoided.

The more traditional adverse impact scenario is illustrated in *Geller v. Markham* (1980) and *Leftwich v. Harris-Stowe* (1983). Both employers used cost cutting as a business necessity defense, and both employers lost because of a DOL regulation (Sec. 860.103(h)) subsequently adopted by the EEOC. The regulation states:

> A general assertion that the average cost of employing older workers as a group is higher than the average cost of employing younger workers as a group will not be recognized as a differentiation under the terms and provisions of the Act, unless one of the other statutory exceptions applies. To classify or group employees solely on the basis of age for the purpose of comparing costs, or for any other purpose, necessarily rests on the assumption that the age factor alone may be used to justify a differentiation—an assumption plainly contrary to the purpose of Congress in enacting it. Differentials so based would serve only to perpetuate and promote the very discrimination at which the act is directed.

In Geller, a 55-year-old art teacher applied for a "sudden opening" and began teaching. She was then replaced by a 25-year-old who applied shortly thereafter. The reason for Geller's release was a school district policy stating:

> Except in special situations, and to the extent possible, teachers needed in West Hartford next year will be recruited at levels below the *sixth step* of the salary schedule. [emphasis added]

A statistician showed that within the district, teachers over age 40 were statistically more likely to have reached the "sixth step" than teachers under 40. The 2nd Circuit then rejected the cost-cutting defense based on the DOL regulation cited above. The school also argued that age was not the determining factor in Geller's exclusion, but the court ruled that this defense is reserved for disparate treatment.

In Leftwich, faculty size was reduced from 51 to 34. Individual professors were classified as tenured or nontenured, and retention decisions were made separately within these classifications. A 47-year-old white biologist (Leftwich) was released in favor of a 33-year-old white biologist (nontenured) and 62-year-old black biologist (tenured). Leftwich had stronger credentials than either colleague, and filed Title

VII (reverse discrimination) and ADEA charges. But the age case was easier to make because the 33-year-old was unopposed. That is, Leftwich faced competition only because he was tenured. In fact, Leftwich was told he was a "victim of tenure density."

The average age of tenured faculty was significantly higher than the average age of nontenured faculty. However, the average age of retained versus released faculty was about the same. The 8th Circuit rejected a bottom-line equality in age based on the Supreme Court's ruling in *Connecticut v. Teal* (1982) (discussed in Chapter 2). The Court also rejected the cost-cutting defense based on the previously cited DOL regulation. In addition, the Court stated:

> to the extent that the defendants in fact utilized their selection plan in an attempt to increase the quality of the college's faculty, they have failed to establish that the plan was necessary to achieve their goal.

In other words, the only justification for using a tenure criterion would be to improve a faculty. Because Leftwich was academically stronger than either of his colleagues, this argument was not even attempted.

Adverse Impact Plus Disparate Treatment

The Westinghouse I (1983) and Bordens (1984) cases discussed in Section III of this chapter combined adverse impact with disparate treatment. At first blush, offering severance to one group and early retirement to another group smacks of facial discrimination. However, the policy was neutral. Indeed, in Bordens the district court accepted adverse impact and rejected disparate treatment, and the 9th Circuit affirmed on adverse impact and reversed on disparate treatment.

Westinghouse II (1990) bordered on contempt. Employees were given a choice between severance versus early retirement, with the possibility of recall if the choice was severance. Thus the policy had a differential effect on (say) a 35-year-old with only 5 years of service versus a 60-year-old with 20 to 30 years of service. Obviously, the older employee had more to lose. This was the rationale used by the 3rd Circuit in Westinghouse II before the Supreme Court ordered reconsideration of the case in light of its Betts ruling.

The remedies awarded in many of the earlier cases are immaterial. The Thurston ruling clarified that liquidated damages require knowledge of violation, or reckless disregard. The Geller employers used a naive city-wide policy, and the Leftwich employers followed the advice of a consultant who naively believed that bottom-line balance was acceptable. As for the advertisers, they used common language in an era not too far removed from tolerated (not tolerable) facial discrimination (e.g., "male" vs. "female" want ads). But Bordens and Westinghouse I and II would beg for liquidated damages, even under Thurston rules.

PATTERN OR PRACTICE

Pattern or practice is rarer than adverse impact. But when it does occur the rules are the same as in Title VII. The following discussion illustrates two ploys; one an obvious vestige of the past and the other a realistic concern for the future.

In *Hodgson v. First Federal* (1972), the DOL sued on behalf of Betty Hall, a 47-year-old woman who applied and was rejected for the position of bank teller. A personnel officer wrote that Hall was "too old for teller" on Hall's personnel file. A DOL investigation revealed that among 35 recently hired tellers, not one was 40 or older. Also, there was other damaging evidence (e.g., documents referencing moderately intelligent females "ages 21 to 24"). The bank lost.

In *Mistretta v. Sandia* (1980), the company was forced into a RIF because of cutbacks in federal funding. But the company focused its RIF on employees aged 52 to 64, a case made at the prima facie level with bottom-line statistics. The company was forced to defend not only the overall pattern charge, but also each of 15 individual charges (of which 14 were lost). Of course, by Title VII traditions the individual charges required productive defenses.

The bank scenario is the vestige; the type of case the DOL specialized in under the Equal Pay Act. But the Mistretta scenario is still plausible. If an employer intentionally screens out older applicants or employees, bottom-line statistics will likely reveal the ploy. Moreover, even though a pattern attack requires only a productive defense, the true danger is having to defend against multiple claims. With 15 or more individuous charges, it would be difficult to make a reasonable articulation applying to all cases, because in a ploy the only common denominator is age. Needless to say, a proven pattern charge implies liquidated damages even by Thurston rules.

McDONNELL-BURDINE SCENARIOS

As in Title VII, attacks with persuasive evidence (i.e., documents, witnesses, etc.) forces a persuasive defense. This principle was supported for ADEA in the Supreme Court's ruling in *TWA v. Thurston* (1985). Of course, as noted in Chapter 2, Title VII plaintiffs rarely use factual evidence, and the same is true for ADEA plaintiffs. The McDonnell-Burdine formula is therefore used more than any other prescription, but its use in ADEA poses difficulties for discriminatory discharge, the most frequent ADEA complaint.

Reexamination of McDonnell-Burdine

The reader will recall from Chapter 2 that in *McDonnell Douglas v. Green* (1973), Justice Powell established the following four steps for prima facie disparate treatment:

(i) that he belongs to a racial majority; (ii) that he applied and was qualified for the job for which the employer was seeking applications; (iii) that, despite his qualifications, he was rejected; and (iv) that, after his rejection, the position remained open and the employer continued to seek applicants from persons of complainant's qualifications.

For example, in *Hodgson v. First Federal* (1972) Betty Hall could have asserted: (a) she is protected by ADEA; (b) she applied and was qualified to be a bank teller; (c) she was rejected; and (d) the search for tellers continued. Of course, the DOL chose a different attack.

There is an inherent problem in RIFs, even in Title VII. In RIFs, employees are not necessarily replaced, or at least not immediately. Thus a modified version of McDonnell-Burdine is required. For example, as stated by the 3rd Circuit in *Massarsky v. General Motors* (1983), the plaintiff must show that:

he is a member of the protected class and that he was laid off from a job for which he was qualified while *others not in the protected class* were treated more favorably. [emphasis added]

Thus only the first two steps (protection and qualification) are used. And in lieu of steps 3 and 4, the plaintiff must provide circumstantial or direct evidence implying that nonprotected employees were differentially treated (e.g., in reassignment, benefits, etc.).

With age, there is an additional problem noted in Section II of this chapter. Even if the four steps apply, the protected class is not dichotomous. For example, after *McDonnell v. Green,* the steps were wrongly applied in *Wilson v. Sealtest* (1974) and *Price v. Maryland* (1977), both of which were 5th Circuit cases. The 5th Circuit demanded evidence of replacement by a younger person in Wilson, and evidence of a replacement from outside the protected age range in Price. But the 5th Circuit altered its own rigid construction of McDonnell-Burdine in *Marshall v. Goodyear* (1977), and then later in *McCortsin v. U.S. Steel* (1980). Indeed, in McCortsin, the 5th Circuit stated that McDonnell-Burdine is not the "alpha and omega of possible tests." More specifically, the Court reasoned:

> A mechanistic application of the McDonnell prima facie test is especially dangerous in the context of age discrimination. Seldom will a sixty-year-old be replaced by a person in the twenties. Rather the sixty-year-old will be replaced by a fifty-five-year-old, who in turn. . . . Eventually, a person outside the protected class will be elevated but rarely to the position of the one fired. This is especially true in management and technical fields where knowledge and experience, the product of years, are necessary prerequisites to appointment of persons on high rungs of the corporate ladder.

Of course, the ruling echoes the 1st Circuit ruling in *Loeb v. Textron* (1979) cited in Section II of the chapter.

Special Problems for Juries

ADEA was the first statute to evaluate McDonnell-Burdine scenarios using jury trials. In general, the district court judge hears the prima facie evidence and determines whether to dismiss or continue the trial. Then the jury hears all the evidence and the judge instructs the jury regarding the McDonnell-Burdine burdens. *Loeb v. Textron* (1979) was a critical case because it tackled the jury issue in the context of another important issue—mixed motive.

Loeb was transferred to a new job. Three years later, he was fired by a new (32-year-old) supervisor who displayed evidence of age bias. Loeb charged age bias and the defense pleaded poor performance. The jury was instructed to evaluate three things: (a) the McDonnell-Burdine steps; (b) whether the defendant proved a legal motive; and

(c) regarding this proof, whether age was **a factor** in Loeb's discharge (i.e., not the **determining** factor). Loeb won in district court.

The 1st Circuit evaluated the case in light of *Sweeney v. Keene State* (1978), the Supreme Court case following *Furnco v. Waters* (1978). The defendant challenged the lower court's application of McDonnell-Burdine, reasoning that a jury cannot understand the scenario. The 1st Circuit disagreed, stating:

> The central issue is whether . . . the plaintiff was discharged "because of his age." . . . Whether the jury is also instructed that the plaintiff must establish the four elements . . . will depend on whether the plaintiff's age discrimination claim is primarily provable in McDonnell Douglas terms.

The 1st Circuit also rejected the lower court's requirement that the defense prove the legal motive. All that is necessary in any McDonnell-Burdine scenario is a productive defense.

Regarding the mixed-motive instruction, the 1st Circuit echoed the going standard in Title VII cases, stating:

> to find that age was a factor that affected the decision is not equivalent to finding that age was the *determinative factor*. [emphasis added]

Obviously, the district court was victimized by confusion regarding the terms *articulate* versus *prove*. Recall that in *McDonnell v. Green* the Supreme Court required an "articulation" of a legal motive, but in *Furnco v. Waters* (1978), the Supreme Court used the term *prove* instead of *articulate*. Thus the district court demanded that the defendant "prove" the legal motive. The 1st Circuit corrected this mistake based on *Sweeney v. Keene State* (1978), where the Supreme Court affirmed the "articulation" standard.

The bottom line is that the jury must understand that in a McDonnell-Burdine scenario, age must be the determining factor for exclusion; not a factor, and not the sole factor. Normally, mixed-motive cases are started with factual evidence of the illegal motive (as in *Price Waterhouse v. Hopkins*, 1989). However, if the plaintiff only implies an illegal motive, as in McDonnell-Burdine, the defendant need only articulate an alternative, shifting the burden of factual proof of pretext to the plaintiff.

Sample Cases

Obviously, there are numerous sample cases to choose from. Recent estimates suggest that ADEA accounts for 15% to 20% of all EEO claims, and most ADEA scenarios with substantive charges (i.e., nonprocedural issues) use McDonnell-Burdine in one form or another. Therefore two cases will be used, one to illustrate a traditional discharge scenario (*Wildman v. Lerner Stores,* 1985), and one to illustrate the RIF scenario (*Berndt v. Kaiser Aluminum,* 1986).

In Wildman, Lerner stores changed ownership. The new owner, Margolis, engaged in a youth movement and often joked with Wildman about retirement. Ironically, Margolis was the same age as Wildman (61). Then, at a business meeting, Margolis asked Wildman to resign. Wildman wrote a letter requesting a 1.5 million dollar settlement or reinstatement, and Margolis fired him for cause. The prima facie case used all four McDonnell-Burdine steps (Wildman was replaced by a 31-year-old). Margolis claimed that Wildman was fired because he failed to discharge an employee who had broken some rules. Although the articulation was factual, the jury deemed it a pretext.

In Berndt, Kaiser laid off salesmen for acceptable economic reasons. But Berndt, then 51, was not considered for reassignment, whereas younger salesman were. The 3rd Circuit applied the RIF modification of the McDonnell-Burdine formula. Thus Berndt established: (a) protection; and (b) qualification; and then (c) provided evidence implying that younger laid-off salesmen received preferential treatment. The defendant articulated that Berndt was not qualified for other positions, but Berndt had sufficient factual proof that the reason was pretext, and the jury believed Berndt.

Other Issues

McDonnell-Burdine cases have also served as the major vehicle for deciding important issues on remedies. Jury trials predominate in ADEA, particularly in disparate treatment cases. The instructions for merits are separate from those for liquidated damages. Moreover, the judge must decide on affirmative awards. For example, in the cases cited above, front pay awards by district court judges were affirmed by both the 3rd Circuit (Wildman) and the 1st Circuit (Berndt).

Clearly, the jury decides whether the liquidated damages are deserved. The judge, however, must affirm the correctness of the dollar amounts, and there is an ADEA-specific issue regarding the relationship between liquidated damages and front pay awards. Generally, judges award front pay (which can be for several years) in lieu of liquidated damages. Furthermore, because liquidated damages are designed to punish **retrospective** violations, even when liquidated damages and front pay are awarded, front pay is not doubled because it is a **prospective** remedy. These issues are discussed in the two cases cited above, as well as in *Whittlesey v. Union Carbide* (1984), *EEOC v. Prudential* (1984), and *McNeil v. Economics Laboratory* (1986).

------- **BRIEF SUMMARY** -------

Adverse impact is rare, pattern or practice is rarer, and both are smoking guns. Indeed, adverse impact and pattern or practice may be the only ways to convert age into a dichotomous classification. Adverse impact requires either of two difficult defenses (business necessity or a statutory defense), and pattern or practice forces multiple articulations where the only common denominator may be age. Disparate treatment is the most common charge in ADEA cases, and the courts have wrestled with adaptation of the McDonnell-Burdine scenario to discharge, particularly in RIFs, and to juries. All four prima facie steps are used when possible. But at other times, steps 1 and 2 are followed with evidence of peferential treatment because of age. Judges decide whether the case should go to the jury (or be dismissed) and the jury decides the merits of the case and whether liquidated damages are called for. However, judges have the discretion to award affirmative relief (e.g., front pay), which is a prospective remedy that is not doubled.

SECTION VI
STATUTORY DEFENSES

In addition to good faith in EEOC interpretations (common to all EEO statutes), ADEA has five statutory defenses. These defenses are: (a) bona fide occupational qualification (BFOQ); (b) bona fide seniority system (BFSS); (c) bona fide benefit plan (BFBP); (d) "good cause"; and (e) "reasonable factors other than age" (RFOA). Of course, BFOQ and BFSS are referenced in Title VII. However, BFSS is more closely associated with one of the age-specific defenses (BFBP), and good cause is a subset of RFOA. All five defenses are persuasive.

GOOD CAUSE AND RFOA

RFOA is like the "factors other than sex" defense in the Equal Pay Act; it can refer to any reason other than illegal discrimination. Good cause, on the other hand, is restricted to discharge (i.e., firing for cause). Thus it is functionally an RFOA. At first blush it might appear that good cause and RFOA could suffice as productive defenses in the second phase of a McDonnell-Burdine scenario. However, the causes and/or reasonable factors must be established factually. Therefore, because McDonnell-Burdine offers an easier productive defense, good cause and RFOA are generally used in situations in which the plaintiff attacks with persuasive evidence, and/or the defendant denies that age played **any role** in a selection decision.

If good cause or RFOA can be established factually, the courts will generally rule in favor of the defendants. For example, in *Surrisi v. Conwed* (1975), the 7th Circuit ruled that plaintiff failed to "fulfill satisfactorily the business responsibility which had been assigned to him" (he had failed to execute a new sales policy properly). In *Sutton v. Atlantic Richfield* (1981), the 9th Circuit stated:

> instances of Sutton's conduct constituted *reasonable factors other than age* which motivated ARCO's management and also established *good cause* for Sutton's constructive discharge. [emphasis added]

And in *Kaputska v. United Airlines* (1981), the plaintiff was discharged for sexual misconduct.

The Kaputska infraction is an automatic; employers would risk a great deal for failing to discharge a sexual offender. However, not all cases are that clear. For example, Surrisi worked for Conwed for 19 years, having advanced from salesman to national sales manager. His trouble began when a rival became an immediate supervisor, and the company was undergoing changes. The 8th Circuit stated:

> The Court must find . . . that plaintiff has not sustained the burden of proof that he was discharged because of his age. On the other hand, there does seem to be an element of unfairness in discharging [a 52-year-old] who had rendered faithful and, on this record, competent business services for some nineteen years with Conwed's providing some department in the business in which Surrisi could continue to [work]. But, of course, that is not the question before the Court.

In other words, Surrisi only attacked the constructiveness of his discharge (which he proved). Had he also charged preferential treatment relative to younger workers who, under similar conditions, might have been reassigned to other jobs, he might have won.

Sutton, like Surrisi, was a longtime employee who also fought with a superior. Sutton made his prima facie case using McDonnell-Burdine principles, but the company (ARCO) chose not to articulate a productive defense. They valued Sutton's past contributions and despite his intractable behaviors (which ARCO proved), they broke their own policies to provide Sutton with a very attractive early retirement offer that had expired 2 years earlier. Clearly, ARCO took a safe track, whereas Conwed was probably lucky.

BFBP AND BFSS

The major features of the BFBP defense require only a recap. BFSS and BFBP are invariably mentioned in the same breath. Technically, however, the concepts are not synonyms.

Bona Fide Benefit Plans (BFBP)

As noted in Section III of the chapter, the BFBP defense is dictated by Title I of the 1990 Older Workers Act. The Act reverses the Supreme Court's interpretation of "subterfuge," originally defined in McMann (1977) for pre-ADEA plans, and extended in Betts for post-ADEA plans. In both cases, the Supreme Court ruled that the burden of proving "subterfuge" rests with the plaintiff. The OWBPA codifies Sec.1625.10 of the EEOC Regulation, itself a restatement of a prior DOL regulation. The regulation leaves only one defense for age-based discrimination in applicable benefit plans—actuarial cost differences based on age. The concept of "subterfuge" no longer applies.

Bona Fide Seniority Systems (BFSS)

BFSS takes on a different meaning in ADEA relative to Title VII. In the cases surveyed in Chapter 2, the BFSS defense benefited older workers. Nevertheless, the literal meaning of BFSS is the same for both statutes. Thus as stated in Sec.1625.8(a) of the EEOC Regulations:

Though a seniority system may be qualified by such factors as merit, capacity, or ability, any bona fide seniority system must be based on length of service as the primary criterion for the equitable allocation of available employment opportunities and prerogatives among younger and older workers.

The only case the author found separating BFSS from BFBP was *TWA v. Thurston* (1985). And even in Thurston, the defendant used BFBP after the BFSS defense was struck down. However, Thurston is more a BFSS case than a BFBP case.

In Thurston, pilots were legally retired at age 60 (for reasons to be discussed shortly). TWA permitted both disabled pilots under 60 and retired pilots 60 and over to continue to work as flight engineers (the third seat in the cockpit). However, a union agreement dictated that pilots under 60 unfit for flying (for medical reasons) could bump existing flight engineers who were never pilots. But the retired pilots could sit in the third seat only if there was a vacancy (i.e., they could not bump). Speaking for a unanimous Court, Justice Powell stated:

> TWA contends that its discriminatory transfer policy is lawful under the Act because it is part of a "bona fide seniority system." The Court of appeals held that the airline's retirement policy is not mandated by the negotiated seniority plan. We need not address this finding; any seniority system that includes the challenged practice is not "bona fide" under the statute.

In other words, a union cannot collectively bargain away the legitimate rights of its older members.

THE BFOQ DEFENSE

As in Title VII, BFOQ is the only defense to facial discrimination based on age. Furthermore, ADEA tracks Title VII in applying the defense. However, the unique interaction between age and safety has made the BFOQ more palatable in age cases than sex cases. As with Title VII, there are landmark Supreme Court rulings, most notably *Western Airlines v. Criswell* (1985). However, the BFOQ age principles were settled well before Criswell.

Lower Court Traditions

The BFOQ age traditions actually begin with a Title VII race case (*Spurlock v. United Airlines,* 1972). Of course, BFOQ cannot apply to race. But Spurlock involved a key issue for age, namely safety. Spurlock applied and was rejected for pilot training for lacking 500 hours of flight time (he had about half the hours), and for lacking a 4-year college degree (he had a 2-year degree). The airline had no indication that Spurlock was black. Spurlock challenged both the flight-time requirement and the 4-year degree. The degree requirement involved a strong adverse impact attack. But 10th Circuit ruled for the airline, stating:

> When a job requires a small amount of skill and training and the consequences of hiring an unqualified applicant are insignificant, the courts should examine closely any pre-employment standard or criteria which discriminate against minorities. In such a case, the employer should have a heavy burden to demonstrate . . . [business necessity]. On the other hand, when the job clearly requires a high degree of skill and the economic and human risks involved in hiring an unqualified applicant are great, the employer bears a correspondingly lighter burden to show that his employment criteria are job-related.

In other words, in a case decided shortly after Griggs (1971), the 10th Circuit differentiated between coal handling and pilot training based on economics and safety. Both factors were accepted in support of the business necessity defense.

Then, in *Hodgson v. Greyhound* (1974), the 7th Circuit evaluated Greyhound's policy of refusing to hire drivers over age 35. The DOL cited the 5th Circuit ruling in *Weeks v. Southern Bell* (1969), arguing that Greyhound's policy was stereotypical, not factual. The Court replied:

> Unlike Weeks, our concern goes beyond that of the welfare of the job applicant and must include consideration of the well-being and safety of bus passengers and other highway motorists.

The Court also cited the 5th Circuit ruling in *Diaz v. Pan Am* (1971), where a "business convenience" test was rejected in favor of a "business necessity" defense. And for the business necessity defense, the 7th Circuit cited the essential features of the Spurlock. Accordingly:

> Greyhound need only demonstrate . . . a minimal increase in risk of harm for it is enough to show that elimination of the hiring policy might

jeopardize the life of one more person than might otherwise occur under the present hiring practice.

Obviously, many Greyhound bus drivers are well over 35 years of age. But the key to this case is the career of a bus driver. Based on seniority principles, newer drivers start out with more arduous routes and then graduate to easier routes. Greyhound presented statistical evidence revealing that drivers who start at too late an age are too old by the time they graduate to the easier schedules.

The 5th Circuit then accepted similar arguments in *Usery v. Tamiami Trail Tours* (1976), where the cutoff age was 40. The Court stated:

> job qualifications which the employer invokes to justify his discrimination must be reasonably necessary to the essence of his business—here, the safe transportation of bus passengers from one point to another. The greater the safety factor, measured by the likelihood of harm and the probable severity of that harm in case of an accident, the more stringent may be the job qualifications designed to ensure safe driving.

This ruling pre-dated and predicted *Dothard v. Rawlinson* (1977), where the Supreme Court upheld exclusion of women as guards in all-male maximum security prisons. The key issue in Dothard was not individual capabilities, as it was in Weeks. In Weeks, the 5th Circuit had ruled that individual females must have an opportunity to demonstrate their capabilities for telephone line work, unless doing so is "impossible or highly impractical." But public safety was not a critical issue in Weeks as it was in Tamiami. Thus in Tamiami the requirement to prove that a worker is incapable was waived because the bus company proved it was impossible and impractical to test individual differences.

The prior and current rules for BFOQ are clearly written in Sec.1625.6 of the EEOC ADEA Regulations. Mimicking the Title VII BFOQ guidelines, Sec.1625.6 states:

> An employer asserting a BFOQ defense has the burden of proving that (1) the age limit is reasonably necessary to the essence of the business, and either (2) that all or substantially all individuals excluded from the job involved are in fact disqualified, or (3) that some of the individuals so excluded possess a disqualifying trait that cannot be ascertained except by relevance to age. If the employer's objective is the goal of public safety, the employer must prove that the challenged practice does indeed effectuate that goal and that there is no acceptable alternative which would better advance it or equally advance it with less discriminatory impact.

Criterion #3 qualifies criterion #2. To prove that "all or substantially all" should be excluded, the employer has to satisfy the "impossible or highly impractical" standard established in Weeks. Obviously, this standard is more strictly applied when public safety is a consideration, regardless of whether the protected class is sex or age.

Western v. Criswell (1985)

The Supreme Court's McMann (1977) ruling occurred within the same time frame as *Dothard v. Rawlinson*. Using lower court principles just described, the McMann Court upheld a Federal Aviation Administration (FAA) regulation requiring pilots and copilots to retire at age 60. The main issue in Criswell, however, was flight engineering (the third seat), for which there were no FAA restrictions. The plaintiffs challenged Western's failure to reassign retired pilots to the third seat. Interestingly, these charges were based on the 1978 congressional amendment designed to reverse McMann (on issues other than BFOQ). Western failed to prove that age was a BFOQ for flight engineers.

Actually, the Supreme Court had rejected a BFOQ argument for flight engineers in *TWA v. Thurston* (1985), which was decided 2 days before the arguments were heard in Criswell. However, because of technicalities (e.g., jury instructions) and a strong attempt by Western Airlines to justify BFOQ, the Criswell Court thoroughly analyzed the flight engineer position and unanimously ruled that age was not a BFOQ.

In essence, Western argued against the "reasonably necessary" component of BFOQ, which requires a factual basis for claiming the defense. Western argued it should have discretion to use its own "rational basis," and the Supreme Court disagreed. The airline also argued for impossibility/impracticality for medical certification, but the Court opted for individual differences, forcing the airline to prove on a case-by-case basis that a retirable airline pilot or copilot is medically unfit for the third seat. In the words of Justice Stevens:

> When an employee covered by the Act is able to point to reputable businesses in the same industry that choose to eschew reliance on mandatory retirement earlier than age 70 [then the upper limit], when the employer itself relies on individualized testing in similar circumstances, and when the administrative agency with primary responsibility for maintaining airline safety has determined that individualized testing is not impractical for the relevant position, the employer's attempt to

justify its decision on the basis of the contrary opinion of experts . . . is hardly convincing. Even in cases involving public safety, the ADEA plainly does not permit the trier of fact to give complete deference to the employer's decision.

In short, Criswell further codified the lower court rulings in Greyhound and Tamiami, as well as Sec.1625.6 of the EEOC Regulations.

―――――― BRIEF SUMMARY ――――――

All five statutory defenses are affirmative; they require factual proof. Good cause and RFOA are rarely used because employers have a less burdensome defense in McDonnell-Burdine. However, an employee can force good cause or RFOA with persuasive evidence of discrimination. Also, employers can choose these defenses when their evidence is strong. On the other hand, BFBP is limited to issues of benefits and requires cost justification; and BFSS does not have the same meaning in ADEA as in Title VII (because older workers are not usually hurt by seniority agreements unless they relate to benefits). Finally, the BFOQ defense is based on Title VII principles and, at least in ADEA, thrives on public safety issues. Furthermore, when public safety is implicated at a level satisfactory to courts, the principle of impossibility or impracticability is used in lieu of the precedent from sex discrimination cases that individuals should be given the opportunity to display their capabilities.

SECTION VII
COMPLIANCE

Compliance principles discussed in relation to Title VII obviously apply to ADEA. Also, there are certain conclusions from individual case law rulings that are facially true (like avoiding advertising mistakes, and in general, adverse impact or pattern or practice). And because ADEA interacts very closely with ERISA and Internal Revenue Tax Code provisions, larger companies with multiple managers should ensure that EEO and compensation/benefits officers are collectively involved in ADEA-related decisions. Beyond these basic considerations, three major issues demand special attention: (a) misplaced sensitivity regarding age (not insensitivity); (b) properly conducting a RIF; and (c) properly using the early retirement incentive.

MISPLACED SENSITIVITY

It would be a mistake, of course, to permit age-based harassment, just as it would be to permit harassment based on race, religion, sex, national origin, or disability. Furthermore, threats or jokes about age, if documentable, could support pretext in a disparate treatment claim. Thus insensitivity can produce problems.

But the opposite is also true. We should be sensitive to the feelings of all people, but sensitivity should not guard the truth. An employer who discharges an older worker for legitimate reasons and, because of sensitivity, does not convey a true reason (e.g., "your skills have eroded," or "you are unable to learn new skills") risks quite a bit. Telling an employee something else (e.g., "the company is on a youth movement") might spare a person's feelings, but it might also convince a jury that a legitimate reason for termination is pretextual.

The author's opinions on this issue are based on three factors: (a) a distinct feeling in some of the cases that juries were misled into accepting pretext; (b) consultations with managers and supervisors who are in the midst of RIFs; and (c) a gut feeling that there should be more good cause and RFOA defenses even though these defenses are persuasive. However, assuming the author is overstating a problem, it is certainly a smart policy to convey the correct reason for a termination decision, regardless of the protected class.

PROPERLY CONDUCTING A RIF

Hartman and Schnadig (1990) provide the best advice the author has read with regard to RIFs. Their view, based on personal trial experience, is that:

> the widespread approach of having the department head review personnel files and choose the worst performers for layoffs with only perfunctory review by any other official, has several disadvantages: the employer's case depends on one witness whose view of the laid off individual may not be shared by others in the Company; the personnel file to be reviewed may well have damaging, age-related entries. (Hartman & Homer, 1990, p. 188)

Hartman and Schnadig offer several guidelines, including: (a) a written policy on RIFs; (b) a management study explaining why a RIF is needed and how the number of layoffs are calculated; (c) consideration and documentation of alternatives to layoffs, including attrition, job elimination, redistribution of workload, reduced workweek, voluntary leaves, and early retirement; (d) using length of service as a decision rule whenever possible; and (e) charging an internal committee with the individual layoff decisions rather than a department head.

In the author's opinion, all but the fourth guideline are practical. The overall theme, however, is that documentable criteria should be used and they should not be applied by any one person (particularly a department head). The author would only add that conducting a RIF based solely on percentages of protected class members runs counter to any documentable criterion other than affirmative action. And as we will witness in Chapter 7, affirmative action is not a justifiable RIF criterion.

EARLY RETIREMENT

Finally, properly used, affirmative action cannot be challenged with reverse discrimination. The same is true in disability, as we will witness in Chapter 8. There is nothing to prevent an employer from sweetening the pot to induce early retirement, particularly in RIF situations. It is also a better policy than lying to the worker. There are no hard and fast rules, but there is case law indicating how not to do it, and a rule of thumb provided by Congress.

The case law clearly suggests it would be a blunder to state or imply that the employee has a choice between early retirement and discharge. That can only work if there is actual cause for discharge (e.g., *Sutton v. Arco*, 1981). The rule of thumb is in Title II of the Older Workers Act. Although Title II is written as a prescription for waivers, its implications for early retirement are clear. The eight steps in Title II were summarized in Section III of the chapter. All eight steps are important, but the two that are most important are: (a) to provide incentives that are genuine (not options the employee already has, or will soon have), and (b) to indicate clearly in the written agreement that the employee's decision is truly voluntary.

———— CHAPTER SUMMARY ————

ADEA is based on age-specific issues plus principles borrowed from Title VII, and to a lesser degree, FLSA. The protected class (Q1) is continuous, and there are four **statutory** exemptions (tenured faculty, hiring/retiring laws for police/firefighters, bona fide executives, and policy-making officials) and one regulatory exemption (apprentice trainees). The covered entities (**Q2**) mimic Title VII. The covered practices (**Q3**) mimic Title VII, but with extra emphasis on benefits and waivers (same benefits/same cost; nondiscrimination in severance; and eight criteria for waiver). The administrative procedures (**Q4**) follow mainly from Title VII, but with ADEA-specific rules to speed up claims. The remedies (**Q5**) include injunction, back pay, liquidated damages, lawyer fees, and affirmative relief. Jury trials are available for pay and damages for nonfederal employees, but federal employees are not eligible for jury trials or damages. All Title VII attack/defense balances (**Q6**) apply, but ADEA is mainly a disparate treatment statute (adverse impact and pattern or practice cases are very difficult to defend). The McDonnell-Burdine scenario uses all four prima facie steps when possible, but often (particularly in RIFs), factual evidence of age discrimination is used in lieu of steps 3 and 4. The five statutory defenses are affirmative. Good cause and RFOA are rarely used because the McDonnell-Burdine defense is less burdensome, and BFBP/BFSS are limited to special circumstances. But the BFOQ scenario is common, and successful, when it is necessary to protect the public safety. Finally, it is recommended that employers not be overly sensitive to age (e.g., not lie about reasons for termination), establish formal and proper procedures for RIFs (never relying on only department heads or bottom-line percentages), and follows Title II principles (from the OWBPA) for early retirement offers.

NOTE

1. It is grammatical to say "the Age Discrimination in Employment Act," and therefore "the ADEA." However, it is common to speak of simply "ADEA" when the acronym is used, much like one speaks of "Title VII" rather than "the Title VII."

7

Executive Order 11246
(Affirmative Action)

CHART 7.1. E.O. 11246

Q1	Q2	Q3	Q4	Q5	Q6
Protection is a misnomer. The Order "prefers" minorities and women	Contractors with more than $10,000 in procurement (Part II) or construction (Part III)	Affirmative action based on under-utilization Recruitment, training, and promotion should be the focus; never discharge	OFCCP reviews AAPs, takes complaints, & has special programs for larger companies	Main threat is to privilege of contracting with federal government OFCCP may also make affected class rulings OFCCP may enforce remedies	Balances are not important because court cases are reviews of DOL final rulings that approve or reverse Administrative Law rulings

(Q1): What classes of people are protected (or have rights)?
(Q2): What business entities are covered (or have duties)?
(Q3): What employment practices are covered?
(Q4): Is the law administered, and if so, how?
(Q5): What are the penalties (or remedies) for breaking the law?
(Q6): What are the attacks and defenses used in litigation?

Executive Order 11246 (E.O.11246) was issued by President Johnson in 1965, and was amended by Johnson himself in 1967, by President Nixon in 1969, and by President Carter in 1978. E.O.11246 is a three-part order covering: (I) federal government employees; (II) procurement contractors; and (III) construction contractors. There is also a fourth part with miscellaneous provisions for Parts II and III. The focus of this chapter is on **procurement** contracts in Part II (i.e., goods and services sold to the federal government) and **construction** contracts in Part III (i.e., federal assistance for state and local projects such as highways and buildings).

A major feature of E.O.11246 is the agreement by procurement and construction contractors to comply with the **Equal Opportunity Clause** in Sec.202 of the Executive Order (hereafter referred to as the "EO Clause"). In actuality, the EO Clause has a preamble and nine separable provisions. The preamble states, in part, that:

> *During the performance of this contract,* the contractor agrees as follows . . . [emphasis added]

The emphasized portion replaces language from President Kennedy's preamble to E.O.10925. E.O.10925 is a 1961 precursor to E.O.11246. Kennedy's preamble, in part, states that:

> *In connection with performance of work under this contract,* the contractor agrees as follows . . . [emphasis added]

In other words, Kennedy's order applied only to contracted work, whereas E.O.11246 is broader and applies to the entire plant. For example, a company contracted to build jet fighters must also comply with E.O.11246 when it builds noncontracted commercial aircraft.

Among the nine provisions in the EO Clause, three are written in Sec.202(1) as follows:

> **[1]** The contractor will not discriminate against any employee or applicant for employment because of race, color, religion, sex, or national origin. **[2]** The contractor will take affirmative action to ensure that applicants are employed, and that employees are treated during employment, without regard to their race, color, religion, sex, or national origin. Such action shall include, but not be limited to the following: employment, upgrading, demotion, or transfer; recruitment or recruitment advertising; layoff or termination; rates of pay or other forms of compensation; and selection for training, including apprenticeship. **[3]** The contractor agrees to post in conspicuous places, available to employees and applicants for employment, notices to be provided by the contracting officer setting forth the provisions of this *nondiscrimination clause.* [Numbering and emphasis added]

The reader will note the emphasized term, *nondiscrimination clause*. In actuality, segment **[1]** is the **nondiscrimination provision**, and segment **[2]** is the **affirmative action provision**. Segment **[3]** contains a notice posting requirement common to all EEO statutes and orders.

Segment **[1]** reads like a preamble to Title VII, which is a nondiscrimination statute. In contrast, segment **[2]** requires the employer to take positive (or extra) steps to ensure that underutilized minorities and/or women are recruited, hired, trained, and/or promoted.

Opponents of E.O.11246 regard segments **[1]** and **[2]** as mutually exclusive provisions. For example, according to Thomas Sowell (1984):

> "Equal opportunity" laws and policies require that individuals be judged on their qualification as individuals, without regard to race, sex, age, etc. "Affirmative action" requires that they be judged with regard to such group membership, receiving preferential or compensatory treatment in some cases to achieve a more proportional "representation" in various institutions and occupations. (p. 38)

Sowell's view implies **reverse discrimination** against innocent nonviolators, as well as undeserved benefits for nonvictims.

Proponents of E.O.11246, on the other hand, perceive consistency between segments **[1]** and **[2]**. Their focus is on the history of workplace discrimination, which reveals an uneven distribution of jobs, training, and wages for blacks relative to whites. For example, according to Haywood Burns (1987):

> Little weight is accorded the vital interest a supposedly modern, democratic, pluralistic state has in doing simple justice for its racial minorities. Too much weight is given to the putative interests of so-called innocent parties. Although it is proper for the Court to show concern for all affected parties, it is difficult to see how even the most ordinary and inoffensive white workers, who often got their jobs as a result of a biased job market, are entirely innocent; although they are not directly responsible for the favoritism built into the system, they directly benefit from it. (p. 104)

Burns's view suggests that Title VII-type laws are necessary to curb present and future violations, but affirmative action is also required to correct the lingering effects of past employment discrimination.

From management's perspective, philosophical issues are less important than the facially opposing demands of nondiscrimination versus affirmative action. The main purpose of this chapter, therefore, is to understand how affirmative action and nondiscrimination differ. The chapter contains five Sections. Section I traces the evolution of E.O.11246, Section II focuses on procurement and construction contracts, and Section III focuses on the executive and regulatory authority behind the Order. Section IV presents the longest and most important discussion (on reverse discrimination), and Section V focuses on compliance.

SECTION I
THE EVOLUTION OF E.O.11246

The nondiscrimination and affirmative action provisions of E.O. 11246 evolved separately. Most precursors to E.O.11246 spoke exclusively to nondiscrimination. By the time President Johnson issued E.O. 11246 in 1965, four Presidents had contributed to the core of Johnson's Order. The affirmative action provision was a late addition by President Kennedy in 1961. Furthermore, Kennedy's Order pre-dated all of the EEO statutes discussed in this book. In short, E.O.11246 is the culmination of presidential action in a domain that Congress did not effectively legislate until the Civil Rights Act of 1964.

PRESIDENTS ROOSEVELT AND TRUMAN

The first nondiscrimination order was E.O.8802, issued by President Roosevelt in 1941. According to Sovern (1966), Roosevelt issued the Order to ward off an impending march on Washington. The Order contained the following nondiscrimination provision:

> All contracting agencies of the Government of the United States shall include in all defense contracts hereafter negotiated by them a provision obligating the contractor not to discriminate against any worker because of race, creed, color, or national origin.

Roosevelt's Order applied only to defense contracts. It covered procurement, but not federal assistance; and referenced race, color, creed (religion), and national origin, but not sex. To enforce the Order, Roosevelt created a committee within the Office of Production Management containing influential private sector volunteers. This committee was empowered to receive complaints and make recommendations, but lacked the authority to impose sanctions.

When issued, E.O.8802 lacked formal congressional support, a detail corrected in the War Powers Act of 1941. Nine days after the War Powers Act, Roosevelt issued E.O.9001, which stipulated that the non-discrimination clause applies to all defense contracts, regardless of contractual language. Roosevelt then issued E.O.9346 in 1943. This order created a new committee, which, for political reasons, was moved to the Executive Office of the President. Like the prior committee, the new one could only make recommendations. In 1944, Congress passed the Russell amendment, forcing Roosevelt to obtain congressional funding. Funds were provided with the understanding that the new committee was to finish its work by June 30, 1946.

After Roosevelt's death in 1945, President Truman issued E.O.9964 to fund Roosevelt's second committee to its termination point. But in 1951, backed by the Defense Production Act of 1950, Truman issued E.O.10210, assigning all contracting authority to the Defense Department. Truman also issued E.O.10308, in which the heads of all federal agencies were authorized to obtain contract compliance, a major feature of Johnson's original order. As in all prior orders, there were no sanctions or penalties.

PRESIDENTS EISENHOWER AND KENNEDY

In 1953, President Eisenhower issued E.O.10479, the first nondiscrimination order that was not defense based. Eisenhower created a new committee consisting of nine presidential appointees and one member from each of six federal agencies. Thus like Truman, Eisenhower opted for intra-agency control. Then in 1954 Eisenhower issued E.O. 10557, which contained three novel provisions: (a) coverage of subcontractors, (b) notice posting requirements, and (c) a list of discriminatory acts covering all terms and conditions of employment. These provisions were subsequently adopted by Kennedy and Johnson.

The main precursor to E.O.11246 was E.O.10925, issued by President Kennedy in 1961. This Order contained the first affirmative action provision, which stated:

> The Contractor will take affirmative action to ensure that applicants are employed, and the employees are treated during employment, without regard to their race, creed, color, or national origin.

Except for omission of sex and use of the word "creed" rather than "religion," the reader will recognize this clause as the affirmative action provision in E.O.11246 (i.e., segment [2]).

Kennedy also created a new committee and a list of sanctions and penalties subsequently adopted by President Johnson. However, the sanctions and penalties required **judicial** enforcement. Kennedy's committee was empowered to report unresolvable violations to the Justice Department for prosecution. Although workable in theory, no case was ever prosecuted under this system.

The final precursor to E.O.11246 was E.O.11114, issued by President Kennedy in 1963. It provided first-time coverage of federally assisted construction contracts.

E.O.11246 AS ISSUED AND AMENDED BY PRESIDENT JOHNSON

The 1965 version of E.O.11246 targeted race, color, religion, and national origin. Johnson's 1967 amendment (E.O.11375) added sex. Part II of the Order on procurement borrowed from E.O.10925, and Part III on construction borrowed from E.O.11114. Except for the altered preamble and the ultimate inclusion of sex, the vast majority of words and phrases in the current EO Clause were taken verbatim from E.O.10925.

Johnson also borrowed Kennedy's sanctions and penalties. Johnson dismissed Kennedy's committee, however, and empowered the Secretary of Labor to regulate the Order. Johnson also empowered individual federal agencies to impose the sanctions and penalties. The freedom to impose sanctions and penalties prior to court action is the main reason why E.O.11246 has been far stronger than its precursors.

AMENDMENTS BY PRESIDENTS NIXON AND CARTER

President Nixon did not alter Parts II or III of E.O.11246. E.O. 11478, issued in 1969, altered only Part I on affirmative action in federal agencies. However, Nixon extended Part I beyond race, color, religion, sex, and national origin to include age and disability—the only order or statute that includes all seven of the major classes.

President Carter issued the last formal amendment to E.O.11246 in the Reorganization Plan of 1978 (in E.O.12086). In keeping with Johnson's plan, the OFCCP had, by 1974, issued regulations for compliance with E.O.11246. However, there was inconsistency within the various agencies regarding enforcement. Thus as noted by Schaeffer (1975), a member of the Conference Board, a private research organization:

> Under This Executive Order, each contracting agency in the Federal Government has been given primary responsibility for obtaining compliance by specified types of rules, regulations, and orders relating to employment discrimination issued through the Office of Contract Compliance (OFCC) in the Department of Labor. . . . Some federal agencies have apparently been much stricter in their requirements on contractors than others. Also, companies that are in several different businesses are subject to review by more than one agency. Sometimes they have faced very annoying and time-consuming problems because of conflicting instructions. (p. 30)

Carter's Reorganization Plan #1 of 1978 eliminated the enforcement powers of the individual federal agencies and added them to the already existing powers of the Secretary of Labor. Thus at the close of Carter's administration, the OFCCP was undoubtedly the most feared federal agency addressing discrimination in the workplace.

E.O.11246 UNDER PRESIDENTS REAGAN AND BUSH

President Reagan was a strong opponent of affirmative action, and President Bush has followed suit. Indeed, on the eve of the Civil Rights Act of 1991, it was reported that a Bush advisor had drafted an order to revoke E.O.11246. The Order is probably safe from formal revocation, because Congress has consistently supported affirmative action. However, Reagan and Bush have weakened E.O.11246 in three other ways. First, OFCCP funds and staff have been trimmed and the agency has been asked to soften its regulatory requirements. Second, the EEOC and Justice Department have actively opposed affirmative action in amicus briefs in several recent reverse discrimination cases. Finally, Reagan and Bush account for five of the current justices on the Supreme Court, none of whom is particularly friendly to affirmative action.

───── **BRIEF SUMMARY** ─────

E.O.11246 did not emerge full-blown in 1965. Most substantive provisions were established before the Civil Rights Act of 1964. Roosevelt and Truman used war powers to write and expanded the original EO Clause for defense procurement contractors. Eisenhower issued the first orders independently of war powers, and codified the basic terms and conditions in the EO Clause as well as the notice posting requirement. Kennedy introduced the affirmative action provision and also extended coverage to construction contractors. Johnson built on Kennedy's orders in 1965, and in 1967 added sex as a referenced class. Most importantly, the 1965 order established sanctions and penalties enforceable by federal agencies, and Carter's 1978 Reorganization Plan shifted all administrative and enforcement powers to the DOL. Nixon only amended Part I of E.O.11246 (not a topic of concern in this chapter), and the Reagan and Bush administrations have taken actions that, as we will witness in Section IV of this chapter, threaten the future of affirmative action for minorities and women.

SECTION II
REQUIREMENTS FOR PROCUREMENT
AND CONSTRUCTION CONTRACTORS

The six dimensions are depicted in Chart 7.1. In comparison to Title VII, E.O.11246 **protects (Q1)** preferred groups rather than whole classes (i.e., minorities and women), and the **covered entities (Q2)** include most procurement and construction contractors doing $10,000 or more worth of business with the federal government. The key **covered practice (Q3)** is affirmative action, not nondiscrimination, and the **administrative (Q4)** powers of the OFCCP include those previously cited for the EEOC plus the power to sanction and penalize. The critical **remedies (Q5)** (or sanctions and penalties) include but are not limited to suspension, cancellation, and debarment, as well as monetary awards for affected classes of employees. Finally, **attack/defense balances (Q6)** are not very relevant to E.O.11246, because court actions arise under much different circumstances than in Title VII.

Given the special attributes of an executive order relative to a congressional statute, the following discussion will de-emphasize the dimensions in favor of minimal obligations for procurement and construction contractors, additional obligations for procurement contractors, additional obligations for construction contractors, and OFCCP authority. The dimensions, however, will be used to compare E.O.11246 to Title VII.

MINIMAL OBLIGATIONS
FOR ALL COVERED CONTRACTORS

Compliance with the EO Clause is a *minimal* obligation for contractors with more than $10,000 dollars in federal contracts, unless otherwise exempted. This holds for procurement contracts and construction contracts.

The Nine Provisions in the EO Clause

Three of the nine provisions of the EO clause were reprinted in the overview to the chapter and include: (a) nondiscrimination, (b) affirmative action, and (c) notice posting. These provisions are contained in Sec.202(1). The remaining six provisions are contained, one each, in Sections 202(2) through 202(7), and include:

Sec.202(2): a statement regarding equal employment opportunity in all advertisements and solicitations

Sec.202(3): notification to unions of the contractors obligations under E.O.11246

Sec.202(4): compliance with the Order, and rules, regulations, and orders of the Secretary of Labor

Sec.202(5): furnishing requested information and reports by the Secretary of Labor, and permitting access to books, records, and accounts

Sec.202(6): agreement to sanctions for noncompliance, including cancellation, termination, suspension, and debarment

Sec.202(7): inclusion of all aforementioned provisions in subcontracts and purchase orders

As we will witness shortly, the affirmative action provision in Sec. 202(1) supersedes its counterpart on nondiscrimination. Moreover, affirmative action implies **preference,** *not* **protection.** Thus unlike Title VII, which protects all groups in any protected class, E.O.11246 provides exclusive privileges for groups who are historical victims of the pattern or practice of discrimination. These preferred groups include blacks, Hispanics, American Indians, Asian Americans, and women.

Exemptions

The key exemption is for contracts of $10,000 or less. Other exemptions include work outside the United States, work by religiously affiliated educational institutions, work deemed in the interest of national security (by agency heads), facilities deemed separate and distinct from the main activities of the contract (by the OFCCP), and subdivisions within state and local governments that do not participate in the contract. Most of these exemptions are straightforward. However, the exemption for subdivisions within state and local governments has been the subject of recent litigation. Specifically, Sec.60-1.5(a)(4) of the OFCCP Regulations states:

> The requirements of the Equal Opportunity Clause in any contract or subcontract with a state or local government . . . shall not be applicable to any agency, instrumentality or subdivision of such government which does not participate in work on or under the contract or subcontract.

In other words, a housing authority contract would presumably exempt the transit authority, since these are different subdivisions of local government. But in *Board of Governors v. DOL* (1990), the 4th Circuit ruled that branch campuses of a state university system are not **subdivisions** within the meaning of Sec.60-1.5(a)(4).

More specifically, the Secretary of Labor had cancelled all federal contracts for the North Carolina State University system because two branch campuses refused to submit to OFCCP compliance reviews. Five of the 16 branches had no federal funds, including the 2 that refused to be examined. The district court ruled in favor of the university system, viewing the branch campuses as legitimate subdivisions. But, in a divided decision, the 4th Circuit reversed, deeming the Board of Governors of the State University a central authority for all campuses, and the recipient of the federal funding. In other words, state university systems are a single state agency.

ADDITIONAL OBLIGATIONS FOR PROCUREMENT CONTRACTORS

Part II of E.O.11246 applies to private, state, and local "government contracts." According to Sec.60-1.3 of the OFCCP regulations, a "government contract" is:

any agreement or modification thereof between any contracting agency and any person for the furnishing of supplies or services for the use of real or personal property, including lease arrangements.

This definition applies to both prime contractors and subcontractors, regardless of the number of employees in the facility. Furthermore, large contracts are subject to obligations other than and in addition to compliance with the EO Clause.

Thresholds for Added Obligations

Procurement contractors with 50 or more employees must submit **EEO-1 Reports** and write **affirmative action plans** (AAPs) if they satisfy any of four additional criteria: (a) a contract value of $50,000 or more; (b) government bills of lading expected to reach $50,000 or more within any 12-month period; (c) serving as a depository of federal funds; or (d) issuing and paying for United States savings bonds and notes.

Most procurement contractors subject to EEO-1 and AAP obligations qualify under the 50 employee/$50,000 rule. Furthermore, dollar value dictates when an AAP is due. Contracts for one million dollars or more must have preapproved AAPs. Otherwise AAPs may be written within 120 days after the award. In 1982 the OFCCP proposed regulations to raise the thresholds for the postapproval from 50 employees and $50,000 to 500 employees and one million dollars. These regulations, however, were not finalized during the Reagan or Bush administrations, and are not likely to be finalized during the Clinton administration.

Work Force and Availability Analyses

The AAP requirement was adopted in the original (1968) OFCCP Regulations, and updated in 1971 (in "Revised Order No.4"). The AAP requires **goals** and **timetables** for correcting **underutilization** of minorities and women in the work force. Underutilization means:

> fewer minorities or women in a particular job group than would reasonably be expected by their availability.

To define underutilization, the contractor must conduct and compare both a **work force analysis** and an **availability analysis**. These analyses must be updated on a yearly basis.

In the work force analysis, each job title is listed as it appears in a collective bargaining agreement or on payroll records. Jobs are then ranked in pay from lowest to highest. Wherever applicable, lines of progressions must be shown. If there are no reasonable lines of progression, job titles and pay should be listed by department, job family, or discipline. Finally, for each job title the number of males and females that are black, Hispanic, American Indian, and Asian American must be calculated and listed.

The availability analysis requires eight steps. Specifically, the contractor must determine:

(1) minority and female population in the immediate labor area; (2) percentage of unemployed minorities and females in the immediate area; (3) percentage of minorities and females in the workforce relative to the percentage of minorities and females in immediate area; (4) availability of minorities and females in the immediate area having the requisite skills to perform the work; (5) availability of minorities and females having the requisite skills in an area in which the contractor can reasonably recruit; (6) availability of minorities and females within the workforce that can be trained or transferred; (7) availability of institutions to train the requisite skill within the immediate vicinity; and (8) degree of training required to bring minorities up to the requisite level of skills for all job titles.

One critical issue in the availability analysis is the **immediate labor area**. For example, Timken is famous for successfully fighting an OFCCP debarment order. The OFCCP ruled that the immediate labor area for Timken encompassed a 25-mile zone. In *Timken v. Vaughn* (1976), an Ohio district court blocked the debarment order because it failed to consider the commuting patterns of citizens in the region (few if any ever commuted 25 miles).

A second critical issue concerns multiestablishment contractors with central administrative offices (i.e., headquarters). According to Order #83a1 issued by the OFCCP in 1988, all positions filled at a central headquarters must be included in the headquarters' AAP.

Correcting Underutilization

Correction applies only to **qualified** job applicants or employees. If an individual is not qualified, the issue reverts to training necessary to make the individual qualified. Thus most corrective procedures involve special recruitment efforts, but they can also include training programs to qualify individuals for job entry and/or promotion. Contractors should not hire or promote unqualified applicants, and non-preferred applicants should not be discharged or demoted to make room for preferred applicants.

Equally as important, the goals and timetables are temporary and flexible targets, rather than fixed quotas. Or as stated in Sec.60-2.12(e) of the OFCCP Regulations:

> Goals may not be rigid and inflexible quotas which must be met, but must be targets reasonably attainable by means of applying every *good faith effort* to make all aspects of the entire affirmative action program work. [emphasis added]

Thus the failure to achieve goals is acceptable given a good faith effort. Also, once the goals are reached the plan has been fulfilled. In other words, an AAP should never be used to maintain a balanced work force, either prior to a determination of underutilization or after the goals of an AAP have been achieved.

ADDITIONAL OBLIGATIONS FOR CONSTRUCTION CONTRACTORS

Part III of E.O.11246 applies to private, state, and local "federal assistance construction contracts." According to Sec.60-1.3 of the OFCCP Regulations, *construction* is defined as:

> the construction, rehabilitation, alteration, conversion, extension, demolition or repair of buildings, highways, or other changes or improvements to real property.

Because construction contracts are usually multimillion dollar ventures, they invariably require the EEO-1 Reports and AAPs, and virtually all AAPs require preapproval.

Historically, the OFCCP has been more directive with construction contracts than procurement contracts. From 1967 through 1970 the OFCCP imposed its own plans. From 1970 through 1978 construction contractors were encouraged to develop preapproved "hometown" plans. After 1978 the OFCCP offered a third alternative termed the "Standard Federal Equal Employment Opportunity Contract Specifications" clause.

OFCCP Imposed Plans

The prototypic example of the OFCCP imposed plan is the "Philadelphia Plan." In the summer of 1969, the OFCCP issued two orders applying to construction contracts of $500,000 or more in the five-county area surrounding Philadelphia. The orders established the following four standards for construction AAPs:

> (1) The current extent of minority group participation in the trade. (2) The availability of minority group persons for employment in such trade. (3) The need for training programs in the area and/or the need to assure demand for those in or from existing training programs. (4) The impact of the program upon the existing labor force.

In the Philadelphia Plan, the OFCCP imposed a 4-year timetable for six trades (ironworkers, plumbers and pipe fitters, steamfitters, sheetmetal workers, electrical workers, and elevator workers). For example, for ironworkers, target hiring goals for minorities were set at 5%-9% for 1970, 11%-15% for 1971, 16%-20% for 1972, and 22%-26% for 1973. The Philadelphia plan was challenged and upheld in *Contractors Assoc. of Eastern Pa. v. Secretary of Labor* (1971).

Preapproved Hometown Plans

By 1970 the OFCCP had imposed plans in a number of other major cities, the most notable ones being Washington, D.C., St. Louis, Atlanta, and Camden (New Jersey). Because each plan was unique and involved a great deal of effort (investigations, hearings, etc.), the OFCCP encouraged other communities to develop **hometown** plans. By 1973 approximately 50 hometown plans were developed.

The prototypic example of a hometown plan is the "Boston Plan," which implicated 13 construction companies and 145 general contractors responsible for about 80% of all construction work in the Commonwealth of Massachusetts. The plan, approved in 1970, was developed by representatives of the unions, the contractors, and the minority community. Its trades, goals, and timetables were comparable to those of the Philadelphia Plan. The Boston Plan was challenged and upheld in *Associated General Contractors, Inc. v. Altshuler* (1973).

The Standard EEO Contract Specifications Clause

Construction contractors are still free to create and follow hometown plans. Because of the nature of the construction industry, however (e.g., contracts across state and community lines), hometown plans can be confusing, containing contradictory goals and timetables for different trades in different regions. The **Standard Clause**, an OFCCP regulation finalized in 1978, permits construction contractors to receive preapproval from the OFCCP on an individual contract basis. The clause, as outlined in Sec.60-4.3 of the OFCCP regulations, stipulates the following seven provisions:

> (1) working environments free of harassment, intimidation, and coercion; (2) job availability notification to minority/female recruitment sources; (3) special records for minority/female referrals and applicants; (4) report to the OFCCP of discriminatory union practices; (5) participation in special training efforts or development of on-the-job training opportunities; (6) communication of the contractor's EEO policies within the company and throughout the community; and (7) an annual audit of the contractor's EEO efforts.

OFCCP ENFORCEMENT

The OFCCP uses reviews and other methods to determine if contractors are in compliance with E.O.11246. When contractors do not comply, the OFCCP can impose a variety of sanctions and penalties. However, the contractor may contest an OFCCP ruling, whereas affected applicants and employees may only file complaints.

Compliance Reviews

Sections 205 through 208 of E.O.11246 authorize the Secretary of Labor to investigate contract facilities. The OFCCP's main investigatory tool is the **compliance review**. Compliance reviews are generally reserved for contracts that have not been preapproved. Currently, the applicable OFCCP Regulations for compliance reviews are contained in Revised Rule #4, published in 1974. If selected, the contractor faces the prospect of a three-step review.

Step 1 is a "desk audit," in which the contractor furnishes AAP and EEO-1 data. The audit focuses on the work force analysis, to ensure that the eight steps in Revised Order #4 are properly met, and that the AAP sets appropriate goals and timetables. If there are issues of confidentiality, the contractor may use codes and pay range indexes in lieu of names, reasons for termination, and actual pay data.

If the desk audit indicates noncompliance, the OFCCP may conduct an "on-site review" (step 2). The review must be based on a recent desk audit. Furthermore, the review cannot be conducted within 24 months of a prior review unless there is evidence of continued noncompliance.

Finally, if complex deficiencies arise during an on-site review, a compliance officer may take company data **off site** (step 3).

If steps 2 and/or 3 are taken, the compliance officer must provide feedback to the contractor. The main purpose of the review is to gain voluntary commitment to correct violations (i.e., a signed conciliation agreement). If an agreement cannot be reached, the OFCCP may impose its sanctions and penalties.

Other Methods of Investigation

In addition to compliance reviews, the OFCCP also uses a formal complaint process and self-monitoring. In accordance with Sec.60-1.21 of the OFCCP regulations, any person (i.e., individual, group, etc.) may file a complaint alleging a violation. Complaints must be filed within 180 days of an alleged violation, unless the violation is continuous or the OFCCP finds "good cause" for extending the limit. OFCCP regulations dictate that complaints must be resolved informally. If informal means fail, however, the OFCCP may impose its sanctions and penalties.

Self-monitoring is a special procedure used with major corporations such as AT&T, General Motors, and IBM. These companies contribute trend reports to the national self-monitoring report system (NSMRS). Contributors to NSMRS are exempt from compliance reviews during the duration of their contracts, as long as the trends reported are indicative of compliance with the Order.

Sanctions and Penalties

The sanctions and penalties for noncompliance are specified in Sec.209(a)(1) through Sec.209(a)(6) of E.O.11246. They include (a) blacklisting (publishing the names of noncompliant contractors and unions); (b) recommendations to the Justice Department for litigation to enforce the provisions of the EO Clause; (c) recommendations to the EEOC to pursue Title VII violations; (d) recommendations to the Justice Department for litigation of criminal violations (e.g., for falsification of documents); (e) cancellation, termination, or suspension of contracts; and (f) revoking the privilege of applying for contracts (i.e., debarment).

Among these sanctions and penalties, cancellation, termination, suspension, and/or debarment are obviously the most extreme. The OFCCP has debarred less than 30 contractors in its entire history (see Leonard, 1990). However, the threat is sufficient to motivate voluntary compliance with E.O.11246.

On the other hand, the OFCCP has frequently used its authority to trigger Justice Department litigation in the federal courts (i.e., sanction #2 above). In addition, Sec.209(a)(2) of E.O.11246 permits the OFCCP to initiate "appropriate proceedings" to enforce the Order. In response, the OFCCP has issued Sec.60-2.1(b), which provides monetary relief for "affected classes" of victims of noncompliance.

For example, in *United States v. Duquesne Light Co.* (1976), the Justice Department sued to enforce an OFCCP order for back pay to an affected class of minorities and women. Duquesne refused to comply because back pay is not on the list of sanctions and penalties specified in Sec.209 of the Order. However, a Pennsylvania district court supported Sec.60-2.1(b) of the OFCCP Regulations, stating:

> By its reference to "appropriate proceedings," Sec.209(a)(2) confers on the government discretion to invoke the equitable powers of this Court. Absent a congressional limitation upon those powers, the government may seek any remedy which will effectuate the purposes of this Order.

A similar case was recently tried to the same conclusion in *United States v. Whitney National Bank of New Orleans* (1987).

Contractor Rights and Privileges

Whether initiated by compliance review or complaint, the OFCCP must attempt conciliation. If conciliation fails, the OFCCP may, of course, impose sanctions and penalties. But the contractor may request a hearing by an administrative law judge (ALJ). The ALJ's ruling serves as a recommendation to the Secretary of Labor. A final ruling by the Secretary exhausts the OFCCP administrative procedures and serves as the starting point for federal court action.

The requirement to exhaust administrative procedures was affirmed by the 10th Circuit in *St. Regis Paper Company v. Marshall* (1979). In 1976 (i.e., prior to Reorganization Plan #1), the General Services Administration (GSA) ordered St. Regis to correct continuing violations affecting a class of women. St. Regis responded, but the GSA rejected the response and invoked an affected class ruling. Rather than exhausting its administrative options, the company filed suit in federal district court. The district court dismissed the suit and the 10th Circuit affirmed. The company argued that further administrative procedures would involve needless expense and would be futile in view of the GSA's prior ruling. The 10th Circuit disagreed, ruling that:

> Plaintiff's assertion that it would be subjected to needless expense if required to pursue its administrative remedy is . . . unconvincing. We refuse to assume that administrative authorities will arbitrarily deny plaintiff relief to which he is entitled . . . and an administrative hearing cannot be "futile" where plaintiff will be afforded a full opportunity to present evidence and argue its position.

Individual Complaints

Finally, an employee may file an individual complaint. But unlike Title VII, the employee has no private right of action. Interestingly, this ruling was initially invoked in two cases involving Kennedy's E.O.10925 (*Farmer v. Philadelphia Electric,* 1964; *Farkas v. Texas Instrument,* 1967). In both cases, individuals sought relief for individuous acts of racial discrimination. The 3rd Circuit dodged the issue by ordering Farmer to file a complaint with the President's committee. However, the 5th Circuit dismissed the case for "failure to show a cause of action" (i.e., failure to raise a federal question). The same ruling has been rendered in claims initiated under E.O.11246 (e.g., *Utley v. Varian Associates,* 1987).

TITLE VII, E.O.11246,
AND THE SIX DIMENSIONS

Facially, Title VII and E.O.11246 appear to **protect (Q1)** the same classes—race, color, religion, sex, and national origin. However, where Title VII protects all groups in each class, E.O.11246 protects only preferred groups, including blacks, Hispanics, American Indians, Asian Americans, and women.

Title VII and E.O.11246 apply to private, state, and local **entities (Q2)**. However, where Title VII focuses on businesses affecting commerce and employers with 15 or more employees, E.O.11246 focuses on procurement contractors (Part II) and federally assisted construction contractors (Part III) with more than $10,000 in contracts.

Facially, Title VII and E.O.11246 **prohibit (Q3)** discrimination in the terms and conditions of employment. But in reality, Title VII focuses on individuous acts where violators and victims are both identifiable. In contrast, E.O.11246 focuses on the continuing effects of past violations, permitting preferred treatment of potential nonvictims at the expense of potential nonviolators. Thus E.O.11246 advocates special efforts to recruit, hire, train, and promote members within its preferred groups, but only when evidence (e.g., from an AAP) indicates underutilization of qualified or trainable applicants.

The **administrative (Q4)** duties of the EEOC and OFCCP are facially parallel. Both offer interpretative guidance, investigate patterns of discrimination, and administer to prerequisites for federal court action. Furthermore, during an investigation both are charged with resolving disputes via conference and conciliation. However, because of its extra enforcement powers, the OFCCP probably has an easier time encouraging voluntary compliance.

Facially, the remedies in E.O.11246 and Title VII are different. Title VII remedies **(Q5)** focus on injunction, back pay, and affirmative relief (e.g., reinstatement or front pay), whereas E.O.11246 focuses on the threat of suspension, cancellation, and debarment. Thus Title VII remedies are designed to restore the individual, whereas E.O.11246 penalties and sanctions are designed to redirect the contractor. These differences are important, but there are also some similarities. The OFCCP can make affected class rulings resulting in back pay awards for individuals. More importantly, a Title VII violation can lead to court ordered affirmative action.

Finally, the **attack/defense balances (Q6)**, so critical to Title VII cases, are only mildly important to E.O.11246. The standards used in administrative law pre-date Title VII traditions. Additionally, only a small percentage of cases heard by administrative law judges are ultimately tried in the federal courts.

——— **BRIEF SUMMARY** ———

Parts II (procurement) and III (construction) of E.O.11246 protect special groups as opposed to entire classes, and place minimal obligations on most private, state, and local contractors doing business with the federal government. Additional obligations are placed on larger contractors, and strong regulatory powers are granted to the OFCCP. Federal court action is a last resort, given failure of OFCCP and the Secretary of Labor to gain conciliation. In short, E.O.11246 is vastly different than Title VII, and these differences are accentuated within the six dimensions.

SECTION III
EXECUTIVE AND REGULATORY AUTHORITY

E.O.11246 has been directly attacked with challenges to the President's authority to issue E.O.11246 and challenges to the OFCCP's authority to regulate E.O.11246. Executive authority has been supported in the courts, and for the most part, so has regulatory authority. However, some limits have been placed on the OFCCP.

EXECUTIVE AUTHORITY

Presidential authority to issue executive orders is not absolute. Indeed, there have been successful challenges in other areas. For example, in 1952 President Truman issued E.O.10340 to prevent a nationwide steelworkers' strike. The Supreme Court reviewed the Order in *Youngstown v. Sawyer* (1952), and deemed it unconstitutional. The Supreme Court did not rule on E.O.11246 until 1974. However, boundaries outlined in *Youngstown v. Sawyer* prompted the lower courts to conclude that E.O.11246 is a valid exercise of executive authority.

The Youngstown Ruling

In Youngstown, six concurrences formed a majority ruling. The most influential of these concurrences was by Justice Jackson, who focused on three tests of executive authority.

In test #1, the President "acts pursuant to an expressed or implied authorization of Congress." Here, executive authority is at its peak. For example, Carter's Reorganization Plan of 1978 was pursuant to the Reorganization Act of 1977.

In test #2, executive authority is weakened by orders written independently of congressional approval (i.e., neither authorization nor contradiction). According to Justice Jackson, test #2 creates a "zone of twilight" because of the possibility of concurrent executive and legislative jurisdiction, with no clear lines of authority.

Executive authority is weakest, however, in test #3. Here the President "takes measures incompatible with the expressed or implied will of Congress." According to Justice Jackson, "at stake is the equilibrium established by our constitutional system."

Basically, Truman's attempt to prevent the steelworkers' strike was struck down on the basis of test #3. However, E.O.11246 has been generally supported on the basis of test #1.

Court Rulings

The President's authority to issue nondiscrimination orders was first addressed in *Farmer v. Philadelphia Electric* (1964) and *Farkas v. Texas Instrument* (1967). For example, citing each order from E.O.8802 through E.O.10295, the Farkas Court concluded that:

> Executive orders and regulations requiring nondiscrimination provisions have the force and effect of laws.

Executive authority was again addressed by the 3rd Circuit (the Farmer Court) in *Contractors Association v. Schultz* (1971) and the 5th Circuit (the Farkas Court) in *United States v. New Orleans Public Service Inc. (NOPSI)* (1977). In Contractors, the previously noted challenge to the Philadelphia Plan, the 3rd Circuit evaluated the limits of executive power based on *Youngstown v. Sawyer* and concluded that E.O.11246 is valid because Congress:

> aware of Presidential action with respect to federally assisted construction projects since June of 1963, has continued to make appropriations for such projects.

The NOPSI challenge was more direct. NOPSI had a state-approved monopoly on electric power in the New Orleans area. Thus federal installations in the area had no other source of power. NOPSI refused to sign the EO Clause because it did not voluntarily seek to do business with the federal government. The 5th Circuit upheld the President's authority to issue E.O.11246, as well as NOPSI's minimal obligation to comply with the Order. The court concluded that:

> NOPSI's monopoly exists only because of local legislative action. The supremacy clause of the Constitution obviously cannot countenance such a result. We hold, therefore, that the Government can compel NOPSI to comply with the equal opportunity obligations of Executive Order 11246, even though the company has not expressly consented to be bound by that Order.

The 5th Circuit also rendered the same ruling in *United States v. Mississippi Power & Light* (1977), a companion case to NOPSI.

OFCCP AUTHORITY

Valid executive authority is necessary, but not sufficient for the validity of the OFCCP regulations. Most of the OFCCP regulations have the force and effect of law. For example, E.O.11246 does not mention "affected class," "imposed plans," or "hometown plans," three products of OFCCP regulations that have been challenged and upheld in the federal courts. But the OFCCP has exceeded its authority in two areas; its selection procedures for compliance reviews, and its policies on disclosing information to third parties.

Boundary Conditions for OFCCP Authority

A federal agency regulation must pass two tests to have the force and effect of law. As summarized by the Supreme Court in *Chrysler v. Brown* (1979), a regulation:

> must be [1] a "substantive" or "legislative type" ruling affecting individual rights and obligations . . . and [2] it must be the product of congressional grant of legislative authority, promulgated in conformity with procedural requirements imposed by Congress. [numbering added]

"Substantive" laws (test #1) outline rights and duties of parties. This contrasts with adjective laws, which define procedures to create and interpret substantive laws. For example, Sec.712(a) of Title VII expressly authorizes the EEOC to:

> issue, amend or rescind *procedural* regulations to carry out the provisions of this Title. [emphasis added]

Thus technically speaking the EEOC Guidelines are procedural, whereas the OFCCP Regulations are substantive. However, as we witnessed in Chapters 2 and 3, EEOC Title VII Regulations are treated with deference (i.e., as if they are regulations).

Test #2 reduces to adherence to the Administrative Procedures Act of 1946 (APA), which was designed by Congress to curb potential excesses by federal agencies. Among other things, the APA requires publication of a regulation in the Federal Register, and the provision of at least 30 days for intervention by interested parties prior to publication in the Federal Register.

Limitations on Authority in Compliance Reviews

In Sec.60-60.3(b) of the OFCCP Regulations it is noted that companies are selected for compliance reviews via "approved methods of priority selection." The 5th Circuit has twice ruled on the OFCCP selection process. Both cases are sequels to the 1977 NOPSI and Mississippi Power cases discussed earlier.

In 1981, NOPSI and Mississippi Power were codefendants against the United States for refusing to submit to compliance reviews. Recall that both companies lost battles to invalidate E.O.11246 in 1977. In the 1981 sequel, the 5th Circuit affirmed that E.O.11246 is "a proper exercise of congressionally delegated authority." But at the same time the court questioned and ultimately overturned the OFCCP's decision to conduct compliance reviews on these two companies. The court ruled that compliance reviews should be (a) congressionally backed; (b) limited in scope; and (c) reasonably based. The court concluded that the reviews were congressionally backed and limited in scope, but questioned whether they were reasonable. According to the 5th Circuit:

> The search will be reasonable if based on either (1) specific evidence of violation, (2) "a showing that reasonable legislative or administrative standards for conducting an . . . inspection are satisfied with respect to a particular establishment," . . . or (3) a showing that a search is "pursuant to an administrative plan containing specific neutral criteria."

In the 1984 sequel to these cases, the 5th Circuit concluded that the OFCCP's decision to investigate the two power companies was not reasonable when matched against the three criteria outlined in its 1981 ruling. In short, the OFCCP cannot arbitrarily review AAPs. In reading these two cases, one is left with the impression that the OFCCP was retaliating against NOPSI and Mississippi Power for their earlier challenges, and the 5th Circuit found this to be unreasonable.

Limitations on Authority to Disclosure Information

Obviously, in a compliance review the OFCCP evaluates sensitive documents. A key issue addressed by the Supreme Court in *Chrysler v. Brown* (1979) concerned whether such documents are available to third parties under the Freedom of Information Act (FOIA) of 1966, as amended by the Privacy Act of 1974.

Chrysler employees sought access to the company's AAP. Pursuant to its own regulations in Sections 60.40-1 through 60.40-4, the OFCCP authorized release. Chrysler sued to prevent disclosure based on FOIA and the Trade Secrets Act of 1948, and won an apparent victory. The Supreme Court issued three important rulings. First, FOIA is a "disclosure statute," meaning it cannot be used to prevent disclosure. Second, the relevant OFCCP regulations were deemed unlawful because they were not consistent with the meaning of a congressional statute (the Trade Secrets Act). But third, Chrysler does not have a private right to sue under the Trade Secrets Act.

To simplify an otherwise overly complicated issue, the Supreme Court struck down the OFCCP regulations as the basis for disclosure, but at the same time entrusted the OFCCP (and other federal agencies) to decide disclosure issues in accordance with the Administrative Procedures Act. Lower courts have subsequently interpreted the Chrysler ruling to mean the OFCCP must decide whether to disclose, and the federal courts must review whether the OFCCP's decisions are, in the words of the Chrysler Court, "arbitrary, capricious, an abuse of discretion, or otherwise not in accordance with law."

In general, the lower courts have backed the OFCCP in their rulings to release EEO-1 and AAP data (see *General Dynamics v. Marshall,* 1979, & *CNA v. Donovan,* 1987). However, it is clear that the OFCCP does not have as free a hand in releasing information as it does in extracting back pay or in approving AAPs.

─────── **BRIEF SUMMARY** ───────

Prior to any of the reverse discrimination rulings by the Supreme Court, the lower courts had deemed E.O.11246 a valid exercise of executive authority based on boundaries conditions established by the Supreme Court in *Youngstown v. Sawyer.* The prevailing lower court ruling is that E.O.11246 has congressional approval (Justice Jackson's test #1). OFCCP regulations are generally legally forceful, but not unlimited. But the limitations discussed above fall into the category of wrist slapping. Basically, the OFCCP must avoid arbitrary and capricious attempts to investigate companies and disclose information. But within those boundaries, the OFCCP exercises a great deal of legal authority.

SECTION IV
SUPREME COURT REVERSE DISCRIMINATION RULINGS

Prior to its ruling in *Regents v. Bakke* (1978), the Supreme Court had virtually ignored reverse discrimination. For example, in *DeFunis v. Odegaard* (1974), a white applicant rejected from law school challenged the admission of 36 minority applicants who had lower test scores and grades than himself. A state court ordered DeFunis's admission and the Washington State Supreme Court reversed. By the time the U.S. Supreme Court heard the case, DeFunis had nearly completed the program. Rather than decide the (14th Amendment) issue, a majority of five justices issued an unsigned (per curium) ruling that the case was moot.

In 1976, the Supreme Court rendered a reverse discrimination ruling in *McDonald v. Santa Fe Transportation,* a Title VII/Sec.1981 case cited earlier in Chapters 2 and 4. In Santa Fe, two white employees were discharged for stealing, whereas a black employee who also stole was retained. But this was a single, individuous act without affirmative action implications.

However, between 1978 and 1990, the Supreme Court issued 12 reverse discrimination rulings that, collectively, define the current status of stronger challenges to affirmative action than those witnessed in Section III of the chapter. These rulings are complex enough. But they are also complicated by four nonsubstantive factors: (a) the changing composition of the Court; (b) the changing opinions of individual justices; (c) variation among issues addressed in these cases; and (d) variation among statutes used to attack affirmative action.

For purposes of exposition, the cases will be discussed in their historical order. To simplify the material the rulings will be divided into five groupings (A through E), each followed by a Brief Summary analysis. A more detailed analysis considering all 12 cases will be provided afterwards.

GROUP A: BAKKE, WEBER, AND FULLILOVE

The Bakke Court consisted of six justices whose tenure spanned all 12 cases (Blackmun, Brennan, Marshall, Rehnquist, Stevens, & White) and three who resigned at varying periods after Fullilove (Burger, Powell, & Stewart). All nine justices heard Bakke and Fullilove, but two (Powell & Stevens) did not participate in the Weber case.

Regents v. Bakke (1978)

Allan Bakke issued 14th Amendment and Title VI (not Title VII) challenges to the admissions policy by a state university medical school. The facts of the case were that the University of California at Davis voluntarily reserved 16 of 100 seats for minority applicants and poor whites.[1] Denied admission in two successive years, Bakke charged that his equal rights were unprotected, since minorities could apply for any of 100 seats, whereas he could apply for any of only 84 seats.

Interpreting the California Constitution, the 14th Amendment, and Title VI, a state court ruled: (a) the Davis plan contained an illegal quota; and (b) race can play no role in admissions. But Bakke was denied admission because he could not prove he would have been admitted, absent the plan. The California Supreme Court, interpreting only the 14th Amendment, affirmed the two lower court rulings, but ordered Bakke's admission because the school could not prove Bakke would have been rejected, absent the plan. Applying a **strict scrutiny** analysis, the court ruled: (a) the state has a **compelling interest** to fight segregation; but (b) its solution was *not* **narrowly tailored** (i.e., not the least intrusive method of satisfying the interest).

The U.S. Supreme Court ruling was a 4-4-1 split containing: (a) a plurality of Brennan, Blackmun, Marshall, and White who believed the plan passed the strict scrutiny test under the 14th Amendment; (b) a plurality of Stevens, Burger, Rehnquist, and Stewart who believed Bakke's rights were violated under Title VI (and therefore saw no need to evaluate the 14th Amendment charge); and (c) Powell, who partially agreed with both pluralities. According to Haywood Burns (1987):

> With four justices upholding the plan, four opposed, and Powell somewhere in the middle, it turned out to be something of a $4\frac{1}{2} - 4\frac{1}{2}$ decision. (p. 102)

Nevertheless, two majority rulings emerged. First, Powell plus the Stevens plurality ruled that the plan contained an illegal quota. But second, Powell plus the Brennan plurality ruled that race can be considered in admissions (thus overruling both California courts).

Two other factors are worth noting. First, the Brennan plurality favored a **moderate** standard of scrutiny in 14th Amendment cases (i.e., less than "strict scrutiny," but greater than "rational basis"). Relative to the strict scrutiny analysis, moderate scrutiny would require: (a) an important state interest rather than an interest that is compelling; and (b) a reasonably related solution rather than a solution that is narrowly tailored. But Powell favored strict scrutiny, and the Stevens plurality did not rule on any 14th Amendment issues. Therefore, the level of scrutiny in 14th Amendment cases was left for another day.

Second, although agreeing that race can be a factor in admissions, Powell disliked **quotas**. He offered the "Harvard Plan" as an example of proper consideration of minority issues, stating:

> In such an admissions program, race or ethnic background may be deemed a "plus" in a particular applicant's file, yet it does not insulate the individual from comparison with all other candidates for available seats.

In other words, all other credentials being equal, an extra plus for being a minority candidate is a legitimate basis for acceptance. Interestingly, the Brennan plurality rejected Powell's reasoning in Bakke, but three of its members (Blackmun, Brennan, & Marshall) later supported this reasoning in *Johnson v. Transportation Agency* (1987).

United Steelworkers v. Weber (1979)

Brian Weber issued a Title VII challenge to a voluntary AAP by a private employer. Kaiser Aluminum required prior craft experience in its skilled workers, but the unions who taught those skills had a history of excluding blacks. For example, in Weber's plant, only 5 of 273 skilled workers (1.83%) were black, relative to 39% in the local black labor force. Kaiser entered a master collective bargaining agreement for all of its plants, the end result being in-house training programs that reserved 50% of all new training slots for black employees. Weber filed his suit when several slots were subsequently awarded to black employees with less seniority than himself.

The district court held that Kaiser's AAP violated Title VII, and the 5th Circuit affirmed, ruling that all employment preferences based on race, even those based on bona fide AAPs, are illegal. In a 5-2 ruling, Justice Brennan, speaking for Blackmun, Marshall, Stewart, and White, ruled that the Kaiser AAP is consistent with the legislative history of the 1964 version of Title VII, stating:

> The purposes of the plan mirror those of the statute [Title VII]. Both were designed to break down old patterns of racial segregation. . . . At the same time, the plan does not unnecessarily trammel the interest of white employees. The plan does not require the discharge of white workers. . . . Nor does the plan create an absolute bar to the advancement

of white employees . . . [finally] the plan is a temporary measure . . . not intended to maintain racial balance, but simply to eliminate manifest racial imbalance.

In other words, an AAP may serve as a legitimate productive phase 2 defense to a prima facie disparate treatment attack when: (a) there is evidence of past discrimination (judicial or otherwise); (b) the AAP does not "trammel" the interests of white employees (e.g., no discharges); and (c) the AAP is temporary and designed to eliminate racial imbalance rather than to maintain racial balance.

Weber's prima facie charge was based on Sec.703(j) of Title VII which states:

> Nothing contained in this title shall be interpreted to *require* any employer . . . to grant preferential treatment to any individual or to any group because of race, color . . . on account of an imbalance which may exist with respect to the total number or percentage of persons of any race, color . . . [emphasis added]

But Brennan rejected the charge, ruling that Congress did not require affirmative action, but did permit it.

The dissent focused on: (a) the "explicit language" of Sec.703(d) of Title VII, which prohibits discrimination in the terms and conditions of employment (including training); and (b) their reading of the 1964 legislative history of Title VII, which, in the words of Justice Burger, speaking for Rehnquist:

> makes equally clear that the supporters and opponents of Title VII reached an agreement about the statute's intended effect. That agreement, expressed so clearly in the language of the statue that no one should doubt its meaning, forecloses the reading which the Court gives this statute today.

Interestingly, neither Brennan nor Burger discussed the 1972 EEO Act amendments to Title VII. E.O.11246 was not yet issued in 1964. But in the debates prior to the EEO Act of 1972, E.O.11246 was a focal point, and most legislators favored Brennan's viewpoint. For example, Senator Ervin twice offered to amend Title VII so that it precluded racial preference under any circumstance. Both amendments were voted down by nearly 70% of the Senate.

Fullilove v. Klutznick (1980)

In the Public Works Act of 1977, Congress ordered a 10% set aside of federal funds for minority business enterprises (MBEs) whose owners are "Negroes, Spanish-speaking, Orientals, Indians, Eskimos, and Aleuts." The Act was challenged by several contracting associations under both the 5th and 14th Amendments. The lower courts upheld the Act, and the Supreme Court affirmed in a 6-3 ruling.

The majority was formed by two 3-person pluralities. Burger, speaking for Powell and White, ruled that Congress had authority to pass the Act. Burger also ruled that the Act passed strict scrutiny under both the 5th and 14th Amendments. That is, Congress demonstrated its compelling interest by documenting discrimination in the construction industry, and the plan was deemed narrowly tailored even though its burdens were shared by innocent parties. Marshall, speaking for Blackmun and Brennan, concurred, but argued for moderate scrutiny.

In a separate concurrence, Powell clarified his agreement with Burger, stating:

> The Government [has] a legitimate interest in ameliorating the disabling effects of identified discrimination. . . . The existence of illegal discrimination justifies the imposition of a remedy that "make[s] persons whole for injuries suffered on account of unlawful . . . discrimination." . . . A critical inquiry, therefore, is whether the [Public Works Act] was enacted as a means of redressing such discrimination. But this Court has never approved race-conscious remedies absent judicial, administrative, or legislative findings of constitutional or statutory violations.

In other words, Powell was protecting his Bakke opinion, where he repudiated quotas. In Fullilove, Powell deemed that a 10% set aside, clearly a quota, was legal because the Public Works Act redressed identifiable, unlawful discrimination.

The dissent consisted of Stevens speaking for Rehnquist, and Stevens speaking for himself. Speaking for Rehnquist, Stevens issued a hard line, stating:

> The equal protection standard of the Constitution has one clear and central meaning—it absolutely prohibits individuous discrimination by government. That standard must be met by every State under the Equal Protection Clause of the Fourteenth Amendment . . . [and] . . . by the United States itself under the Due Process Clause of the Fifth Amendment. . . . Under our Constitution, any official action that treats a person

differently on account of his race or ethnic origin is inherently suspect
and presumptively invalid.

But speaking for himself, Stevens forecast a future change in attitude
toward affirmative action by stating:

> It is up to Congress to demonstrate that its unique statutory preference
> is justified by a relevant characteristic that is shared by the members of
> the preferred class. In my opinion, because it has failed to make that dem-
> onstration, it has also failed to discharge its duty to govern impartially
> embodied in the Fifth Amendment to the United States Constitution.

In other words, Stevens believed that discrimination in the construction industry should be remedied, but he viewed set asides for only a
small portion of the minority population as being inadequate.

--------- **BRIEF SUMMARY** ---------

Weber was clearly a landmark ruling, affirming the primary meaning behind
E.O.11246: that employers voluntarily assess and correct patterns of discrimination in hiring and training. The other two cases are of lesser value.
The Bakke ruling, though famous by name, settled nothing; it merely raised
one question regarding the definition of a quota and another question
regarding the proper standard for scrutiny in 14th Amendment cases. The
Fullilove ruling affirmed Congress's authority to order affirmative action,
but like Bakke, left the standard for scrutiny unresolved.

GROUP B: STOTTS AND WYGANT

Stotts and Wygant contained three new variables: (a) O'Connor's
replacement of Stewart on the bench; (b) layoffs; and (c) amicus briefs
by the United States expressing the Reagan administration's opposition to affirmative action. Stotts was a Title VII BFSS case and Wygant
was a 14th Amendment strict scrutiny case. Both rulings were, at the
time, strong victories for the Reagan administration.

Firefighters Local Union No. 1784 v. Stotts (1984)

Carl Stotts, a black firefighter, filed a Title VII suit against the Mem-
phis Fire Department alleging a pattern or practice of discrimination
in hiring and promotion. The fire department and its black firefight-

ers carved out a formal consent decree to remedy the pattern of discrimination, but the decree also absolved the fire department of any guilt. Subsequently, in the face of budget cuts and a layoff, a federal district court enjoined the city from using its "last hired, first fired" layoff policy. The decree was then modified and approved again. But as a result, senior white firefighters were laid off who, otherwise, would have been retained.

The union, silent on the original decree, challenged the court injunction, asserting that it contradicted a bona fide seniority system (BFSS); a Title VII violation. The district court rejected the union's charge, ruling that the effects of the seniority system were discriminatory, and that the seniority system was not bona fide. The 6th Circuit ruled that the seniority system was bona fide, but upheld the injunction. The Supreme Court reversed because the 6th Circuit deemed the seniority system bona fide.

Although the Supreme Court vote was 6-3 to reverse, it was functionally 5-0, with four abstentions. That is, four justices debated only procedural issues relating to temporary injunctions. Within this framework, Justice Stevens believed that the district court had abused its discretion, and concurred with the majority judgment to reverse. Justice Blackmun, speaking for Brennan and Marshall, believed the district court had not abused its discretion, and dissented.

The critical ruling was rendered by Justice White, speaking for Burger, O'Connor, Powell, and Rehnquist. According to White:

> Title VII protects bona fide seniority systems, and it is inappropriate to deny an innocent employee the benefits of his seniority in order to provide a remedy in a pattern or practice suit such as this.

White also cited the 1977 Teamsters case discussed in Chapter 2. In Teamsters, the Supreme Court limited the award of retroactive seniority to actual victims of the pattern of discrimination. Of course, the fire department had approved the original decree in order to avoid a court battle on Stott's Title VII pattern charges. And as noted in Blackmun's dissent, had Stotts won in court, the black firefighters would have been entitled to retroactive seniority, as in Teamsters. But the fire department was absolved of any guilt in the original decree.

Wygant v. Jackson Board of Education (1986)

To avoid community-wide disturbances, a collective bargaining agreement with a teachers union was amended to preserve seniority rights in the event of layoff, but with the provision that the percentage of minority teachers remain unchanged. Then, in a subsequent layoff, two tenured white teachers were discharged and two untenured black teachers were retained. The white teachers filed suit under Title VII and the 14th Amendment, but the Title VII charges were dropped for failure to comply with EEOC procedures.

The district court and the 6th Circuit upheld the provision on grounds that societal discrimination justifies a need for role models for black students. Speaking for Burger, Rehnquist, White, and in part, O'Connor, Justice Powell reversed the lower court rulings using the strict scrutiny test. Citing the 1977 Hazelwood pattern or practice case discussed in Chapter 2, Powell stated:

> This Court never has held that societal discrimination alone is sufficient to justify a racial classification. Rather the Court has insisted upon some proof of prior discrimination by the governmental unit involved before allowing limited use of racial classifications in order to remedy such discrimination.

Recall that the Supreme Court had struck down role modeling in Hazelwood in the context of Title VII. In Wygant, Powell ruled that role modeling, for the sake of correcting past societal discrimination, does not pass the strict scrutiny test in a 14th Amendment challenge. Powell did not view role modeling as a compelling state interest. Just as important, he did not view the bargaining agreement as narrowly tailored because it permitted senior labor union members to "waive the constitutional rights" of its junior members.

There were two dissents. Justice Marshall, speaking for Brennan and Blackmun, again pleaded for moderate scrutiny. Marshall asserted that the bargaining agreement was substantially related to important governmental objectives. Interestingly, Stevens, in his lone dissent, altered his earlier opinions by arguing that cultural diversity could serve a "valid public purpose" if adopted with "fair procedures" and if given "narrow breadth."

Ultimately, however, it was the concurrence by O'Connor that decided the case. O'Connor might have supported the bargaining provision as "narrowly tailored" had it directly related to a compelling state interest (i.e., had there been evidence of prior discrimination). Like Powell, she did not accept role modeling as a compelling interest.

─────── **BRIEF SUMMARY** ───────

In retrospect, Stotts and Wygant illustrate the "trammeling" effects of layoffs. Affirmative action lost to a BFSS in a Title VII case (Stotts), and to a strict scrutiny test in a 14th Amendment case (Wygant). Indeed, Wygant was the first time a majority of justices expressed preference for strict scrutiny over moderate scrutiny. The Stotts and Wygant rulings also revealed that White had turned into an opponent of affirmative action. On the other hand, O'Connor, expected to be more conservative than the justice she replaced (Stewart), spelled out circumstances under which she would support affirmative action; a stark contrast to Rehnquist, who clearly would not support affirmative action under any circumstances.

───────────────────────

GROUP C: CLEVELAND
AND SHEET METAL WORKERS

After Stotts and Wygant, Bradford Reynolds, the Solicitor General, established a plan to dismantle AAPs throughout the country. However, he was stopped cold after the nine justices who decided Stotts and Wygant issued the Cleveland and Sheet Metal rulings in 1986 (on the same day). Both were crushing defeats for the Reagan administration. As in Stotts, Cleveland involved a consent decree. But the Sheet Metal case involved a new issue for the Supreme Court: court ordered affirmative action after a Title VII violation.

Local No. 93 (Firefighters) v. Cleveland (1986)

In 1970, the city of Cleveland lost a pattern suit to minority police officers. In 1975, the city lost a similar suit to minority firefighters. Thus when sued again by minority firefighters in 1980, the city admitted its guilt and agreed to conciliate. The Vanguards, who represented the minority firefighters, challenged the promotional system. A consent decree was issued to placate the Vanguards but it was challenged by Local No.93 (the union). The decree was modified to placate the union, but the union sued anyway. The final decree established promotional goals for qualified applicants over a 4-year interval. The 6th Circuit upheld the decree because of the city's admission of guilt, and the Supreme Court affirmed in a 6-3 ruling.

The gist of the union's challenge was a portion of Sec.706(g) of Title VII that states:

> No order of the court shall require the admission or reinstatement of an individual as a member of a union, or the hiring, reinstatement, or promotion of an individual as an employee, or . . . for any reason other than discrimination on account of race, color, religion, sex, or national origin or in violation of section 2000-e-3(a) of this title.

The union interpreted this to mean that courts may not award relief of any kind to individuals who are not victims of illegal discrimination.

Justice Brennan, speaking for Blackmun, Marshall, O'Connor, Powell, and Stevens, concluded that Sec.706(g) applies to race-conscious relief only "after a trial, but not to relief awarded in a consent decree." According to Brennan:

> Because Sec.706(g) is not concerned with voluntary agreements by employers or unions to provide race-conscious relief, there is no inconsistency between it and a consent decree providing such relief, although the court might be barred from ordering the same relief after a trial, or as in Stotts, in disputed proceedings to modify a decree entered upon consent.

Basically, Brennan's ruling reduced to three points: (a) the union had its due process; (b) it raised no substantive issues (as were raised in Stotts); and (c) it was not legally obligated to do anything.

The narrowness of this ruling must be emphasized. In a separate concurrence, Justice O'Connor, who concurred in full with the majority ruling, stated:

> the validity of race-conscious relief provided in a consent decree is to be assessed for consistency with the provisions of Sec.703, such as Sec.703(a) and Sec.703(d), which were at issue in . . . [Weber] . . . and in the case of a public employer, for consistency with the 14th Amendment.

In other words, parties to a consent decree cannot voluntarily agree to break the law. Clearly, O'Connor, who voted against affirmative action in both Stotts and Wygant, voted differently in Cleveland because unlike Stotts, the union had failed to show any substantive violations.

Dissents were issued by Justice White, speaking for himself, and Justice Rehnquist, speaking for Burger. All three believed that consent decrees are not immune to Sec.706(g), and that relief for nonvictims, whether by decree or court order, is challengeable under Title VII. The difference between White versus Rehnquist and Burger was that White would approve relief for nonvictims if the violations are "egregious"; Rehnquist and Burger would not do so under any circumstances.

Two other issues are worth noting. First, as in Stotts and Wygant, the Justice Department issued an amicus brief representing the Reagan administration's opposition to affirmative action. Brennan noted that the justice department "took exactly the opposite opinion in *Steelworkers v. Weber.*" Second, Brennan paid deference to Sections 1601.1 and 1601.8 of the EEOC Guidelines on Affirmative Action suggesting that although they do not have the force and effect of law, they "constitute a body of experience and informed judgment to which courts and litigants may properly resort to guidance." These Guidelines will be discussed further in Section V of this chapter.

Local 28 (Sheet Metal Workers) v. EEOC (1986)

In Cleveland, a majority of the Court avoided ruling directly on Sec.706(g) of Title VII. In Sheet Metal Workers, the Court had no choice. A district court in New York found Local 29 (the union) guilty of a pattern of discrimination in hiring, and ordered a 29% nonwhite membership goal. On two subsequent occasions, the district court held the union in contempt for not obeying the court's orders. The 2nd Circuit affirmed the 29% goal, ruling that the union was guilty of long-standing egregious violations, and that there were no violations under Title VII or the 5th Amendment. The same lineup as in Cleveland affirmed the 2nd Circuit ruling, except this time O'Connor partially concurred and partially dissented.

The central issue in this case was the one avoided in Cleveland; authorization of relief to **nonvictims**. Justice Brennan, speaking for the same lineup as in Cleveland, stated:

> We reject this argument, and hold that Sec.706(g) does not prohibit a court from ordering, in appropriate circumstances, affirmative race-conscious relief as a remedy for past discrimination. Specifically, we hold that such relief may be appropriate where an employer or a labor union has engaged in persistent or *egregious* discrimination, or where necessary to dissipate the lingering effects of pervasive discrimination. [emphasis added]

Brennan's ruling focused on the portion of Sec.706(g) that states:

> If the court finds that the respondent has intentionally engaged in or is intentionally engaging in an unlawful employment practice . . . the court may enjoin the respondent from engaging in such unlawful employment practice, and *order such affirmative action as may be appropriate.* [emphasis added]

The dissent by Justice Rehnquist (for Burger) was the same as in Cleveland; no relief for nonvictims regardless of anything. Justice White, on the other hand, accepted the lower court rulings that egregious violations had been committed, and Brennan's belief that under such circumstances, relief for nonvictims is possible. However, he felt the award in this case was excessive because it was a quota; a point agreed to by O'Connor in her partial dissent.

One other factor is worth noting. The EEOC, who inherited this case from the Justice Department, filed an amicus brief against itself and for the union. The reason for noting this, of course, is that Clarence Thomas, the newest member of the Supreme Court, was the head of the EEOC at the time the brief was filed. Whether the brief represents Thomas's personal view or conciliation to a President bent on terminating affirmative action remains to be seen.

─────── **BRIEF SUMMARY** ───────

Cleveland and Sheet Metal were critical rulings because they prevented E.O.11246 from becoming a pure nondiscrimination statute. They also prevented Title VII affirmative action remedies from being severely limited. Although not cited in the discussion above, numerous lower court precedents were at stake, a fact noted by Justice Brennan. For example, in *Rios v. Steamfitters* (1974), the 2nd Circuit affirmed a district court order for a 30% "racial goal," reasoning that: *Where there had been a pattern of long-continued and egregious racial discrimination under which qualified nonwhite applicants were precluded from gaining membership in [the] union and where [the] union, despite opportunity afforded after issuance of preliminary relief, had failed to take any meaningful steps to eradicate effects of its past discrimination, imposition of [a] racial goal on [the] union was not an abuse of discretion.* In short, affirmative action remedies for egregious violations was already a Title VII tradition in the lower courts. The issue for the future, however, is whether "goals" will be perceived as quotas even for egregious violations, given the current relatively conservative composition of the Supreme Court.

GROUP D: PARADISE AND JOHNSON

The Paradise and Johnson rulings were handed down within 30 days of each other, each less than a year after the Cleveland and Sheet Metal rulings. Burger had resigned as Chief Justice, Rehnquist was elevated to Burger's seat, and Scalia had assumed Rehnquist's seat. Paradise involved a 14th Amendment challenge to a court ordered AAP, and Johnson involved a Title VII challenge to a voluntary AAP. The Johnson case was the first and only reverse discrimination Supreme Court case involving sex. Although both Paradise and Johnson were victories for E.O.11246, both contained ominous caveats for the future.

United States v. Paradise (1987)

In 1972, the Alabama Department of Public Safety was found guilty of a 40-year pattern of discrimination. The district court imposed a hiring quota and also enjoined the department from discriminating in promotions. But as of 1979, there were no blacks in upper ranks. The district court then approved a decree requiring a promotional procedure that: (a) produced no adverse impact; and (b) was consistent with the EEOC Uniform Guidelines. As of 1981, there were still no blacks in upper ranks. The district court then imposed stricter promotional quotas for qualified black candidates, and the United States challenged the order under the 14th Amendment. The 11th Circuit affirmed the order, as did the Supreme Court in a 5-4 ruling.

Brennan spoke for Blackmun, Powell, and Marshall. Stevens concurred separately in what was mainly an attack on the dissenting opinion of O'Connor, who spoke for Rehnquist and Scalia. Although White spoke for himself, he presented only a four-line dissent agreeing with O'Connor. Based on a strict scrutiny test, all nine justices agreed that the state had a compelling interest in alleviating the pattern of discrimination. The key to the majority ruling was Powell who, writing separately, believed that the promotional quota was narrowly tailored based on the following five criteria:

> (i) the efficacy of alternative remedies; (ii) the planned duration of the remedy; (iii) the relationship between the percentage of minority workers to be employed and the percentage of minority group members in the relevant population or work force; (iv) the availability of waiver provisions if the hiring plan could not be met; and (v) the effect of the remedy upon innocent third parties.

There were two main issues in the dissent. First, the original trial in 1972 dealt only with hiring. But second and more importantly, there was the issue of quotas per se. O'Connor stated her own prior objections to quotas, as well as White's, in the Sheet Metal case. According to O'Connor:

> In Sheet Metal Workers, I observed that "it is completely unrealistic to assume that individuals of each race will gravitate with mathematical exactitude to each employer or union absent unlawful discrimination." Thus, a rigid quota is impermissible because it adopts "an unjustified conclusion about the precise extent to which past discrimination has lingering effects," or . . . an unjustified prediction about what would happen in the future in the absence of continuing discrimination. Even more flexible "goals," however, also may trammel unnecessarily the rights of nonminorities. Racially preferential treatment of nonvictims, therefore, should only be ordered "where such remedies are truly necessary." Thus, "the creation of racial preferences by courts, even in the more limited form of goals rather than quotas, must be done sparingly and only where manifestly necessary."

In short, four justices warned that even where there is a clear-cut compelling state interest in a 14th Amendment case, it would take a drastic circumstance for them to agree that quotas are an appropriate, narrowly tailored remedy.

Johnson v. Transportation Agency (1987)

In *Johnson v. Transportation Agency,* a state agency did essentially what Powell had proposed in Bakke—it treated sex as a plus for candidates otherwise deemed equally qualified for promotion. The agency had 238 skilled craft workers, all male. Additionally, females were underrepresented throughout the agency, and were segregated into five of seven job categories. The AAP was developed to achieve:

> a statistically measurable yearly improvement in hiring, training and promotion of minorities and women throughout the Agency in all major job classifications where they are underrepresented.

When a craft job opened, there were seven finalists for promotion, including Diane Joyce and Paul Johnson. Johnson, a male, was rated slightly higher than Joyce, a female, and was recommended for promotion by the three supervisors providing the ratings. But the director,

with input from an affirmative action officer whom Joyce had peti-
tioned, ordered his subordinate to choose any of the seven finalists.

After Joyce was selected, Johnson filed Title a VII claim that sex was
the "determining factor in [Joyce's] selection." The district court agreed
with Johnson, but the 9th Circuit reversed. The Supreme Court affirmed the 9th Circuit in a 6-3 ruling. As in Weber, the Court treated
the AAP as a productive defense in a disparate treatment scenario.
Justice Brennan, speaking for Blackmun, Marshall, Powell, and Stevens,
echoed Powell's idiosyncratic words from Bakke, stating:

> The Agency's Plan thus set aside no specific number of positions for
> minorities and women, but authorized the consideration of ethnicity
> or sex as a factor when evaluating qualified candidates for jobs in which
> members of such groups were poorly represented.

O'Connor, in a separate but full concurrence, saw no difference
with respect to rules for deciding Title VII versus 14th Amendment
reverse discrimination cases, and was satisfied that the agency:

> had a firm basis for adopting an affirmative action program. . . . [W]hen
> compared to the percentage of women in the qualified work force, the
> statistical disparity would have been sufficient for a prima facie Title
> VII case . . . [the agency's] affirmative action plan as implemented in
> this instance . . . satisfies the requirements of Weber and Wygant.

White, Scalia, and Rehnquist dissented. For White, this was a reversal from his concurrence in Weber. He disagreed with O'Connor's
assessment of the statistical disparity, stating:

> My understanding of Weber was, and is, the employer's plan did not
> violate Title VII because it was designed to remedy the intentional and
> systematic exclusion of blacks. . . . That is how I understood "tradition-
> ally segregated jobs" . . . The Court now interprets it to mean nothing
> more than a manifest imbalance between one identifiable group and
> another in an employer's labor force.

White then stated for the written record that he would now vote in
favor of overturning the Weber ruling.

Scalia, speaking for Rehnquist, agreed with White and included
their votes for overturning Weber. Of course, Rehnquist had consistently opposed affirmative action, and Scalia was known to oppose
affirmative action as a D.C. Circuit Court judge. According to Scalia:

as a result of the present [decision], Title VII, which was designed to establish a color-blind and gender-blind workplace, has been converted into a powerful engine of racism and sexism.

Clearly, the keys to the majority ruling were Stevens, Powell, and O'Connor. For Powell, the AAP was quite harmonious with his earlier opinion in Bakke, and for Stevens it was a change in heart (which he admitted) relative to Bakke. But for O'Connor, it was a clear-cut statement that her partial dissent in Sheet Metal and her full dissent in Paradise were a function of her belief that quotas can never serve as an appropriate remedy.

———— BRIEF SUMMARY ————

Based on the majority rulings, both cases represent affirmations of prior victories for E.O. 11246. Paradise affirms Sheet Metal and Johnson extends Weber. However, Powell, the key vote in Paradise, resigned after the 1986-1987 term. He was replaced by Kennedy, who is as strongly opposed to affirmative action as Rehnquist and Scalia. Assuming therefore that Kennedy would join White, Scalia, and Rehnquist, there are now four justices on the Court who might overturn Weber if given the opportunity.

GROUP E: CROSON, WILKS, AND METRO BROADCASTING

The last three cases were decided during the 1989 and 1990 terms. Croson involved a successful 14th Amendment challenge to affirmative action legislated by state government; Wilks involved a (temporarily) successful Title VII challenge to a consent decree; and Metro Broadcasting involved an unsuccessful 5th Amendment challenge to affirmative action legislated by Congress.

City of Richmond v. Croson Company (1989)

In Fullilove, the Supreme Court approved a congressional 10% set aside for minority business enterprises (MBEs) under the 5th Amendment. In Croson, the City of Richmond established a 30% set aside for MBEs. The city was 50% black and, historically, less than 1% of construction contracts had been awarded to local black companies. Croson was denied a contract even though it was the sole bidder. Using the

14th Amendment, the company challenged the plan unsuccessfully in both lower federal courts. However, the Supreme Court reversed in a 6-3 ruling.

As in prior 14th Amendment cases, Marshall, speaking for Blackmun and Brennan, argued for moderate scrutiny. However, six justices agreed that the majority in Wygant had established the precedent of strict scrutiny in 14th Amendment cases. Although there were several concurring opinions, Kennedy, Rehnquist, Scalia, Stevens, and White agreed with Justice O'Connor's assessment that there was neither: (a) a compelling state interest; nor (b) a narrowly tailored solution. On the issue of compelling interest, O'Connor stated:

> Like the "role model" theory employed in Wygant, a generalized assertion that there has been past discrimination in an entire industry provides no guidance for a legislative body to determine the precise scope of injury it seeks to remedy.

On the issue of narrow tailoring, O'Connor stated:

> the 30% quota cannot be said to be narrowly tailored to any goal, except perhaps outright racial balancing. It rests upon the "completely unrealistic" assumption that minorities will choose a particular trade in lockstep proportional to their representation in the local population.

Martin v. Wilks (1989)

Wilks was a firefighter/consent decree case in which the National Association for the Advancement of Colored People (NAACP) sued the City of Birmingham, and the city consented to hiring and promotional goals to head off the litigation. The white firefighters objected to the decree, but otherwise did not participate in its formulation. They then challenged the decree under both Title VII and the 14th Amendment. The district court dismissed the challenge as an "impermissible collateral attack." The 11th Circuit reversed.

In a controversial 5-4 ruling, the Supreme Court affirmed the 11th Circuit ruling. Justice Rehnquist, speaking for Kennedy, O'Connor, Scalia, and White, ruled that the white firefighters were not given an opportunity to intervene as the decree was fashioned. Justice Stevens, speaking for Blackmun, Brennan, and Marshall, dissented, arguing that the white firefighters had the opportunity to intervene in timely fashion and failed to do so.

However, Congress reversed Rehnquist's ruling. Thus Sec.108 of the Civil Rights Act of 1991 states:

> an employment practice that implements and is within the scope of a litigated or consent judgment or order that resolves a claim of employment discrimination under the Constitution or Federal civil rights laws may not be challenged . . . [if] . . . actual notice of the proposed judgment or order . . . was available . . . [and] . . . an opportunity was available to present objections to such judgment or order by a future date certain.

Metro Broadcasting v. FCC (1990)

In 1978, the Federal Communications Commission (FCC) adopted two regulations for broadcast licenses: (a) enhancement credits for minority broadcasters; and (b) a "distress sale" policy for troubled majority broadcasters to avoid hearings and other red tape by assigning their licenses directly to minority businesses. These policies were subsequently codified by Congress. Metro joined two 5th Amendment challenges: (a) by a majority broadcaster denied a license because of enhancement credits; and (b) by a minority broadcaster denied a license because the lower court failed to endorse the distress sale policy.

Given the composition of the Supreme Court and its recent rulings on reverse discrimination, the Metro ruling is perhaps the most remarkable of those rendered to date. As noted in the June 30, 1990 issue of *Congressional Quarterly:*

> The ruling came on the last day of the 1989-90 term. When Chief Justice Rehnquist announced that the decision in the long-awaited case would be read by Justice William J. Brennan Jr., observers in the courtroom were astonished, including Justice Department officials who had come expecting to hear the court strike down the race-preference policy, as the department had sought.

Of course, Kennedy, Rehnquist, O'Connor, and Scalia would overturn the FCC policies and Blackmun, Brennan, and Marshall would not. Stevens, reversing his Fullilove opinion, was also in favor of the policies. But the shocker was White, who fully concurred with the majority.

The majority ruling was twofold. First, Justice Brennan, speaking for Blackmun, Marshall, Stevens, and White, ruled that moderate scrutiny, although unacceptable in 14th Amendment cases such as Wygant, was the proper level of scrutiny under the 5th Amendment. Second, Justice Stevens, speaking separately, echoed his Wygant ruling and suggested that cultural diversity is a legitimate business interest.

Also of interest was one of the two dissents. Kennedy, speaking for Scalia, likened the majority ruling to: (a) exhuming and rearranging *Plessy v. Ferguson*, the 1897 "separate but equal" case later overturned in the landmark *Brown v. Board of Education* (1954) case; (b) policy statements issued by the Apartheid South African Government; and (c) Roosevelt's internment of Japanese Americans during World War II. If any readers doubt that Kennedy or Scalia would vote to overturn any affirmative action ruling, they are urged to read this dissent.

―――――― **BRIEF SUMMARY** ――――――

Croson represents an unsurprising failure to extend Fullilove to state and local entities, and Metro represents a surprising extension within the federal domain. Wilks was one of the original six cases that motivated the failed Civil Rights Restoration Act of 1990. Congress was able to achieve its objectives with respect to Wilks in the 1991 Act. The key difference between Croson versus Metro was the Court's willingness to apply moderate scrutiny to congressional statutes, but to maintain a strict scrutiny standard for statutes issued at the state or local level. However, it is doubtful that the Croson plan would have survived even moderate scrutiny.

A SUMMARY EVALUATION
OF ALL 12 CASES

Stare decisis is a valued Supreme Court tradition. But on the issue of reverse discrimination, individual justices have marked out forbidden territory. Therefore it is necessary to consider the current Court composition, as well as substantive issues and relevant statutes.

Current Composition of the Supreme Court

With the resignations of Brennan and Marshall and the anticipated resignation of Blackmun (who is 83 years old), only one justice will remain with favorable views on affirmative action: Justice Stevens, a relatively recent supporter. Kennedy, Rehnquist, and Scalia oppose any affirmative action remedy, and White joins them as threats to the landmark Weber ruling. O'Connor is a strong supporter of strict scrutiny, regardless of the challenge, and a strong opponent of quotas. But she favors affirmative remedies when a compelling interest is demonstrated and the remedy is narrowly tailored. White supports remedies for nonvictims for egregious violations, but like O'Connor, opposes quotas. Any characterization of Justices Souter or Thomas is, of course, speculative. Nevertheless, it is difficult to expect that they will be friends of E.O.11246.

In short, the current Court leans away from affirmative action remedies. However, this is not a guarantee that critical precedents will be overturned. To begin with, the Court itself is not overly anxious to hear new cases. The following quote is from the April 20, 1992, issue of *USA Today:*

> The justices passed up two chances to reenter the debate over government [AAPs] that help minorities gain jobs and government contracts. The court left intact an [AAP] aimed at increasing the number of black police officers in Philadelphia. . . . In a second case, the justices let stand a San Francisco plan to funnel more public works contracts to companies run by minorities and women. "It shows they're not looking for the first opportunity to reopen the wounds" on affirmative action, say Eric Schnapper, lawyer for the NAACP Legal Defense and Education Fund.

Another factor to consider is that Supreme Court justices are not always predictable. Blackmun, for example, was a Nixon appointee who routinely joined Burger for the first several years of his tenure, and White was a "liberal" Kennedy appointee. Burger, clearly a "conservative," wrote the Griggs ruling. And as recently as the last week of June 1992, Scalia and Kennedy, close comrades (and jogging partners), disagreed vehemently on a 1st Amendment prayer issue and on the issue of a woman's right to an abortion. Perhaps it is easy for coalitions to hang together when they are in the minority and not so easy when they become the majority.

In the author's opinion, three assumptions should be made. First, the current precedents live and are **judicial law**. But second, it is best to interpret those precedents consistently with the two middle sectors of the current Court; O'Connor and White. Third, Congress supports affirmative action and is ready to fight for Supreme Court precedents. For example, Sec.116 of the Civil Rights Act of 1991 states:

> Nothing in the amendments made by this title shall be construed to affect court-ordered remedies, affirmative action, or conciliation agreements that are in accordance with the law.

Although neutral in tone, court-ordered remedies and conciliation agreements are supported within Title VII, as well as in majority rulings in cases such as Weber, Cleveland, Sheet Metal Workers, Paradise, and Johnson. Also, the Wilks ruling is reversed.

The Current Precedents

Under current precedents, voluntary AAPs by private or public employers are valid, especially if they address underutilization in recruitment, training, and promotion, but certainly not discharge. The same holds for AAPs established via court order or consent decree. On the other hand, Congress has the authority to legislate AAPs under moderate scrutiny, but state and local legislation must pass strict scrutiny. Clearly, selection decisions inconsistent with a bona fide seniority systems will fail any test.

On a more global level, the philosophical goals of affirmative action are clearly challengeable. That is, E.O. 11246 speaks to correcting past societal injustices via redistribution. But an AAP based solely on past societal injustice cannot stand up to any of the judicial precedents. There must be some evidence of underutilization. Furthermore, even with such evidence, statistical quotas in lieu of alternative remedies (e.g., "pluses") are risky.

Legal Bases for Challenges

The two main laws in reverse discrimination suits are Title VII and the 14th Amendment. The 5th Amendment applies to rare occasions when Congress enacts affirmative action legislation. And Title VI, a statute prohibiting discrimination in federal contracts based on race, color, or national origin (but not religion or sex), enjoyed only a brief and relatively minor moment in Bakke.

Title VII applies to reverse discrimination charges against all entities, whereas the 14th Amendment applies to only state and local entities. Currently, it would appear that **strict scrutiny** applies to 14th Amendment challenges and also to Title VII. It would be fair to say that an employer who engages in affirmative action with no basis is merely maintaining a balanced work force and therefore is not protected by Title VII, the 14th Amendment, or E.O.11246.

SECTION V
COMPLIANCE

Operationally, the dilemma is that OFCCP regulations are expressed in terms of statistical balance, whereas federal and constitutional laws prohibit statistical quotas. Therefore it is critical to find an acceptable common ground between nondiscrimination and affirmative action. It is also possible to take a different approach; that cultural diversity may be establishable as a business necessity. The idea was first noted by Justice Stevens in Wygant and more recently in Metro.

COMMON GROUND BASED ON CASE LAW

EEO laws focus exclusively on nondiscrimination, whereas E.O.11246 is synonymous with affirmative action. Therefore the common ground must be inferred from cracks and crevices.

The Nondiscrimination Viewpoint

Most of the "egregious" violations seen in the last section stem from the **pattern or practice** of discrimination in recruitment, hiring, training, and promotion. Thus entry decisions should be carefully scrutinized before upstream decisions are made. Valuable lessons are contained in Title VII cases reviewed in Chapter 2, particularly *Furnco v. Waters* (1978) and *Connecticut v. Teal* (1982). From the perspective of nondiscrimination laws, the perfectly balanced work force provides a false aura of insulation, because the likelihood of statistical exactitude is quite low. Indeed, statistical exactitude may alert a plaintiff or an agency to a nondiscrimination violation.

Recall that in Furnco the numbers matched well, and yet the rights of the excluded black employee were still protected. In Teal, the bottom-line percentages favored blacks, and yet each step of a multiple hurdle procedure was scrutinized in accordance with the principles of adverse impact. We witnessed a similar ruling in the age discrimination literature (*Leftwich v. Harris-Stowe*, 1983).

As an aside, President Bush feared the Restoration Act of 1990 because it was a "quota bill." But strong civil rights laws do not compel employers to fashion quotas; they merely scare them into doing so. Thus a strong law that would induce fear would also illegalize that motive. EEO rulings reveal that bottom-line statistical disparities can produce and/or add to a prima facie attack. But statistical imbalances can exist for legitimate business reasons, in which case they are legal.

The Affirmative Action Viewpoint

The critical affirmative action principles are expressed in **Revised Rule No.4** of the OFCCP regulations. E.O.11246 does not rest on statistical imbalance within the work force. The work force must be compared to the **relevant labor force**. This principle is consistent with the Supreme Court's ruling in *Hazelwood v. United States* (1977), a major pattern or practice suit.

For jobs most people can perform, the relevant labor force is probably the immediate surrounding population. Documented statistical discrepancies for such jobs imply a safe and simple strategy—enhanced recruitment. Companies should be particularly wary of word-of-mouth recruitment, which can easily create a pattern of discrimination and perpetuate the effects of an already existing pattern. The company can safely engage in affirmative advertisement and recruitment efforts without trammeling the rights of anyone, if all populations are recruited.

For skills that require training, enhanced recruitment is only part of the solution. Obviously, all qualified people should be recruited. But no law prevents a company from supporting an external training program for special populations. For in-house training, no law prevents special training for remedial knowledge that normally produces adverse impact (e.g., reading, writing, math, etc.). Individuals who have the knowledge cannot challenge simply because they cannot benefit from the training.

For skilled jobs that attract nonlocal workers (e.g., college teachers, engineers, etc.), it is dangerous to recruit in any one place. For example, companies that visit only well-to-do schools may be guilty of adverse impact. Additionally, companies that rely on one method of recruitment may miss the opportunity to attract the largest possible pool of qualified applicants.

Nondiscrimination and Affirmative Action Combined

No law requires selection of unqualified workers and no law requires preference to **maintain** a balanced work force. Affirmative action is a cure for **underutilization**, and nondiscrimination means remedies to correct **individuous** wrongs. But when the violations are egregious, nonvictims can benefit from affirmative action. The worst mistake is to wait for a pattern or practice suit; the company should take voluntary action.

Nondiscrimination and **voluntary** affirmative action converged in Weber and then later in *Johnson v. Transportation.* In Weber, Kaiser Aluminum committed an **egregious** violation; the company hired only those skilled workers trained by a discriminatory union. Kaiser's remedy was characterized by: (a) a collectively bargained agreement; with (b) no internal union issues; (c) no issues relating to consent decrees or court orders; and (d) a remedy for workers who could not have received the training (i.e., actual victims). Furthermore, the AAP was temporary and at worst delayed, but did not preclude advancement of nonminority employees. However, it did involve an obvious quota.

In *Johnson v. Transportation,* there was also an egregious pattern violation. The Transportation agency used something akin to the "plus" system advocated by Justice Powell in his Bakke ruling for a group of candidates that were deemed qualified for promotion. The case could be made that Diane Joyce was an identifiable victim. The problem, however, was the implication from lower level decision makers that Joyce would not have been promoted but for her sex.

Extracting the best from Weber and Johnson, it is possible that egregious violations are correctable via quotas for workers who are victims of these violations, but not for all selection decisions. Weber involved training and Johnson involved promotion; neither case involved discharge, and certainly neither case opposed a seniority agreement. Judging from surrounding Supreme Court rulings, Kaiser could have used a safer strategy, even for training. Kaiser could have first used a "plus" system, with minority status as one plus and seniority as another plus. The workers chosen for in-house training, both black and white, were not the ones selected or rejected by the union. They were the ones trying to obtain the skills previously provided by the union. Therefore all affected workers were in the same boat.

On a more general level, it is safest to ensure, regardless of the selection decision, that all employees or applicants are at a certain level of qualification, and that goals in an AAP are not fulfilled strictly by the percentages. Goals can represent good faith guesses regarding what a fair plus/minus system can generate when it is used. If the company is guilty of an egregious violation (and therefore faces the prospect of a pattern charge), it can try two pluses (or three pluses) for minorities and/or women. A quota, if needed at all, should always be a last resort.

In short, using the legal language, nonwillful underutilization constitutes a "rational basis" for affirmative action, and a plus/minus system is usually a fitting solution. If the underutilization is egregious (e.g., reflects a pattern of discrimination), then the basis is more compelling and a quota solution is narrowly tailored if the plus/minus system is not working or is not likely to work. A good strategy is to confirm the basis and the solution with collectively bargained agreements from all concerned parties. This will at least head off the pattern suit, a critical concern.

COMMON GROUND BASED ON EEOC GUIDANCE

Affirmative action requires identification of underutilization; not documentation of causes. Causes should not be included in the AAP because the AAP can be viewed by the OFCCP and EEOC and may be requested by third parties under the Freedom of Information Act. But there is another strategy; the EEOC blessing. Part 1608 of the EEOC Guidelines covers "Affirmative Action Appropriate Under Title VII."

Overview of the EEOC Guidelines

The purpose of the Guidelines is stated in Sec.1601 (b) as follows:

The Commission believes that by the enactment of Title VII Congress did not intend to expose those who comply with the Act to charges that they are violating the very statute they are seeking to implement. Such a result would immobilize or reduce the efforts of many who would otherwise take action to improve the opportunities of minorities and women with litigation, thus frustrating the Congressional intent to encourage voluntary action and increasing the prospect of Title VII litigation. The Commission believes it is now necessary to clarify and *harmonize* the principles of Title VII. [emphasis added]

In other words, the Guidelines are written to "harmonize" Title VII and E.O.11246, or to find common ground. Presumably anything that would be common ground for Title VII would also satisfy the Equal Protection Clause of the 14th Amendment.

More importantly, Sec.1608.1(d) provides the "good faith" Title VII defense. More specifically:

> [T]hese Guidelines state the circumstances under which the Commission will recognize that a person subject to Title VII is entitled to assert that actions are taken "in good faith, in conformity with, and in reliance upon a written interpretation or opinion of the Commission," including reliance upon the interpretation and opinion contained in these Guidelines, and thereby invoke the protection of Section 713(b)(1) of Title VII.

In other words, conformity with written interpretations by the EEOC limits liability in reverse discrimination cases.

Substantive Features of the EEOC Guidelines

Sec.1608.3 cites three major "circumstances" for affirmative action: (a) "adverse effect"; (b) "effects of prior discriminatory practices"; and (c) "limited labor pool." Of course these circumstances translate into adverse impact, the continued effect of prior discrimination, and artificial restrictions on recruitment for hiring, training, or promotion. Sec.1608.3 also recommends affirmative action in (a) "training plans and programs"; (b) "extensive and focused recruiting activity"; (c) "elimination of adverse impact caused by unvalidated selection criteria"; and (d) "modification through collective bargaining."

Sec.1608.4 expands on three issues related to Revised Rule #4 of the OFCCP regulations. First, the EEOC endorses the "reasonable self analysis," and stresses there is "no mandatory method of conducting a self analysis." Second, the EEOC stresses that affirmative action should have a "reasonable basis" (i.e., from circumstances identified in the self-analysis). And third, the EEOC speaks of "standards of reasonable action," which summarizes the essential feature of harmony between Title VII and E.O.11246 as follows:

> The plan should be tailored to solve the problems which were identified in the self analysis . . . and to ensure that employment systems operate fairly in the future, while avoiding unnecessary restrictions on opportunities for the workforce as a whole. The race, sex, and national origin

conscious provisions of the plan or program should be maintained only
so long as is necessary to achieve these objectives.

In short, an AAP must have a discriminatory reason for being. It
cannot be used simply to maintain work force balance and is considered fulfilled once its goals are achieved.

A final point to note is that a Title VII violation is obviously good
cause for establishing an AAP. However, a Title VII violation is not
necessary to justify an AAP, and an admission of guilt is not necessary
if a Title VII violation does exist. The only prerequisite is that the
AAP be a formally written and dated document.

Caveats

The EEOC Affirmative Action Guidelines were published in 1979,
and therefore were prepared before any Supreme Court rulings on reverse discrimination (preparation is always several years behind). This
is obviously a drawback. However, the Guidelines accurately summarize the OFCCP requirements and present an almost prophetic view
of the 12 Supreme Court rulings on reverse discrimination.

Another drawback is that written interpretations from the EEOC
might open the store to investigation of general EEO violations. This
is true when a single "person" requests EEOC interpretive guidance.
However, it is not necessary to obtain written EEOC interpretations;
correct interpretations of the Guidelines guarantees the good faith
defense. Furthermore, when written interpretations are necessary, it
is probably best to avoid seeking advice as a "person." The safest alternative is to approach the EEOC as a group (e.g., chambers of commerce,
professional organizations, etc.).

CULTURAL DIVERSITY

Finally, a unique approach to the nondiscrimination versus affirmative action dilemma is cultural diversity as a business necessity. In
the 1980s companies began studying work force diversity and some
of the larger ones have conducted studies to validate this job practice,
much like one would validate a paper/pencil test. There is evidence
to suggest that cultural diversity is a competitive advantage. If so, cultural diversity is consistent with business necessity, and does not require an affirmative action justification.

Readers interested in this topic are directed to Cox and Blake (1991) and references cited therein. Cox and Blake advance six arguments relating to: (a) costs; (b) resource acquisition; (c) marketing advantages; (d) creativity; (e) problem solving; and (f) system flexibility. They cite management studies substantiating these benefits. For example, a study by Ortho Pharmaceuticals calculated savings of $500,000 from reduced turnover among women and minorities.

Cultural diversity is obviously a hot topic, as evidenced in conferences and workshops currently offered throughout the country. It must be emphasized that from a legal standpoint, however, cultural diversity would not stand up to a strict scrutiny analysis in a reverse discrimination case unless the company could demonstrate job- relatedness through a validation study.

——— CHAPTER SUMMARY ———

Most of the substantive provisions in Parts II and III of E.O.11246 were established in prior orders. The key contribution by Johnson was to empower agencies to enforce sanctions and penalties, and a key contribution by Carter was to restrict agency control to the DOL. By the dimensions, E.O.11246 protects (Q1) preferred groups (minorities and women) and covers (Q2) procurement (Part II) and construction (Part III) contracts. The key covered practice (Q3) is affirmative action, required only when a work force versus availability analysis reveals underutilization. Corrective action usually involves recruitment, training, and promotion, and should not be applied to termination. AAPs should not be established to maintain statistical balance. The administrative agency (Q4), the OFCCP, may conduct compliance reviews and penalize any contractor not in compliance with the EO Clause, or who has a faulty AAP. The most threatening remedy (Q5) is debarment, but the OFCCP has other threats, including affected class rulings. Attack/Defense balances (Q6) are relatively unimportant, because federal court cases are approved reviews or overruled ALJ decisions. Although executive and regulatory authority has been directly challenged and for the most part defeated, the strongest challenges to E.O.11246 have been in Title VII and/or 14th Amendment reverse discrimination cases. The weight of evidence from 12 Supreme Court rulings, in light of the current court composition, suggests that employers should avoid treating goals as quotas. The AAP should favor milder solutions such as point systems. In general, the employer is safest when applying affirmative action for equally qualified applicants or employees. Otherwise, employers need to seek common ground between the principles of nondiscrimination versus affirmative action. The EEOC Affirmative Action Guidelines are still useful in this regard, despite their age. The Guidelines also provide a good faith defense. Finally, employers should investigate the possibility of validating the effects of culturally diverse efforts within their own companies.

NOTE

1. No poor white applicant was ever admitted under the Davis Plan.

8

The Americans
With Disabilities Act

CHART 8.1. THE ADA

Q1	Q2	Q3	Q4	Q5	Q6
Qualified (having KSAs) AND Physical/ mental impairment Record of impairment Regarded as being impaired	Private & state/local entities with 25 or more employees on 7/26/92 15 or more employees on 7/26/94	Non-discrimination Reasonable accommodation But no additional affirmative action beyond notice posting	Title VII EEOC procedures	Title VII remedies	Adverse impact Disparate treatment Surmountable barriers

(Q1): What classes of people are protected (or have rights)?
(Q2): What business entities are covered (or have duties)?
(Q3): What employment practices are covered?
(Q4): Is the law administered, and if so, how?
(Q5): What are the penalties (or remedies) for breaking the law?
(Q6): What are the attacks and defenses used in litigation?

The Americans With Disabilities Act (the ADA)[1] enjoyed bipartisan support in Congress, passing 91-6 in the Senate and 377-27 in the House. The ADA was also supported by Presidents Reagan and Bush, and numerous organizations and foundations. The Act contains five titles: (I) Employment; (II) Public Services; (III) Public Accommodations and Services Operated By Private Entities; (IV) Telecommunications; and (V) Miscellaneous Provisions. This chapter focuses on Title I (Employment).

It should be noted that the Rehabilitation Act of 1973 used the term **handicap**. Congress, recognizing the preferences of the protected class, chose the term **disabled** for the ADA. However, there is no difference in meaning between "handicap," as used in the Rehabilitation Act of 1973, and "disabled," as used in the ADA. Furthermore, the term "**Americans** with disabilities" does not imply that only American citizens are protected.

The ADA culminates 72 years of legislation, beginning with the Sears-Smith Act of 1918, which provided training and education for physically disabled World War I veterans. The Smith-Fess Act of 1920 extended Sears-Smith to all physically disabled Americans, and the Social Security Act of 1935 permanently codified Sears-Smith and Smith-Fess. A 1943 amendment added first-time protections for the mentally disabled, and the 1950s and 1960s were marked by various federal and state programs and demonstration projects. Then in 1973 Congress enacted the Rehabilitation Act, a landmark statute.[2] Congress also enacted the Veterans Assistance Act of 1974, on affirmative action for disabled Vietnam veterans. Most recently, disability provisions were included in the Fair Housing Act of 1989.

In spite of these laws, the plight of disabled people has worsened. As approximated by various sources, 43 million Americans are disabled. Among 12 million at traditional working ages (16 to 64), the unemployment rate is greater than 65%. Polls reveal that more than 80% of unemployed disabled people want to work, even at the cost of reduced disability benefits. In 1980, disabled workers earned 23% less than their nondisabled counterparts, a figure that grew to 36% by 1988. Currently, 53% of all disabled adults have household incomes below $15,000, relative to only 25% for counterparts. Finally, disabled people are 3 times less likely to finish high school than their counterparts.

The ADA is depicted in Chart 8.1. As with older people, the major problem is ignorance, not animus. Thus the **protected class (Q1)** is broadly defined to include not only (a) current physical or mental impairments but also (b) a record of physical or mental impairment, and (c) being falsely regarded as being physically or mentally impaired.

In 1978, while amending the Rehabilitation Act of 1973, Congress prayed that model programs for federal entities would trigger widespread voluntary efforts in the private and state/local sectors—a prayer that went unanswered. Federal employees have always been well protected by Sec.501 of the Rehabilitation Act. However, private and state/local employees have not been as broadly or as well protected by Sec.504 as federal employees have been by Sec.501. Thus the ADA **covers (Q2)** *only* private and state/local entities, and federal employees continue to enjoy the protections of Sec.501.

The **covered practices (Q3)** include the standard Title VII terms and conditions for nondiscrimination. There are also prohibitions for job criteria that screen out disabled people, and an affirmative requirement to **reasonably accommodate** a known disability that poses a **barrier** to performance of **essential job functions**. But the ADA neither requires nor forbids affirmative action beyond reasonable accommodation and notice posting. There are also special prohibitions, most notably for preemployment inquiries into the medical/psychological status of applicants, and for discriminating against nondisabled people who are related to or closely associated with (e.g., taking care of) disabled people.

The **administrative procedures (Q4)** and **remedies (Q5)** of the ADA mimic Title VII, as amended by the Civil Rights Act of 1991. In Sec.504 of the Rehabilitation Act, the covered private and state/local entities were subject to the procedures and remedies of Title VI (not Title VII), a factor resulting in unforeseen complications. Linkage of the ADA to Title VII creates consistency between the ADA and Sec.501 of the Rehabilitation Act, which also uses the procedures and remedies of Title VII (not Title VI).

Finally, the **attack/defense balances (Q6)** follow from the covered practices and two critical statutory defenses. Thus in addition to adverse impact and disparate treatment,[3] a plaintiff may attack a failure to reasonably accommodate known disability **barriers** to **essential job functions.** An employer may counter that such barriers are **insurmountable** (i.e., accommodations will not permit the disabled person to perform an essential job function), or with either of two statutory defenses: (a) that accommodations impose **undue hardship** on employers; and/or (b) that the disability poses a **direct threat** to worker safety,[4] which cannot be reasonably accommodated.

Title I of the ADA is fueled by Title V of the Rehabilitation Act (both cover employment). Portions of the Rehabilitation Act are amended by the ADA, but the Rehabilitation Act still stands. In fact, as noted in Title V of the ADA, the new Act "does not apply a lesser standard" than the older act. Thus interpretation of the ADA will likely build on case law developed within the Rehabilitation Act.[5] This chapter contains five Sections. Section I will summarize the Rehabilitation Act and preview how ADA captures the strengths of the older statute and overcomes its weaknesses, particularly those in Sec.504. The most difficult ADA dimensions to comprehend are the **protected class (Q1)**, **covered practices (Q3)**, and **attack/defense balances (Q6)**. Therefore Sections II through IV will emphasize these dimensions. Section V contains recommendations for compliance.

SECTION I
OVERVIEW OF THE REHABILITATION ACT OF 1973

There are three core statutes in the Rehabilitation Act: Sec.501, Sec.503, and Sec.504. Each statute uses the same three-part definition of **individual with a handicap** to define **protected class (Q1)**, namely: (a) current physical or mental impairments that substantially limit major life activities; (b) a record of such impairments; and (c) being falsely regarded as being impaired. The statutes differ, however, on the other five dimensions. Sec.503 has only minor implications for the ADA. Indeed, it may be argued that the whole point of the ADA was to create a Sec.501-type statute for private and state/local entities to correct complications and weaknesses in Sec.504.

SEC.501 OF THE REHABILITATION ACT

Sec.501, depicted in Chart 8.2, is strong in every dimension but one; it **covers (Q2)** *only* federal employers. Originally, Sec.501 mandated only affirmative action. Accordingly:

> Each department, agency, and instrumentality (including the United States Postal Service and the Postal Rate Commission) in the executive branch shall . . . submit to the . . . [EEOC] . . . an affirmative action program plan for the hiring, placement, and advancement of handicapped individuals in such department, agency, or instrumentality. Such Plan shall be updated annually, and shall be reviewed annually . . . to provide adequate hiring, placement, and advancement opportunities for handicapped individuals.

Prior to 1978, Sec.501 was enforced by the Civil Service Commission. Control was then passed to the EEOC in Reorganization Plan #1 of 1978. At about the same time, Congress amended the Rehabilitation Act to incorporate into Sec.501 the **covered practices (Q3)**,

CHART 8.2. SEC.501 (REHAB ACT)

Q1	Q2	Q3	Q4	Q5	Q6
Qualified (having KSAs) AND Physical/mental impairment Record of impairment Regarded as being impaired	Most federal executive agencies	Non-discrimination Affirmative action Reasonable accommodation	Title VII EEOC procedures	Title VII remedies	Adverse impact Disparate treatment Surmountable barriers

(Q1): What classes of people are protected (or have rights)?
(Q2): What business entities are covered (or have duties)?
(Q3): What employment practices are covered?
(Q4): Is the law administered, and if so, how?
(Q5): What are the penalties (or remedies) for breaking the law?
(Q6): What are the attacks and defenses used in litigation?

administrative procedures (Q4), and **remedies (Q5)** of Title VII. Or as stated in the Sec.505(a)(1) of the Rehabilitation Act:

> The remedies, procedures, and rights set forth in section 717 of [Title VII], including sections 706(f) through 706(k), shall be available with respect to any complaint under [Sec.501] of this title. . . . *In fashioning an equitable or affirmative action remedy under such section, a court may take into account the reasonableness of the cost of any necessary workplace accommodation, and the availability of alternatives therefore or other appropriate relief in order to achieve an equitable and appropriate remedy.* [emphasis added]

The italicized segment reveals that in addition to incorporating Title VII into Sec.501, Sec.505(a)(1) explicitly added an affirmative requirement to **reasonably accommodate**; a factor critical in making Sec.501 a strong statute.

Concurrently with Sec.505(a)(1), Congress amended *Sec.504* (not Sec.501) to cover federal entities. The motive behind dual Sec.501/504 coverage of federal entities has been hotly debated. To shorten an otherwise long and unnecessary discussion, the most likely motive was that by 1978 the former Department of Health, Education and Welfare (HEW) had established regulations for reasonable accommodation and related requirements for Sec.504, and Congress wanted to ensure that federal employees would benefit from these regulations.

Regardless of motive, the end result was strong protection for federal employees. The only complications of dual Sec.501/504 coverage have been technical in nature. For example, in *Boyd v. U.S. Postal Service* (1985), Boyd failed to exhaust EEOC administrative procedures and was precluded from suing under Sec.501. He then filed a Sec.504 claim, hoping to gain direct access to federal court. But the 9th Circuit dismissed the case, stating:

> Because Boyd's claim was covered clearly by section 501, with its specific exhaustion requirements imposed by section 501(a)(1), we cannot accept the argument that he should be able to invoke section 504 to circumvent those exhaustion requirements.

In general, the circuit courts agree that federal employees must exhaust EEOC procedures regardless of whether claims are based on Sec.501 or Sec.504. But many courts have permitted dual Sec.501/ Sec.504 claims once EEOC procedures have been exhausted. As we will witness later, dual Sec.501/504 rulings have had critical implications for the ADA. In particular, the **surmountable barrier attack (Q6)** has been easier for courts to evaluate in Sec.501 than Sec.504 because of the statutory requirement in Sec.501 for **reasonable accommodation**.

SEC.503 OF THE REHABILITATION ACT

Sec.503, depicted in Chart 8.3, **covers (Q2)** procurement and construction contractors, and the **covered practice (Q3)** is affirmative action. In other words, Sec.503 does for disabled people what Parts II and III of E.O.11246 do for minorities and women. But unlike E.O. 11246, which was issued under independent executive authority, Congress delegated the executive authority for Sec.503. Not surprisingly, that authority was passed on to the Secretary of Labor and ultimately to the OFCCP. According to Sec.503(a):

> Any contract in excess of $2,500 entered into by any Federal department or agency for the procurement of personal property and nonpersonal

CHART 8.3. SEC.503 (REHAB ACT)

Q1	Q2	Q3	Q4	Q5	Q6
Qualified (having KSAs) AND Physical/ mental impairment Record of impairment Regarded as being impaired	Contractors with more than $2,500 in procure- ment or con- struction contracts	Affirmative action as in E.O.11246	Most proce- dural features of E.O.11246	Most reme- dial features of E.O.11246	Surmountable barriers

(Q1): What classes of people are protected (or have rights)?
(Q2): What business entities are covered (or have duties)?
(Q3): What employment practices are covered?
(Q4): Is the law administered, and if so, how?
(Q5): What are the penalties (or remedies) for breaking the law?
(Q6): What are the attacks and defenses used in litigation?

services (including construction) for the United States shall contain a provision requiring . . . affirmative action to employ and advance the employment of qualified handicapped individuals as defined in section 706(8) of this title. . . . The President shall implement the provisions of this section by promulgating regulations.

The OFCCP enforces Sec.503 with **administrative procedures (Q4)** and **sanctions and penalties (Q5)** similar to E.O.11246. For example, the OFCCP requires compliance with a six-part equal opportunity clause and written affirmative action plans from contractors with 50 or more employees and $50,000 or more in contracts. The penalties and sanctions are, at least theoretically, as threatening as in E.O.11246.

Attack/defense balances (Q6), however, are more important in Sec.503 than in E.O.11246. Although federal court actions result from appeals of final rulings made by the Secretary of Labor (as in E.O. 11246), an appeal that involves disability barriers to essential job functions follows the same rules in Sec.503 as in Sec.501. That is, the employer must demonstrate that the barrier is insurmountable (i.e., no accommodation will work) or that accommodations that permit performance of essential job functions impose undue hardships on the employer and/or pose a direct (and nonaccommodatable) threat to worker safety.

Finally, it should be noted that reverse discrimination, the main fuel for court challenges to E.O.11246, has *not* been a major by-product in Sec.503. That is, the facially opposing demands of nondiscrimination versus affirmative action witnessed in Chapter 7 have been easier to resolve for disabled people than for minorities and women.

SEC.504 OF THE REHABILITATION ACT

Sec.504, depicted in Chart 8.4, is a complicated, hybrid statute. Its **covered entities (Q2)** are recipients of federal assistance grants of any dollar value, as well as the federal agencies that administer these grants. The **covered practices (Q3)** apply to discrimination "solely by reason of" handicap (i.e., *not* affirmative action). As a result of an early landmark Supreme Court ruling (*Southeastern v. Davis,* 1979), an attempt to incorporate affirmative action into Sec.504 via HEW regulations was invalidated by the Supreme Court. This weakened, at least initially, the surmountable **barrier attack (Q6)**. The **procedures (Q4)** and **remedies (Q5)** are in accordance with Title VI (not Title VII). According to Sec.504(a):

> No *otherwise qualified* handicapped individual in the United States, as defined in section 706(8) of this title shall, solely by reason of his handicap, be excluded from participation in, be denied the benefits of, or be subjected to discrimination under any program or activity receiving Federal financial assistance or under any program or activity conducted by any Executive agency or by the United States Postal Service. *The head of each agency shall promulgate such regulations as may be necessary to carry out the amendments to this section* made by the Rehabilitation, Comprehensive Services, and Developmental Disabilities Act of 1978. [emphasis added]

Three critical events are responsible for the complications and weaknesses of Sec.504. In order of importance, they are: (a) the aforementioned 1979 Supreme Court *Southeastern v. Davis* ruling; (b) a 1978 amendment incorporating Title VI into Sec.504 at the same time that Title VII was incorporated into Sec.501; and (c) the initial failure in 1973 of the HEW to issue Sec.504 regulations.

CHART 8.4. SEC. 504 (REHAB ACT)

Q1	Q2	Q3	Q4	Q5	Q6
Otherwise qualified (having KSAs) AND Physical/ mental impairment Record of impairment Regarded as being impaired	Any private or state/ local agency having federal assistance funds in any amount	Non-discrimination But no additional affirmative action beyond notice posting	Title VI procedures (not Title VII)	Same as pre-1991 Title VII remedies	Adverse impact Disparate treatment Surmountable barriers

(Q1): What classes of people are protected (or have rights)?
(Q2): What business entities are covered (or have duties)?
(Q3): What employment practices are covered?
(Q4): Is the law administered, and if so, how?
(Q5): What are the penalties (or remedies) for breaking the law?
(Q6): What are the attacks and defenses used in litigation?

Southeastern Community College v. Davis (1979)

Sec.504 protects **otherwise qualified** individuals (the first segment underlined in Sec.504(a)). This does not alter the basic three-part definition of **individual with handicaps**. In Davis, however, the Supreme Court interpreted "otherwise qualified" to mean qualified **in spite of** rather than **except for** a handicap. At the same time, the Court invalidated an HEW affirmative action regulation.

The interpretation of "otherwise qualified" within in the ADA is being qualified **except for** a disability; or having the knowledge, skills, and abilities (KSAs) and other requisites to perform essential functions of a job, **with or without** reasonable accommodation. Thus it is when a disability interferes with essential job functions that reasonable accommodation is required; unless, of course, an accommodation imposes a direct and nonaccommodatable threat to worker safety or undue hardship. However, at the time of the Davis ruling, this was not the ascribed meaning in Sec.504. For example, according to Mack Player's (1981) interpretation of Davis:

> The Court has held that under Sec.504 "an otherwise qualified person is one who is able to meet . . . requirements in spite of his handicap," including physical requirements legitimate and necessary for performance of the duties. . . . *Thus, an employer is under no duty to hire a handicapped individual who is unable adequately to perform the job requirements.* [emphasis added] (pp. 341-342)

Hindsight reveals that this interpretation is questionable. More recent Sec.504 rulings suggest that the Supreme Court treated Davis's physical impairment as one of the prerequisite KSAs for being "otherwise qualified" because the Court perceived no way to accommodate Davis without **substantially** altering the Southeastern nursing program (which would constitute an undue hardship under ADA standards).

The reference to Player is not a criticism. To the contrary, Player is an exceptional author and a professor who specializes in personnel law. But the quote illustrates that many experts misinterpreted the Davis ruling. Furthermore, in reference to Sec.503, which has an affirmative action requirement, Player stated:

> The Court in Southeastern Community College v. Davis, supra, noted the difference in language between Sec.504, which only proscribes discrimination, and the language of Sec.503, which specifically authorizes "affirmative action" obligations. This power granted by Sec.503, the Court suggested, could serve as authority to require reasonable accommodation" that would reach the level of *substantial modification.* [emphasis added] (p. 348)

This is also a questionable interpretation. The term *substantial modification* ultimately proved to be the Supreme Court's code term for **undue hardship**. No statute, not even the ADA, forces accommodations that require substantial modifications that raise to the level of undue hardship on the employer.

Ironically, there would appear to be no inherent connection between **reasonable accommodation** and other forms of **affirmative action** (e.g., correction for underutilization of the protected class). However, as we will witness below, in many dual Sec.501/504 cases the courts used affirmative action to rationalize a reasonable accommodation requirement in Sec.501 where, at least by implication, reasonable accommodation would not have been permitted by Sec.504. This is a very complicated issue to be featured in Section III of this chapter. For present purposes, it is sufficient to know that Sec.504 is weak because reasonable accommodation is not statutorily mandated, thus undermining the critical **surmountable barrier attack (Q6)**.

Sec.505(a)(2): Incorporation of Title VI

The second critical event was Sec.505(a)(2), a 1978 amendment that bonded Sec.504 to Title VI at the same time that Sec.505(a)(1) bonded Sec.501 to Title VII. As stated in Sec.505(a)(2):

> The remedies, procedures, and rights set forth in Title VI of the Civil Rights Act of 1964 shall be available to any person aggrieved by any act or failure to act by any recipient of Federal assistance or Federal provider of such assistance under [Sec.504] of this title.

The choice by Congress of Title VI seemed logical at the time. Sec.504 was designed to cover more than just employment discrimination. In this broader context, the statutory prohibitions in Sec.504 mimic Title IX, a 1972 statute on sex discrimination in colleges and universities. Title IX, in turn, mimics Title VI, a 1964 statute on discrimination based on race, color, or national origin in all federal assistance contracts. However, there were three major unforeseen complications related to the Sec.504/Title VI connection.

Complication #1 involved Sec.604 of Title VI, which limits coverage of Title VI as follows:

> Nothing contained in this title shall be construed to authorize action under this title by any department or agency with respect to any employment practice of any employer, employment agency, or labor organization except where a *primary objective of the Federal financial assistance is to provide employment.* [emphasis added]

When applied literally to Sec.504, coverage does not extend to contracts designed for nonemployment purposes. For example, in *Sabol v. Bd. of Educ. of Willingboro, County of Burlington* (1981), a teacher injured in a car accident was fired because his principal did not believe he could perform in a wheelchair and crutches. The teacher was deemed not protected by Sec.504 because the grant to the school did not relate to employment. However, the Supreme Court struck down rulings such as Sabol in *Consolidated Rail Corporation (Conrail) v. Darrone* (1984).

A second complication occurred in *Grove City College v. Bell* (1984), where the Supreme Court ruled that Title IX and related statutes (such as Sec.504) apply only to funded programs. In other words, if funded only for Program A, a grantee could legally discriminate against handicapped individuals in Program B. However, Congress reversed the Grove City ruling in the Civil Rights Restoration Act of 1987.

The third complication involved state employees. Individual claims against state agencies are plentiful because state schools, colleges, and social service agencies receive a great deal of federal assistance. But in *Atascadero State Hospital v. Scanlon* (1985), a 5-4 majority ruled that the state of California had not consented to being sued, and that Congress did not use its 14th Amendment powers to override 11th Amendment immunity in Sec.504. However, the ADA explicitly neutralizes this ruling.

Delayed HEW Regulations

Finally, in 1973 Sec.504 granted administrative control to agency heads. The HEW, the largest agency, was expected to issue coordinating regulations to guide the other agencies. But by 1976, despite an executive order, no regulations were issued. In *Cherry v. Matthews* (1976) a district court ordered regulations, which were then written toward the end of Ford's administration and published during Carter's administration. But as of 1986, more than two thirds of these federal agencies had yet to issue final regulations.

Generally, the HEW regulations require employers with 15 or more employees to establish internal grievance procedures. In other words, employees are encouraged to use internal procedures before petitioning for the **procedures (Q4)** and **remedies (Q5)** from the appropriate federal agency. But there is a major drawback; the administrative remedies in HEW regulations are designed more to punish an offending employer than to relieve an affected employee.

Consequently, claimants have flocked to the private right of action implied in Title VI, which was approved by the Supreme Court in *Conrail v. Darrone* (1984). Generally, the Darrone ruling permitted direct access to federal district court, a privilege reserved for private and state/local entities (federal employees must exhaust EEOC procedures). The Darrone ruling also limited Title VI claimants to **equitable relief**. Or as stated by the Darrone Court:

> Without determining the extent to which money damages are available
> under Sec.504, we think it clear that Sec.504 authorizes a plaintiff who
> alleges intentional discrimination to bring an *equitable* action for back-
> pay. [emphasis added]

Victorious Sec.504 plaintiffs can thus receive back pay, injunctions,
reinstatement (or front pay), but not compensatory and punitive damages. Attorney fees are recoverable in accordance with Sec.505(b),
another 1978 amendment enacted together with Sections 505(a)(1)
and 505(a)(2). In other words, the Title VI remedies are basically the
same as the pre-1991 Title VII remedies.

IMPLICATIONS FOR THE ADA

Referring again to Chart 8.1, the ADA **protects (Q1)** all **qualified
individual[s] with a disability**. This is a major change relative to Sec.504
because the word *otherwise* is not included in the definition of "qualified
individual with a disability."[6] Generally, as noted earlier, disabled individuals are qualified if they have the prerequisite KSAs to perform essential functions of a job, with or without reasonable accommodation.

The ADA **covers (Q2)** private and state/local entities in **industries
affecting commerce**. This is an expansion of coverage relative to
Sec.504, which covered only federal grantees. Since July 26, 1992, and
extending 2 years, the ADA covers employers with 25 or more employees for 20 or more weeks of the current or prior year. Beginning on
July 26, 1994, the number is reduced from 25 to 15. Traditional Title
VII exemptions (e.g., religious institutions, Indian reservations) and
more recent extensions (e.g., employees of overseas American subsidiaries) also apply in the ADA.

The **covered practices (Q3)** contain the traditional Title VII nondiscrimination prohibitions, plus the affirmative requirements noted
earlier. But in addition, the ADA codifies a number of prohibitions
from the Sec.504 HEW regulations. For example, the employer must
avoid preemployment **medical** inquiries, and in general, disability inquiries of any kind. However, screening for illegal drug use is not
considered a medical exam according to the statute, and neither is an
agility test (according to the EEOC ADA Regulations).

The **administrative procedures (Q4)** mimic Title VII, which means
that in contrast to Sec.504, Title VII-type EEOC filing requirements must

be exhausted. Employers must also heed EEOC regulations authorized by Congress, and finalized on July 26, 1991. The EEOC regulations contain an appendix on Interpretive Guidance, and a *Technical Assistance Manual* was published in January of 1992.

The **remedies (Q5)** also mimic Title VII as amended by the Civil Rights Act of 1991. The pre-1991 remedies include injunction, back pay, reinstatement (with reasonable accommodation) or front pay, and lawyer fees, which are consistent with the remedies in Sec.504. However, the Civil Rights Act of 1991 adds compensatory and punitive damages for intentional discrimination, as determined by a jury.

Finally, the ADA codifies two **attacks (Q6)**; adverse impact and surmountable barriers. As we will witness later in the chapter, adverse impact is codified by explicit references to job criteria that screen out individuals with disabilities, and surmountable barriers is codified by statutory reference to failure to reasonably accommodate. Disparate treatment is both implied by statutory reference to terms and conditions of employment, and codified within the EEOC ADA Regulations.

In short, the ADA borrows from the basic three-part definition of "individual with handicaps" (i.e., the **protected class (Q1)** in the Rehabilitation Act), and eliminates **covered entity (Q2)** problems relating to both 11th Amendment immunity (which is clearly overridden) and Title VI (which is clearly irrelevant to the ADA). The reference to Title VII also provides clear **administrative procedures (Q4)** and **remedies (Q5)**, and the ADA mandates that the **covered practices (Q3)** include reasonable accommodation, thus codifying a connection between reasonable accommodation and undue hardship within the **attack/defense balances (Q6)**.

───────── **BRIEF SUMMARY** ─────────

Among the three Rehabilitation Act statutes, the key precursors to the ADA are Sec.501 and Sec.504. Sec.503 is an E.O.11246-type affirmative action statute providing only a limited perspective on the ADA. On the other hand, Sec.501 provides strong Title VII-type protections and affirmative action in federal sectors, whereas Sec.504 provides much weaker and confusing Title VI-type protections in selected private and state/local sectors. Thus in effect, the ADA spreads the strong features of Sec.501 deeply into the private and state/local sectors, and does so without an explicit requirement for affirmative action beyond reasonable accommodation and notice posting.

SECTION II
FOCUS ON THE PROTECTED CLASS (Q1)

As noted previously, the ADA **protects (Q1)** "qualified individual[s] with a disability." To understand the entire phrase, it is necessary to separate the term *individual with a disability* from the term *qualified*. To understand the phrase's overall protections it is also necessary to discuss separately issues relating to infectious diseases and to alcohol and drug abuse.

"INDIVIDUAL WITH A DISABILITY"

Sec.3 of the ADA provides the aforementioned three-part definition of **individual with a disability** (Parts A, B, & C). Accordingly:

> The term "disability" means, with respect to the individual: **(a)** a physical or mental impairment that substantially limits one or more of the major life activities of such individual; **(b)** a record of such an impairment; or **(c)** being regarded as having such an impairment.

The language is taken almost verbatim from Sec.8(B), a 1974 amendment to Title V of the Rehabilitation Act.

Part A: Substantially Limiting Impairments

Part A has two prongs: (1) a physical or mental impairment and (2) a substantial limitation of a major life activity. There are no exhaustive lists for impairments or activities. However, in accordance with Sec. 1630.2 of the EEOC regulations:

Physical impairments include, but are not limited to physiological disorders and conditions, cosmetic disfigurement, and anatomical loss. Typical examples are cerebral palsy, epilepsy, muscular dystrophy, multiple sclerosis, cancer, heart disease, and diabetes.

Mental impairments include but are not limited to mental retardation, organic brain syndrome, emotional or mental illness, and learning disabilities. Typical examples are schizophrenia, depression, any kind of brain trauma, and dyslexia. Expressly omitted are sexual preference, sexual or gambling disorders, and drug-induced psychosis.

Major life activities include, but are not limited to seeing, hearing, walking, caring for oneself, learning, breathing, and—of course—working. And to **substantially limit** means to **significantly restrict**. Factors to be considered include: (a) nature and severity of impairment, (b) expected or actual duration of impairment, and (c) expected or actual long-term impact on the individual. Factor 1 excludes minor impairments such as a trick knee, and factors 2 and 3 exclude temporary impairments such as broken bones (unless, of course, broken bones lead to a more severe, long-range consequence such as arthritis).

Two other points must be noted. First, restrictions must be evaluated relative to **average** people. For example, a professional athlete who suffers a career-ending knee injury is not considered disabled if, after recuperation, he can walk or run as well as most other people in the population.

Second, exclusion from a single job is *not* a significant restriction when the major life activity is **working**. For example, acrophobia (a fear of heights) is clearly a mental impairment. But in *Forrisi v. Bowen* (1986), the 4th Circuit ruled that an acrophobic was not substantially limited by his inability to work on upper floors of a building. The court ruled that:

> Far from being regarded as having a "substantial limitation" in employability, Forrisi was seen as unsuited for one position in one plant—and nothing more.

In other words, the substantial limitation has to be broad, implicating many jobs, a ruling reinforced in Sec.1630.(2) of the EEOC Regulations, where it is plainly stated that "[t]he inability to perform a single, particular job does not constitute a substantial limitation in the major life activity of working."

Part B: History of Impairment

Part B covers individuals recuperated from impairments cited in Part A. According to Sec.1630.(2) of the EEOC Regulations, a record of impairment means:

> [having] a history of, or has been misclassified as having, a mental or physical impairment that substantially limits one or more major life activities.

In general, Part B protects individuals from unproven fears associated with having had a disease or having been a patient. A classic example is provided in *Allen v. Heckler* (1985), where the D.C. circuit supported a previously hospitalized mental patient because:

[discrimination] occurs against those who at one time had a disabling condition. The handicap that these people face is the continuing stigma of being a former psychiatric patient; this disability does not disappear on discharge from the hospital.

This "stigma" is also captured in the Supreme Court's ruling in *School Board v. Arline* (1987), a landmark case involving a teacher with a history of tuberculosis. Accordingly:

The fact that some persons who have contagious diseases may pose a serious threat to others under certain circumstances does not justify excluding from the coverage of the Act all persons with actual or perceived contagious diseases. Such exclusion would mean that those accused of being contagious would never have the opportunity to have their condition evaluated in light of medical evidence and a determination made as to whether they were "otherwise qualified." Rather, they would be vulnerable to discrimination on the basis of mythology—precisely the type of injury Congress sought to prevent.

The Arline ruling has critical implications for infectious diseases, and therefore will be discussed in greater detail below.

Part C: Falsely Regarded as Impaired

Part C also addresses "mythology" and "stigmas." It protects individuals who are fully capable, but are falsely thought to be, or treated as if they are, incapable. Examples include but are not limited to burn victims and people erroneously thought to be drug addicts. The EEOC also provides an example of an employee rumored to carry the HIV virus that causes AIDS. It should be noted, however, that being **treated as being** is not the same as being **falsely diagnosed**. The false diagnosis belongs to the Part B definition above.

A case law example of the Part C definition is provided in *E. E. Black v. Marshall* (1980),[7] where a plaintiff was excluded from apprenticeship carpentry when a preemployment medical exam (not allowed in the ADA) revealed a congenital back disorder. The plaintiff was not currently impaired in accordance with Part A, and his prior history did not justify protection under Part B (he had two relatively minor workplace episodes). But he was protected under Part C because his exclusion was based on the unfounded fear that he would someday become disabled (and receive workers' compensation benefits). The court ruled that a "perceived impairment prevented Mr. Crosby from securing the job he wanted." The ruling should be taken in context. There was no evidence of an active impairment or that one was imminent. The court suggested that medical evidence indicating (say) an 90% risk of an imminent impairment (e.g., heart attack) would have resulted in a different ruling.

BEING "QUALIFIED"

Not all "individual[s] with a disability" are **qualified** under the ADA. According to Sec.101(8):

> The term "qualified individual with a disability" means an individual with a disability who, with or without reasonable accommodation, can perform the *essential functions* of the employment position that such individual holds or desires. [emphasis added]

Clearly, the focus is on **essential functions** of a job. Employers should not exclude or chill disabled employees because of what the EEOC terms **marginal** job duties.

Sec.1630.2(m) of the EEOC Interpretive Guidelines advocates a two-step inquiry for determining qualification:

> The first step is to determine if the individual satisfies the prerequisites for the position, such as possessing the appropriate educational background, employment experience, skill, licenses, etc.

For example, disabled individuals who are unlicensed may be excluded from jobs requiring licenses—just like anyone else (e.g., teaching).

> The second step is to determine whether or not the individual can perform the essential functions of the position held or desired with or without reasonable accommodation.

Thus for those who have a license (and other prerequisite KSAs), the emphasis shifts to determining whether disabilities serve as barriers to performance of essential job functions.

Even the Sec.504 term *otherwise qualified* has been redefined, as suggested in Note 6. For example, in Sec.1630.9 of the Interpretive Guidelines for the ADA, the EEOC states:

The term "otherwise qualified" is intended to make clear that the obligation to make reasonable accommodation is owed only to an individual with a disability who is qualified within the meaning of Sec.1630.2(m) in that he or she satisfies all the skill, experience, education and other job-related selection criteria. An individual with a disability is "otherwise qualified," in other words, if he or she is qualified for a job, except that, because of the disability, he or she needs a reasonable accommodation to perform the job's essential functions.

Thus it is clear that in the ADA an individual with a disability must have prerequisite KSAs **in spite** of the disability, but given the prerequisites, that individual is qualified **except for** the disability.

INFECTIOUS DISEASES

Special statutory language is devoted to **communicable diseases** and **food handling**. Accordingly, Sec.103(d)(2) of the ADA states:

In any case in which an individual has an infectious or communicable disease that is transmitted to others through the handling of food, that is included on the list developed by the Secretary of Health and Human Services under paragraph (1), and which cannot be eliminated by *reasonable accommodation,* a covered entity may refuse to assign or continue to assign such individual to a job involving food handling. [emphasis added]

This has been a very controversial issue. For example, how does an employer reasonably accommodate a person who is actively infectious? Furthermore, Sec.103(d)(3) permits states and municipalities to uphold even stricter standards than the ADA.

On a more general level, the issue of communicable (or infectious) diseases extends beyond food handling to include any worker in any job. Historically, the critical issues for infectious diseases were addressed in the aforementioned *School Board v. Arline* (1987) case. In Arline, a teacher with a history of tuberculosis was discharged after her third relapse. The school board contended that Arline was discharged not because of her disease, but because her disease was infectious. This argument is reflected in the minority ruling by Justice Rehnquist, who, speaking for Scalia, stated:

The record in this case leaves no doubt that Arline was discharged because of the contagious nature of tuberculosis, and not because of any diminished physical or mental capabilities resulting from her condition. Thus, in the language of Sec.504, the central question here is whether discrimination on the basis of contagiousness constitutes discrimination "by reason of . . . handicap."

This is precisely what the school board contended—that Arline should not be protected because her disease did not impair her physically or mentally, but instead threatened others.

However, Justice Brennan, speaking for a majority of seven, disagreed, stating:

> We do not agree . . . [that] the contagious effects of a disease can be meaningfully distinguished from the disease's physical effects on a claimant. . . . It would be unfair to allow an employer to seize upon the effects of a disease on others and the effects of a disease on a patient and use that distinction to justify discriminatory treatment.

Interestingly, Brennan cited but did not rule on AIDS. However, the 9th Circuit, interpreting the Arline ruling, treated a school teacher with AIDS much like the Supreme Court treated Arline (*Chalk v. U.S. District Court*, 1988). The Chalk ruling was recently supported by the 11th Circuit (*Doe v. Garrett*, 1990) and is clearly supported within the EEOC ADA Regulations. A practice forecasted by the EEOC concerns singling out *suspected* AIDS victims for blood tests; a practice that the EEOC clearly perceives as being illegal.

Subsequent to the Arline ruling, Congress, in 1988, amended the definition of "individual with handicaps" in the Rehabilitation Act so that it does *not* include:

> an individual who has a currently contagious disease or infection and who, by reason of such disease or infection, would constitute a *direct threat* to the health or safety of other individuals or who, by reason of the currently contagious disease or infection, is currently unable to perform the duties of the job. [emphasis added]

In other words, by Rehabilitation Act standards, the infectious individual who does *not* pose a **direct threat** to worker safety, and is able to perform his or her job, is "otherwise qualified."

This amendment is bolstered in two ways in the ADA. First, Sec.101.(3) of the ADA states that the term *direct threat* means:

a *significant risk* to the health or safety of others that cannot be eliminated by reasonable accommodation. [emphasis added]

Second, Sec.1630.2(r) of the EEOC ADA Interpretive Guidelines defines as **significant risk:**

[1] The duration of risk; [2] the nature and severity of potential harm; [3] the likelihood that the potential harm will occur; and [4] the *imminence* of the potential harm. [emphasis added]

Returning to Arline, it could be argued that while she was infectious (i.e., during a relapse), the potential harm posed by Arline was **imminent.** Indeed, as noted in Headnote 7.5 in the Arline ruling:

A person who poses a significant risk of communicating an infectious disease to others in the workplace will not be "otherwise qualified" for his or her job within the meaning of [Sec.504] . . . if reasonable accommodation will not eliminate that risk; *the Act does not require a school board to place a teacher with active, contagious tuberculoses in a classroom with elementary school children.* [emphasis added]

Thus the reasonable accommodation for Arline would likely reduce to unpaid leave to permit recovery from infectiousness.

More generally, it would seem to be imprudent for an employer to establish a general rule that **automatically** precludes the hiring or continued employment of an individual with an infectious disease. Rather, both the Arline ruling and the ADA's statutory definition of **direct threat** would seem to dictate a case-by-case consideration of individuals with infectious diseases, thus preventing exclusion based *only* on "stigmas" and "myths."

DRUGS AND ALCOHOL

The Rehabilitation Act does not treat drug and alcohol abuse expansively. In contrast, the ADA contains a great deal of statutory language pertaining to illegal drugs and, to a lesser degree, alcohol abuse. Relative to the Rehabilitation Act, the picture for illegal drugs is much clearer than the picture for alcohol abuse.

Drugs and Alcohol in the Rehabilitation Act

In 1978 Congress amended the definition of individual with a handicap in Sec.503 and 504 so that it:

> does *not* include any individual who is an *alcoholic or drug abuser* whose current use of alcohol or drugs prevents such individual from performing the duties of the job in question or whose employment, by reason of such *current alcohol or drug abuse,* would constitute a *direct threat* to property or the safety of others. [emphasis added]

In other words, the amendment covered only current abuse, did not define alcohol or drug abuse, did not distinguish between alcohol and drug abuse, and did not reference recovery from addiction. Thus the courts had to decide a number of important issues, particularly **direct threat** and **recovery**.

On the issue of **direct threat**, just 41 days prior to the enactment of the ADA the 5th Circuit upheld the firing of an alcoholic FBI agent who was deemed a threat to the safety of himself and others (*Butler v. Thornburgh,* 1990). The same ruling was made by the 8th Circuit in *Crewe v. U.S. Office of Personnel Management* (1987) for an alcoholic mathematician. It should be noted, however, that in both cases the employees were given ample opportunity to benefit from rehabilitation before they were terminated.

Furthermore, in *Rodgers v. Lehman* (1989) the 4th Circuit ruled that alcoholism is a handicap within the meaning of the Rehabilitation Act, and supported the following four accommodations: (a) notifying the employee of available counseling services upon evidence of poor job performance; (b) offering a "firm choice" between treatment versus discipline if poor job performance continues; (c) imposing progressive discipline for the alcoholic in outpatient treatment who continues to drink; and (d) offering the alcoholic who quits outpatient treatment the option of inpatient treatment. If after accommodation #4 the individual relapses, discharge is considered appropriate.

On the issue of **recovery**, in *Wallace v. Veterans Administration* (1988), a Kansas district court ruled that a nurse who was a rehabilitated drug addict could be reasonably accommodated by job restructuring (i.e., not having to administer drugs). In *Nisperos v. Buck* (1989), a California district court ruled similarly for a federal government lawyer (i.e., in cases regarding drug laws).

Clearly, the above rulings on **recovery** are consistent with ADA statutory language as it regards illegal drugs or alcohol. However, the rulings on **direct threat**, as they relate to alcohol abuse, are more difficult to evaluate.

ADA Language Regarding Illegal Drugs

Statutory language regarding drug abuse is relatively clear. Unlike the Rehabilitation Act, the ADA contains a definition for **illegal use of drugs**. According to Sec.101(6)(a), the term means:

> the use of drugs, the possession or distribution of which is unlawful under the Controlled Substances Act (21 U.S.C. 812). Such term does not include the use of a drug taken under supervision by a licensed health care professional, or other uses authorized by the Controlled Substances Act or other provisions of Federal law.

The language is intended to distinguish commonly known illegal drugs such as cocaine and heroin from legal use of prescription drugs. Also, it is illegal to use, possess, *or* sell illegal drugs.

The ADA also distinguishes between current users versus those who are in or who have completed rehabilitation programs. Thus Sec.104(a) of the ADA states:

> For purposes of [Title I], the term "qualified individual with a disability" shall not include any employee or applicant who is currently engaging in the illegal use of drugs, when the covered entity acts on the basis of such use.

But Sec.104(b) of the ADA includes in the definition of "qualified individual with a disability" any individual who:

> (1) has successfully completed a supervised drug rehabilitation program and is no longer engaging in illegal use of drugs, or has otherwise been rehabilitated successfully and is no longer engaged in such use; (2) is participating in a supervised rehabilitation program and is no longer engaging in such use; or (3) is erroneously regarded as engaging in such use, but is not engaging in such use.

Thus aside from narrow exemptions in Sec.101.6(a), it is clear that an employer can refuse to hire or may discharge current users of illegal drugs, but rehabilitated or rehabilitating drug addicts are "qualified individuals with a disability," and the same would apply, quite obviously, to rehabilitated or rehabilitating alcoholics.[8]

Additionally, Sec.104(d)(1) explicitly states that drug testing is *not* a medical exam, and Sec.104(b) states:

> it shall not be a violation of this Act for a covered entity to adopt or administer *reasonable policies or procedures,* including but not limited to drug testing, designed to ensure that an individual . . . is no longer engaging in the illegal use of drugs. [emphasis added]

In other words, the ADA neither encourages nor discourages drug testing; it merely permits it. But employers who engage in drug testing should use **reasonable policies or procedures** to avoid discrimination in the process of drug testing (e.g., testing some but not others when there is no evidence of cause).

ADA Language Regarding Alcohol

The ADA contains no language that defines alcoholism or alcohol abuse, and does not contain language that would **automatically** exclude any current user of alcohol from the definition of "qualified individual with a disability."

Most of the statutory language regarding alcoholism and alcohol abuse also references illegal use of drugs. For example, Sec.105(c) of the ADA states that a covered entity:

> (1) may prohibit the illegal use of drugs and the use of alcohol at the workplace by all employees; (2) may require that employees shall not be under the influence of alcohol or be engaging in the illegal use of drugs at the workplace; (3) may require that employees behave in conformance with the requirements established under the Drug-Free Workplace Act of 1988 . . . ; (4) may hold an employee who engages in the illegal use of drugs or who is an alcoholic to the same qualification standards of employment . . . [as] other employees.

There is also a fifth subsection in Sec.105(c) that permits employers to comply with stiffer standards established by the Department of Defense, Nuclear Regulatory Commission, and Department of Transportation.[9]

Thus what is clear regarding alcohol (and illegal drugs) is that the employer can insist on: (a) an alcohol-free workplace; (b) that an employee be free from the effects of alcohol while on the job; and (c) that the alcohol abuser be held to the same standard of performance and conduct as other employees.

What is *not* clear is the status of the abuser who uses alcohol on his or her own time and is never drunk or under the influence on the employer's time, particularly when the employer is not bound by any of the federal statutes or regulations cited in Sec.104(c)(5) of the ADA. Unfortunately, there is no clarification in any specific section of the ADA; nor is there clarification in the EEOC ADA Regulations.

For example, Sec.512 of the ADA entitled "Amendments To The Rehabilitation Act" incorporates most of the explicit references to illegal drugs cited above into the Rehabilitation Act. However, in Sec. 512(a)(v) of these amendments it is stated that:

> For purposes of sections 503 and 504 as such sections relate to employment, the term "individual with handicaps" does not include any individual who is an alcoholic whose current use of alcohol prevents such individual from performing the duties of the job in question or whose employment, by reason of such current alcohol abuse, would constitute a direct threat to property or the safety of others.

On a word-by-word basis the language here is exactly the same as in the aforementioned 1978 amendment to the Rehabilitation Act, except that it excludes reference to drug abuse.

Regarding the EEOC Regulations, Sec.1630.16(b) of the Interpretive Guidance on "Regulation of Alcohol and Drugs" states:

> This provision permits employers to establish or comply with certain standards regulating the use of drugs and alcohol in the workplace. It also allows employers to hold alcoholics and persons who engage in the illegal use of drugs to the same performance and conduct standards to which it holds all of its other employees. Individuals disabled by alcoholism are entitled to the same protections accorded other individuals with disabilities under this part. As noted above, individuals currently engaging in the illegal use of drugs are not individuals with disabilities for purposes of part 1630 when the employer acts on the basis of such use.

In other words, there a clear affirmation of statutory language regarding the illegal use of drugs, but there is a relatively vague statement specifying that alcoholics *are* "individuals with disabilities."

According to Hartman and Homer's (1991) interpretation of the ADA and the EEOC ADA Regulations:

> it should be noted that the exclusion from the [ADA's] protections is limited to illegal drug users and does not apply to *alcohol abusers.*

Accordingly, while an employer may prohibit employees from consuming or being under the influence of alcohol at the workplace, and may hold alcohol abusers to the same performance and conduct standards as other employees, an employer may not take adverse action against an applicant or employee based upon their abuse of alcohol during off duty hours. [emphasis added] (p. 184)

Hartman and Homer are experienced EEO lawyers, and therefore their opinions merit some deference. Nevertheless, the issue is probably not as cut and dried as these authors suggest. For example, there are different levels of **alcohol abuse**. Certainly, a person who is physically dependent and who drinks is in a different category than one who is not physically dependent but who abuses alcohol on weekends. This issue will be explored further in Section V of the chapter.

─────── **BRIEF SUMMARY** ───────

Individuals are *disabled* if they (a) have a current physical or mental impairment that substantially limits a major life activity; (b) have a record of such impairment; or (c) are falsely regarded as being impaired. Individuals are *qualified* if they have the KSAs required to perform essential job functions. To be protected (**Q1**), the individual must be both disabled and qualified. The protected class includes alcohol abuse and infectious diseases, as well as rehabilitated (or rehabilitating) drug addicts and alcoholics, but does not include current illegal drug use, drug-induced psychoses, sexual preference, and sexual or gambling disorders. Employers may use drug tests, and may refuse to hire or may discharge any current user of illegal drugs. However, individuals with infectious diseases should be treated on a case-by-case basis. Recommendations regarding alcohol abusers are reserved for Section V of the chapter.

SECTION III
FOCUS ON COVERED PRACTICES (Q3)

As noted earlier, the ADA **covered practices (Q3)** include general prohibitions from Title VII plus explicit language regarding adverse impact. The prohibitions also include disability-specific concepts, such as association with disabled people, failure to reasonably accommodate, and prohibited preemployment medical exams and inquiries. The following discussion overviews the ADA covered practices and then focuses on **reasonable accommodation** within Sec.504, Sec.501, and the ADA.

OVERVIEW OF THE ADA
COVERED PRACTICES (Q3)

The **covered practices (Q3)** are contained in Sec.102 of the ADA. Sec.102(a) contains the **General Rule** for discrimination, which contains Title VII-type language specifying that:

> No covered entity shall discriminate against a qualified individual with a disability of such individual in regard to job application procedures, the hiring, advancement, or discharge of employees, employee compensation, job training, and other terms, conditions, and privileges of employment.

Like Title VII, the ADA also prohibits segregation and classification (Sec.102(b)(1)), and contractual arrangements (e.g., unions) that are discriminatory against disabled people (Sec.102(b)(2)).

Explicit language regarding adverse impact is contained in Sec.103 (b)(3), which prohibits:

> utilizing standards, criteria, or methods of administration—(A) that have the effect of discrimination on the basis of disability; or (B) that perpetuate the discrimination of others who are subject to common administrative control.

Sec.103(b)(2) is bolstered by Sec.103(b)(6) and Sec.103(b)(7). Thus Sec.103(b)(6) prohibits:

> [U]sing qualification standards, employment tests or other selection criteria that screen out or tend to screen out an individual with a disability or a class of individuals with a disability unless the standard, test or other selection criteria, as used by the covered entity is shown to be job-related and consistent with business necessity.

And Sec.103(b)(7) prohibits:

> [F]ailing to select and administer tests concerning employment in the most effective manner to ensure that, when such test is administered to a job applicant or employee who has a disability that impairs sensory, manual, or speaking skills, such test results accurately reflect the skills,

aptitudes, or whatever other factor of such applicant or employee that such test purports to measure, rather than reflecting the impaired sensory, manual, or speaking skills of such employee or applicant (except where such skills are the factors that the test purports to measure).

The disability-specific prohibitions are contained in Sec.103(b)(4), Sec.103(b)(5), and Sec.103(c). Sec.103(b)(4) contains the prohibition against association. Accordingly, the term "discriminates" includes:

[E]xcluding or otherwise denying equal jobs or benefits to a qualified individual because of the known disability of an individual with whom the qualified individual is known to have a relationship or association.

Failure to make reasonable accommodation is covered in Sec.103 (b)(5) which prohibits:

(A) not making reasonable accommodations to the known physical or mental limitations of an otherwise qualified individual with a disability who is an applicant or employee, unless such covered entity can demonstrate that the accommodation would impose an undue hardship . . . ; or (B) denying employment opportunities to a job applicant or employee who is an otherwise qualified individual with a disability, if such denial is based on the need of such covered entity to make reasonable accommodation to the physical or mental impairments of the employee or applicant.

And the prohibition against preemployment medical exams and inquiries is contained in Sec.102(C)(2)(A), which states:

Except as provided in paragraph (3), a covered entity shall not conduct a medical examination or make inquiries of a job applicant as to whether such applicant is an individual with a disability or as to the nature or severity of such disability.

The exception in paragraph (3) is that:

A covered entity may require a medical examination after an offer of employment has been made to a job applicant and prior to the commencement of the employment duties of such applicant, and may condition an offer of employment of the results of such examination if: (A) all entering employees are subjected to such examination regardless of disability [and] (B) information obtained regarding the medical condition . . . is collected and maintained on separate forms and in separate

medical files and is treated as a confidential record . . . [and] (C) the
results of such examination are used only in accordance with this title.

In other words: (a) medical exams and inquiries prior to a job offer
is prohibited; (b) the postoffer exam must be given to all employees;
(c) medical information must be kept in confidence;[10] and (d) exclusions based on medical information must be job-related and consistent
with business necessity. However, the covered entity may conduct voluntary medical examinations that are necessary for employment health
programs.

REASONABLE ACCOMMODATION IN SEC.504

Much of the disability-specific statutory language within the ADA
follows from the Sec.504 HEW regulations cited earlier in the chapter.
For example, the preemployment prohibitions stem from Sec.84.14 of
the HEW regulations that state an employer may *not:*

conduct a pre-employment medical examination or may not make preemployment inquiries of an applicant as to whether the applicant is a
handicapped person or as to the nature or severity of the handicap. A
recipient may, however, make pre-employment inquiry into the applicant's ability to perform job-related functions.

And the failure to reasonably accommodate stems from Sec.84.12 of
the HEW regulations, which states:

where reasonable accommodation *does not overcome* the effects of a
person's handicap, or where reasonable accommodation causes *undue
hardship* on the employer, failure to hire or promote the handicapped
person will not be considered discrimination. [emphasis added]

Sec.84.12 clearly pinpoints the need for reasonable accommodation
if (a) the accommodation suffices to overcome the effects of a disability (i.e., disability **barriers** to employment); and (b) it does not impose
undue hardships on the employer.

Most HEW regulations have been upheld in the courts. For example,
Sec.84.14 on preemployment prohibitions was supported in *Doe v.
Syracuse* (1981), where an applicant excluded from substitute teaching
was queried about a prior mental illness (a nervous breakdown).

However, Sec.84.14 on failure to reasonably accommodate has enjoyed only mixed success in Sec.504 cases. For example, just prior to the Supreme Court's ruling in *Southeastern v. Davis,* a Missouri district court ruled that a handicapped person should be treated like any other applicant (*Carmi v. Metro. St. Louis Sewer District,* 1979). More specifically, the court stated:

> The term "otherwise qualified" . . . does not mean that a handicapped individual must be hired despite his handicap; the statute prohibits the nonhiring of a handicapped individual when the disability does not prevent the individual from performing the job.

As noted by Player (1981), Carmi's employer was "not discriminating because of the handicap, but because of the inability to perform necessary job elements" (p. 343). This type of ruling, of course, was ultimately struck down in *School Board v. Arline* (1987), where it was held that discrimination against the effects of a handicap is tantamount to discrimination against the handicap itself.

The Carmi Court clearly misinterpreted the meaning of **otherwise qualified,** even by the standards of *Southeastern v. Davis* (1979). But there was good reason for Player (1981) and others to believe that the Supreme Court affirmed Carmi in Davis. Davis clearly contained a hard message. But Davis also contained a softer message. The Supreme Court clarified its Davis ruling in *Alexander v. Choate* (1985) and again in *School Board v. Arline* (1987). However, even prior to the Choate and Arline rulings, lower courts seemed to follow the Davis message that best fit the merits of individual Sec.504 cases.

Southeastern v. Davis (1979)—Revisited

Frances Davis had a serious hearing impairment; she could only read lips. She was denied admission to nursing school because an audiologist advised that her impairment would endanger patients. The audiologist also advised that even with intensive individual attention Davis could not fully participate in the program. Thus the program would have required modifications in order for Davis to graduate, and this was viewed as a reduction in academic standards.

The district court ruled that Davis was not an "otherwise qualified handicapped individual." The court deemed Davis a **threat** to the safety and health of others, and that Sec.504 required her to be qualified **in spite** of her handicap.

Before appeal HEW issued its final regulations, which the 4th Circuit accepted as law. The 4th Circuit then overruled the district court for two reasons. First, the college failed to review Davis's academic credentials independently of her impairment. Second, the college was obliged to apply **affirmative conduct** to modify the nursing program, even if such modifications were expensive.

But a unanimous Supreme Court agreed with the district court, and rejected both 4th Circuit rulings. Justice Powell issued the hard message cited in most references to Sec.504. Accordingly:

> The [4th Circuit] believed that "otherwise qualified" persons protected by Sec.504 include those who would be able to meet the requirements of a particular program in every respect *except* as to limitations imposed by their handicaps. . . . We think . . . [a]n otherwise qualified person is one who is able to meet all of a program's requirements *in spite* of his handicap. [emphasis added]

Powell also invalidated HEW's affirmative action requirement, as previously noted.[11] However, his ruling seemed to confuse "affirmative action" with "affirmative conduct" (the term used by the 4th Circuit in its ruling). That is, doing something extra (e.g., posting notices) is affirmative, but does not necessarily imply affirmative action as defined in E.O.11246 (e.g., written plans with goals and timetables). According to Powell:

> an interpretation of the regulations that required extensive modifications necessary to include respondent in the nursing program would raise grave doubts about their validity. If these [affirmative action] regulations were to require substantial adjustments in existing programs beyond those necessary to eliminate discrimination against otherwise qualified individuals, they would do more than clarify the meaning of Sec.504. Instead, they would constitute an unauthorized extension of the obligation imposed by the statute.

The softer message by Powell reads as follows:

> We do not suggest that the line between a lawful refusal to extend affirmative action and illegal discrimination against handicapped persons always will be clear. It is possible to envision situations where an insistence on continuing past requirements and practices might arbitrarily deprive genuinely qualified handicapped persons of the opportunity to participate in a covered program. Technological advances can be expected to enhance opportunities to rehabilitate the handicapped or otherwise

to qualify them for some useful employment. Such advances also may enable attainment of these goals *without imposing undue financial and administrative burdens* upon a state. Identification of those instances where a refusal to accommodate the needs of a disabled person amounts to discrimination against the handicapped *continues to be an important responsibility of HEW.* [emphasis added]

Thus Powell upheld the HEW regulations aside from affirmative action, and suggested that reasonable accommodations that do not rise to **undue burdens** may be required in some cases. As previously noted, "undue burdens" ultimately proved to be a code term for **undue hardship**.

Supreme Court Clarifications of the Davis Ruling

The facts in *Alexander v. Choate* (1985) were conceptually unconnected to facts in Davis (the state of Tennessee wanted to reduce Medicaid-related hospital payments from 20 to 14 days). Reaching beyond the Court's principal ruling in Choate (that Medicaid reductions do not constitute adverse impact), Justice Marshall, speaking for the unanimous Court, issued the following footnote:

In Davis, we stated that Sec.504 does not impose an "affirmative action" obligation . . . Our use of the term "affirmative action" . . . has been severely criticized for failing to appreciate the difference between affirmative action and reasonable accommodation; the former refer[s] to a remedial policy for the victims of past discrimination, while the latter relates to elimination of existing obstacles against the handicapped. . . . Regardless . . . it is clear from the context of Davis that the term *"affirmative action" referred to those "changes," "adjustments," or "modifications" to existing programs that would be "substantial".* . . *or that would constitute "fundamental alteration[s] in the nature of a program"* . . . *rather than to those changes that would be reasonable accommodations.* [emphasis added]

The italicized segment implies that reasonable accommodations are lawful as stated in Sec.84.12 of the HEW Regulations, but that **substantial** modifications cannot be justified.

Then, in *School Board v. Arline* (1987), Justice Brennan issued the following footnote:

"An otherwise qualified person is one who is able to meet all of a program's requirements *in spite* of the handicap" . . . . In the employment context, an otherwise qualified person is one who can perform the *essential functions* of the job in question. . . . When a handicapped person is not able to perform the essential functions of the job, the court must also consider whether any *"reasonable accommodation"* by the employer would enable the handicapped person to perform those functions. Accommodation is *not reasonable* if it either imposes *"undue financial and administrative burdens"* on the grantee . . . or requires *"a fundamental alteration in the nature of the program."* [emphasis added]

In other words, Brennan maintained the **in spite of** criterion for **otherwise qualified** from *Southeastern v. Davis,* but suggested that in the employment context, accommodations must be provided for barriers to performance of **essential job functions** unless such accommodations impose **undue burdens** (i.e., undue hardship) on the employer.

Thus in retrospect Frances Davis faced both obstacles implied by Sec.84.12 of the HEW regulations: (a) an **insurmountable barrier;** and (b) imposition of **undue hardship.** Unfortunately, no accommodations would have permitted Davis to hear well enough to participate in the nursing program as constructed, and modification of the nursing program would have constituted an undue hardship. In addition, even if the accommodations proposed by Davis were acceptable, it could be argued that Davis's poor hearing would pose a **direct threat** to the safety of her patients (i.e., the ruling of the district court in the Davis case).

Lower Court Sec.504 Rulings

Most lower courts viewed Davis as a special case where a direct and nonaccommodatable threat to health and safety poses undue hardship. When faced with circumstances analogous to Davis, the courts issued Powell's hard message. When faced with different circumstances, the courts issued Powell's softer message.

Doe v. New York University (NYU) (1981) illustrates the hard message. Doe was denied readmission into medical school for psychiatric reasons (she had attempted suicide on several occasions). Interpreting Davis, the 2nd Circuit stated:

Turning to the Act's term "otherwise qualified handicapped individual," it is now clear that this refers to a person who is qualified in *spite* of her handicap and that an institution is not required to disregard the disabilities of a handicapped applicant . . . if the handicap could reasonably be viewed as posing a substantial risk that the applicant would be unable to meet its reasonable standards, the institution is not obligated by the Act to alter, dilute or bend them to admit the handicapped applicant. [italics in original]

Doe was clearly a threat to herself, other students, and ultimately, her patients. Her suicide attempts involved wrist slashing and she routinely used blood letting to relieve tension.

Strathie v. Department of Transportation (1983) illustrates the softer message. This case directly addressed Sec.84.12, the core HEW regulation cited above. Strathie was hired and trained as a school bus driver and had worked one day. He was suspended, however, because of a Transportation Department regulation prohibiting hearing aids. Interpreting Davis, the 3rd Circuit stated:

> In [Davis], the United States Supreme Court held that an "otherwise qualified" handicapped individual is one who can meet all of a program's requirements in spite of his handicap. In dictum, however, the Court indicated that an individual may be "otherwise qualified" in some instances even though he cannot meet all of a program's requirements. This is the case when an existing program to accommodate the handicapped individual would be unreasonable, and thereby discriminatory.

Clearly, Strathie posed no greater danger to passengers than a driver wearing eyeglasses. The court examined reasons why Strathie's hearing aid posed a **direct threat** to safety, and ruled that each one could be reasonably accommodated without undue hardship.

Another illustration of Powell's softer message was provided by the 11th Circuit in *Stutts v. Freeman* (1983). Stutts was a dual Sec.501/504 case evaluated exclusively via Sec.504 principles. The facts of the case were that Stutts, a dyslexic, was excluded from the position of heavy equipment operator because of low scores on the GATB (General Aptitude Test Battery). Stutts did not challenge the test, but rather the fact that it was not administered orally. The district court dismissed the claim based on Davis. The 11th Circuit overruled, suggesting that Davis only applies when there is a threat to safety. More specifically, the court stated:

> Davis does not control . . . the Supreme Court held that a nursing school was not compelled . . . to admit an applicant with a serious hearing disability. It was found that the ability to hear was a *necessary qualification* for being a nurse. . . . In this case TVA has not shown that the ability to read is a necessary *physical qualification,* or that, if Mr. Stutts

needs accommodation, it would be an unreasonable burden. "The ultimate test is whether, with or without reasonable accommodation, a handicapped individual who meets all employment criteria except for the challenged discriminatory criteria 'can perform the essential functions of the position in question without *endangering* the health and safety of the individuals and others'." [emphasis added]

The last sentence (in quotes) is from *Prewitt v. U.S. Postal Service* (1981), a case to be featured shortly. More importantly for present purposes, the 11th Circuit interpreted Davis to mean that hearing is a prerequisite KSA for nursing because otherwise, patients would be endangered. However, for heavy equipment operation, reading is not a prerequisite and nobody would be endangered.

REASONABLE ACCOMMODATION IN SEC.501

The Supreme Court has never directly ruled on Sec.501. However, the implications of Davis are that the statutory language in Sec.501 permits a natural bypass to the Davis definition of "otherwise qualified." Supporting this statutory language is Sec.1613.702(f), a Sec.501 EEOC regulation that states:

"Qualified handicapped person" means with respect to employment, a handicapped person who, with or without accommodation, can perform the essential functions of the position in question without endangering the health and safety of [himself or others and] . . . meets the experience and/or education requirements . . . of the position in question.

The EEOC borrowed Sec.1613.702(f) from HEW. But obviously, the HEW regulation was negated to some extent by the Davis Court's definition of "otherwise qualified." Clearly, the EEOC regulation defines "qualified" as being **except for,** *not* **in spite** of the handicap.

The landmark ruling is *Prewitt v. Postal* (1981), a dual Sec.501/504 case cited above in *Stutts v. Freeman*. Prewitt is recognized for three major precedents: (a) application of adverse impact to handicaps; (b) creation of the **surmountable barrier** scenario; and (c) the use of Sec.501 to accomplish what is theoretically prohibited in Sec.504. The implications for adverse impact and surmountable barriers will be reserved for Section IV of this chapter. The following discussion focuses on precedent #3, and on post-Prewitt hard versus softer rulings.

Prewitt v. U.S. Postal Service (1981)

Prewitt was a Vietnam veteran who suffered wartime wounds leaving him with little mobility in his left arm and shoulder. He had worked as a carrier/clerk in the Jackson, Mississippi, post office prior to 1970. In 1978, after an 8-year self-imposed layoff, he applied for a similar position in the Greenville, Mississippi, post office. The job description for carrier/clerk listed duties that were neutral but that adversely impacted Prewitt. For example, the job required "arduous physical exertion involving prolonged standing, throwing, reaching, and . . . lifting sacks of mail up to 70 pounds."

Prewitt scored 82.8 on a written test; a score increased by 10 points because of his veteran status. But even as the number two person on the hiring list, he was excluded because of prior medical diagnoses. The fact that he had previously performed the clerk/carrier job was deemed irrelevant. The employer ordered Prewitt to take a medical exam and Prewitt refused. The district court dismissed the case because of Prewitt's refusal. But the 5th Circuit overruled because, in its view, Prewitt was excluded because of job requirements, not because of his refusal to submit to a medical exam.

The 5th Circuit presented its view of the "Davis rationale," which was that:

> employers subject to the Rehabilitation Act need not hire handicapped individuals who cannot fully perform the work, even with accommodation. However, while Davis demonstrates that only individuals who are qualified "in spite of" their handicaps need be hired, *Griggs* and its progeny dictate that the employer must bear the burden of proving that the physical criteria are job related. [emphasis added]

In other words, the Court ruled that the 70-pound lifting requirement was subject to adverse impact scrutiny regardless of whether Prewitt was "otherwise qualified" to do the lifting.

But the 5th Circuit relied on the Sec.501 affirmative action requirement to rule on whether Prewitt must be reasonably accommodated if the lifting requirement is job related. Focusing on health and safety issues cited in Sec.1613.702(f) of the EEOC regulations, the Court supported another EEOC regulation (Sec.1613.704) containing reasonable accommodation versus undue hardship criteria similar to those in the HEW regulations, and similar to those ultimately adopted in the ADA.

"Hard" Rulings Subsequent to Prewitt

Two commonly cited post-Prewitt cases illustrate a critical point: when there is undue hardship, affirmative action is irrelevant, even in Sec.501. The cases are *Treadwell v. Alexander* (1983) and *Gardner v. Morris* (1985). Indeed, the Treadwell and Gardner rulings read much like the Supreme Court's ruling in *Southeastern v. Davis.*

In Treadwell, a retired Air Force colonel was excluded from the job of park technician with the Army Corps of Engineers. Treadwell had a history of nervous breakdown and heart problems (a quadruple coronary bypass). The job description had physical demands (e.g., all-day patrols) that the employer deemed insurmountable via reasonable accommodation. Citing Prewitt, the 11th Circuit stated:

> Once a plaintiff shows an employer denied him employment because of physical condition, the burden of persuasion shifts to the federal employer to show that the criteria used are job related and that plaintiff could not safely perform the essentials of the job.

The Court ruled that the challenged job function is essential. Then, citing Davis, the Court ruled that even with the Sec.501 affirmative action requirement, modifying the position for another technician to perform one of Treadwell's essential functions would impose undue hardship, because the Corps employed only four park technicians.

In Gardner, an Army engineer with a history of manic depression sought a transfer to Saudi Arabia. His condition, however, required medication and close medical supervision. The medical facilities in Saudi Arabia were not conducive to Gardner's needs. Based on Prewitt, the 8th Circuit stated that:

> Although Gardner brought this action under Sections 501 and 504, we have considered carefully the scope of protection and the allocations of burdens under both sections and we conclude that the relief afforded a successful plaintiff under Sec.501 is equal to or greater than that provided under Sec.504.

The Court then ruled that: (a) without modern medical facilities, Gardner was a threat to himself; and (b) it would pose an undue hardship for the Army Corps to provide such facilities.

"Softer" Rulings Subsequent to Prewitt

The softer Sec.501 rulings do not differ radically in outcome from the softer Sec.504 rulings cited earlier. But most of these rulings connect the need for accommodation to unique Sec.501 requirements. The most frequently cited post-Prewitt cases illustrating this point are *Hall v. U.S. Postal Service* (1988) and *Arneson v. Heckler* (1989).

In Hall, a mail carrier could no longer perform her duties after a car accident. But Hall had occasionally clerked inside the post office. Based on those experiences, Hall believed she could successfully clerk. She was excluded, however, because the job description had the 70-pound lifting requirement, and a physician recommended that she could not do the job "without serious risk to her health." Borrowing from Davis, the 6th Circuit ruled that:

> *federal employers* have an *affirmative obligation* to make reasonable accommodations for handicapped employees. The burden is on the employer to present credible evidence that reasonable accommodation is not possible in a particular situation. [emphasis added]

In Arneson, the 8th Circuit evaluated apraxia, a neurological disorder that impairs concentration and cognitive and motor performance. The Court echoed its prior ruling in *Gardner v. Morris,* stating:

> Arneson is only required to provide evidence sufficient to make "at least a *facial showing* that reasonable accommodation is possible. . . . At that point, the burden shifts to the SSA to prove that it is unable to accommodate Arneson.

The "facial showing" was originally espoused in Prewitt and adopted by the 8th Circuit in Gardner. As we will witness in Section IV of this chapter, it is an essential component to shifting a burden of persuasion to the defendant in the **surmountable barrier** scenario.

As for the case, Arneson, with accommodation, had been an adequate claims representative for the Social Security Administration (SSA). But after volunteering for a new post, Arneson's work deteriorated and he was fired for cause. The SSA contended that despite his past record of accomplishment, further accommodations would impose undue hardship (e.g., requiring another representative to, in effect, do Arneson's job). Two 8th Circuit judges felt that the proposed accommodations were reasonable, and one dissenting judge ruled much like the 11th Circuit in Treadwell and the 8th Circuit in Gardner.

REASONABLE ACCOMMODATION
IN THE ADA

The ADA statute and its EEOC Regulations clearly endorse the **except for** criterion used in Sec.501. But, as noted earlier, the ADA provides these protections without referencing or requiring affirmative action beyond reasonable accommodation and notice posting. As stated in Sec.101(9) of the ADA, reasonable accommodations may include:

> **(A)** making existing facilities used by employees readily accessible to and usable by individuals with disabilities; and **(B)** job-restructuring, part-time or modified work schedules, reassignment to a vacant position, acquisition or modification of equipment or devices, appropriate adjustment or modifications of examinations, training materials or policies, the provision of qualified readers or interpreters, and other similar accommodations for individuals with disabilities.

Furthermore, reasonable accommodations are required for **known** physical or mental limitations of otherwise qualified individuals. Thus applicants must request accommodation, and the employer must provide them for qualified individuals as defined by the **except for** criterion, unless doing so would impose **undue hardship**, or create a **direct threat** that cannot be reasonably accommodated. Undue hardship will be discussed in Section IV of the chapter.

———— BRIEF SUMMARY ————

The ADA stipulates that any individual having prerequisite KSAs for essential job functions is qualified *with or without* reasonable accommodation. This standard was used in Sec.501 rulings based on statutory language. But for Sec.504, the Supreme Court defined the "otherwise qualified individual with a handicap" as being qualified *in spite of* the handicap. Having no affirmative action backup, Sec.504 placed a seemingly heavier burden on plaintiffs, courts, and legal scholars. The ADA avoids the Sec.504 versus Sec.501 confusions in two ways: (a) it redefines otherwise qualified to mean qualified *except for* the disability; and (b) it makes reasonable accommodation an affirmative requirement of the statute without requiring or prohibiting additional affirmative action beyond notice posting.

SECTION IV
Focus on Attack/Defense Balances (Q6)

For purposes of exposition, attacks based on **disparate treatment, adverse impact**, and **surmountable barriers** will be treated separately below. However, multiple attacks can occur in any one case. For example, most adverse impact cases in the Rehabilitation Act case law literature were combined cases in which adverse impact was step 1 and surmountable barriers was step 2. And in one of these cases (*Prewitt v. Postal,* 1981), all three attacks were evaluated.

In general, there is a burden on the plaintiff to prove he or she is both qualified and disabled. That is, the plaintiff must have the prerequisite KSAs for the job, and must be a person with a disability. In addition, there must be some connection between the disability and being excluded from work. That is, the person must be excluded because of the disability, because of some job criterion that impacts the disability, and/or because of failure to reasonably accommodate the disability that interferes with an essential job function.

FOCUS ON DISPARATE TREATMENT

According to Sec.1630.15 of the ADA Interpretive Guidelines entitled "Disparate Treatment Defenses," the EEOC states:

> The crux of the defense to this type of charge is that the individual was treated differently not because of his or her disability, but for a legitimate nondiscriminatory reason . . . unrelated to the individual's disability.

The EEOC cites the two major cases reviewed that fueled the McDonnell-Burdine Scenario, namely *McDonnell v. Green* (1973) and *Texas v. Burdine* (1981). Of course, McDonnell-Burdine is not a mandatory disparate treatment scenario, but other scenarios (e.g., direct evidence of disparate treatment) place a heavier initial burden on the plaintiff.

Another disparate treatment scenario defined by the EEOC references employer policies that, under Title VII, might be construed as **facial** discrimination. For example, in Sec.1630.15 of the ADA Interpretive Guidelines, the EEOC states:

> Disparate treatment has also occurred where an employer has a policy
> of not hiring individuals with AIDS regardless of the individuals'
> qualifications.

Under such circumstances, McDonnell-Burdine is inappropriate because
having hired **regardless** of qualifications is direct evidence of disparate treatment. Therefore, the employer would probably have to appeal
to **direct threat**, which, as we witnessed earlier, has reasonable accommodation (and thus undue hardship) complications.

Regarding McDonnell-Burdine, the reader will recall from Chapter
2 that the plaintiff **produces** evidence of prima facie discrimination
in phase 1 (by demonstrating protected class membership, qualification
for the job, rejection, and continuation of the search). The defendant
then **produces** (or **articulates**) an alternative to discrimination in
phase 2. The scenario then reduces to phase 3, in which the plaintiff
attempts to **persuade** the court that the phase 2 production is pretext.

Interestingly, the EEOC cites *Prewitt v. Postal* (1981) as an example
of disparate treatment. Clearly, disparate treatment was not the major
feature in this case. Rather, the employer tried to skirt other issues (i.e.,
adverse impact and reasonable accommodation) with the articulation
that Prewitt was passed over not because of disability, but because of
failure to adhere to an employer request (to be medically examined).
The court viewed this argument as pretext.

Of course, by ADA standards, the medical exam would have to be
conditioned to a job offer; all other applicants would have to be medically examined; and exclusion based on medical data would have to
be justified by job-relatedness and consistency with business necessity.

A better example of McDonnell-Burdine is *Norcross v. Sneed* (1985),
a Sec.504 case. In Norcross, a blind woman finished second in the
search for a librarian. She had established prima facie discrimination
by showing she was protected and otherwise qualified for the job, and
that she was passed over in favor of another applicant. But the 8th
Circuit accepted the defendant's articulation that the favored applicant was more qualified. Norcross then appealed for affirmative action
in lieu of pretext, and was denied.

It should be noted, however, that relative to other Sec.504 cases summarized earlier, Norcross was unique. Reasonable accommodation
was not an issue because Norcross was an accomplished librarian who
was treated as "otherwise qualified" *with* reasonable accommodation.
Or as stated by 8th Circuit:

there are at least two different types of suits. In one category, the defendant acknowledges relying on the plaintiff's handicap in reaching the employment decision. . . . In the second category, the defendant denies relying on handicap in reaching the employment decision. The case before us falls in this category.

Norcross lost in a two-person race after having beaten out several other applicants. Had the ultimate victor not applied for the job, it would have undoubtedly gone to Norcross.

In other words, an employer can determine that another nondisabled applicant is more qualified than a disabled and reasonably accommodated applicant. The ADA does not guarantee a disabled and accommodated applicant a job; nor does it require an affirmative action hiring decision.

On the other hand, it is difficult to envision a court using McDonnell-Burdine prescriptions if a **qualified individual with a disability** requests accommodation and an employer refuses to oblige. Clearly, the ADA prohibits this refusal. Or as stated in Sec. 1630.15(d) of the EEOC ADA Interpretive Guidelines:

> an employer cannot simply assert that a needed accommodation will cause it undue hardship . . . and thereupon be relieved of the duty to provide accommodation. Rather an employer will have to present evidence and demonstrate that the accommodation will, in fact, cause it undue hardship.

The same logic would also hold, quite obviously, if the defense is a direct threat to worker safety, because reasonable accommodation is also implied in this defense.

FOCUS ON ADVERSE IMPACT

Recall from Chapter 2 that in Title VII adverse impact, the plaintiff shifts a burden of **persuasion**, not production. For example, in *Griggs v. Duke Power* (1971), either of two job criteria had a statistically negative impact on blacks; a much higher proportion of blacks than whites were excluded from being coal handlers for lacking a high school degree, and achieving low test scores. The defendant could not prove that these job criteria were job related, and lost the case.

To a large extent, the ADA is an adverse impact statute. Congress was less concerned with animus toward the disabled than with stereotypes regarding what disabled people cannot do, and with job criteria that disproportionately screen out disabled people. However, the rules for ADA adverse impact are likely to be somewhat different from the rules for Title VII adverse impact, both in terms of attack and defense.

The Prima Facie Attack

In Sec.1630.(b) and (c) of the ADA Interpretive Guidelines, the EEOC states:

> Disparate impact means . . . that uniformly applied criteria have an adverse impact on an *individual* with a disability or a disproportionately negative impact on a *class* of individuals with a disability. [emphasis added]

This language implies an extra consideration relative to Title VII. In Title VII, a whole **class of individuals** must be disproportionately impacted. The EEOC supports this Title VII requirement for the ADA, but in addition provides a vehicle for the **individual** to prove adverse impact independently of class considerations.

Moreover, case law from the Rehabilitation Act suggests prima facie proof of adverse impact can be made without statistics in either a class action or an individual case. The **class action** scenario is illustrated by *Strathie v. Department of Transportation* (1983), where a job criterion (prohibition of hearing aids) clearly impacted both Strathie and anyone else wearing a hearing aid. Strathie did not have to provide statistical evidence because it was facially evident that anyone with a hearing aid would be precluded from eligibility for the job of bus driver.

The **individual** case scenario is illustrated in *Prewitt v. Postal* (1981), where Prewitt challenged a weight-lifting criterion (a similar scenario existed in *Hall v. U.S. Postal Service,* 1988). Rather than providing statistical evidence, Prewitt provided factual evidence that he was: (a) qualified except for the disability; (b) that the disability prevented him from meeting job criteria; and (c) that the criteria adversely impacted him and people like him. On the issue of statistical evidence, the 5th Circuit reasoned:

> In our opinion, in the disparate impact context, there should be only minor differences in the application of the Griggs principles to handicap discrimination claims. One difference, however, is that, when assessing the

disparate impact of a facially neutral criterion, courts must be careful not to group all handicapped persons into one class, or even into broad subclasses. This is because the *"the fact that an employer employs fifteen epileptics is not necessarily probative of whether he or she has discriminated against a blind person."* [emphasis added]

The quoted and italicized portion at the end reflects the reason why this conclusion was drawn. The postal service had argued that they had a good record in hiring disabled people. The response, of course, was that what a business does with "blind" people is unrelated to what it does, or has previously done with respect to "epileptics."

But there may be times where statistical proof is the preferred way for plaintiffs to make the case. For example, in *Alexander v. Choate* (1985), the plaintiff provided statistical evidence that a reduction in Medicaid benefits would have a statistically negative impact on disabled people. The Supreme Court did not accept the argument, but only because it felt that the state was not obligated to ensure that such benefits must equally affect all people.

The Phase 2 Defense

Once a plaintiff has established prima facie adverse impact, the burden of defense rests upon statutory ADA language. Thus according to Sec.103(a) of the ADA:

It may be a defense to a charge of discrimination under this Act that an alleged application of standards, tests, or selection criteria that screen out or otherwise deny a job or benefit to an individual with a disability has been shown to be *job-related* and *consistent with business necessity,* and such performance cannot be accomplished by reasonable accommodation, as required under this Act. [emphasis added]

The reader will recall that Title VII adverse impact defenses rely to a large extent on the *Uniform Guidelines on Personnel Selection.* But the *Uniform Guidelines* do not apply to the Rehabilitation Act, and do not apply to the ADA. As noted in Sec.1630.10 of the EEOC ADA Regulations, "job relatedness" and "consistency with business necessity" follow from the HEW standards set for Sec.504. Overall, the standards are not the same as in the *Uniform Guidelines.*

The reasons are twofold. First, disability aside, the case law history on adverse impact reveals job criteria that are not likely to adversely impact disabled people because they represent all races, colors, religions, national origins, ages, and both sexes. Thus a test that disproportionately screens (say) blacks will not screen disabled people unless there is something about the test or its administration procedures that connects to disability (e.g., *Stutts v. Freeman*, 1983).

Second, where there is comparability, the *Uniform Guideline* standards are not sufficient to provide equal opportunity for disabled people. For example, a weight-lifting requirement could adversely impact both women and disabled people. If the requirement is valid by *Uniform Guideline* standards, the women have no case. However, for disabled people there is the residual question of whether the job could be done given reasonable accommodation.

The same reasoning applies to a test that measures prerequisite KSAs for work. *What* the test measures must be distinguished from *how* it measures. For example, in *Stutts v. Freeman* the job-relatedness of the GATB was not the core issue. Rather, Stutts's dyslexia prevented him from demonstrating his talents given the format of the test.

Thus job-relatedness is necessary for consistency with business necessity. Intuitively, a test that is not related to job performance cannot relate to essential functions of a job. However, job relatedness is only a preliminary issue if there are barriers to optimal test performance that, themselves, are unrelated to the job. Stutts's dyslexia interfered with his ability to read test questions, and reading was not related to the job (heavy equipment operator). Stutts requested an oral exam, thereby notifying the employer of his need for reasonable accommodation. The ultimate issue in Stutts, therefore, was failure to reasonably accommodate.

FOCUS ON SURMOUNTABLE BARRIER SCENARIOS

Clearly, a major difference between Title VII and the ADA is that some disabled people require affirmative extras in order to have an equal opportunity to work. Several affirmative extras are written into the statute; most notably, reasonable accommodation. The key statutory defense implied by reasonable accommodation is **undue hardship**. Once again, a key reference case is *Prewitt v. Postal* (1981).

In addition to proving qualification, connection of the disability to essential job functions, and adverse impact, Prewitt was required to provide a "facial showing" or "plausible reasons to believe" that the barriers are surmountable. This part, however, is a production, not a persuasion.

Undoubtedly, the defendant could try to prove **insurmountability** at this juncture. If pushed to a phase 2 defense, however, the issue would likely reduce to undue hardship, as it did in Prewitt and other cases cited earlier (e.g., *Treadwell v. Alexander*, 1983; *Gardner v. Morris*, 1985; *Arneson v. Heckler*, 1989; etc.).

Statutory ADA Language

As codified in Sec.101(10)(A) of the ADA, the "in general" definition of **undue hardship** is "an action requiring significant difficulty or expense"; that is, undue hardship reduces to either or both of two factors: (a) financial cost and (b) work efficiency. The illustrative "factors to be considered" for undue hardship are fourfold. As codified in Sec.101(10)(B) of the ADA, they are:

> (i) the nature and cost of the accommodation needed under this Act; (ii) the overall financial resources of the facility or facilities involved in the provision of the reasonable accommodation; (iii) the overall financial resources of the covered entity; the overall size of the business of a covered entity with respect to the number of its employees; the number, type, and location of its facilities; and (iv) the type of operation or operations of the covered entity including the composition, structure, and functions of the workforce of such entity; the geographic separateness, administrative, or fiscal relationship of the facility or facilities in question to the covered entity.

Clearly, factors (i) through (iii) speak to a ratio of cost of accommodation divided by the resources of the provider of reasonable accommodation. Factor (iv) speaks to a variety of ways that work efficiency might be retarded.

Additionally, although not defined as undue hardship, direct threat to safety and health can be considered as a similar burden. Direct threat applies to all disabilities, but most notably to infectious diseases and alcohol abuse. Clearly, the threat must exist despite reasonable accommodation (i.e., be insurmountable). Therefore, by definition, direct threat can invoke undue hardship.

Focus on Financial Cost

The most frequently cited cost case in the Rehabilitation Act is *Nelson v. Thornburgh* (1983). In Nelson, three blind income maintenance workers for the Pennsylvania Department of Public Welfare (DPW) were paying for private readers. The employees earned about $20,000 per year and required approximately $6,000 per year in reading accommodations. The workers requested funding from the DPW. Interpreting *Prewitt v. Postal,* the court reasoned that:

> in view of DPW's [3 billion dollar] administrative budget, the modest cost of providing half-time readers, and the ease of adopting that accommodation without any disruption of DPW's services, it is apparent that DPW has not met its burden of showing undue hardship.

The critical factors to note are: (a) the ratio of cost of accommodation to salary was *not* that critical; and (b) neither was the number of employees that require accommodation. In addition, it should be noted that the EEOC ADA Regulations permit an employee (and other sources such as state and federal grants) to offset employer costs for reasonable accommodations, as was done by the Nelson plaintiffs.

Interestingly, Congress debated a recipe relating cost of accommodation to salary, namely limiting the cost to 10% of the salary. However, it became obvious that this recipe would adversely impact lower paying jobs; the very jobs many disabled people would compete for. Had Congress codified an explicit ratio for cost of accommodation divided by financial assets of the company, the cost factor would be easier to understand. But is clear that even a well-funded entity cannot be driven to excess (e.g., building medical facilities where none previously existed—*Gardner v. Morris,* 1985). If there is a magical rule or ratio possible, the courts will have to create it.

Focus on Work Efficiency

Other factors, however, suggest that cost is the lesser of the two concerns. First, several public and private foundations have outlined reasons why 90%-95% of all accommodations will require costs of $500 or less. Second, Sec.501 and Sec.504 rulings suggest that most contests will test work efficiency issues more than cost.

For example, the U.S. Postal Service undoubtedly has more funds than the Pennsylvania DPW. But in cases such as Prewitt and Hall, accommodations worth $25 or less were opposed. In *Dexler v. Tisch* (1987), for example, a dwarf wanted only a stool. The court ruled that the stool was an undue hardship because the postal service provided evidence that even if Dexler could safely perform his functions on a stool, he would slow down the entire operation.

Other examples of undue hardship include modifying or eliminating an essential job function (or school function as in Davis), and shifting duties among workers when the work force is small (Treadwell). It might also be unduly hard for a company to provide an accommodation that counters a bona fide collective bargaining agreement (e.g., *Bey v. Bolger,* 1982). And although the author did not find an affirming case, the same could possibly hold for a bona fide seniority system.

There are many other cases in the literature. But in general, noncost factors reduce to maintaining the fundamental purpose and goals of the business and the effect of accommodations on other workers (their productivity, not their attitudes).

──────── **BRIEF SUMMARY** ────────

Based on ADA statutory language, ADA Regulations, and relevant Rehabilitation Act case law, certain assumptions are viable regarding the likely attack/defense balances (Q6) in the ADA. First, disparate treatment scenarios following the McDonnell-Burdine scenario are most likely to occur when the employer contends there are reasons other than disability for excluding a disabled person. However, disparate treatment for general policies (e.g., a no-hiring policy for AIDS) will likely trigger the direct threat defense, and refusal to reasonably accommodate will likely trigger surmountable barrier scenarios. Second, the attack/defense rules for adverse impact will likely be different relative to Title VII. Plaintiffs can rely on either factual evidence that a job criterion precludes an individual or a class from a job, or on statistical evidence. And the defense to adverse impact goes beyond job relatedness to issues of reasonable accommodation. Third, reasonable accommodation raises the issue of undue hardship, which has a cost component (accommodation cost matched against employer resources) and a work efficiency component (the fundamental nature of the business and the effects on worker performance). Unfortunately, there are no recipes.

SECTION V
COMPLIANCE WITH THE ADA

Compliance with the ADA requires an understanding of the rights and privileges of disabled people versus the responsibilities of the employer. However, the employer should also realize that disabled people have responsibilities that most other protected classes in other statutes do not have. The following discussion focuses on properly conceptualizing the ADA; understanding the meaning of essential job functions; understanding the preemployment prohibitions; use of affirmative action policies; and miscellaneous considerations.

CONCEPTUALIZING THE ADA

Title I of the ADA is designed to provide equal opportunity for disabled people in the work place. For some disabled people, this means following the general principles of **nondiscrimination** espoused in Title VII and ADEA. But for others, equal opportunity requires extra **affirmative** considerations, most notably, reasonable accommodation. Thus to some extent there are parallels between discrimination based on disability and discrimination based on religion.

Recall from Chapter 3 that many Title VII religious discrimination cases involve failure to reasonably accommodate a sincerely held religious belief. But Title VII also covers nonaccommodation issues such as religious harassment. The same is true with disability. The statute covers reasonable accommodation, but in nonaccommodation cases traditional Title VII considerations apply (e.g., *Norcross v. Sneed*).

In addition, religious accommodation features neutral practices that adversely impact religious beliefs. These are ordinary and necessary practices that hardly seem discriminatory (e.g., working on Saturday). The same is true of adverse impact against the disabled. Job criteria that most of us would take for granted (e.g., standing, seeing, hearing, etc.) can serve as barriers to work.

Finally, religious people with prerequisite KSAs must be accommodated for sincerely held beliefs, beliefs must connect to job requirements, and employers must know that a need for accommodation exists. Also, a believer must join in identifying accommodations and accept any accommodation that overcomes the religious barrier—not just the best one or the most preferred one. Similarly, disabled people must have the KSAs for essential job functions, and accommodations are required only if disabilities interfere with one or more of these essential functions. Disabled people must also request accommodations, cooperate in identifying them, and accept any that are sufficient to overcome barriers to performance of the essential job functions.

Thus a responsibility is placed on religious and disabled people that is not seen in traditional Title VII or ADEA nondiscrimination cases.

The applicant or employee must make the employer aware of discriminatory job criteria and the need for reasonable accommodation. This principle was strongly supported by Congress in the legislative history of the ADA. As summarized by Perritt (1990):

> the committees reporting the ADA endorsed the idea that an employee or applicant cannot recover without showing that she asserted the right to have reasonable accommodation made and the employer denied the request. Thus, the ADA does not impose liability for purely neutral employer actions that, unbeknownst to the employer, have a prohibited effect on the disabled. Rather the Act prohibits only conscious decisions to impose or to continue employment practices that have the prohibited effect. (pp. 49-50)

Similar conclusions are drawn by Ogletree, Deakens, Nash, Smoak, and Stewart (1992).

On the other hand, disability has higher thresholds than religion in two places. First, it is difficult to imagine an insurmountable religious barrier. Some accommodation will likely suffice; time off, altered shifts, swapping, and so forth. But accommodations for disability can fail, as for example in the unfortunate case of Frances Davis. Second, the undue hardship requirement in religious accommodation is "de minimis." Thus any additional cost in dollars or work efficiency is sufficient to justify undue hardship. The ADA standard is far beyond "de minimis."

Nevertheless, religious accommodation establishes two boundary conditions for disability accommodation. First, employers cannot be attacked blindly; the accommodations are for **known** limitations. Surmountable barrier claims, therefore, should never come as a surprise. Second, because accommodation generally requires a case-by-case consideration, there should be less class action suits than in Title VII. Logically, disability occurs in different degrees, and different accommodations may be required even for similar disabilities. Class actions are most likely to occur in "need not apply" cases (e.g., people with AIDS need not apply) or where state or local laws imply classwide impacts (e.g., no hearing aids allowed).

JOB DESCRIPTION AND SPECIFICATION

The employer is free to establish the essential functions of a job. However, the employer must ensure that the advertised functions of the job reflect the actual functions of the job. Or as stated in Sec. 1630.(n) of the EEOC ADA Interpretive Guidelines:

> The inquiry into whether a particular function is essential initially focuses on whether the employer actually requires employees in the position to perform the functions that the employer asserts are essential. For example, an employer may state that typing is an essential function of a position. If, in fact, the employer has never required any employee in that position to type, this will be evidence that typing is not actually an essential function of the position.

In short, the EEOC will pay deference to formally written job descriptions, but documents that are incorrect are self-incriminating. Therefore it is critical to know the essential job functions and the KSAs needed to perform these functions.

Essential Functions

The essential functions come first. The EEOC defines as essential functions: (a) jobs that contain only one function; (b) functions only a limited number of employees can perform; and (c) functions that are highly specialized. Some jobs satisfy the first criterion, but most jobs can be broken down into major duty areas, and major duty areas can be further divided into critical job tasks. Within this framework, traditional job analysis procedures conducted or supervised by competent professionals overkill the demands of the EEOC and the statute. Therefore, the author recommends them.

There are many job analysis techniques; some focus on jobs, some on workers, and some on both. The author recommends Levine's (1983) text because of its clear and humorous presentation of the various techniques, and his procedures for combining work and worker issues. Larger entities, however, may have to rely on less labor-intensive techniques discussed by Levine and others (e.g., Cascio, 1991; Landy, 1991; Muchinsky, 1990; Schneider & Schmidt, 1986).

Levine advocates a two-step approach. First, job tasks are defined in terms of: (a) action; (b) with or without equipment; for (c) a purpose. For example, an assembler may inspect a product (action) using a microscope (equipment) to search for defects (purpose). Second, tasks are then rated on three dimensions: (a) task criticality; (b) task complexity; and (c) time required for task completion. The criticality and complexity ratings are more important than time spent. For example, a law officer may only occasionally make a forcible arrest. The forcible arrest procedure is complex, however, and the consequences of failing to perform this task properly can be dreadful.

The fundamental goal of any job analysis procedure is therefore consistent with a fundamental goal of the ADA; to separate essential versus nonessential job tasks. An employer who excludes an applicant for inability to perform a marginal task will be guilty of what is essentially a cardinal sin (e.g., rejecting a blind applicant who cannot drive because employees occasionally drive to the bank to make deposits).

Specifying the KSAs

Also consistent with both EEOC regulations and accepted job analysis methods is the inherent bond between essential functions and KSAs necessary to perform these functions. Levine, for example, advocates derivation of KSAs from job description data based on four critical factors.

The first two factors speak to job-entry expectancies, and require: (a) a yes/no rating for whether a KSA is a necessary preemployment requirement, and (b) a yes/no rating for whether it is practical to expect applicants to have the KSA. In essence, there is a critical choice: what to expect from applicants at job entry versus what to train applicants to do after they are hired. The other two factors require numerical ratings, namely: (c) the extent to which trouble is expected if a given KSA is ignored; and (d) to extent to which a given KSA distinguishes between average versus superior workers.

Generally, an adequate job specification will isolate KSAs that require special attention (e.g., abilities to sit, stand, see, hear, lift, read, write, etc.). If such abilities are truly necessary for the job, accommodations must be made; if not, they should be eliminated, because they represent the types of criteria that can produce adverse impact based on disability.

Working Conditions

Working conditions are almost always included in written job analysis documents, but they are usually cursory. Few job analysts are ergonomic experts. However, it may be beneficial to conduct ergonomic analyses. Companies with substantial resources can hire high-level experts. But other options are available, including cooperative arrangements with local nonprofit agencies funded for the purpose of training and placing disabled people. Another alternative is to use experts in occupational health and safety who specialize in evaluating workplaces for conditions that produce or exacerbate physical impairments. This advice is less expensive, and often comes in exchange for other considerations (e.g., joining an insurance plan).

A Special Note on Professional Help

The foregoing discussion was not designed to advocate a particular procedure or consultant, but rather to illustrate critical principles. The specific methods used in job analysis vary, and include inspection of the job, reading of training manuals and other literature, reading of job diaries, if available, and interviews with job incumbents and supervisors. In larger operations, surveys may be required. The specific methods used in ergonomics focus on the relationship between the environment and the worker. These are complex issues that warrant professional attention of some sort.

However, not all companies are wealthy enough to choose among all of the options cited above. Individual consultation can be expensive. But there are alternatives to the $100-$200 dollar-per-hour consultant. There are workshops to train skills. Furthermore, the EEOC recommends cooperative arrangements to promote sharing of expenses. Finally, as noted in prior chapters, it is probably safer for a group or consortium to approach the EEOC on a range of issues than it is for an individual employer to request written interpretations on specific practices.

PREEMPLOYMENT INQUIRIES

The proscriptions of the ADA differentially apply to pre- versus posthiring decisions. Clearly, prehiring requires extra considerations. But the major principle for both pre- and posthiring is to inquire about what an applicant or employee can do; not what he or she cannot do. A given inquiry may be legal or illegal depending upon phrasing. For example, asking "can you do this work?" is legal, whereas asking if anything prevents you from doing the work is not.

Preemployment Prohibitions

The dominant issue is the prohibition against preemployment medical exams and inquiries. Also, the reader should not forget that promotional decisions can be viewed as preemployment. As for the prohibition itself, it applies to *inquiry;* that means suspect inquiries cannot be justified even if they are job related and consistent with business necessity. Furthermore, the prohibition applies to *any* inquiry; not just by medical doctors and psychologists, and not just by people. Therefore, the prohibition includes medical information gleaned from application blanks, background checks, interviews, polygraph tests, and so forth. It also includes any other information from such sources used to infer that a person cannot do the work.

What Strategies Can Be Used?

Two good strategies include: (a) reliance on realistic job previews; and (b) reorganization of selection steps, particularly in complex, multiple hurdle procedures.

Given a focus on ability as opposed to disability (or even inability), the realistic job preview should focus on essential functions; it should not, however, embellish these functions (i.e., it is not realistic to chill an applicant). The preview should include a written statement concerning the ADA, particularly its reasonable accommodation requirement. This is advocated in the EEOC Regulations and therefore serves the good faith function. It also serves another critical function; self-elimination for applicants who dislike the work or feel they cannot do it, even with accommodation.

Multiple hurdle components should be examined and possibly reordered. For example, applications, properly structured interviews, drug testing, and skills testing are more appropriate at the preoffer stage, and medical exams, background checks, polygraphs, and psychological interviews are better left to the postoffer stage. Again, all preoffer procedures should be stripped of reference to medical issues and disability or inability.

Special Situations

Some employers have special requirements. For example, prospective law officers and firefighters must be assessed for physical abilities. Agility testing is quite common in these professions, and the EEOC has explicitly deemed that agility tests are not medical tests. However, agility testing raises three other issues.

First, agility testing is not capacity (or fitness) testing. Agility tests are generally designed to simulate essential job functions (e.g., carrying a weighted dummy 100 feet). Tests of such things as lung capacity or heart recovery are often used in lieu of or in addition to agility tests. Regardless of whether capacity tests are job related and consistent with business necessity, if they are medical in nature they must be reserved for the postoffer stage.[12]

Second, agility testing often precedes training, which precedes employment. A conditional offer of training is not a conditional offer of employment, unless training itself is given probationary paid status. Some police and fire departments do this, but not all of them.

Third, where physical training does not involve sponsorship, failure to test medically prior to training poses an even bigger threat than violation of the ADA: liability for injury or death as a result of testing and/or training. For these and any other circumstances in which agility testing and physical training precedes the job offer, the EEOC has deemed that it is legal to solicit certification from medical doctors that the examinee is fit; that is, a yes/no answer, not a general report.[13]

Additional Considerations for Medical Issues

There are four additional medical considerations. First, the prohibitions against medical exams do not hold for employees participating in voluntary programs (e.g., for health benefits). Second, regardless of when and for what purpose medical information is legally collected, it must be filed in confidence and given only to those with valid reasons for having the information (safety personnel, supervisors, and government officials). Third, whenever an exclusion is based on medical information, it is treated like exclusion for any other reason. Thus it must be job related and consistent with business necessity. Finally, an employer may not single out employees for medical testing based on suspicion of illness.

AFFIRMATIVE ACTION

It is legal to exceed the requirements of the ADA when such practices benefit the disabled; indeed, this practice is encouraged by the statute and the EEOC. This contrasts with preferential treatment of minorities and women in reverse discrimination situations discussed in Chapter 7. Thus employers can impose undue hardships upon themselves. They can restructure work and modify jobs as they see fit, as long as certain other agreements (e.g., collective bargaining and seniority agreements) are not broken. Employers can seek grants and contracts to promote employment of the disabled; they can establish special programs; and they can engage in cooperative relationships with other businesses or agencies. One particular affirmative practice that is also good business is the drug-free workplace.

The federal Drug Free Workplace Act of 1988 is mandatory for some companies (e.g., all defense contractors, transportation agencies, and for any contract worth $25,000 or more), but not for most. However, the Act has been adopted for other reasons, most notably: (a) a drug-free workplace cuts down on accidents, absenteeism, and tardiness, and promotes better work; and/or (b) some states provide worker compensation premium reductions for compliance with the Act. The minimum requirement for a federal drug-free program is drug-free policy. But the spirit of the federal Act goes beyond a written document and includes drug testing, drug education, and employee assistance.

Beyond creating a drug-free working environment and capturing the benefits of such an environment, the author sees another advantage of voluntarily adopting the Act. All states have statewide chambers of commerce. All statewide chambers coordinate drug-free programs through local chambers. A chamber of commerce can provide critical information regarding when employees can be legally drug tested, when they should be tested, and when they must be tested. In addition, some local chambers coordinate employee assistance programs and there is a growing body of data indicative of savings as a result of prevention and rehabilitation through such programs.

MISCELLANEOUS CONSIDERATIONS

It is impossible to anticipate all of the scenarios that will emerge. An unstructured interview can lead to innocuous but dangerous questions. A letter of recommendation can have information an employer would rather not look at. A simple question on an application blank (what college did you graduate from?) can yield an unneeded answer (a college for the blind or hearing impaired). Even EEOC advice (a yes/no medical clearance for agility testing) can create a difficult dilemma (a doctor who does not want to accept the responsibility). These are the true unknowns that will be resolved through litigation.

Certainly, alcoholism and alcohol abuse fit into this category. Neither the statute nor the ADA Regulations are entirely clear on all relevant issues. It is clear that the employee may not drink or be under the influence of alcohol while at work. It is also clear that a rehabilitating or rehabilitated alcoholic is protected by the statute. But as noted earlier in the chapter, it is not clear what the employer should do with the employee who drinks on private time but who can adequately perform the job.

The problem is that neither the statute nor the regulations are specific enough to provide exact prescriptions and proscriptions. Neither are other sources. For example, the DSM-III-R (American Psychological Association, 1987) does not distinguish between alcohol dependence versus dependence on other drugs. And, in a segment entitled "**Patterns of use,**" the DSM III-R describes "three main patterns of Alcohol Abuse or Dependence." These include: (a) "daily intake of large amounts"; (b) "regular heavy drinking limited to weekends"; and (c) "long periods of sobriety interspersed with binges of daily heavy drinking lasting for weeks or months." It seems clear that patterns (a) and (c) would constitute **direct threat** under ADA statutory language. However, pattern (b) might not. Certainly, this is the implication of the quote from Hartman and Homer (1991) cited earlier.

The safest strategy would seem to be technical assistance from the EEOC. Additionally (not alternatively), employers should consider the affirmative benefits of drug education and employee assistance. Where possible and legally permissible, rehabilitation costs might be less expensive that having to rehire and retrain new employees. Also, a company that promotes rehabilitation sends a message to its employees to come forward for help without fear of recrimination.

In the final analysis, however, there is one piece of advice the author believes in more so than any other; having *only* one piece of advice is dangerous. No two lawyers, management consultants, or even federal agency officials fully agree on all issues. Attending one workshop, reading one book, following blindly the advice of any one source—these are dangerous. Having one person in charge of setting policy is also dangerous. Indeed, the healthiest pattern the author has observed in the past 2 years is the sharing of information stimulated by the concern with all EEO laws, but particularly the ADA. Because this is the last substantive section of the last chapter of this book, the author will end on that thought, fully believing it is the best single piece of advice one can give or take.

——— **CHAPTER SUMMARY** ———

A major assumption in this chapter is that Congress created the ADA to have an impact like Sec.501 of the Rehabilitation Act; that is to cut deeply into the private and state/local sectors **(Q2)**, and to make up for the general weakness of Sec.504 of the Rehabilitation Act. The ADA protects **(Q1)** "individuals with disabilities" (current physical/mental impairments, a record of impairment and being regarded as impaired) who are "qualified" (have the necessary KSAs) for essential job functions with or without accommodation. Although the ADA covers **(Q3)** nondiscrimination as in Title VII, it also has affirmative requirements (reasonable accommodation and special prohibitions), but no traditional affirmative action requirements (i.e., correction for underutilization is not required). Title VII EEOC procedures **(Q4)** and remedies **(Q5)** apply, including the expanded remedies in the Civil Rights Act of 1991. The attack/defense balances **(Q6)** include disparate treatment (as in McDonnell-Burdine), adverse impact (with less emphasis on statistical proof), and surmountable barriers (where the focus will be on undue hardship). To comply with the statute, the employer must first understand in general the responsibilities of the disabled person as well as the employer. Beyond that, emphasis should be on understanding the essential features of the work and the KSAs needed to do the work. Ergonomic considerations will also be important. Preemployment inquiries into disability or inability to do work is expressly prohibited. The employer should consider permissible forms of affirmative action, particularly those available in a Drug-Free Workplace Act program. Finally, some issues (e.g., alcohol abuse off premises) are still unclear and may require technical assistance.

NOTES

1. The author has rarely heard "the ADA" referenced as simply "ADA." Thus unlike the Equal Pay Act and the Age Act, which are usually referenced as simply "EPA" or "ADEA," the author will, when using the acronym for the Americans With Disabilities Act, will refer to "the ADA."

2. The Rehabilitation Act was vetoed twice by President Nixon for budgetary reasons. It was signed into law in 1973 only after budget cuts grudgingly agreed to by Congress.

3. ADA statutory language clearly references both adverse impact and failure to reasonably accommodate. However, the statute does not discuss disparate treatment. But, disparate treatment is discussed extensively in the EEOC Interpretive Guidelines,

where references to disparate treatment scenarios from Rehabilitation Act cases are provided.

4. ADA statutory language does not explicitly note to whom the direct threat must be. However, in the introduction to its ADA Regulations, the EEOC states that the threat can be to the disabled individual or other employees. The EEOC maintained this interpretation despite complaints from that such an interpretation would permit discrimination based on naive, paternalistic attitudes.

5. Both the *Congressional Record* and the EEOC ADA Regulations contain numerous references to Congress's desire to incorporate regulations from Sec.504 of the Rehabilitation Act into the ADA.

6. The term *otherwise qualified* is used elsewhere in the ADA statute and in several places in the EEOC ADA Regulations. However, the term now implies qualification with or without reasonable accommodation, as we will witness shortly.

7. *Black v. Marshall* is one of the rare influential Sec.503 cases.

8. Technically speaking, mental health professionals do not use the terms *rehabilitated* or *recovered*. Rather, the individual is seen as "recovering," regardless of how many years have passed since recovery began.

9. For example, in *Traynor v. Turnage* (1988), the Supreme Court unanimously upheld a Veterans Administration regulation defining alcoholism as "willful misconduct." Although this ruling would not apply to the ADA, as written, Sec.105(c) implies that collateral federal laws which have stiffer penalties for alcohol abuse are legal.

10. In particular, Sec.103(B) limits knowledge of legal medical inquiries to "(i) supervisors and managers . . . (ii) first aid and safety personnel . . . and (iii) government officials investigating compliance with the Act."

11. The regulation was Sec.84.44, which is quite lengthy but contains a clear reference to modifying academic requirements and providing auxiliary aids. Literally read, the regulation would force the college to accept the accommodation proposed by Frances Davis.

12. Some forms of fitness testing are not medical. For example, police departments use grip tests that do not, per se, involve medical indicators.

13. The permission referred to has been in writing to various police and fire departments, and in videotapes in which EEOC and Justice Department officials have served on question/answer panels. Interested readers should contact their state law enforcement agency.

List of Cases

Berndt v. Kaiser Aluminum (CA3 1986) 789 F.2d 253

Bey v. Bolger (E.D.Pa. 1982) 540 F.Supp 910

Bd. of Governors, Univ. of North Carolina v. U.S. DOL (CA4 1990) 917 F.2d 812

Bd. of Regents v. Tomanio (1980) 446 US 478

Bd. of Trustees of Keene State College v. Sweeney (1978) 439 US 24

The Board of Regents of the University of Nebraska v. Dawes (CA8 1976) 522 F.2d 380

Boyd v. Ozark Airlines (CA8 1977) 568 F.2d 50

Boyd v. U.S. Postal Service (CA9 1985) 752 F.2d 410

Brady v. Bristol-Meyers, Inc. (CA8 1972) 459 F.2d 621

Brener v. Diagnostic Center Hospital (CA5 1982) 671 F.2d 141

Brennan v. Ace Hardware Corp. (CA8 1974) 495 F.2d 368

Brennan v. City Stores, Inc. (CA5 1973) 479 F.2d 235

Brennan v. Goose Creek Consolidated Ind. School Dist. (CA5 1975) 519 F.2d 53

Brennan v. J. M. Fields,Inc. (CA5 1973) 488 F.2d 443

Brooks v. AFC Industries (S.D.W.Va. 1982) 537 F.Supp 1122

Brown v. Board of Education (1954) 347 US 483

Brown v. Bd. of Regents of the Univ. of Nebraska (Neb. 1986) 640 F.Supp 674

Brown v. Gaston Dyeing Machine Co. (CA5 1972) 457 F.2d 1377

Brown v. General Services Administration (1976) 425 US 820

Brown v. St. Louis Police Department (CA8 1982) 691 F.2d 393

Bundy v. Jackson (D.C.Cir 1981) 641 F.2d 934

Burnett v. Grattan (1984) 468 US 42

Burns v. Southern Pacific Trans. (CA9 1978) 589 F.2d 403

Burton v. Wilmington Parking Authority (1961) 365 US 715

Burwell v. Eastern Airlines (CA4 1980) 633 F.2d 371

Butler v. Thornburgh (CA5 1990) 900 F.2d 871

Butts v. Nichols (S.D. Ia. 1974) 381 F.Supp 573

Caldwell v. The National Brewing Co. (CA5 1971) 443 F.2d 1044

California Federal Savings and Loan Association v. Guerra (1987) 479 US 272

Canton v. Harris (1989) 489 US 378

Cariddi v. K.C. Chiefs (CA2 1977) 890 F.2d 569

Carino v. Univ. of Oklahoma Bd. of Regents (CA10 1984) 750 F.2d 815

Carmi v. Metro. St. Louis Sewer District (E.D. Mo. 1979) 471 F.Supp 119

Carrero v. N.Y.C. Housing Authority (1989) 890 F.2d 569

Carrol v. Tallman (CA7 1979) 604 F.2d 1028

Carroll v. General Accident Insurance Co. Of America (CA5 1990) 891 F.2d 1174

Carter v. Gallagher (CA8 1971) 452 F.2d 315

References for Frequently Cited and Currently Applicable Guidelines and Regulations

Equal Employment Opportunity Commission: Affirmative action appropriate under Title VII of the Civil Rights Act of 1964, as amended (29 C.F.R. 1608)

Equal Employment Opportunity Commission: Age Discrimination in Employment Act (29 C.F.R. 1625)

Equal Employment Opportunity Commission: The Equal Pay Act (29 C.F.R. 1620)

Equal Employment Opportunity Commission: Guidelines on discrimination because of national origin (29 C.F.R. 1606)

Equal Employment Opportunity Commission: Guidelines on discrimination because of religion (29 C.F.R. 1605)

Equal Employment Opportunity Commission: Guidelines on discrimination because of sex (29 C.F.R. 1604)

Equal Employment Opportunity Commission: Record keeping and reporting requirements under Title VII and the ADA (29 C.F.R. 1602)

Equal Employment Opportunity Commission: Regulations to implement the equal employment provisions of the Americans with Disabilities Act (29 C.F.R. 1630)

Equal Employment Opportunity Commission: Uniform guidelines on employee selection procedures (29 C.F.R. 1607)

Office of Contract Compliance Programs: Affirmative action programs, (41 C.F.R. 60-2)

Office of Contract Compliance Programs: Construction contractors: affirmative action requirements (41 C.F.R. 60-4)

Office of Contract Compliance Programs: Contractor evaluation procedures for contractors for supplies and services (41 C.F.R. 60-60)

Office of Contract Compliance Programs: Obligations of contractors and subcontractors (41 C.F.R. 60-1)

Office of Contract Compliance Programs: Rules of practice for administrative proceedings to enforce equal opportunity under Executive Order 11246 (41 C.F.R. 60-30)

358

References for Frequently Cited and Currently Applicable Statutes and Executive Orders

Administrative Procedures Act of 1946 (5 U.S.C. 701)

Age Discrimination in Employment Act of 1967 (29 U.S.C. 631)

Americans With Disabilities Act of 1990 (42 U.S.C. 12101)

Civil Rights Act of 1991 (42 U.S.C. 1981A)

Employee Retirement Income Security Act of 1974 (29 U.S.C. 1001)

Equal Pay Act of 1963 (29 U.S.C. 206(d))

Executive Order 11246 of 1965 (3 CFR Section 167) (Reprinted in 42 U.S.C. 2000e APP at 28-35)

Fair Labor Standards Act of 1938 (29 U.S.C. 204(f))

Freedom of Information Act of 1966 (5 U.S.C. 552)

Immigration Reform and Control Act of 1986 (8 U.S.C. 1324)

National Labor Relations Act of 1935 (29 U.S.C. 141)

Reconstruction Civil Rights Acts of 1866, 1870, and 1871 (42 U.S.C. 1981-1988)

Rehabilitation Act of 1973 (29 U.S.C. 701)

Reorganization Plan No.1 of 1978 (3 C.F.R. 321) (Reprinted in 42 U.S.C. 2000-e4 App at 39-40)

Title VI of the Civil Rights Act of 1964 (42 U.S.C. 2000d)

Title VII of the Civil Rights Act of 1964 (42 U.S.C. 2000e)

Title IX of the Education Amendments of 1972 (38 U.S.C. 1681)

Vietnam Era Veterans' Readjustment Assistance Act of 1974 (38 U.S.C. 2011)

References

American Psychiatric Association. (1987). *Diagnostic and statistical manual of mental disorders DSM-III-R* (3rd ed., rev.). Washington, DC: American Psychiatric Association.

Arvey, R. D. (1979). Unfair discrimination in the employment interview: Legal and psychological aspects. *Psychological Bulletin, 86*(4), 736-765.

Babcock, B. A., Freedman, A. E., Norton, E. H., & Ross, S. C. (1975). *Sex discrimination and the law: Causes and remedies.* Boston: Little, Brown.

Bersoff, D. N. (1988). Should subjective employment devices be scrutinized? *American Psychologist, 43*(12), 1016-1018.

Black, H. C. (1990). *Black's law dictionary.* St. Paul, MN: West Publishing.

Bray, D. W. (1982). The assessment center and the study of lives. *American Psychologist, 37,* 180-189.

Burns, H. (1987). The activism is not affirmative. In H. Schwartz (Ed.), *The Burger years: Rights and wrongs in the Supreme Court: 1969-1986.* New York: Penguin.

Bussey, E. M. (1990). *Federal civil service law and procedures: A basic guide.* Washington, DC: Bureau of National Affairs.

Cascio, W. F. (1976). Turnover, biographical data, and fair employment practice. *Journal of Applied Psychology, 61,* 576-580.

Cascio, W. F. (1991). *Applied psychology and personnel management* (4th ed.). Englewood Cliffs, NJ: Prentice-Hall.

Cascio, W. F., Alexander, R. A., & Barrett, G. V. (1988). Setting cutoff scores: Legal, psychometric, and professional issues and guidelines. *Personnel Psychology, 41,* 1-24.

Cox, T. H., & Blake, S. (1991). Managing cultural diversity: Implications for organizational competitiveness. *Academy of Management Executive, 5*(3), 45-56.

Eskenazi, M., & Gallen, D. (1992). *Sexual harassment: Know your rights.* New York: Carroll & Graf.

Field, H. S., & Holley, W. H. (1982). The relationship of performal appraisal system characteristics to verdicts in selected employment discrimination cases. *Academy of Management Journal, 25*(2), 392-406.

360

Harris, M. M. (1989). Reconsidering the employment interview: A review of recent literature and suggestions for future research. *Personnel Psychology, 42,* 691-726.

Hartman, G. S., & Homer, G. W. (1991). *Current employment law issues.* Winston-Salem, NC: Wake Forest University School of Law Continuing Education.

Hartman, G. S., & Schnadig, R. H. (1990). *Personnel law handbook.* Winston-Salem, NC: Wake Forest University School of Law Continuing Education.

Landy, F. J. (1991). *Psychology of work behavior.* Pacific Grove, CA: Brooks/Cole.

Leonard, J. S. (1990). The impact of affirmative action regulation and equal employment law on black employment. *Journal of Economic Perspectives, 4*(1), 47-63.

Levine, E. L. (1983). *Everything you always wanted to know about job analysis.* Tampa, FL: Mariner.

Mahoney, T. A. (1983). Approaches to the definition of comparable worth. *Academy of Management Review, 8,* 14-22.

Muchinsky, P. M. (1990). *Psychology applied to work: An introduction to industrial and organizational psychology.* Pacific Grove, CA: Brooks/Cole.

Ogletree, Deakens, Nash, Smoak, & Stewart. (1992). *Americans With Disabilities Act: Employee rights and employer obligations.* New York: Matthew Bender.

Player, M. A. (1981). *Federal law of employment discrimination.* St. Paul, MN: West Publishing.

Perritt, H. H., Jr. (1990). *The Americans With Disabilities Act handbook.* New York: John Wiley.

Russell, J. S. (1984). A review of fair employment cases in the field of training. *Personnel Psychology, 37,* 261-276.

Schneider, B., & Schmidt, N. (1986). *Staffing organizations.* Glenview, IL: Scott, Foresman.

Shaeffer, R. G. (1975). Nondiscrimination in employment, 1973-1975. New York: The Conference Board.

Society for Industrial and Organizational Psychology, Inc. (1987). *Principles for the validation and use of personnel selection procedures* (3rd ed.). College Park, MD: Author.

Sovern, M. I. (1966). *Legal restraints on racial discrimination in employment.* New York: Twentieth Century Fund.

Sowell, T. (1984). *Civil rights: Rhetoric or reality?* New York: William Morrow.

Treiman, D. J., & Hartmann, H. I. (1981). *Women, work, and wages: Equal pay for jobs of equal value.* Washington, DC: National Academy Press.

Index

About the Author

Arthur Gutman is Professor of Psychology and past chair of the Personnel Pscyhology program at Florida Institute of Technology. His previous publications are in the areas of learning and memory, training, and statistics. He is a former National Institute of Mental Health Postdoctoral Fellow, and is currently a consultant to the Center for Substance Abuse Prevention on program evaluation. His other major consultations include the U.S. Army and Air Force, Brevard County Police Testing Center, Holmes Regional Medical Center, Harris Corporation, CDM, and COSMOS.